ONE-PUNCH MAN | 10
ONE + YUSUKE MURATA

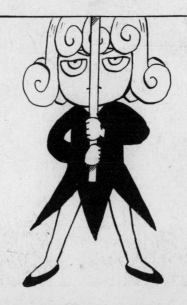

★The stories,
characters and
incidents mentioned
in this publication
are entirely
fictional.

DISCARD

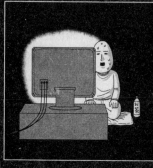

O N E

Saitama! Genos! Monsters?! They're
moving around and talking!

—ONE

Manga creator ONE began *One-Punch Man* as a
webcomic, which quickly went viral, garnering
over 10 million hits. In addition to *One-Punch Man*,
ONE writes and draws the series *Mob Psycho 100*
and *Makai no Ossan*.

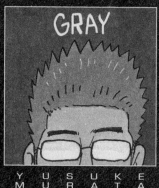

Y U S U K E
M U R A T A

I decided to become a proper old man,
so I stopped dying my gray hair.

—Yusuke Murata

A highly decorated and skilled artist best known
for his work on *Eyeshield 21*, Yusuke Murata won
the 122nd Hop Step Award (1995) for *Partner* and
placed second in the 51st Akatsuka Award (1998)
for *Samui Hanashi*.

ONE-PUNCH MAN 10

STORY BY ONE ART BY YUSUKE MURATA

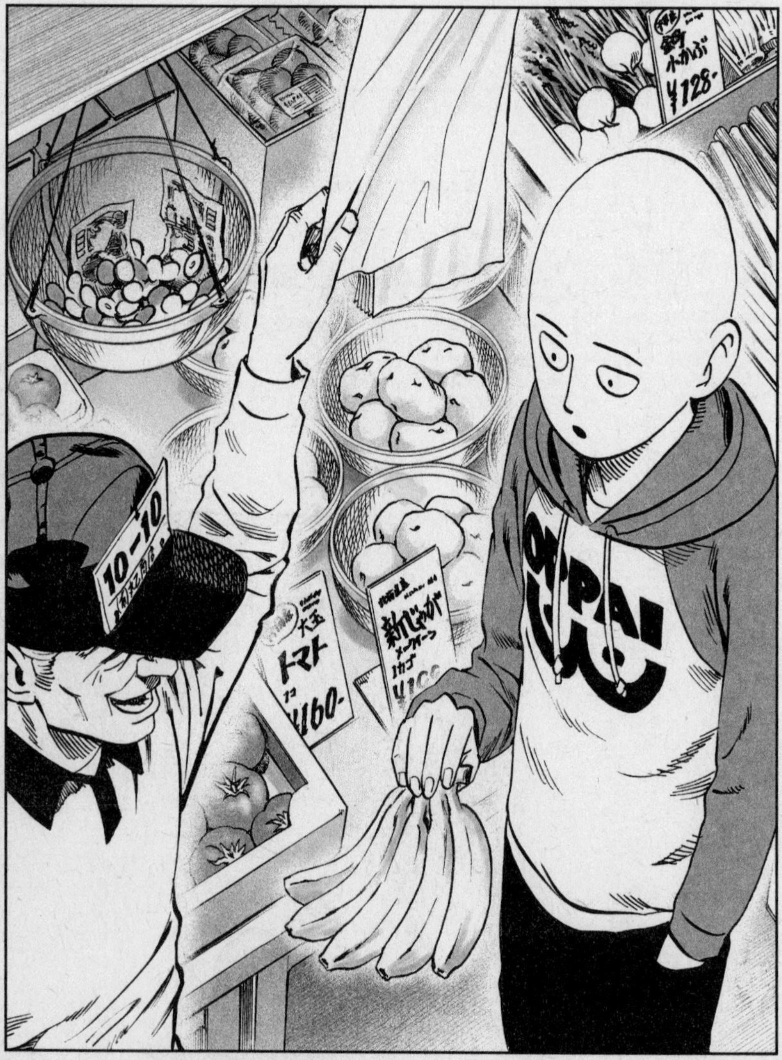
小かぶ
¥128-
10-10
大玉
トマト
¥160-
新じゃが
OPPAI

CHARACTERS

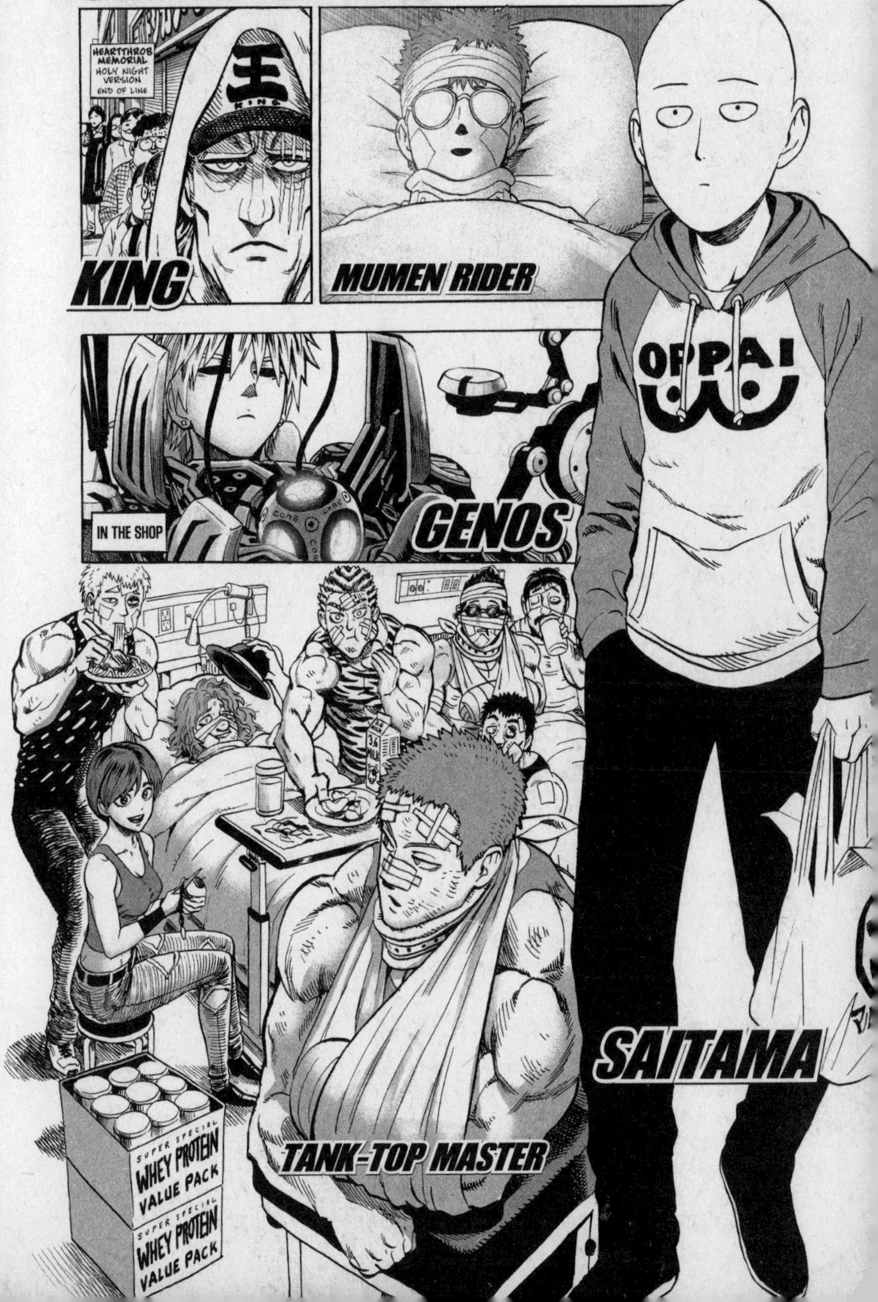
OPPAI
SAITAMA
MUMEN RIDER
KING
HEARTTHROB MEMORIAL HOLY NIGHT VERSION END OF LINE
KING
GENOS
IN THE SHOP
TANK-TOP MASTER
3.6 MILK
SUPER SPECIAL WHEY PROTEIN VALUE PACK
SUPER SPECIAL WHEY PROTEIN VALUE PACK

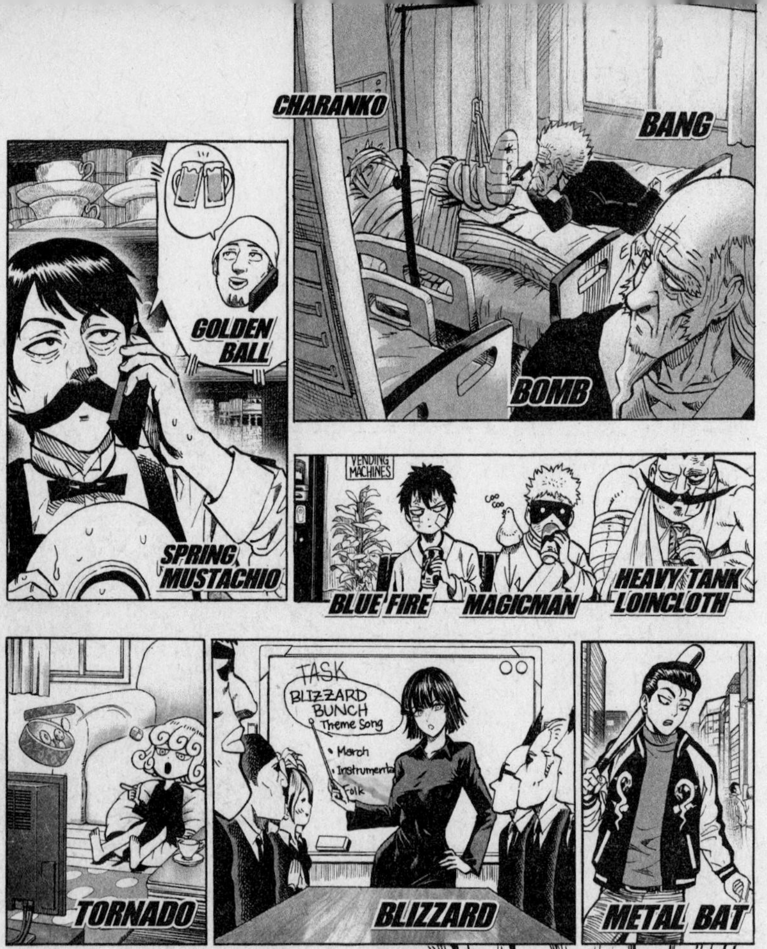
CHARANKO
BANG
BOMB
HEAVY TANK LOINCLOTH
MAGICMAN
VENDING MACHINES
BLUE FIRE
GOLDEN BALL
SPRING MUSTACHIO
METAL BAT
TASK
BLIZZARD BUNCH Theme Song
• March
• Instrumental
• Folk
BLIZZARD
TORNADO

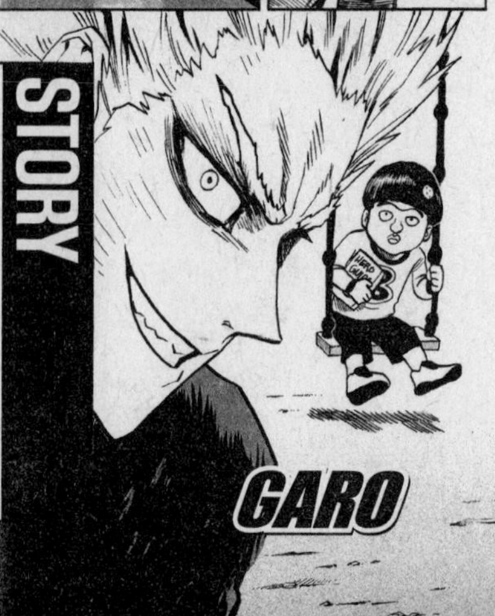
GARO

STORY

A single man arose to face the evil threatening humankind! His name was Saitama. He became a hero for fun!

With one punch, he has resolved every crisis so far, but no one believes he could be so extraordinarily strong.

Together with his pupil, Genos (Class S), Saitama has been active as a hero and risen from Class C to Class B.

One day, a seer predicts a great danger to Earth and dies. Is the increasing number of catastrophes in recent years an omen of this great danger? When the Hero Association seeks cooperation from ne'er-do-wells, a man named Garo, who admires monsters, shows up and begins hunting the heroes instead!

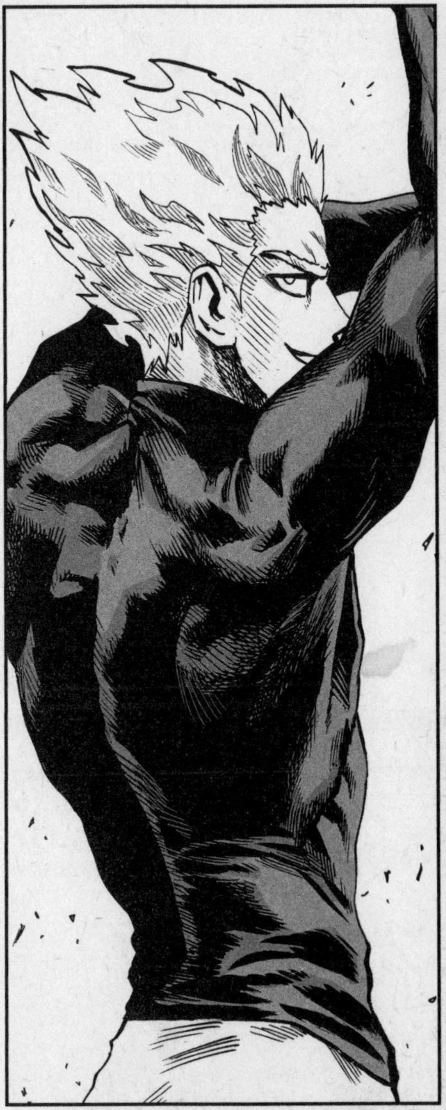

CONTENTS

ONE-PUNCH MAN VOLUME TEN

10

PUMPED UP

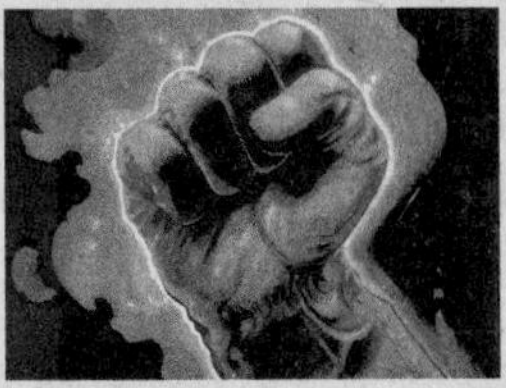

ONE-PUNCH MAN

ONE + YUSUKE MURATA

My name is Saitama. I am a hero. My hobby is heroic exploits. I got too strong. And that makes me sad. I can defeat any enemy with one blow. I lost my hair. And I lost all feeling. I want to feel the rush of battle. I would like to meet an incredibly strong enemy. And I would like to defeat it with one blow. That's because I am One-Punch Man.

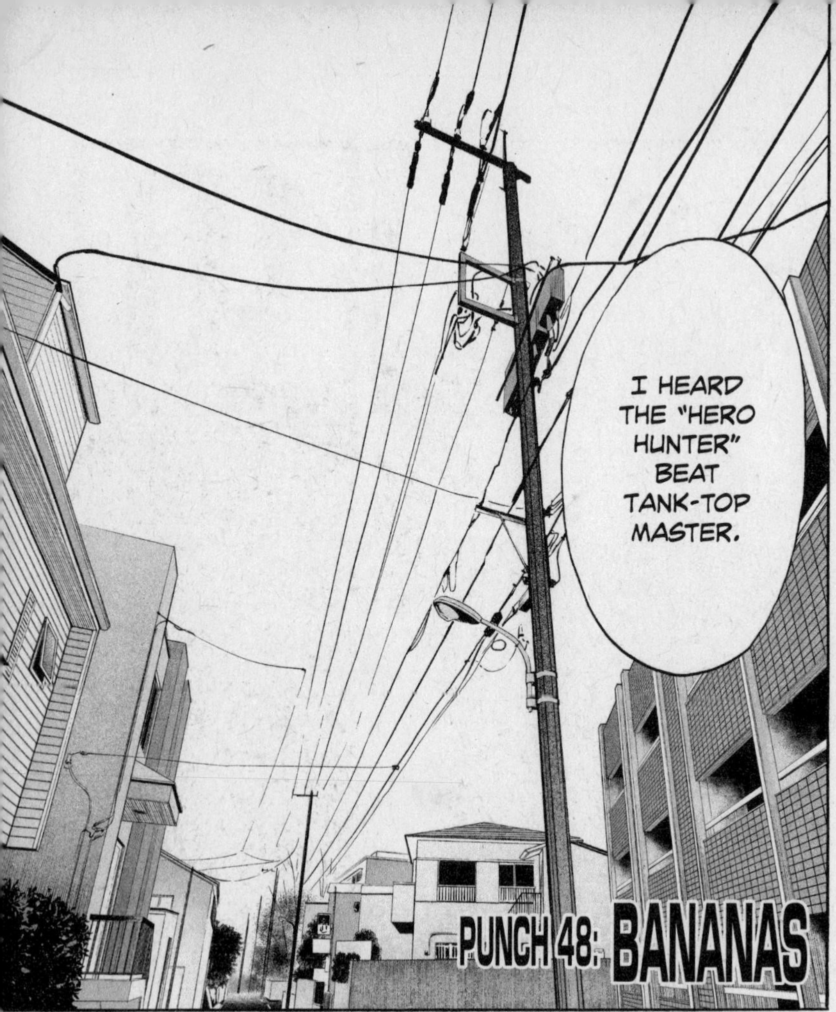
I HEARD THE "HERO HUNTER" BEAT TANK-TOP MASTER.
PUNCH 48: BANANAS

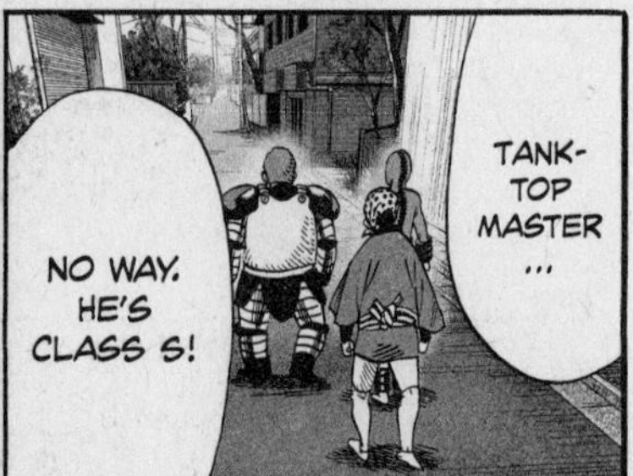
TANK-TOP MASTER ...
NO WAY. HE'S CLASS S!

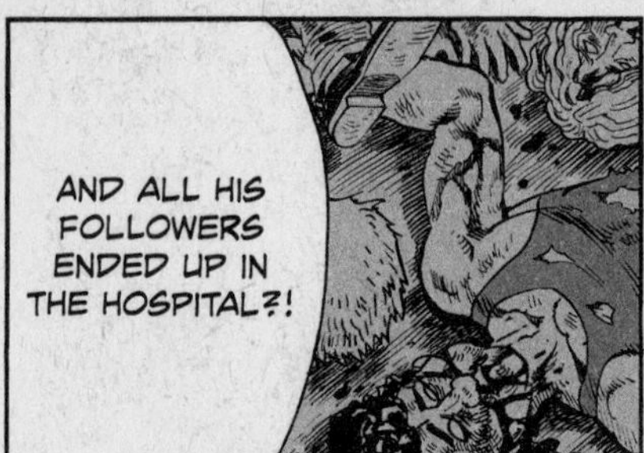
AND ALL HIS FOLLOWERS ENDED UP IN THE HOSPITAL?!

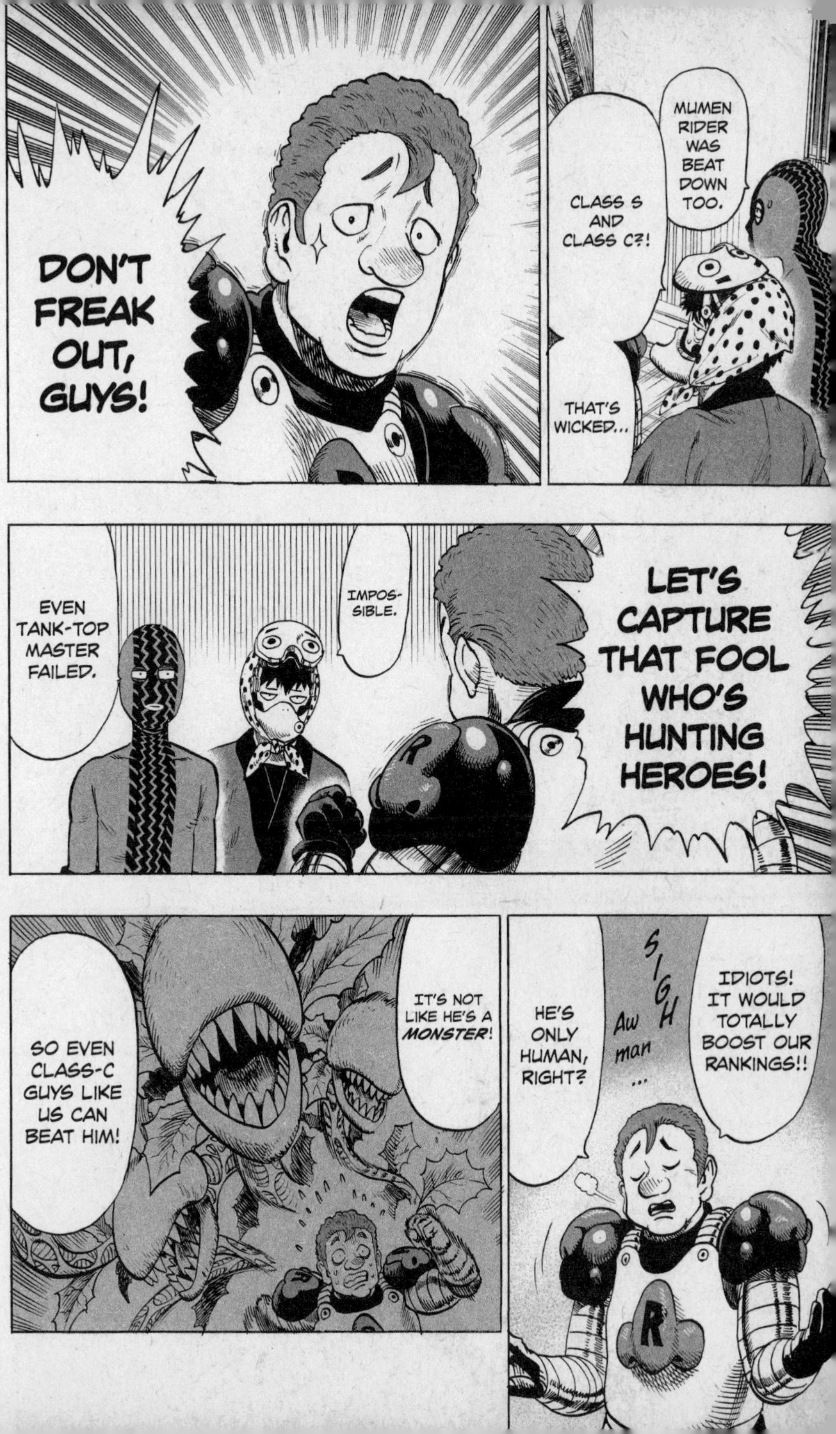
MUMEN RIDER WAS BEAT DOWN TOO.
CLASS S AND CLASS C?!
THAT'S WICKED...
DON'T FREAK OUT, GUYS!
LET'S CAPTURE THAT FOOL WHO'S HUNTING HEROES!
IMPOSSIBLE.
EVEN TANK-TOP MASTER FAILED.
IDIOTS! IT WOULD TOTALLY BOOST OUR RANKINGS!!
SIGH
Aw man...
HE'S ONLY HUMAN, RIGHT?
IT'S NOT LIKE HE'S A MONSTER!
SO EVEN CLASS-C GUYS LIKE US CAN BEAT HIM!

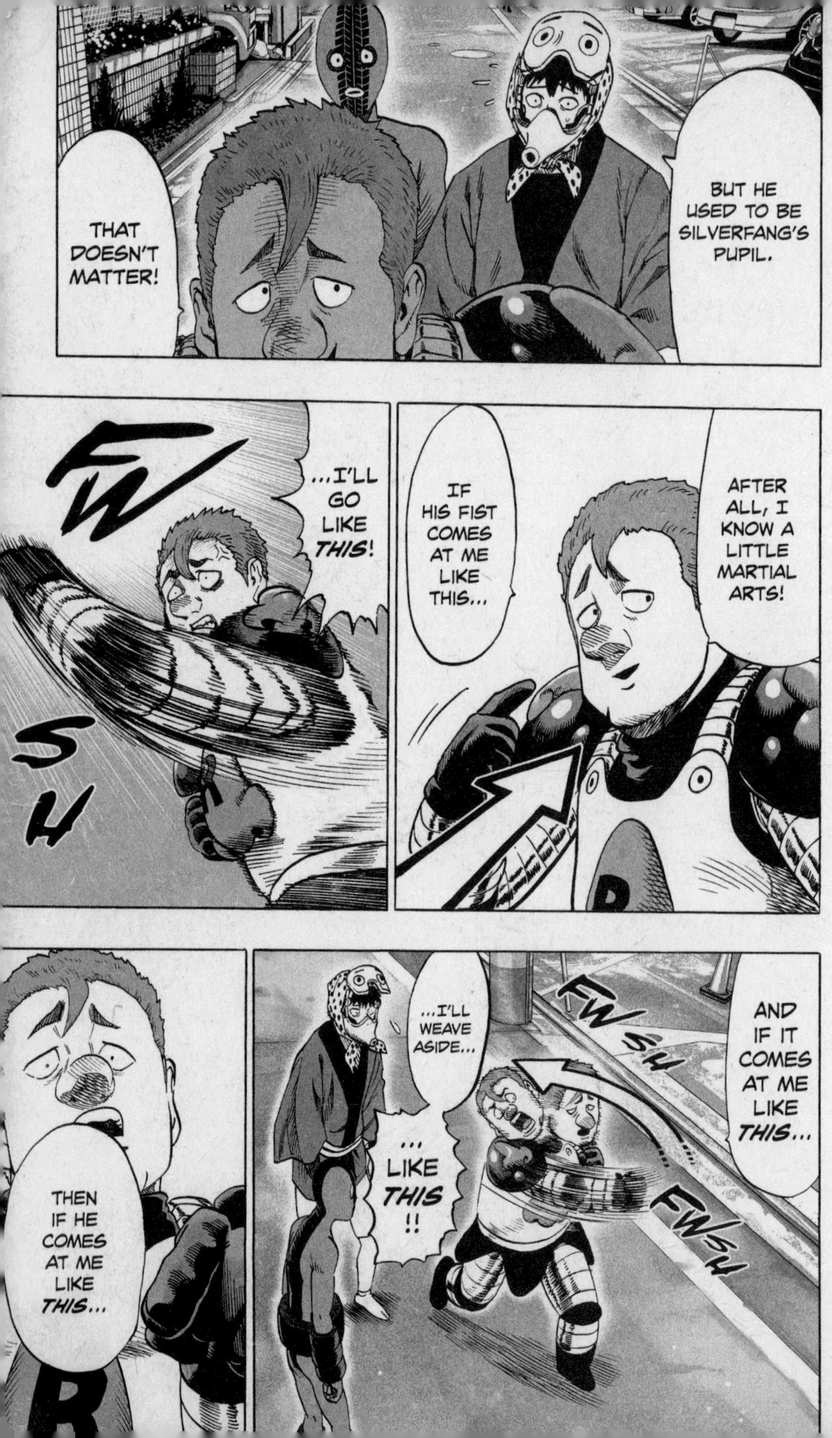
BUT HE USED TO BE SILVERFANG'S PUPIL.
THAT DOESN'T MATTER!
AFTER ALL, I KNOW A LITTLE MARTIAL ARTS!
IF HIS FIST COMES AT ME LIKE THIS...
...I'LL GO LIKE *THIS*!
FW
SH
AND IF IT COMES AT ME LIKE *THIS*...
...I'LL WEAVE ASIDE...
...LIKE *THIS* !!
FWSH
FWSH
THEN IF HE COMES AT ME LIKE *THIS*...

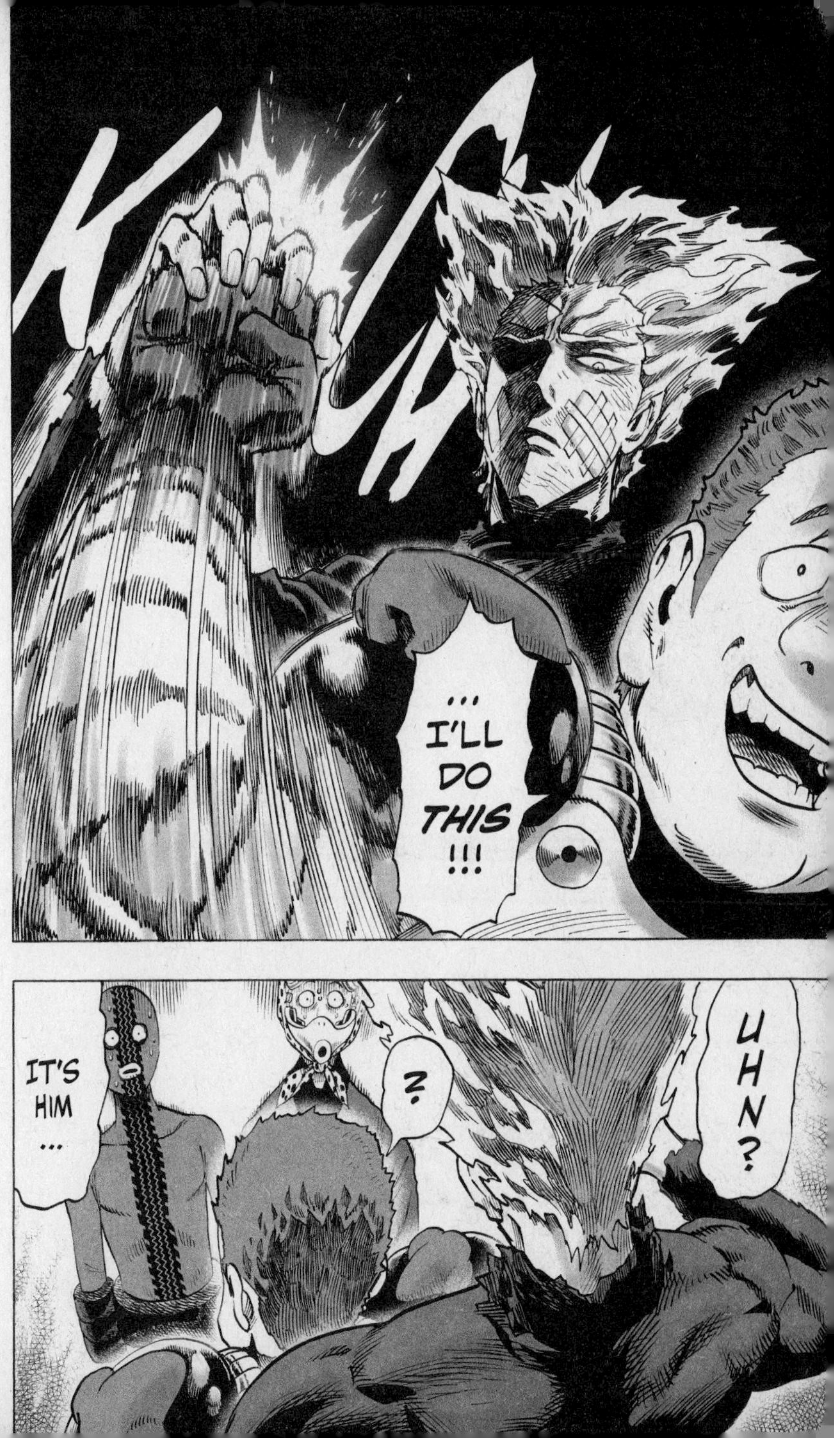
... I'LL DO THIS !!!
UHN?
?
IT'S HIM ...

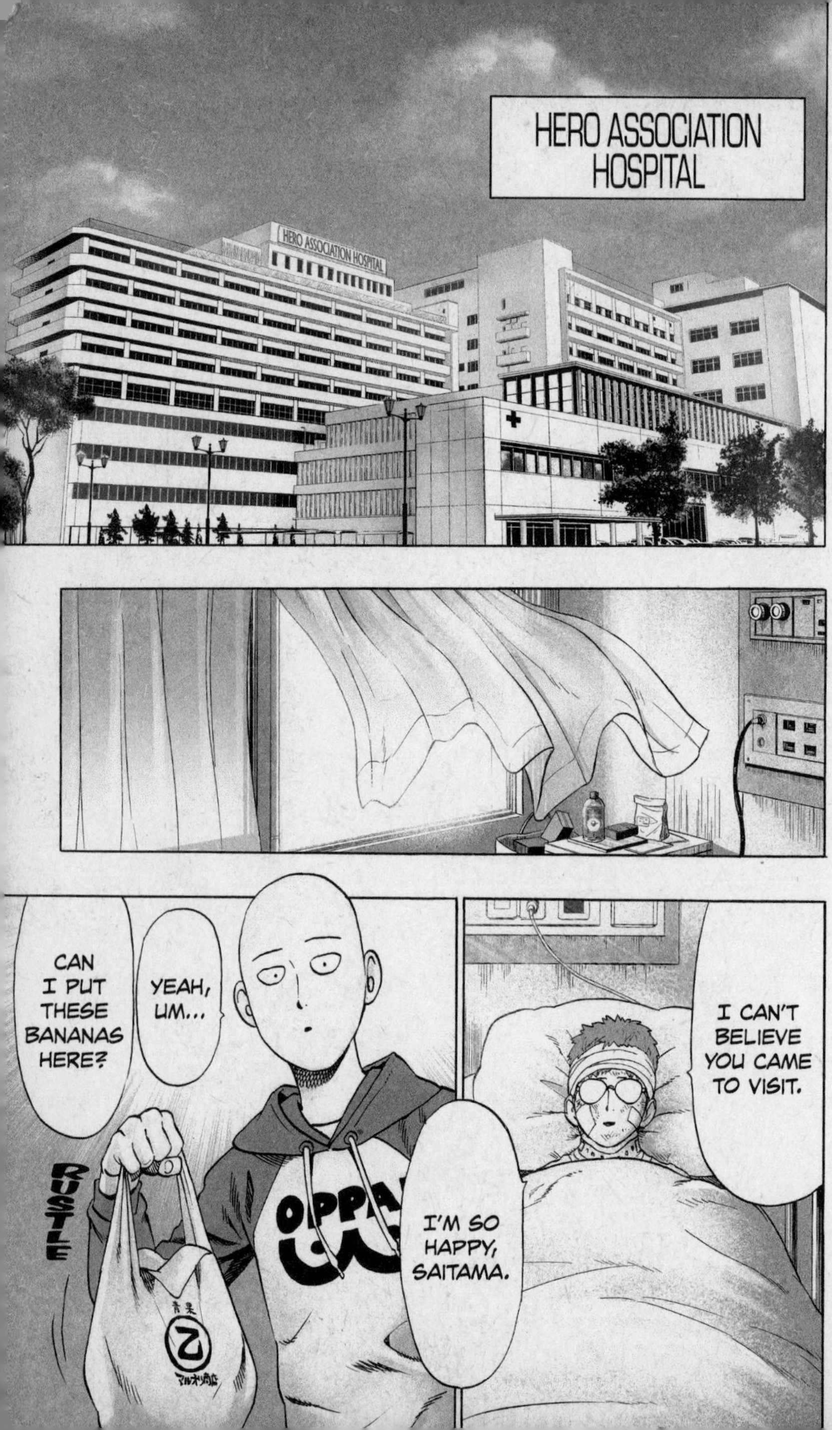
HERO ASSOCIATION HOSPITAL
HERO ASSOCIATION HOSPITAL
I CAN'T BELIEVE YOU CAME TO VISIT.
I'M SO HAPPY, SAITAMA.
YEAH, UM...
CAN I PUT THESE BANANAS HERE?
RUSTLE
OPPAI

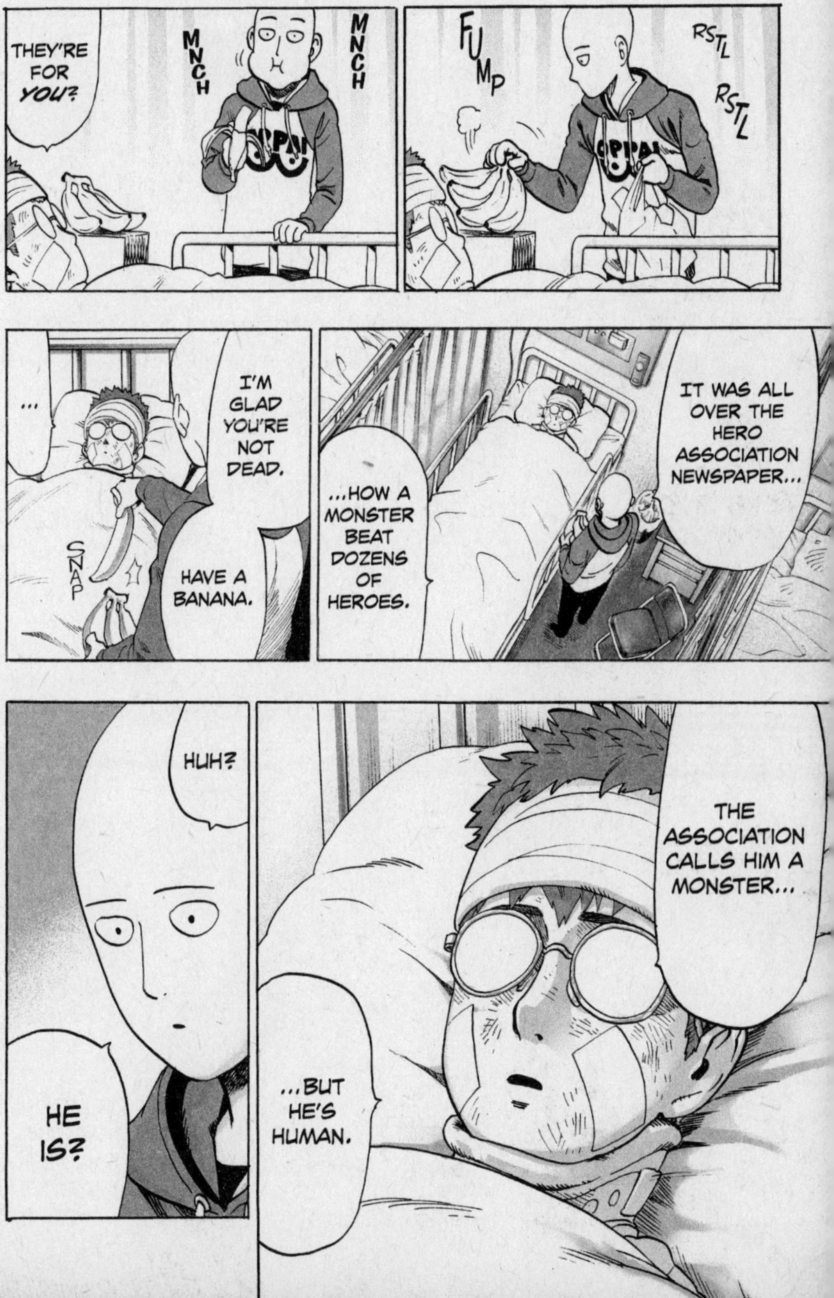
FUMP
RSTL
RSTL
THEY'RE FOR YOU?
MNCH
MNCH
IT WAS ALL OVER THE HERO ASSOCIATION NEWSPAPER...
...HOW A MONSTER BEAT DOZENS OF HEROES.
I'M GLAD YOU'RE NOT DEAD.
...
HAVE A BANANA.
SNAP
THE ASSOCIATION CALLS HIM A MONSTER...
...BUT HE'S HUMAN.
HUH?
HE IS?

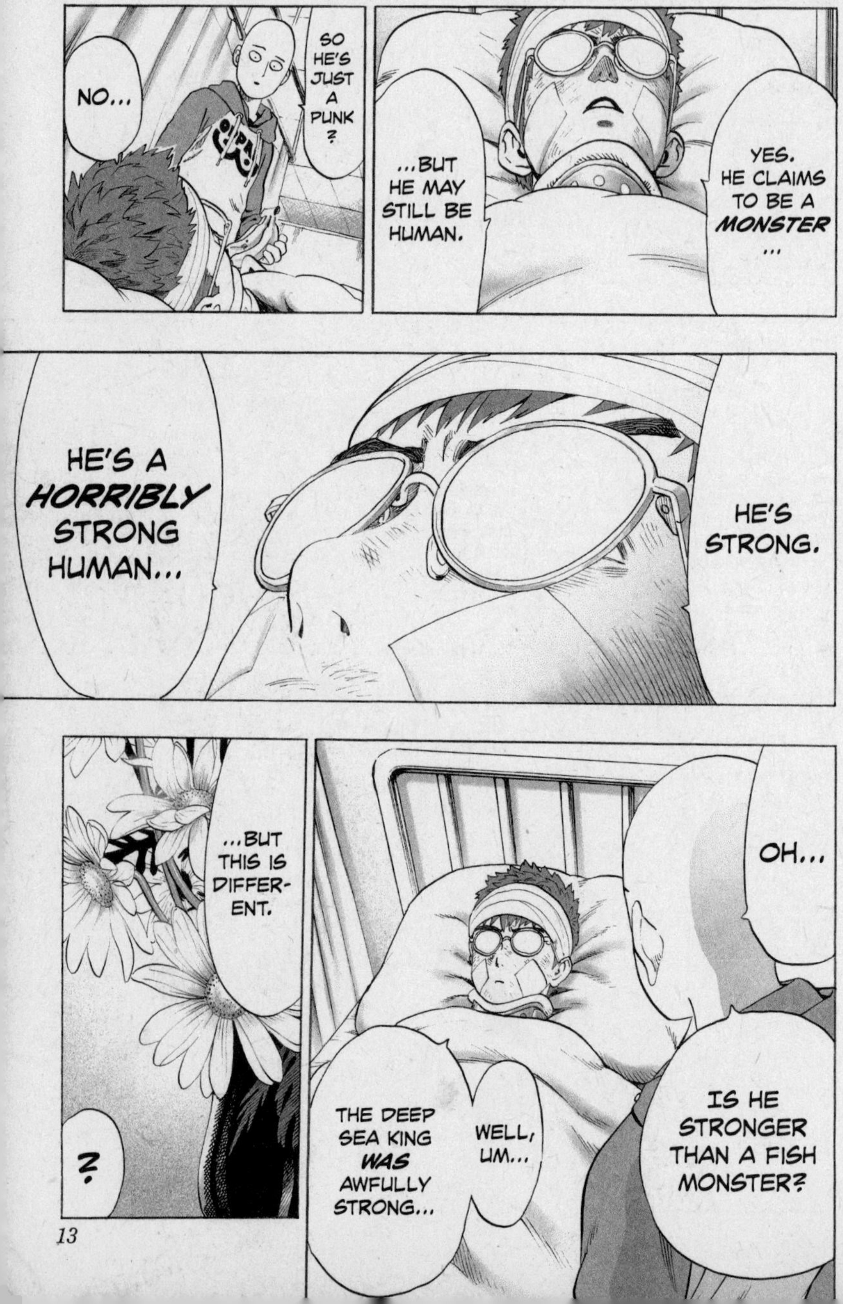
YES. HE CLAIMS TO BE A *MONSTER* ...
...BUT HE MAY STILL BE HUMAN.
SO HE'S JUST A PUNK?
NO...
HE'S STRONG.
HE'S A *HORRIBLY* STRONG HUMAN...
OH...
IS HE STRONGER THAN A FISH MONSTER?
WELL, UM...
THE DEEP SEA KING *WAS* AWFULLY STRONG...
...BUT THIS IS DIFFER-ENT.
?

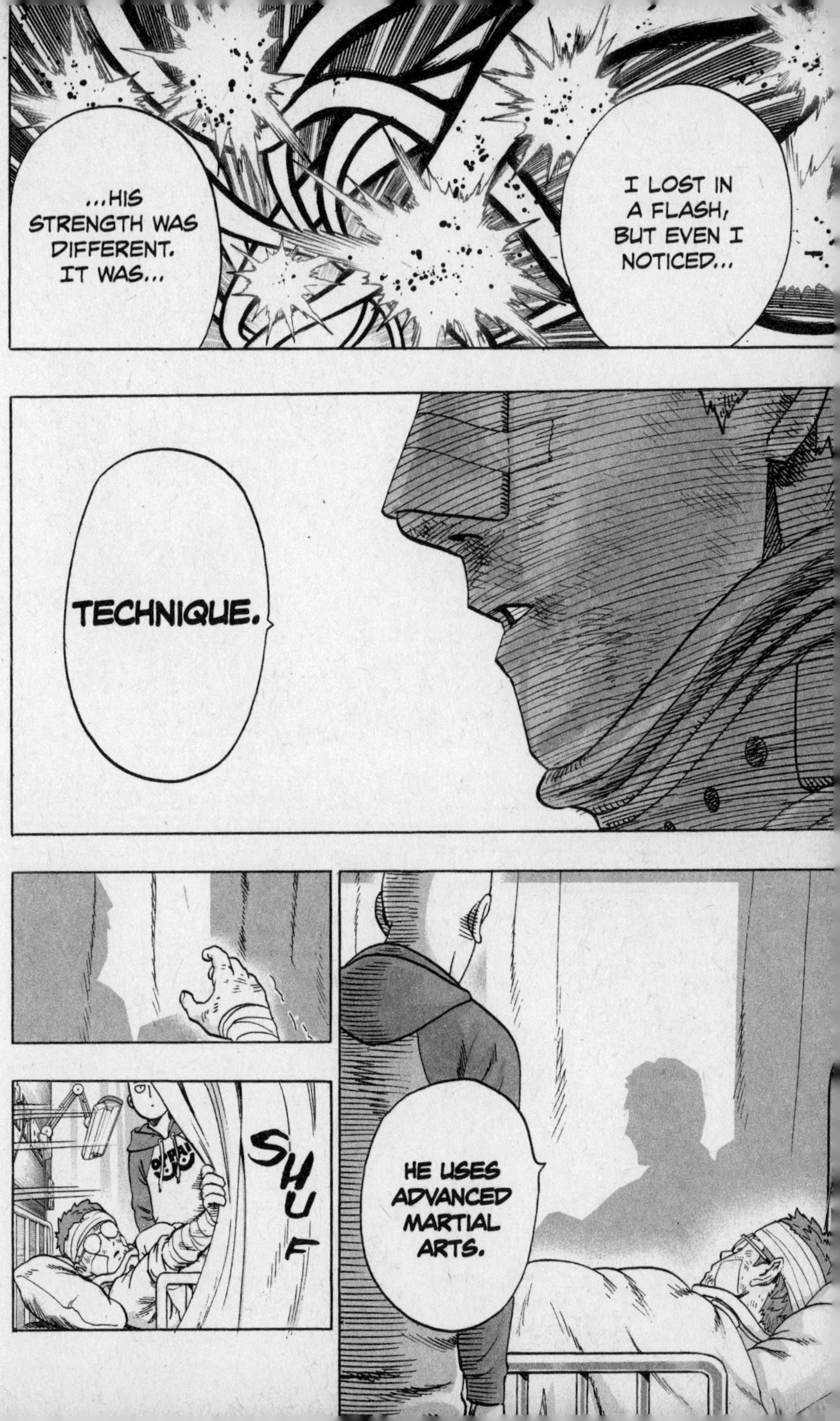
I LOST IN A FLASH, BUT EVEN I NOTICED...
...HIS STRENGTH WAS DIFFERENT. IT WAS...
TECHNIQUE.
HE USES ADVANCED MARTIAL ARTS.
SHUF

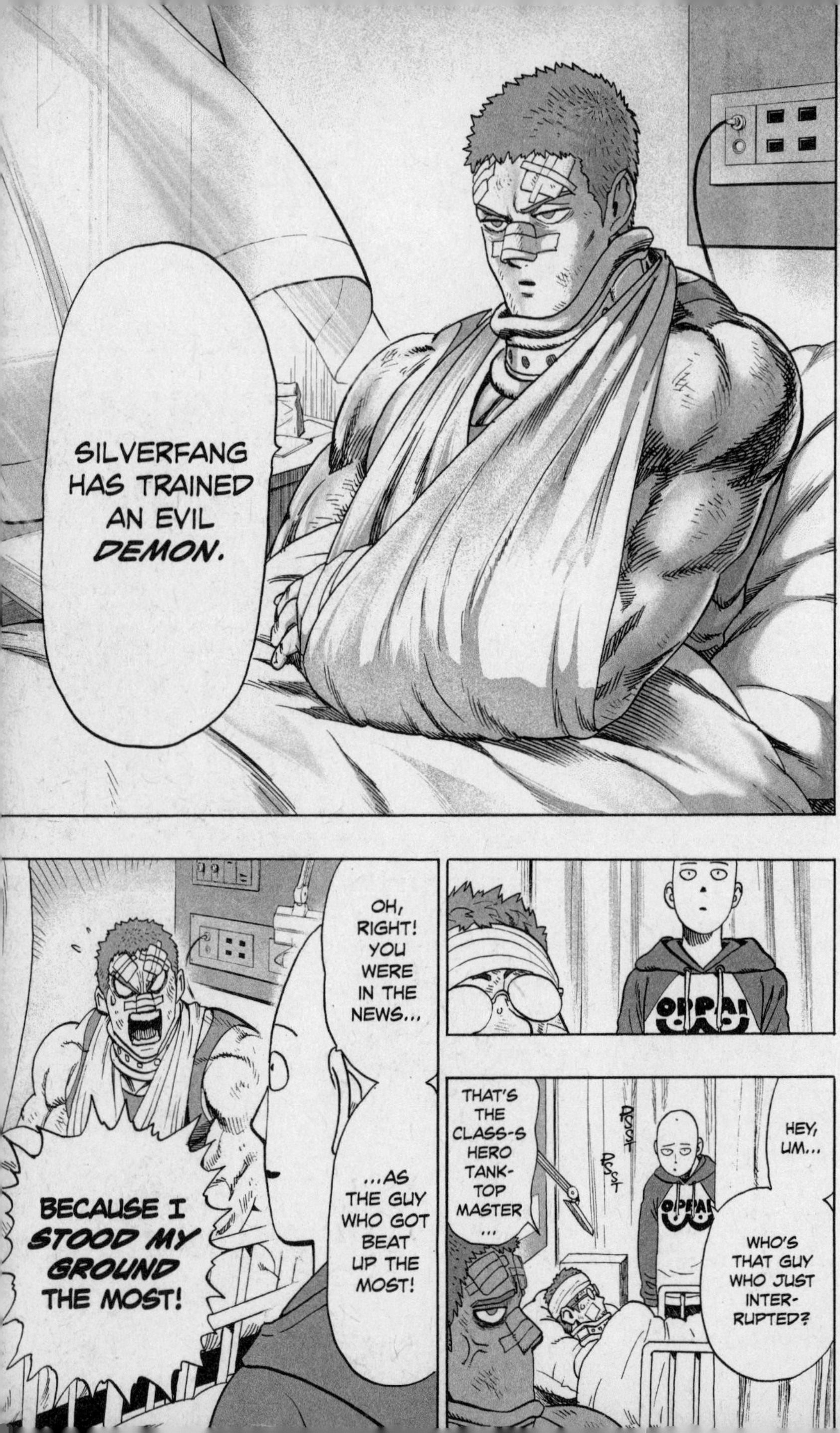
SILVERFANG HAS TRAINED AN EVIL DEMON.
HEY, UM...
WHO'S THAT GUY WHO JUST INTER-RUPTED?
PSSST
PSST
THAT'S THE CLASS-S HERO TANK-TOP MASTER...
OH, RIGHT! YOU WERE IN THE NEWS...
...AS THE GUY WHO GOT BEAT UP THE MOST!
BECAUSE I STOOD MY GROUND THE MOST!

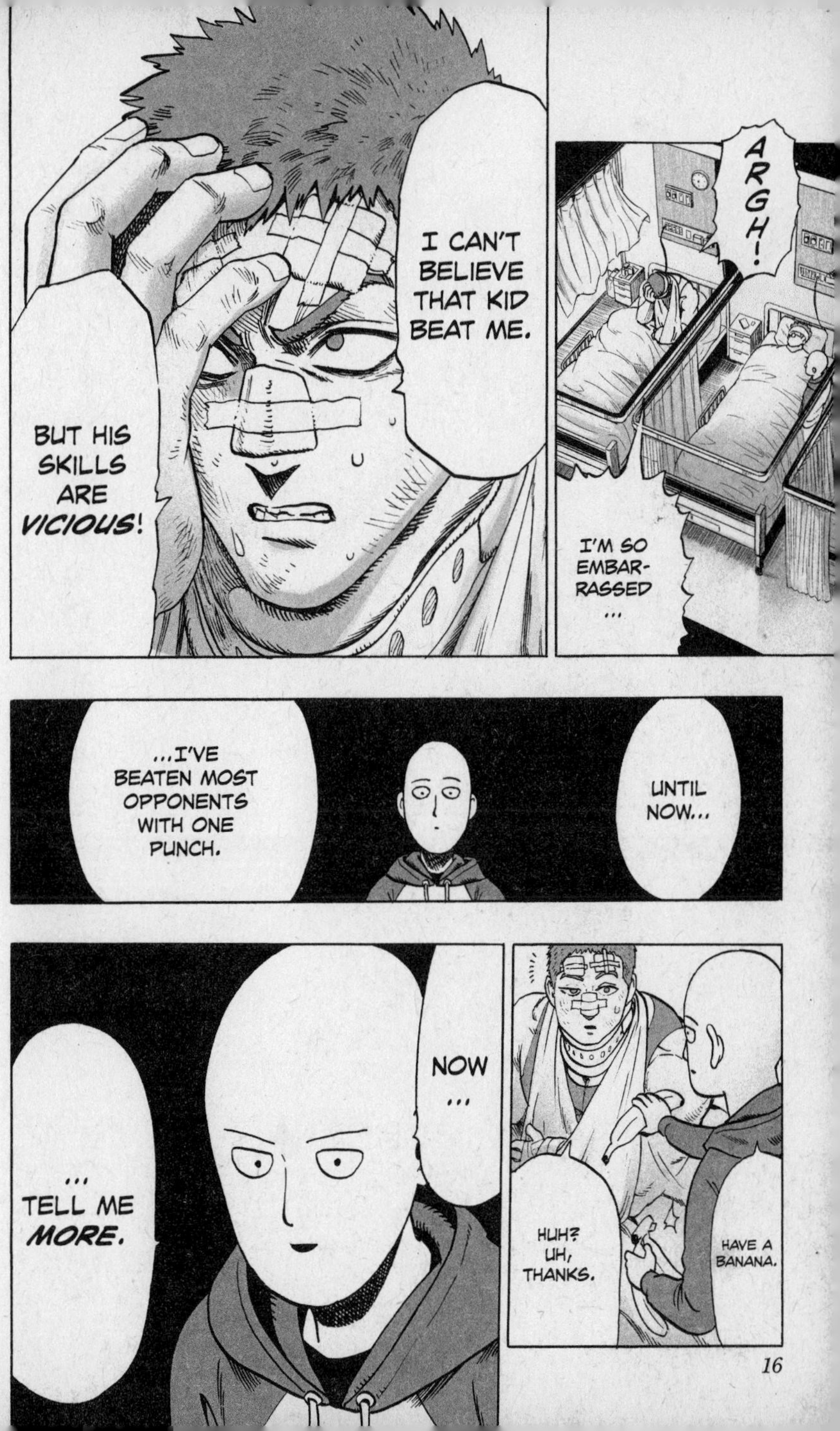
ARGH!
I'M SO EMBAR-RASSED ...
I CAN'T BELIEVE THAT KID BEAT ME.
BUT HIS SKILLS ARE *VICIOUS*!
UNTIL NOW...
...I'VE BEATEN MOST OPPONENTS WITH ONE PUNCH.
HAVE A BANANA.
HUH? UH, THANKS.
NOW ...
... TELL ME *MORE*.

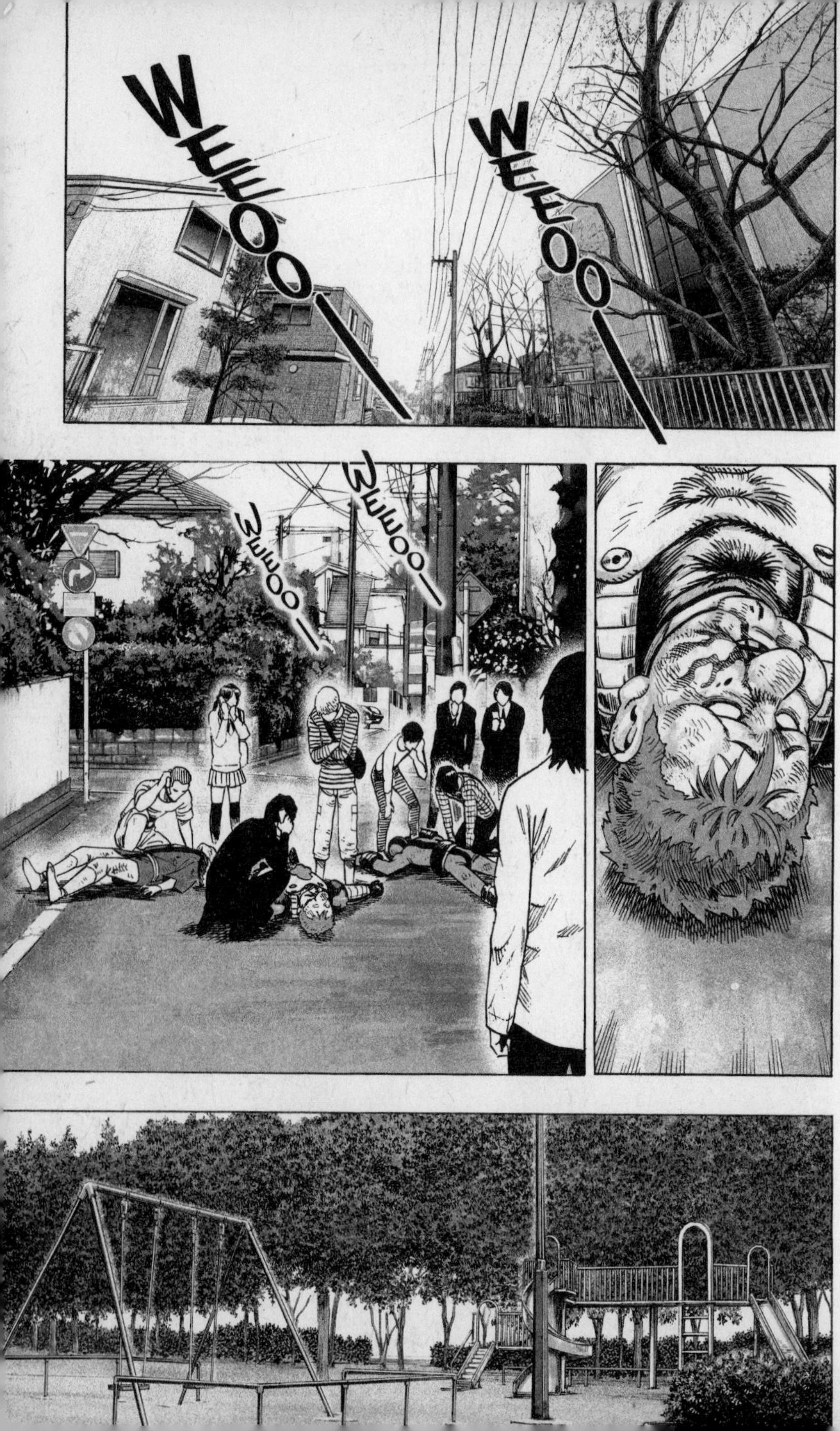
WEEOO—
WEEOO—
WEEOO—
WEEOO—

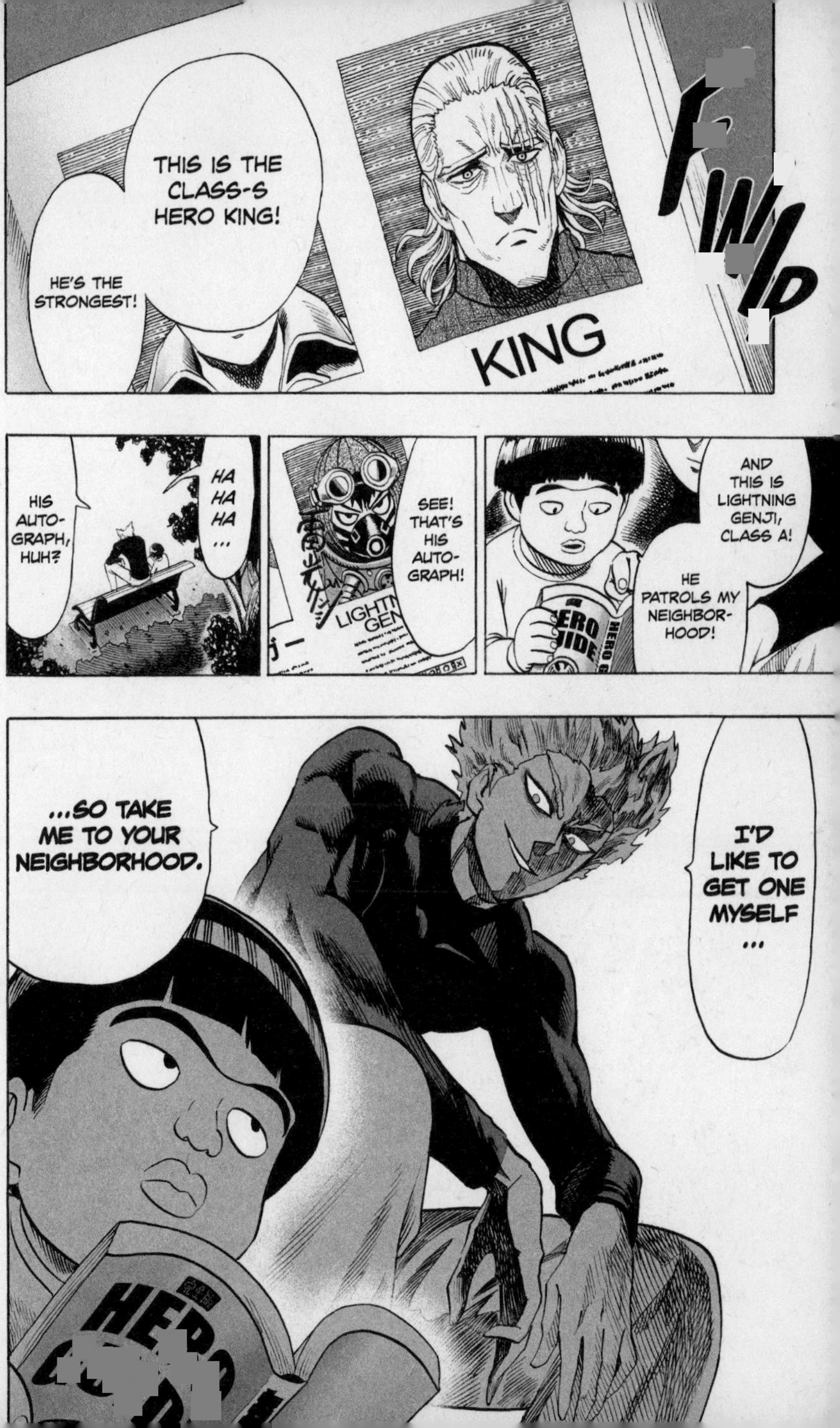
FWIP
KING
THIS IS THE CLASS-S HERO KING!
HE'S THE STRONGEST!
AND THIS IS LIGHTNING GENJI, CLASS A!
HE PATROLS MY NEIGHBORHOOD!
SEE! THAT'S HIS AUTOGRAPH!
HA HA HA ...
HIS AUTOGRAPH, HUH?
I'D LIKE TO GET ONE MYSELF ...
...SO TAKE ME TO YOUR NEIGHBORHOOD.

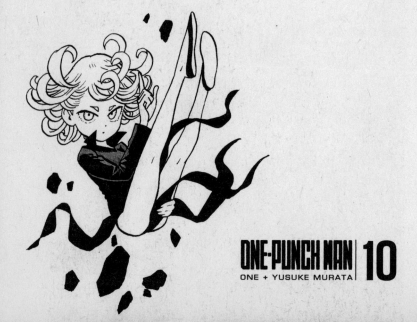

ONE-PUNCH MAN | 10

ONE + YUSUKE MURATA

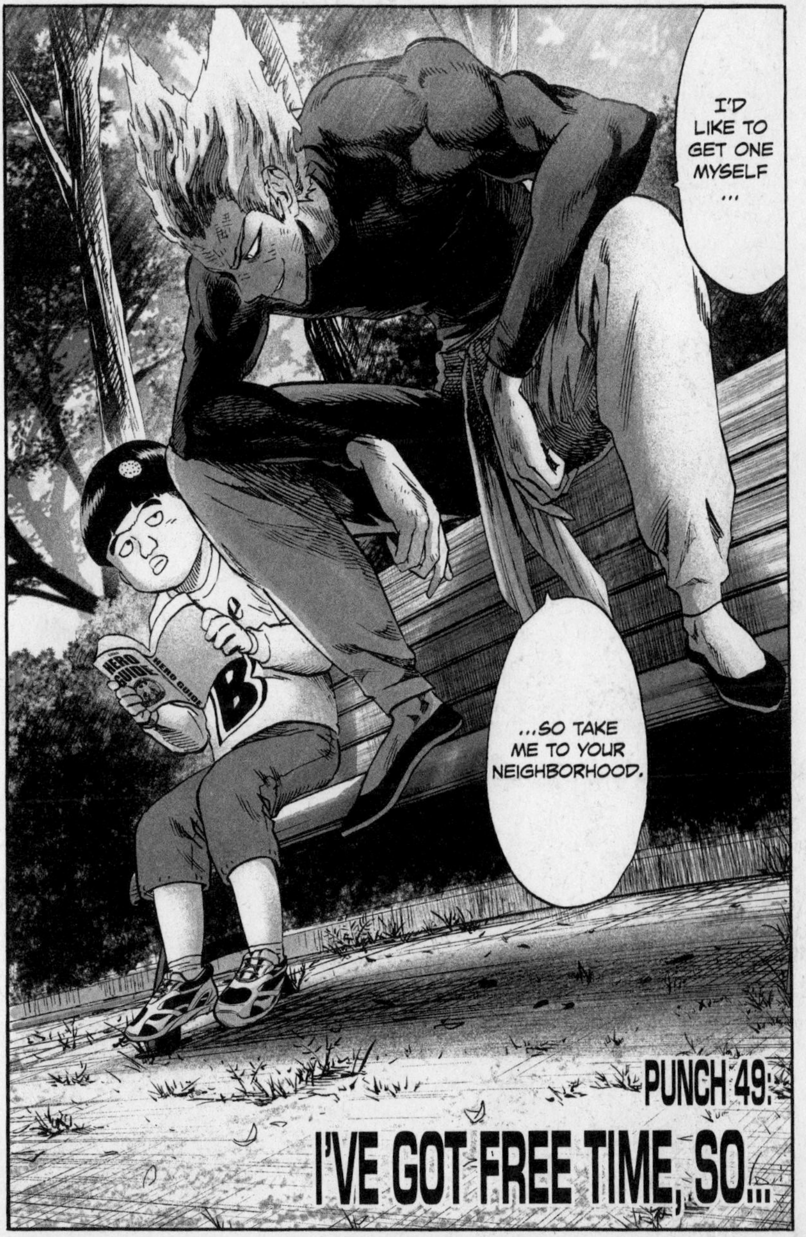
I'D LIKE TO GET ONE MYSELF ...
...SO TAKE ME TO YOUR NEIGHBORHOOD.
HERO GUIDE
PUNCH 49:
I'VE GOT FREE TIME, SO...

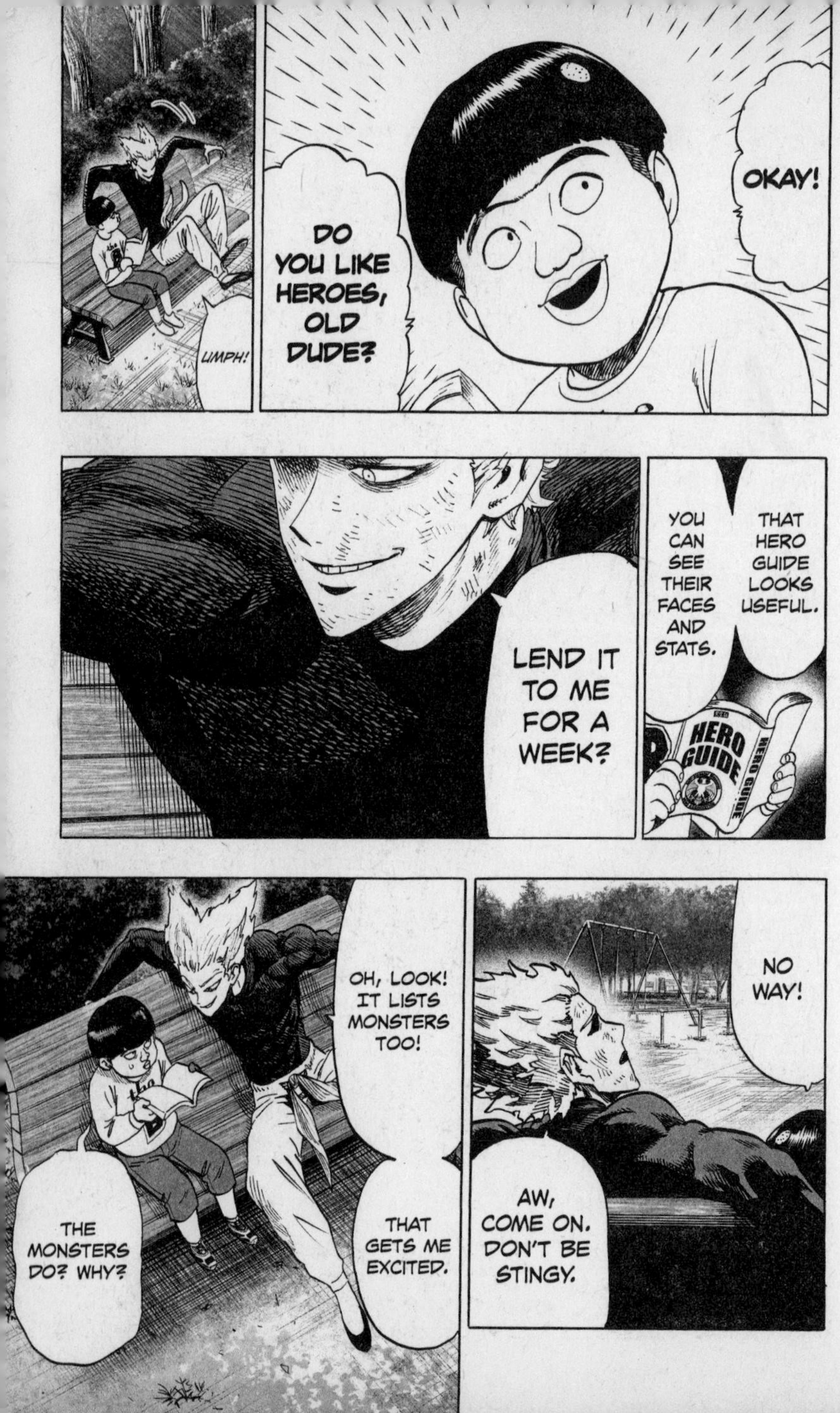
OKAY!
DO YOU LIKE HEROES, OLD DUDE?
UMPH!
THAT HERO GUIDE LOOKS USEFUL.
YOU CAN SEE THEIR FACES AND STATS.
HERO GUIDE
LEND IT TO ME FOR A WEEK?
NO WAY!
AW, COME ON. DON'T BE STINGY.
OH, LOOK! IT LISTS MONSTERS TOO!
THAT GETS ME EXCITED.
THE MONSTERS DO? WHY?

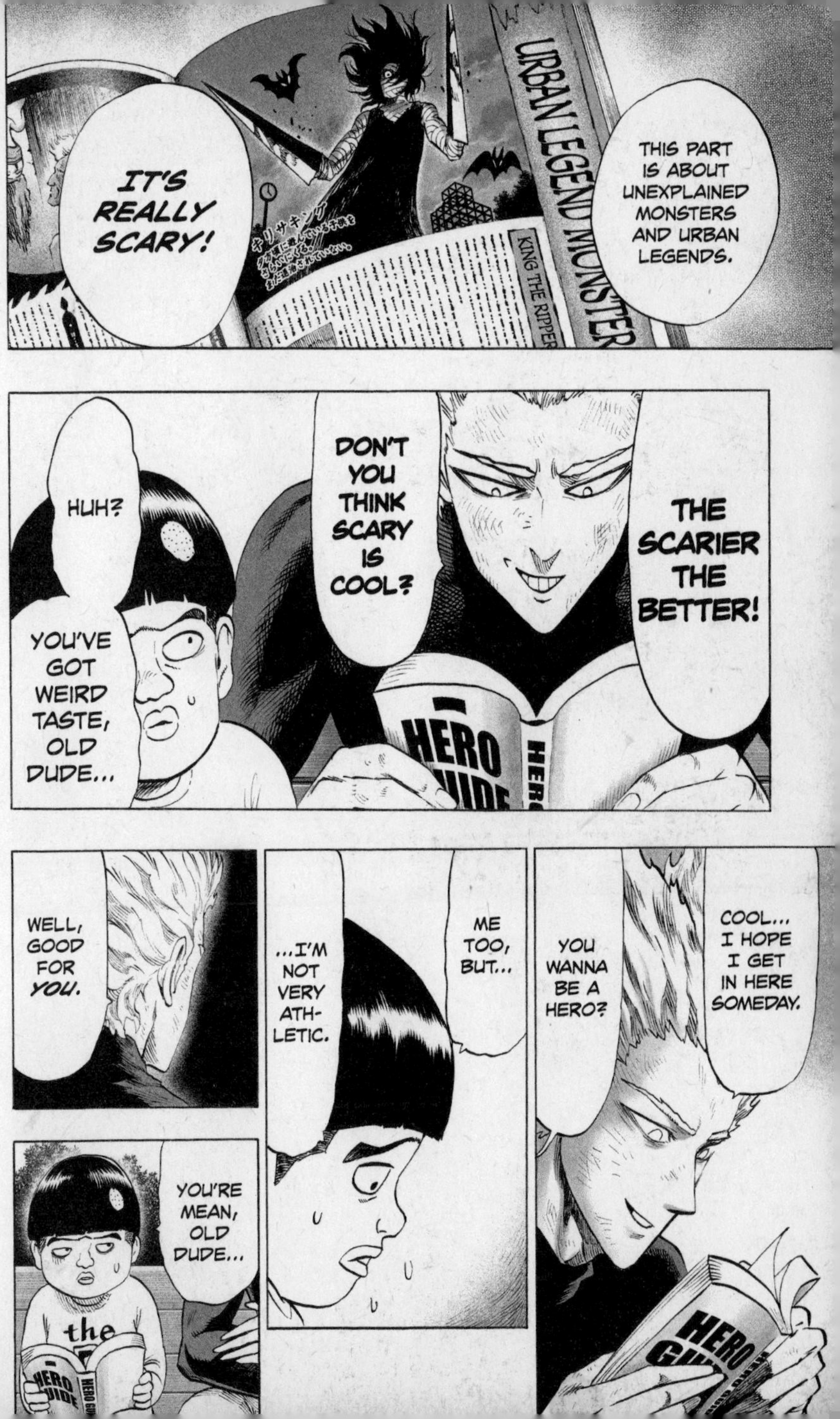
THIS PART IS ABOUT UNEXPLAINED MONSTERS AND URBAN LEGENDS.
URBAN LEGEND MONSTER
KING THE RIPPER
キリサキング
夕方に遊んでいる子供を
さらいにくる。
まだ退治されていない。
IT'S REALLY SCARY!
THE SCARIER THE BETTER!
DON'T YOU THINK SCARY IS COOL?
HUH?
YOU'VE GOT WEIRD TASTE, OLD DUDE...
COOL... I HOPE I GET IN HERE SOMEDAY.
YOU WANNA BE A HERO?
ME TOO, BUT...
...I'M NOT VERY ATHLETIC.
WELL, GOOD FOR *YOU*.
YOU'RE MEAN, OLD DUDE...

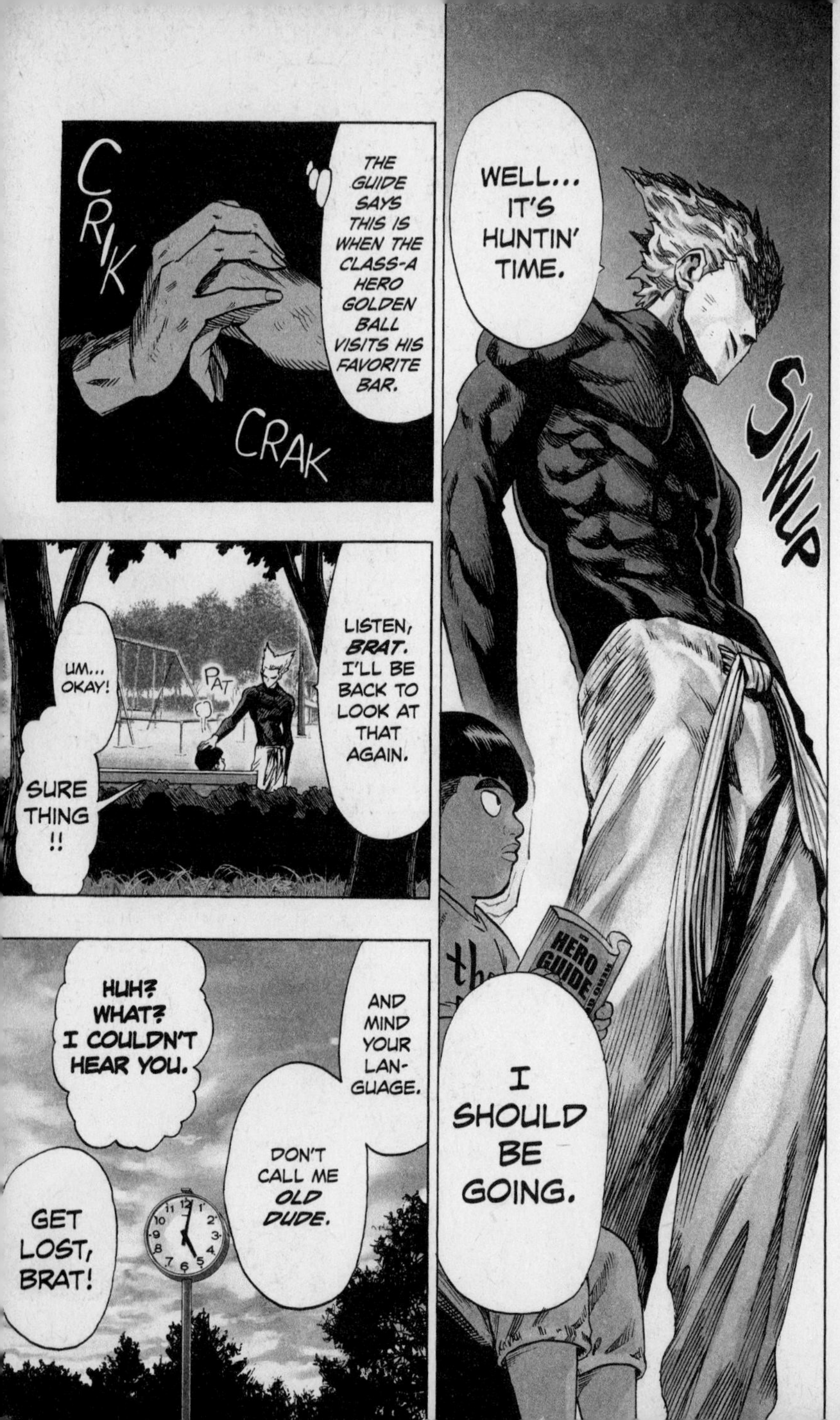
WELL... IT'S HUNTIN' TIME.
SWUP
HERO GUIDE
I SHOULD BE GOING.
THE GUIDE SAYS THIS IS WHEN THE CLASS-A HERO GOLDEN BALL VISITS HIS FAVORITE BAR.
CRIK
CRAK
LISTEN, BRAT. I'LL BE BACK TO LOOK AT THAT AGAIN.
PAT
UM... OKAY!
SURE THING!!
AND MIND YOUR LAN-GUAGE.
HUH? WHAT? I COULDN'T HEAR YOU.
DON'T CALL ME OLD DUDE.
GET LOST, BRAT!

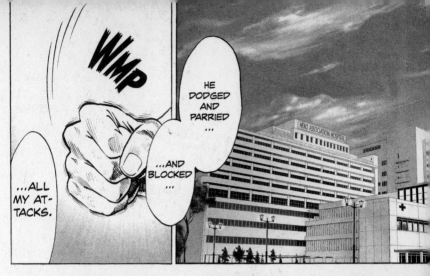

HE DODGED AND PARRIED ...
...AND BLOCKED ...
WMP
...ALL MY AT-TACKS.
NO MATTER HOW STRONG THE ATTACK ...
...IT'S NO USE IF IT DOESN'T HIT ITS MARK.
YEAH, THAT'S TRUE.
HIS COUNTER-ATTACKS AND THROWS ANTICIPATED MY MOVES...
...AND HIS TECHNIQUES RETURNED MY OWN STRENGTH TWOFOLD.
HE ALSO INCAPACI-TATED PHYSICAL FUNCTIONS ...
...WITH THRUSTS TARGETING JOINTS AND VITAL SPOTS.

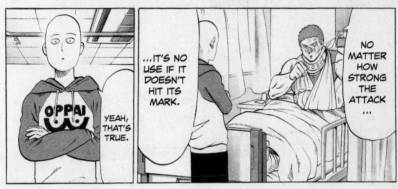

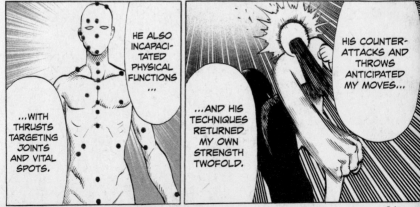

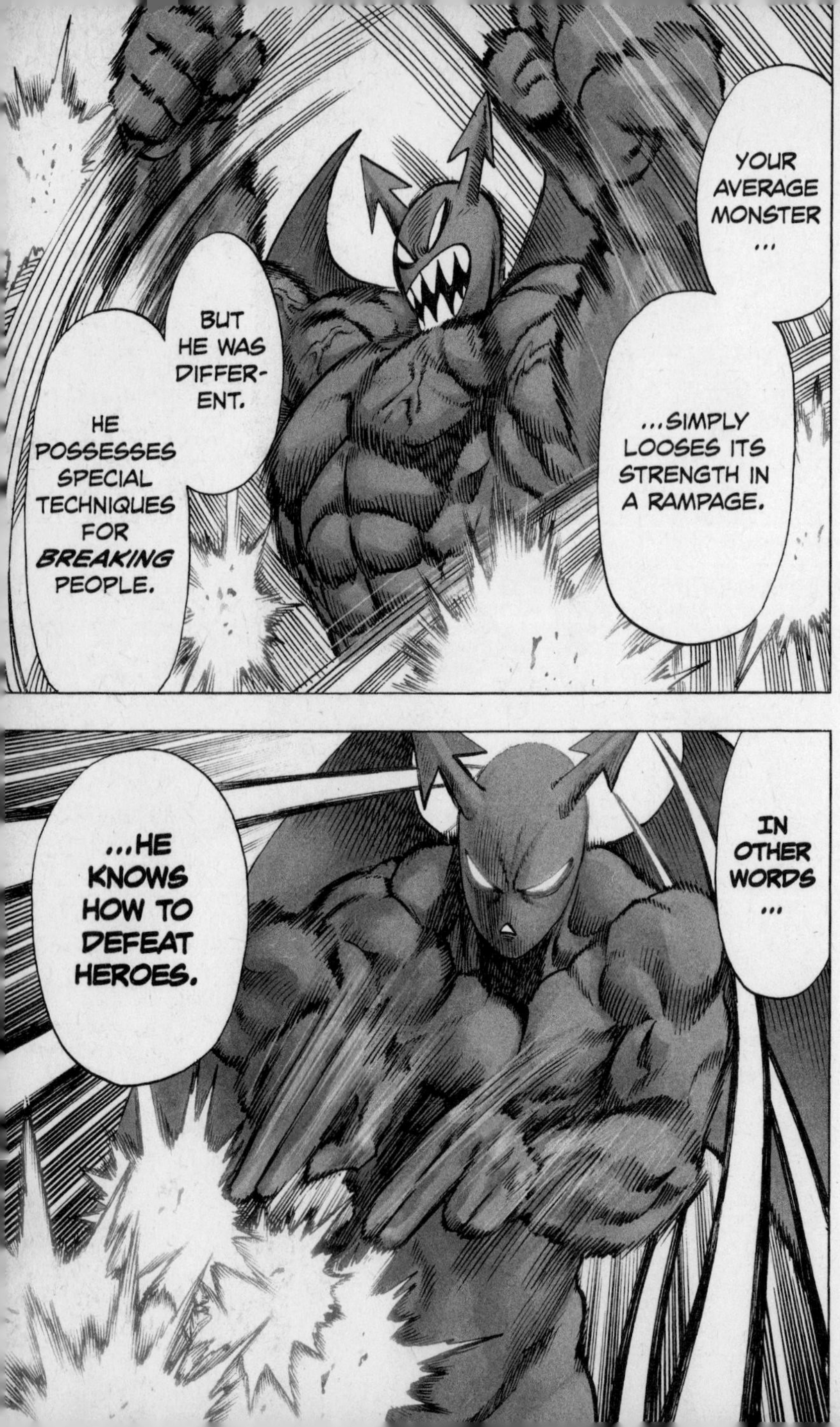
YOUR AVERAGE MONSTER ...
...SIMPLY LOOSES ITS STRENGTH IN A RAMPAGE.
BUT HE WAS DIFFER- ENT.
HE POSSESSES SPECIAL TECHNIQUES FOR *BREAKING* PEOPLE.
IN OTHER WORDS ...
...HE KNOWS HOW TO DEFEAT HEROES.

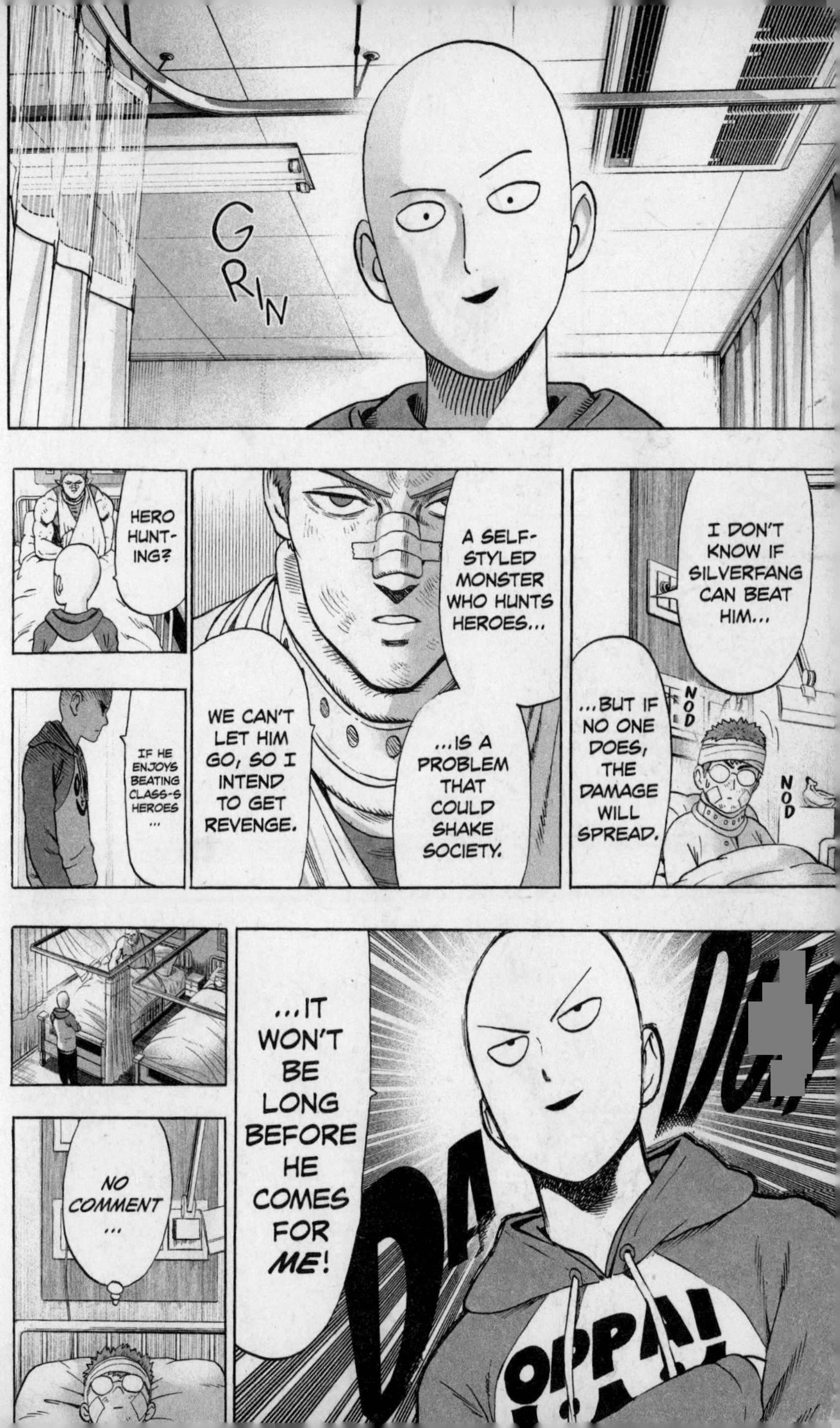
GRIN
I DON'T KNOW IF SILVERFANG CAN BEAT HIM...
...BUT IF NO ONE DOES, THE DAMAGE WILL SPREAD.
NOD
NOD
A SELF-STYLED MONSTER WHO HUNTS HEROES...
...IS A PROBLEM THAT COULD SHAKE SOCIETY.
WE CAN'T LET HIM GO, SO I INTEND TO GET REVENGE.
HERO HUNTING?
IF HE ENJOYS BEATING CLASS-S HEROES ...
...IT WON'T BE LONG BEFORE HE COMES FOR *ME*!
DA
NO COMMENT ...
OPPAI

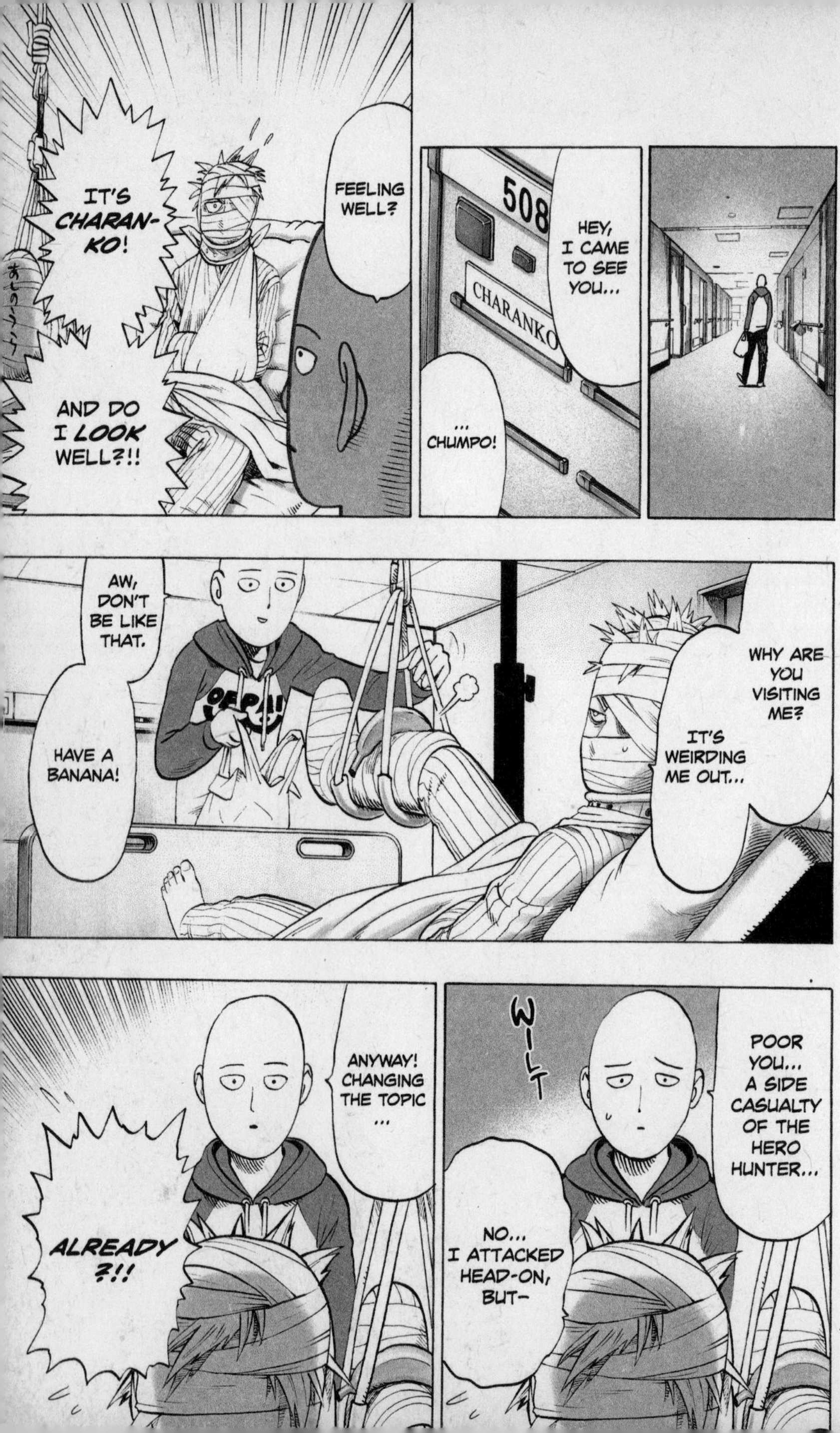
HEY, I CAME TO SEE YOU...
...CHUMPO!
508
CHARANKO
FEELING WELL?
IT'S CHARAN-KO!
AND DO I LOOK WELL?!!
WHY ARE YOU VISITING ME?
IT'S WEIRDING ME OUT...
AW, DON'T BE LIKE THAT.
HAVE A BANANA!
WILT
POOR YOU... A SIDE CASUALTY OF THE HERO HUNTER...
NO... I ATTACKED HEAD-ON, BUT-
ANYWAY! CHANGING THE TOPIC...
ALREADY?!!

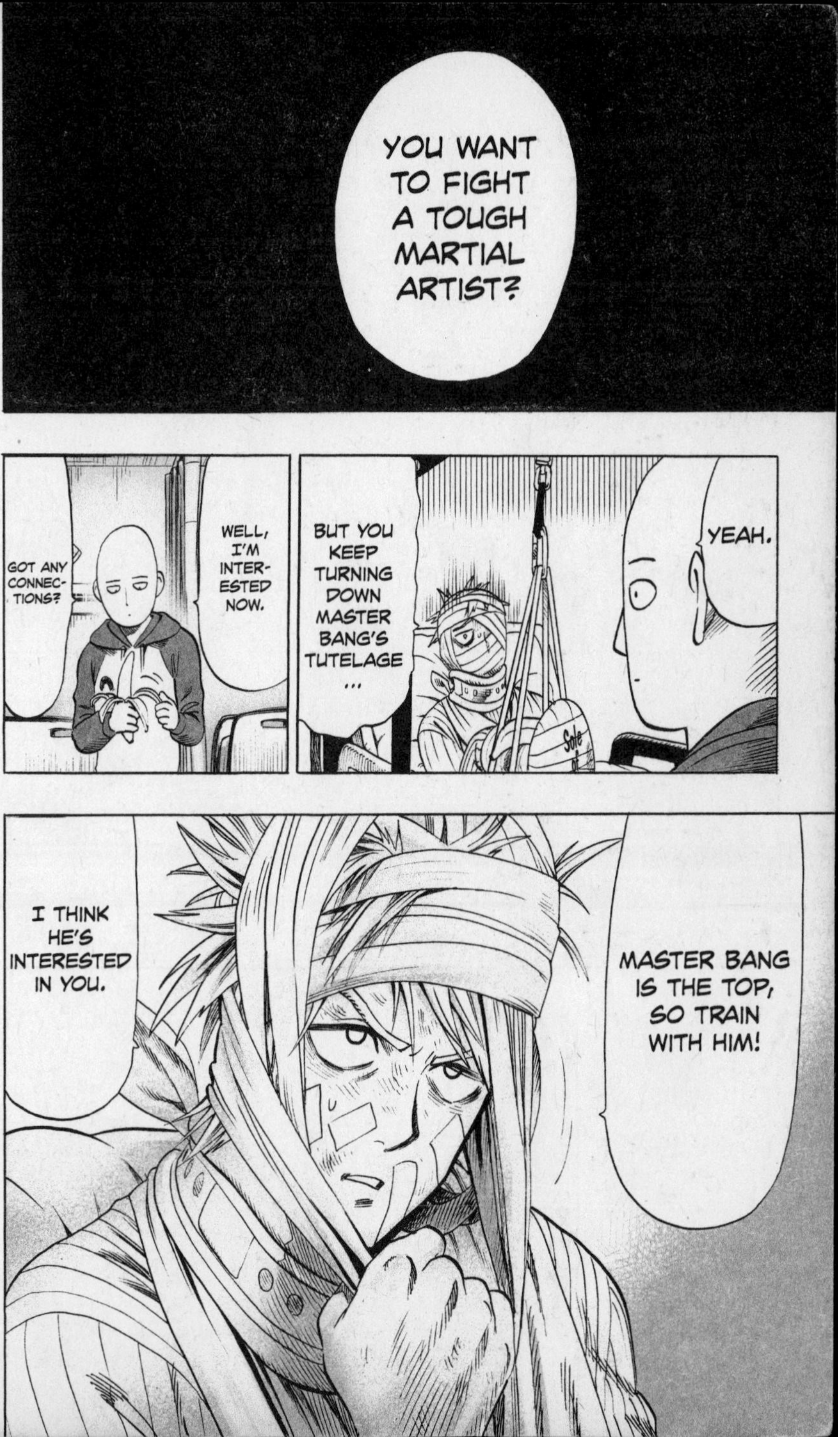
YOU WANT TO FIGHT A TOUGH MARTIAL ARTIST?
YEAH.
BUT YOU KEEP TURNING DOWN MASTER BANG'S TUTELAGE ...
WELL, I'M INTER-ESTED NOW.
GOT ANY CONNEC-TIONS?
MASTER BANG IS THE TOP, SO TRAIN WITH HIM!
I THINK HE'S INTERESTED IN YOU.

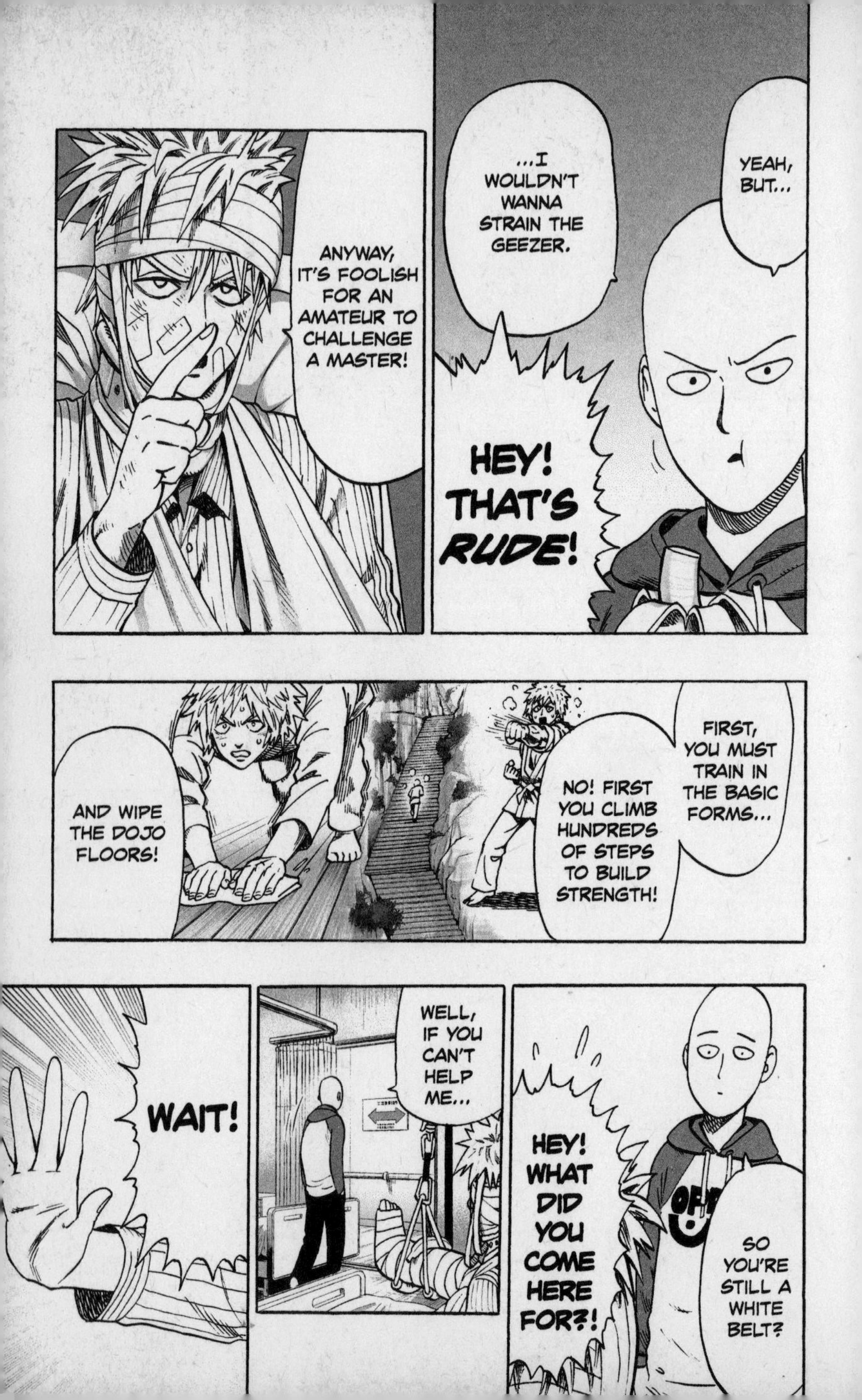
YEAH, BUT...
...I WOULDN'T WANNA STRAIN THE GEEZER.
HEY! THAT'S *RUDE*!
ANYWAY, IT'S FOOLISH FOR AN AMATEUR TO CHALLENGE A MASTER!
FIRST, YOU MUST TRAIN IN THE BASIC FORMS...
NO! FIRST YOU CLIMB HUNDREDS OF STEPS TO BUILD STRENGTH!
AND WIPE THE DOJO FLOORS!
SO YOU'RE STILL A WHITE BELT?
HEY! WHAT DID YOU COME HERE FOR?!
WELL, IF YOU CAN'T HELP ME...
WAIT!

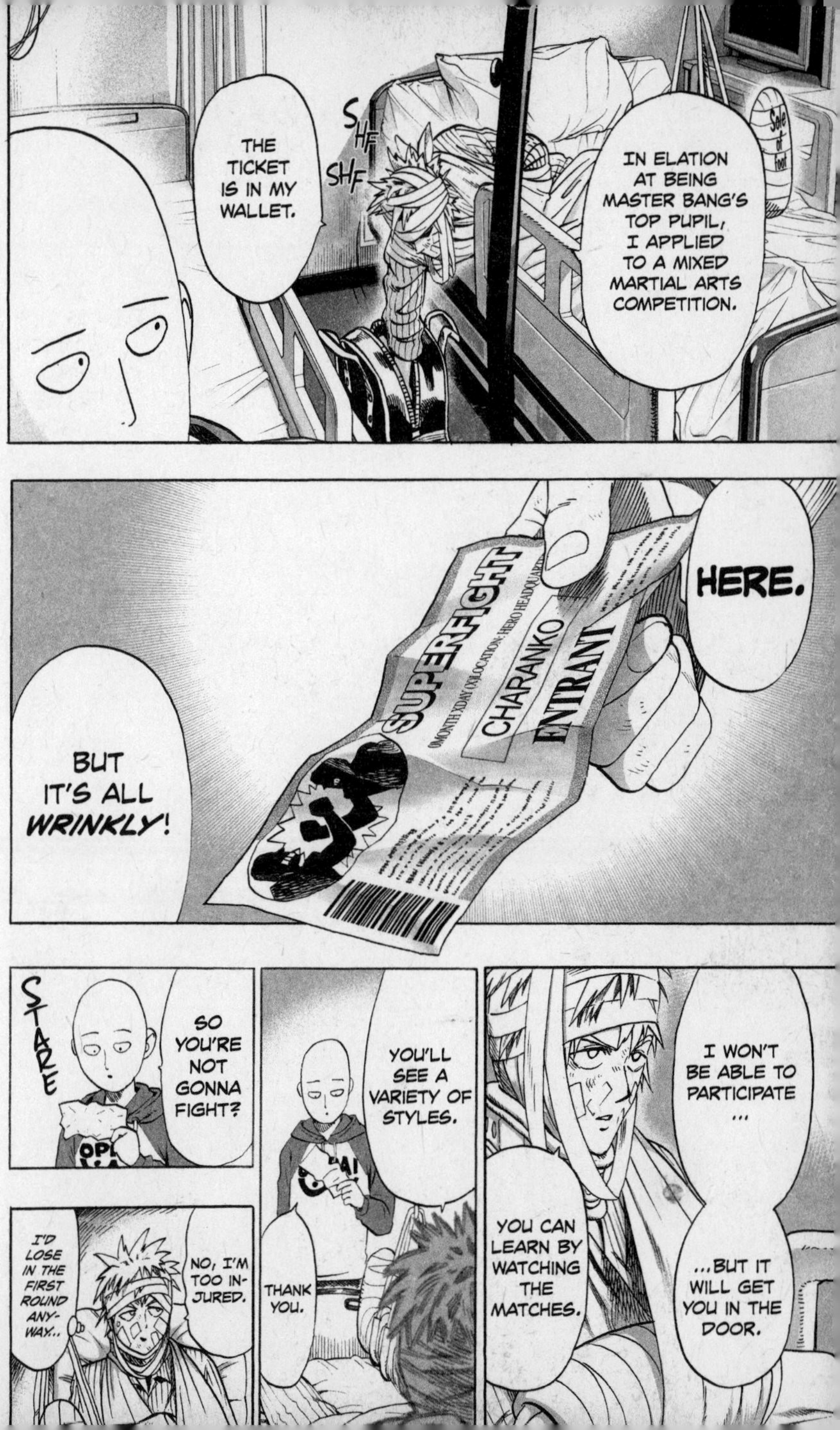
Sole of foot
IN ELATION AT BEING MASTER BANG'S TOP PUPIL, I APPLIED TO A MIXED MARTIAL ARTS COMPETITION.
SHF SHF
THE TICKET IS IN MY WALLET.
HERE.
SUPERFIGHT
CHARANKO
ENTRANT
BUT IT'S ALL WRINKLY!
I WON'T BE ABLE TO PARTICIPATE ...
...BUT IT WILL GET YOU IN THE DOOR.
YOU CAN LEARN BY WATCHING THE MATCHES.
YOU'LL SEE A VARIETY OF STYLES.
THANK YOU.
STARE
SO YOU'RE NOT GONNA FIGHT?
NO, I'M TOO IN-JURED.
I'D LOSE IN THE FIRST ROUND ANY-WAY..

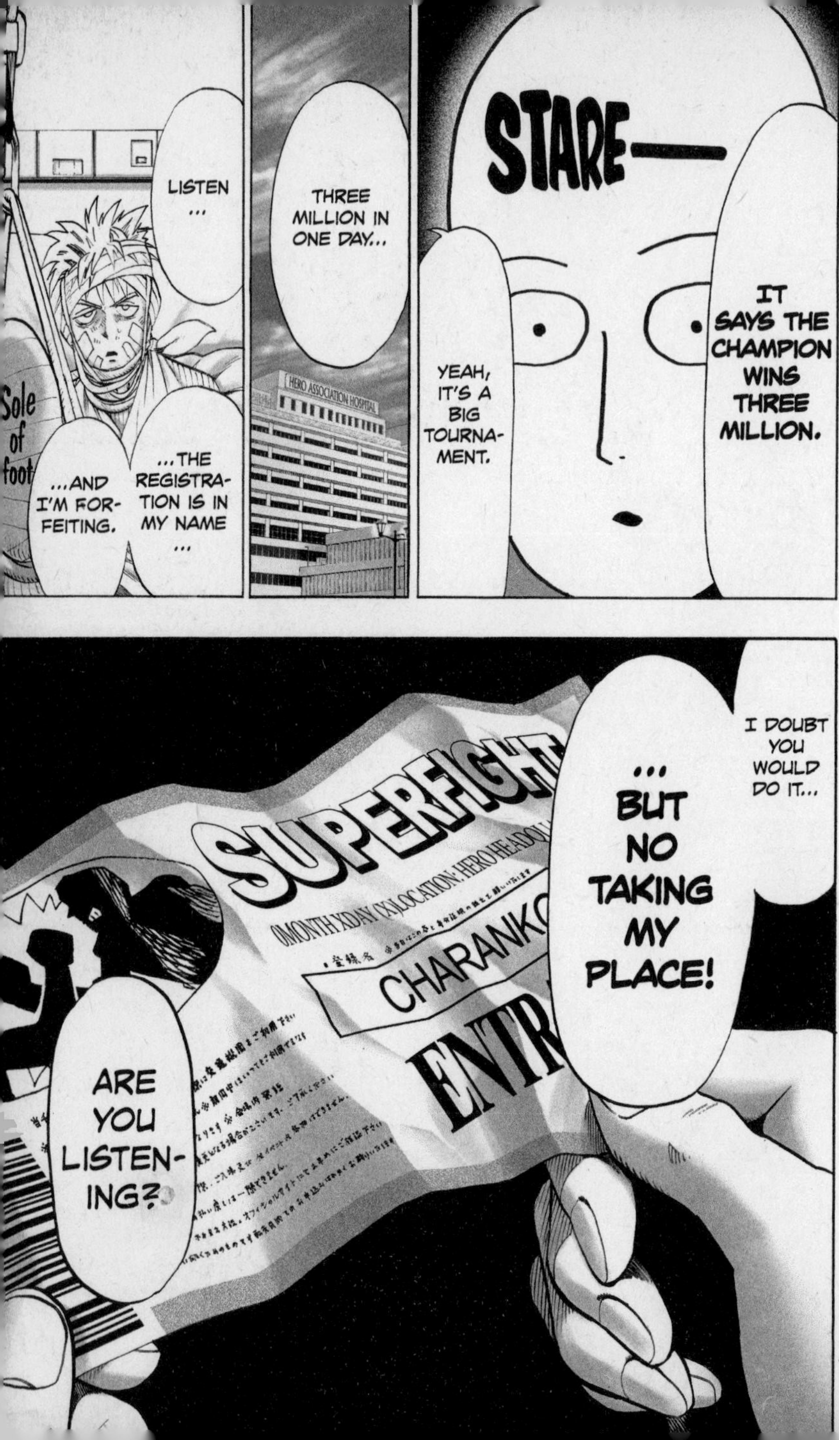
STARE—
IT SAYS THE CHAMPION WINS THREE MILLION.
YEAH, IT'S A BIG TOURNAMENT.
HERO ASSOCIATION HOSPITAL
THREE MILLION IN ONE DAY...
LISTEN ...
...THE REGISTRATION IS IN MY NAME ...
...AND I'M FORFEITING.
Sole of foot
I DOUBT YOU WOULD DO IT...
... BUT NO TAKING MY PLACE!
SUPERFIGHT
0MONTH XDAY (X) LOCATION: HERO HEADQU
CHARANKO
ENTR
ARE YOU LISTENING?

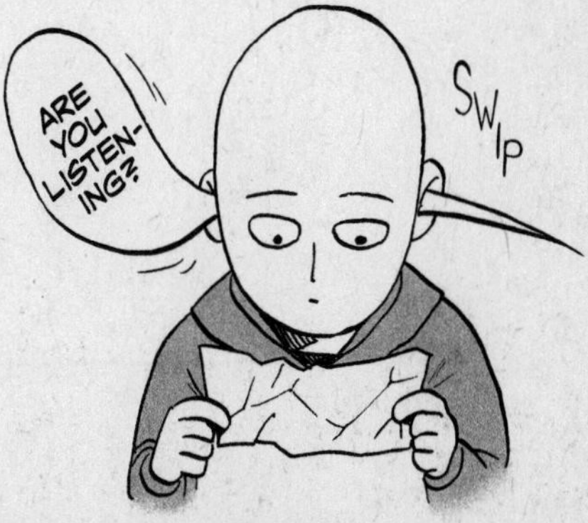
ARE YOU LISTEN-ING?
SWIP

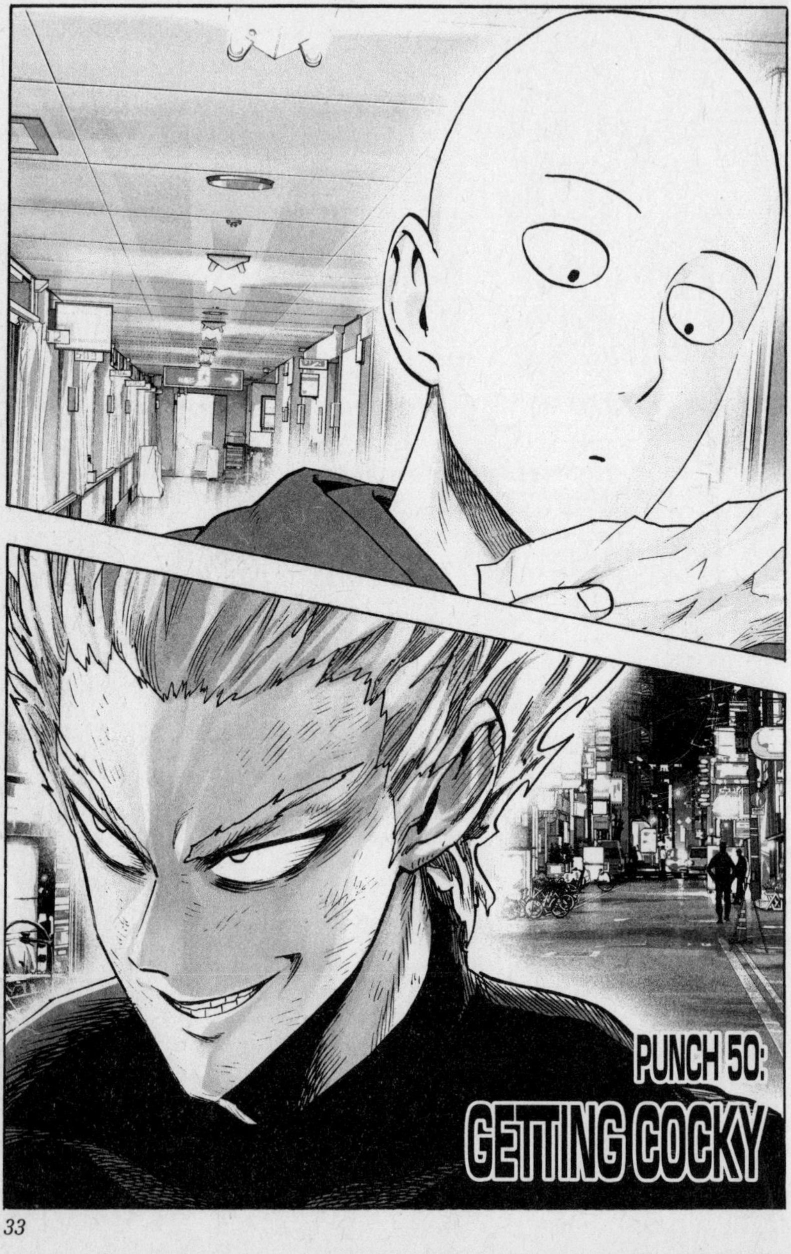
PUNCH 50:
GETTING COCKY

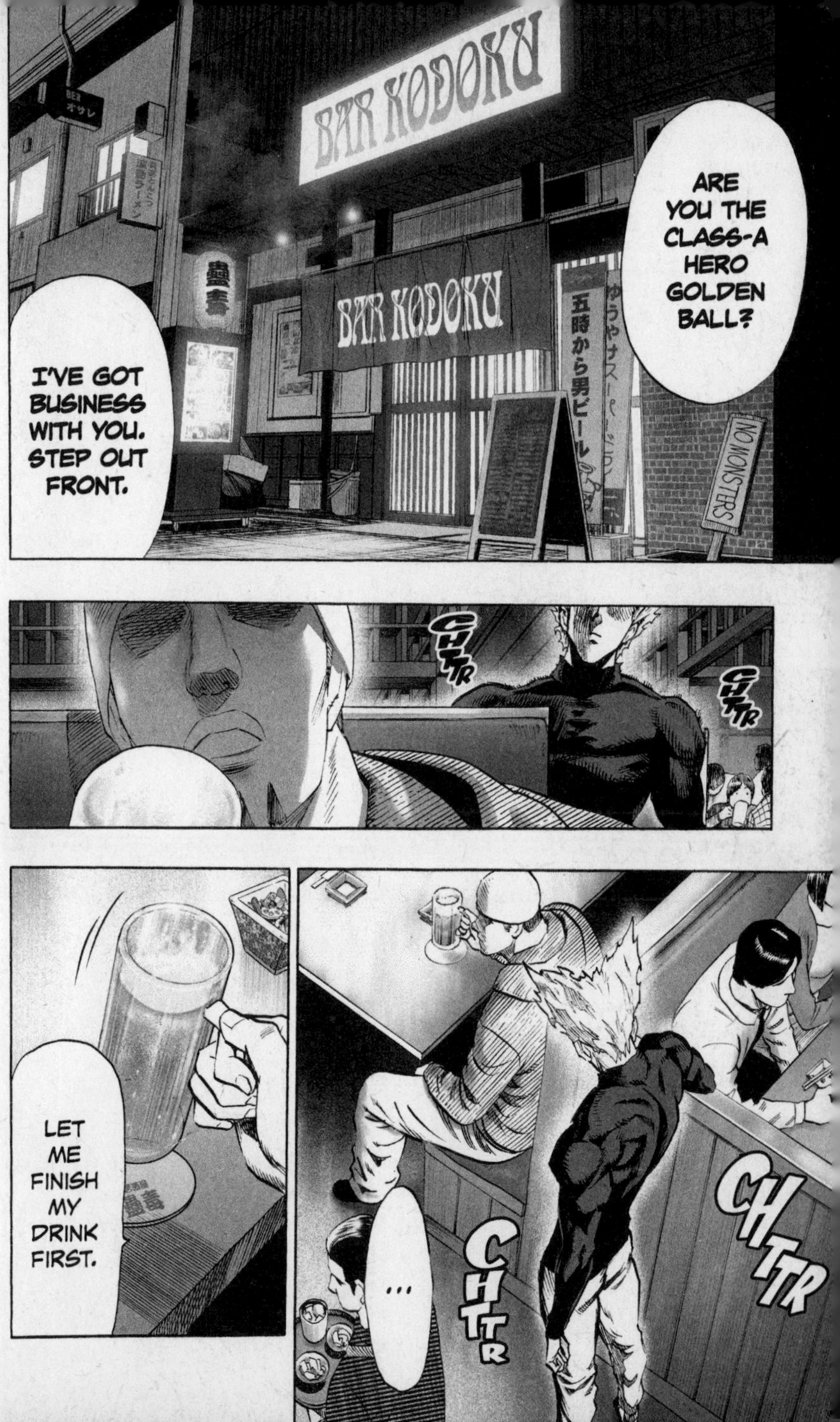
BAR KODOKU
BAR KODOKU
ARE YOU THE CLASS-A HERO GOLDEN BALL?
I'VE GOT BUSINESS WITH YOU. STEP OUT FRONT.
五時から男ビール
NO MONSTERS
CHTTR
CHTTR
CHTTR
CHTTR
...
LET ME FINISH MY DRINK FIRST.

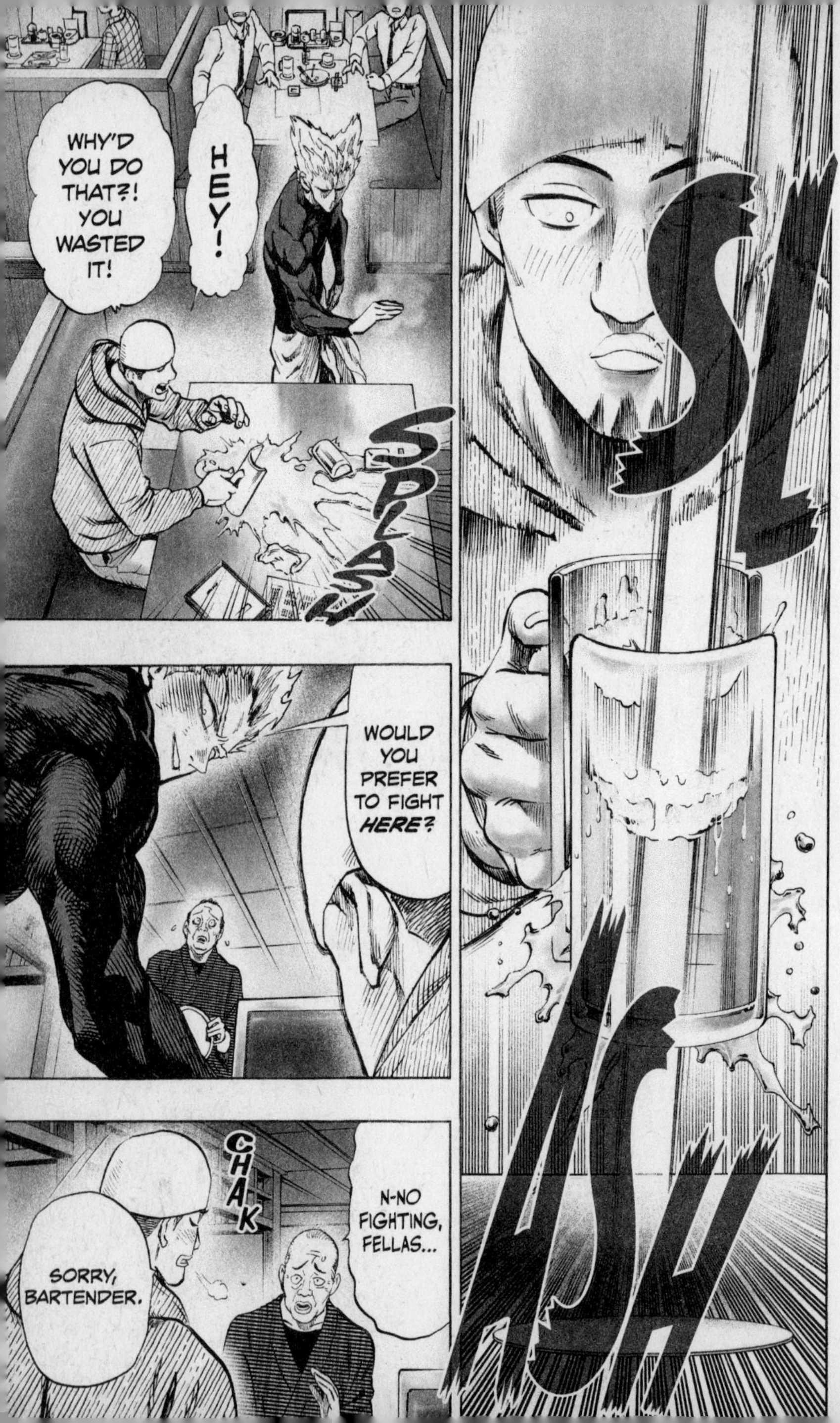
HEY!
WHY'D YOU DO THAT?! YOU WASTED IT!
SPLASH
WOULD YOU PREFER TO FIGHT *HERE?*
N-NO FIGHTING, FELLAS...
CHAK
SORRY, BARTENDER.

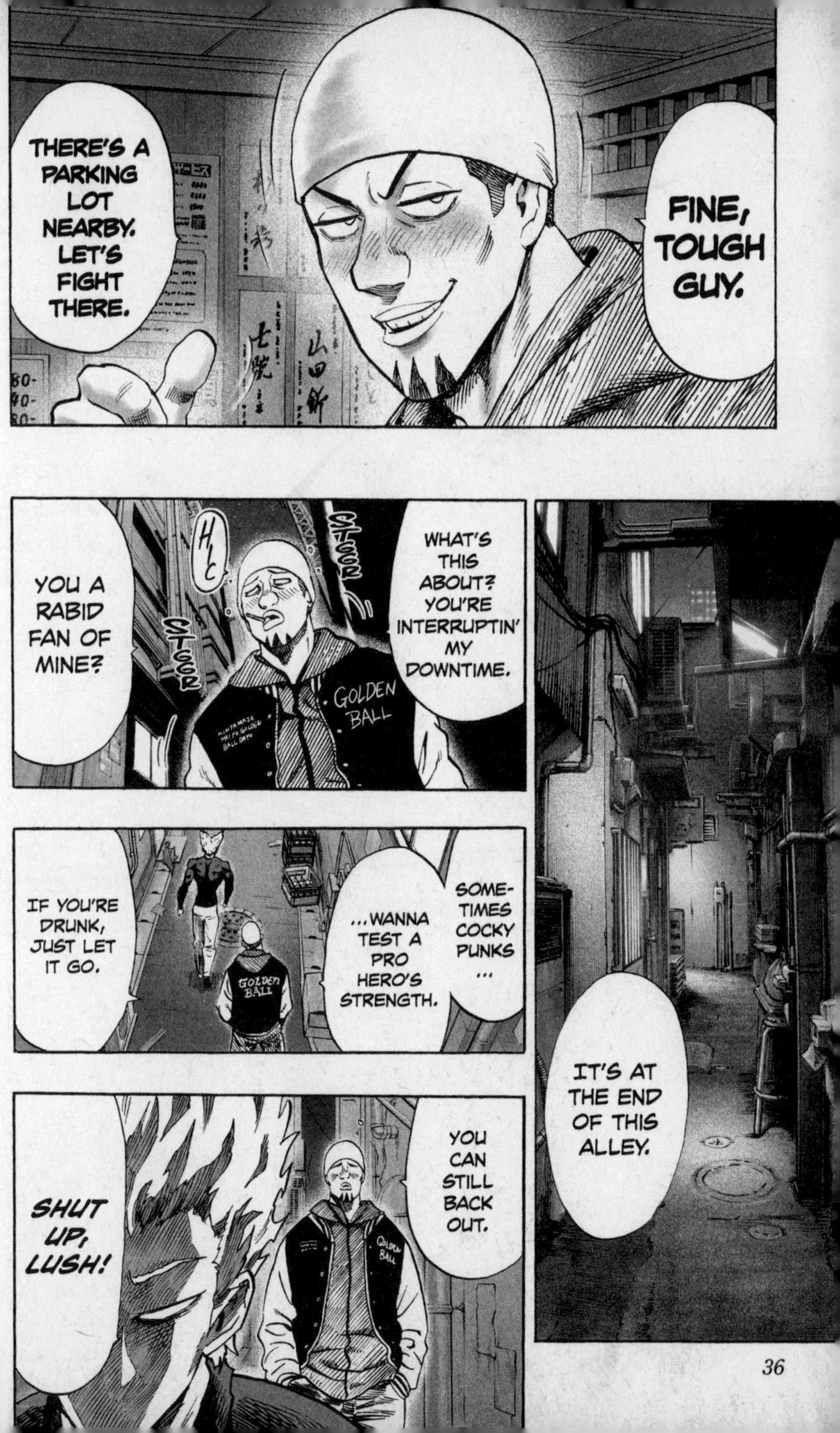
FINE, TOUGH GUY.
THERE'S A PARKING LOT NEARBY. LET'S FIGHT THERE.
IT'S AT THE END OF THIS ALLEY.
STGGR
WHAT'S THIS ABOUT? YOU'RE INTERRUPTIN' MY DOWNTIME.
HIC
STGGR
YOU A RABID FAN OF MINE?
GOLDEN BALL
SOMETIMES COCKY PUNKS...
...WANNA TEST A PRO HERO'S STRENGTH.
IF YOU'RE DRUNK, JUST LET IT GO.
GOLDEN BALL
YOU CAN STILL BACK OUT.
SHUT UP, LUSH!

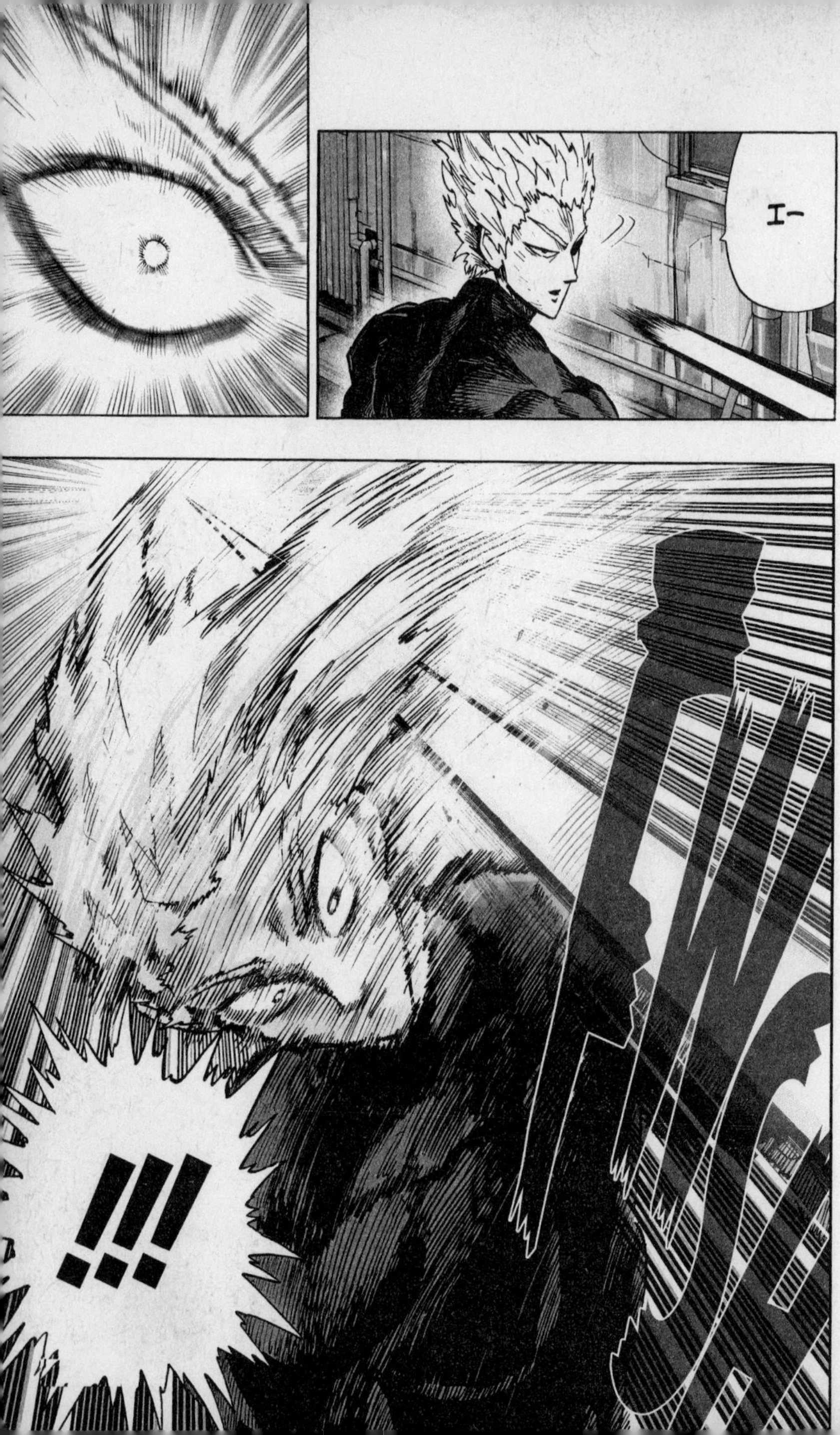
I-
!!!

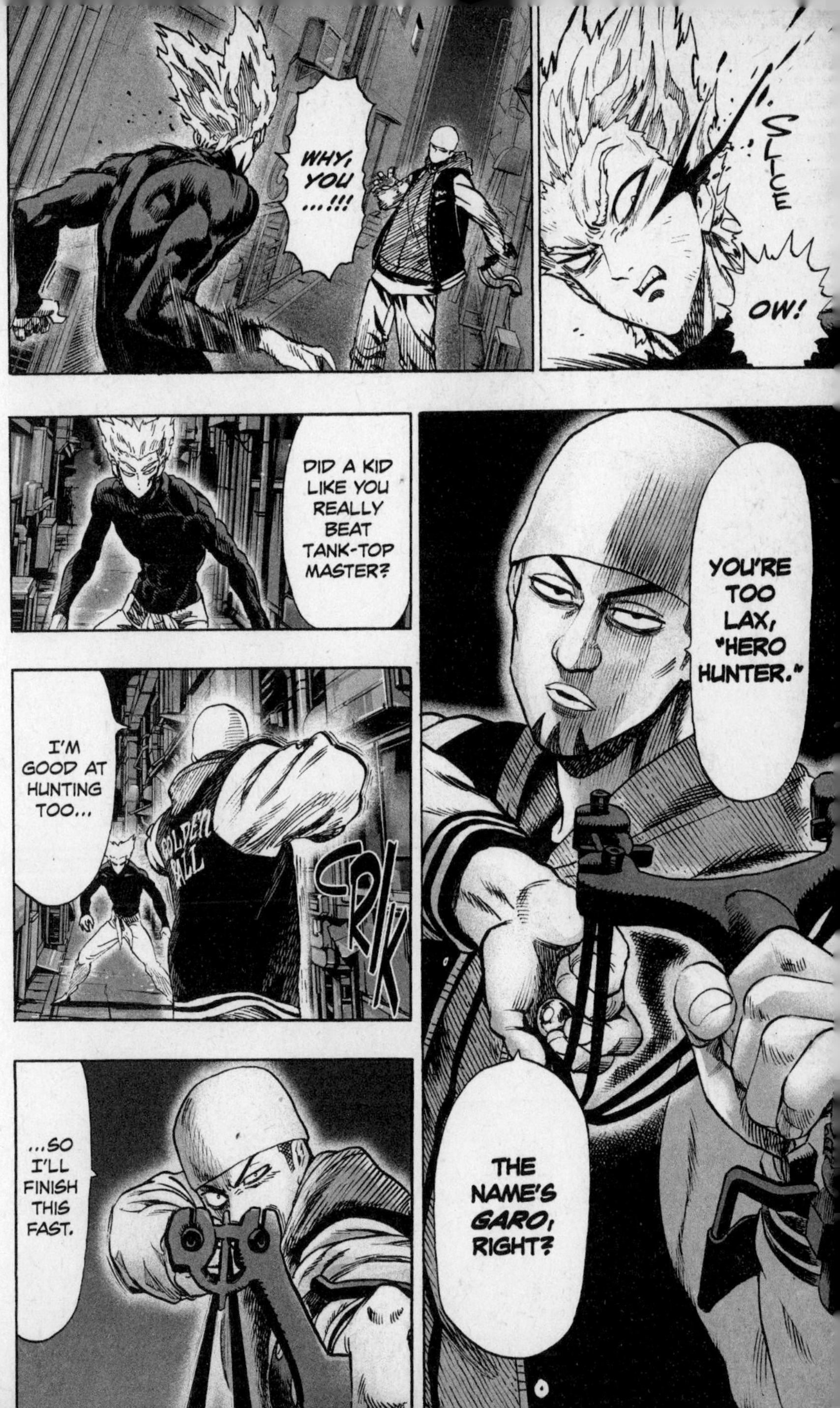
SLICE
OW!
WHY, YOU ...!!!
YOU'RE TOO LAX, "HERO HUNTER."
THE NAME'S *GARO*, RIGHT?
DID A KID LIKE YOU REALLY BEAT TANK-TOP MASTER?
I'M GOOD AT HUNTING TOO...
GOLDEN BALL
CRIK
...SO I'LL FINISH THIS FAST.

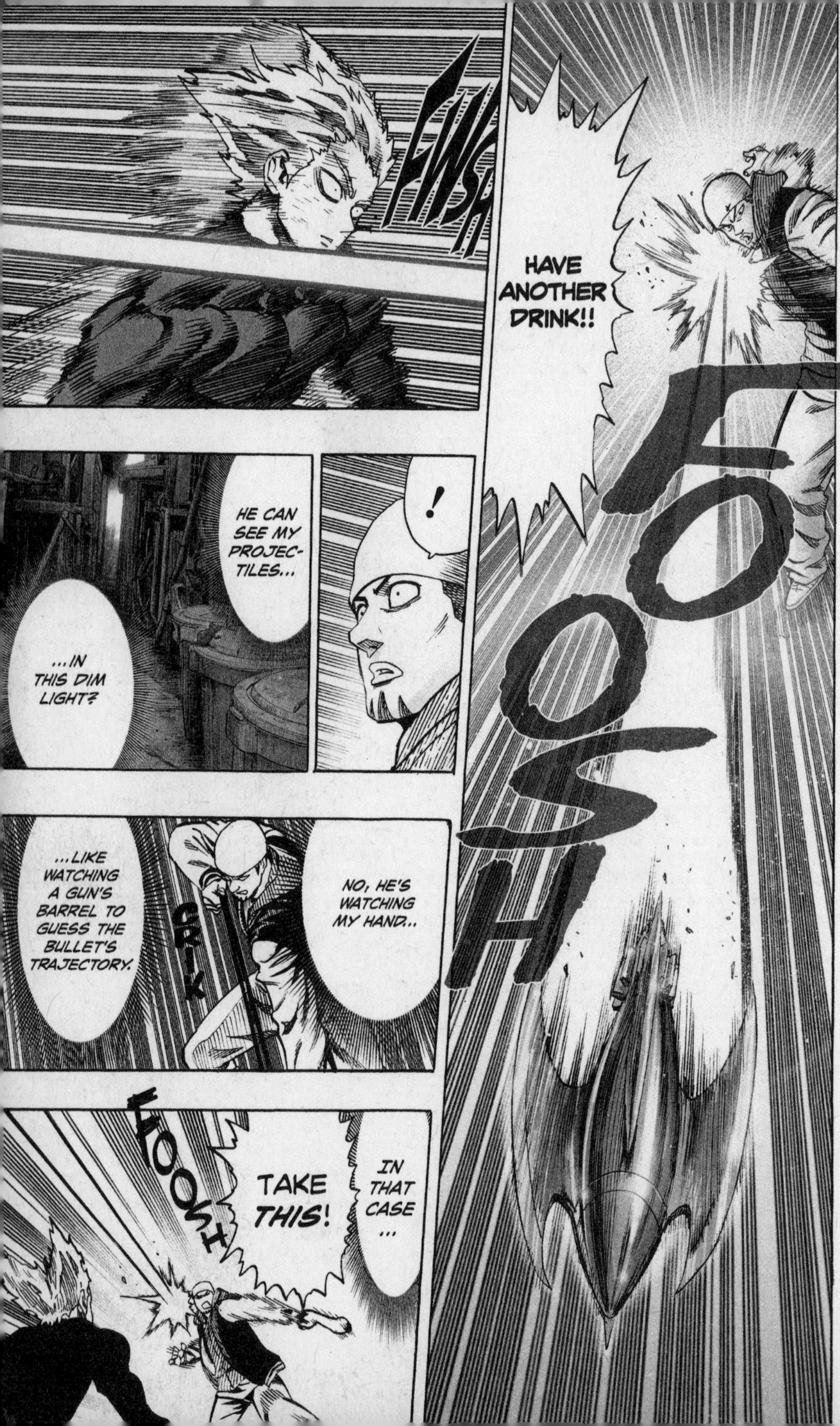
HAVE ANOTHER DRINK!!
FOOSH
FWSH
!
HE CAN SEE MY PROJECTILES...
...IN THIS DIM LIGHT?
NO, HE'S WATCHING MY HAND...
...LIKE WATCHING A GUN'S BARREL TO GUESS THE BULLET'S TRAJECTORY.
GRIK
IN THAT CASE...
TAKE THIS!
KOOSH

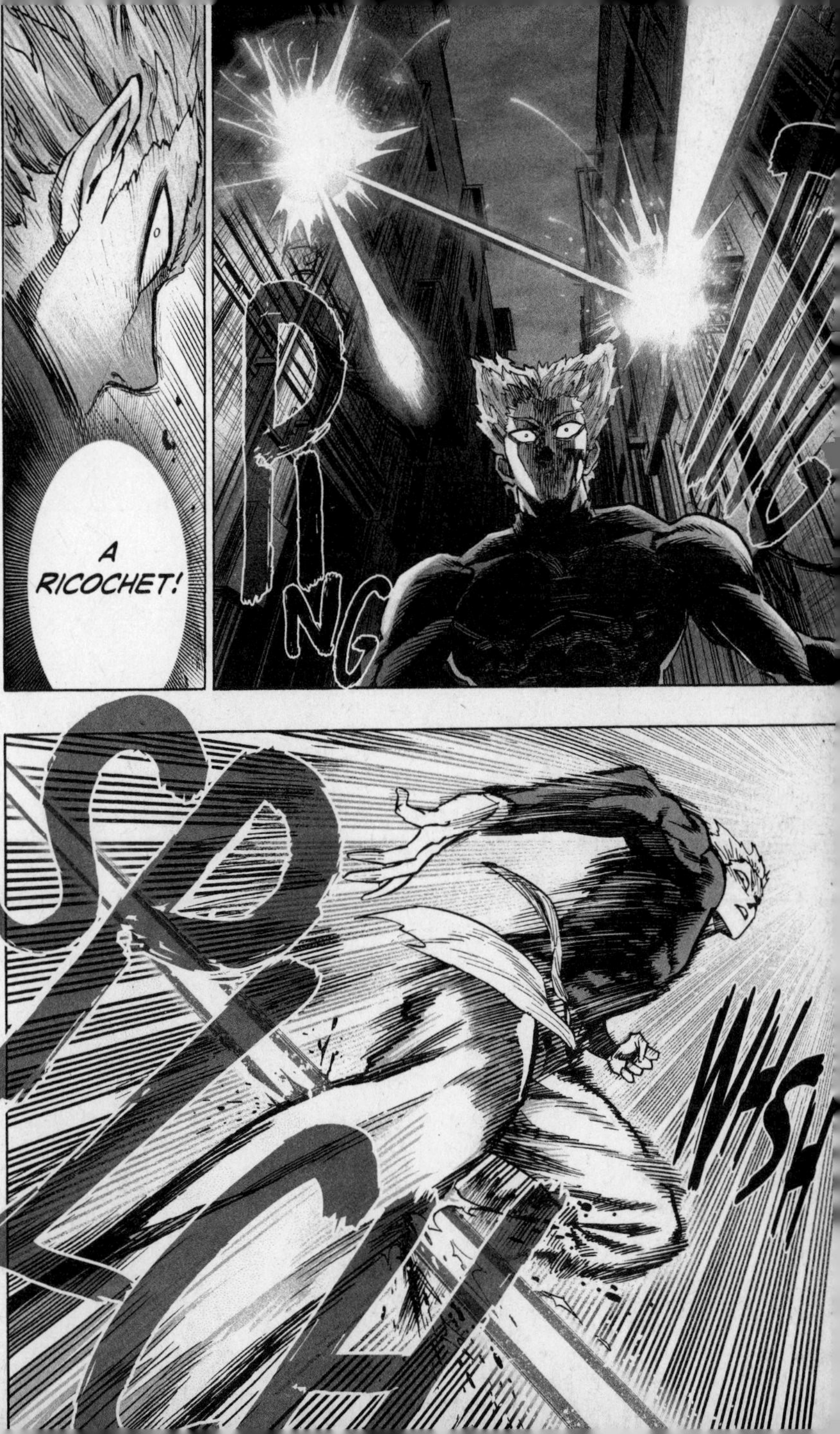
PING
A RICOCHET!
WHSH

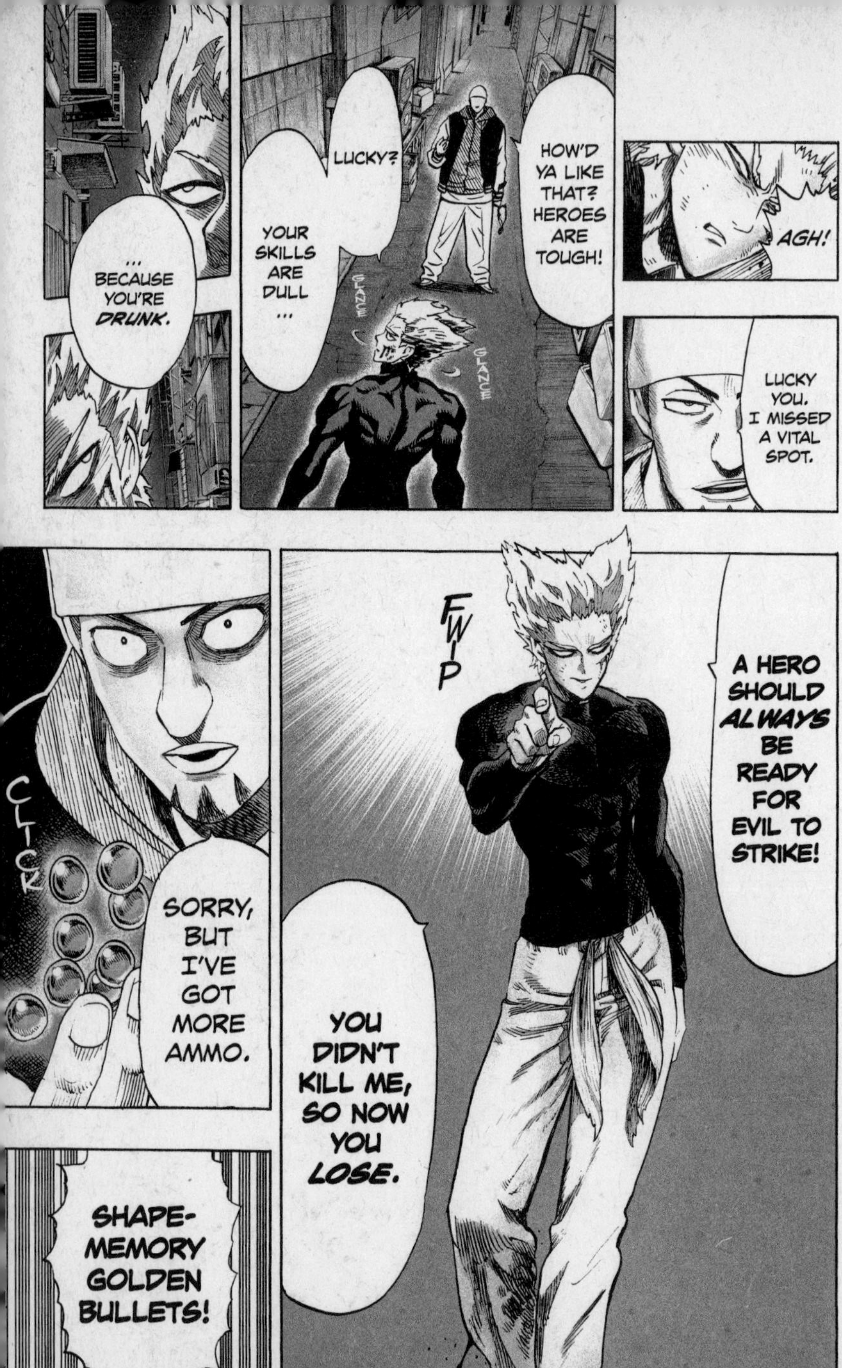
AGH!
LUCKY YOU. I MISSED A VITAL SPOT.
HOW'D YA LIKE THAT? HEROES ARE TOUGH!
LUCKY?
YOUR SKILLS ARE DULL ...
GLANCE
GLANCE
... BECAUSE YOU'RE DRUNK.
FWIP
A HERO SHOULD ALWAYS BE READY FOR EVIL TO STRIKE!
YOU DIDN'T KILL ME, SO NOW YOU LOSE.
CLICK
SORRY, BUT I'VE GOT MORE AMMO.
SHAPE-MEMORY GOLDEN BULLETS!

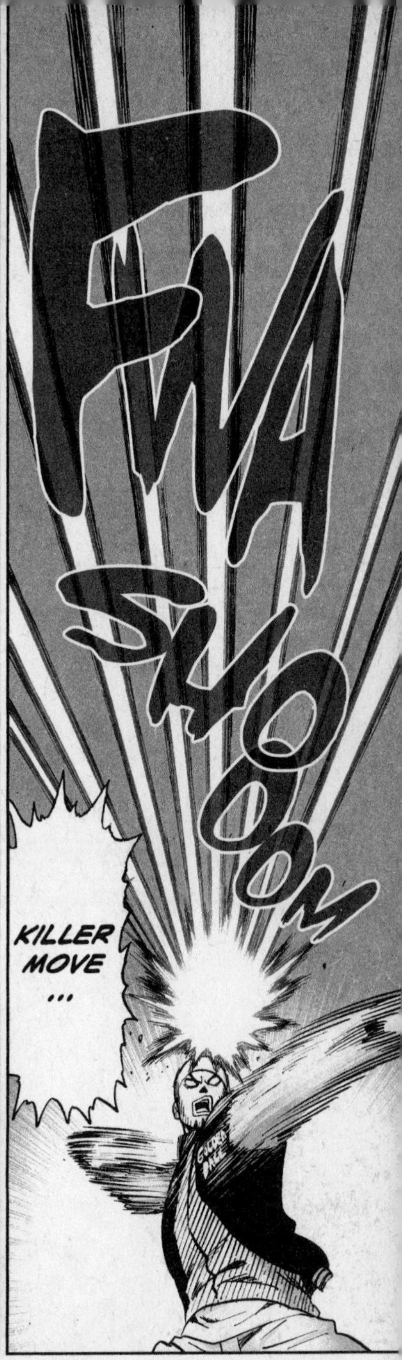
FWA
KILLER MOVE ...
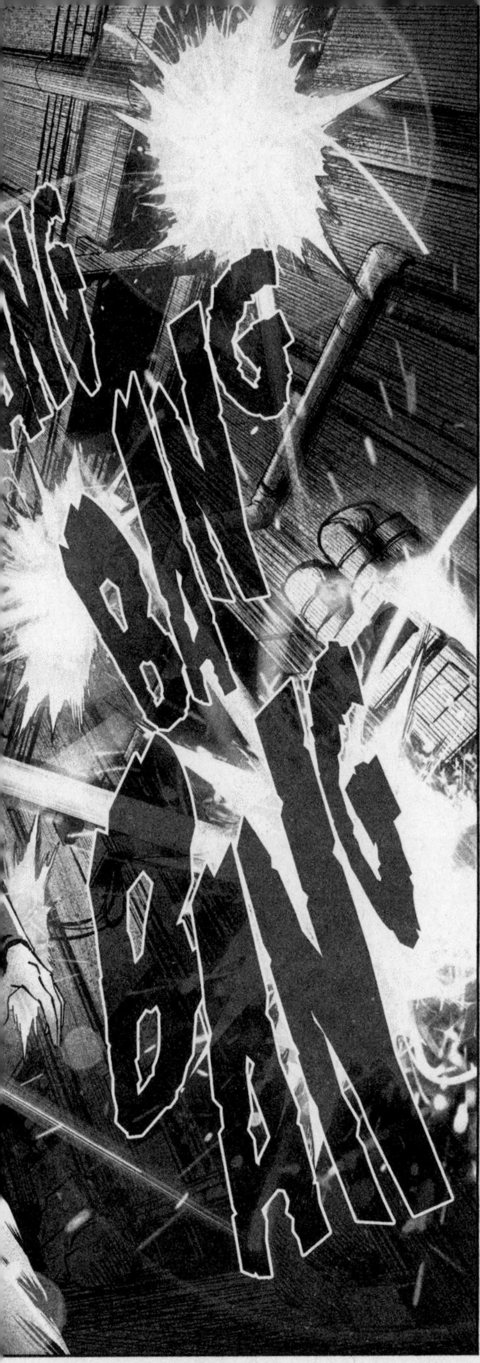
BANG
BANG

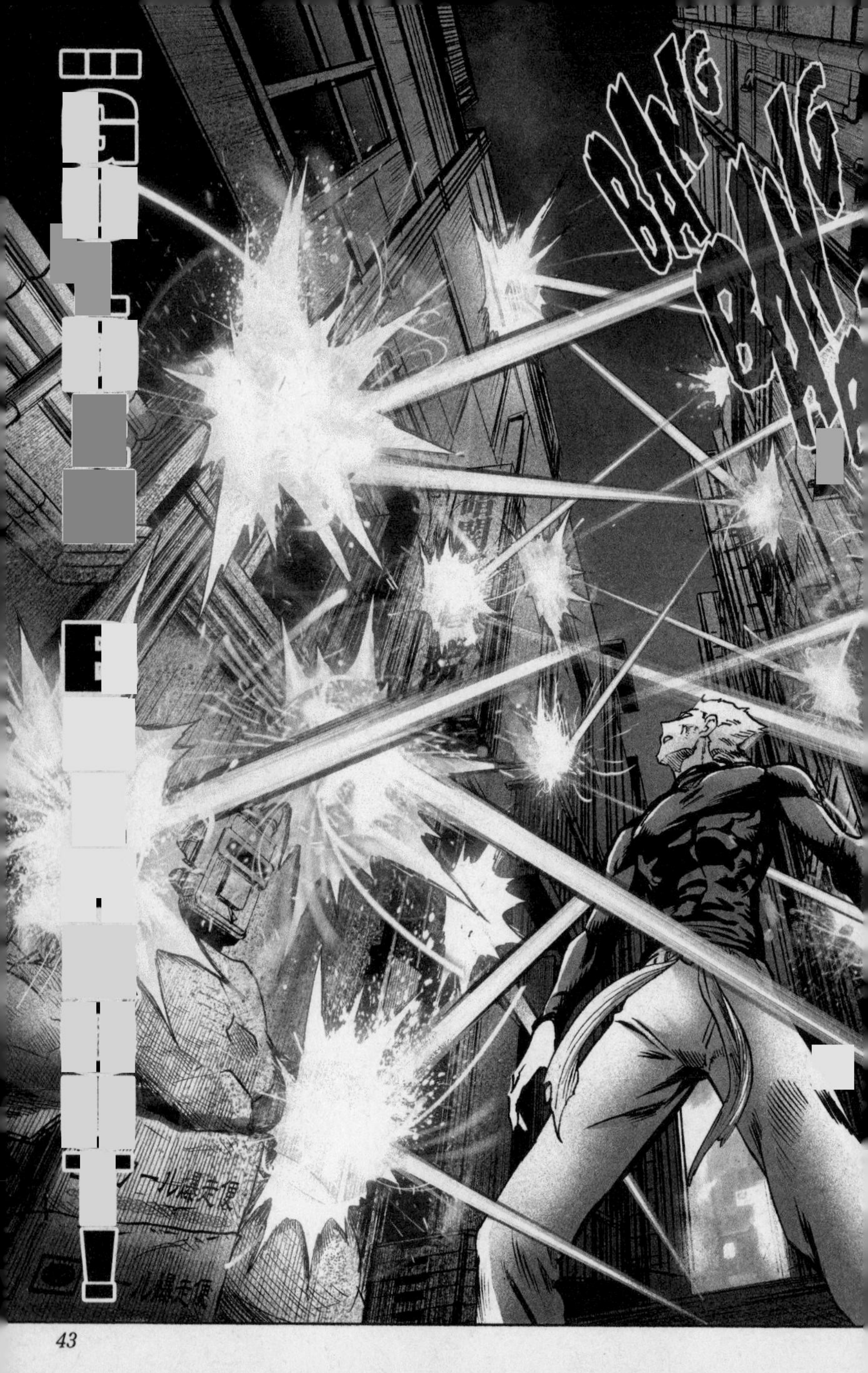
BANG
BANG

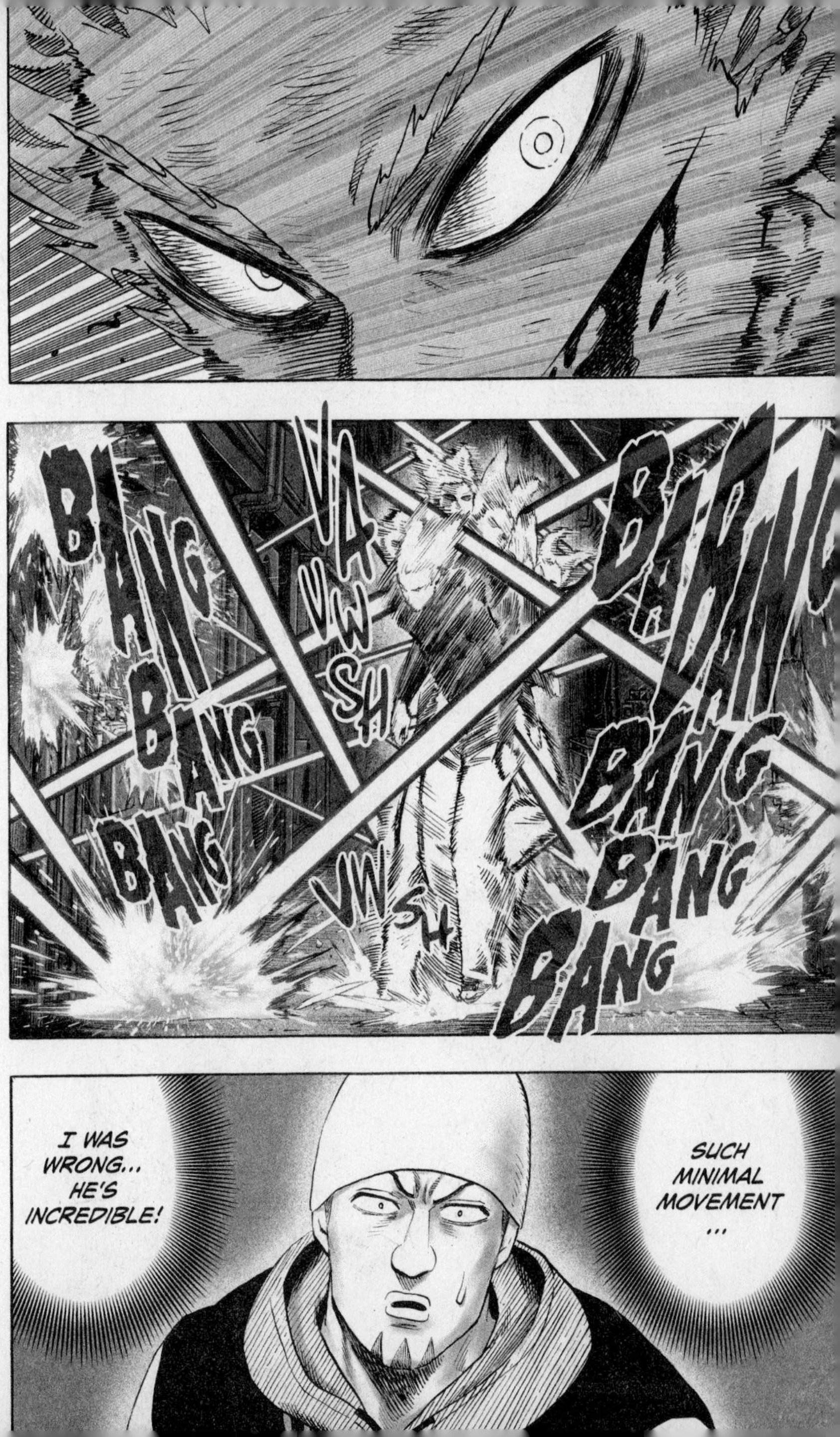
BANG
BANG
BANG
VWWSH
VWSH
BANG
BANG
BANG
SUCH MINIMAL MOVEMENT ...
I WAS WRONG... HE'S INCREDIBLE!

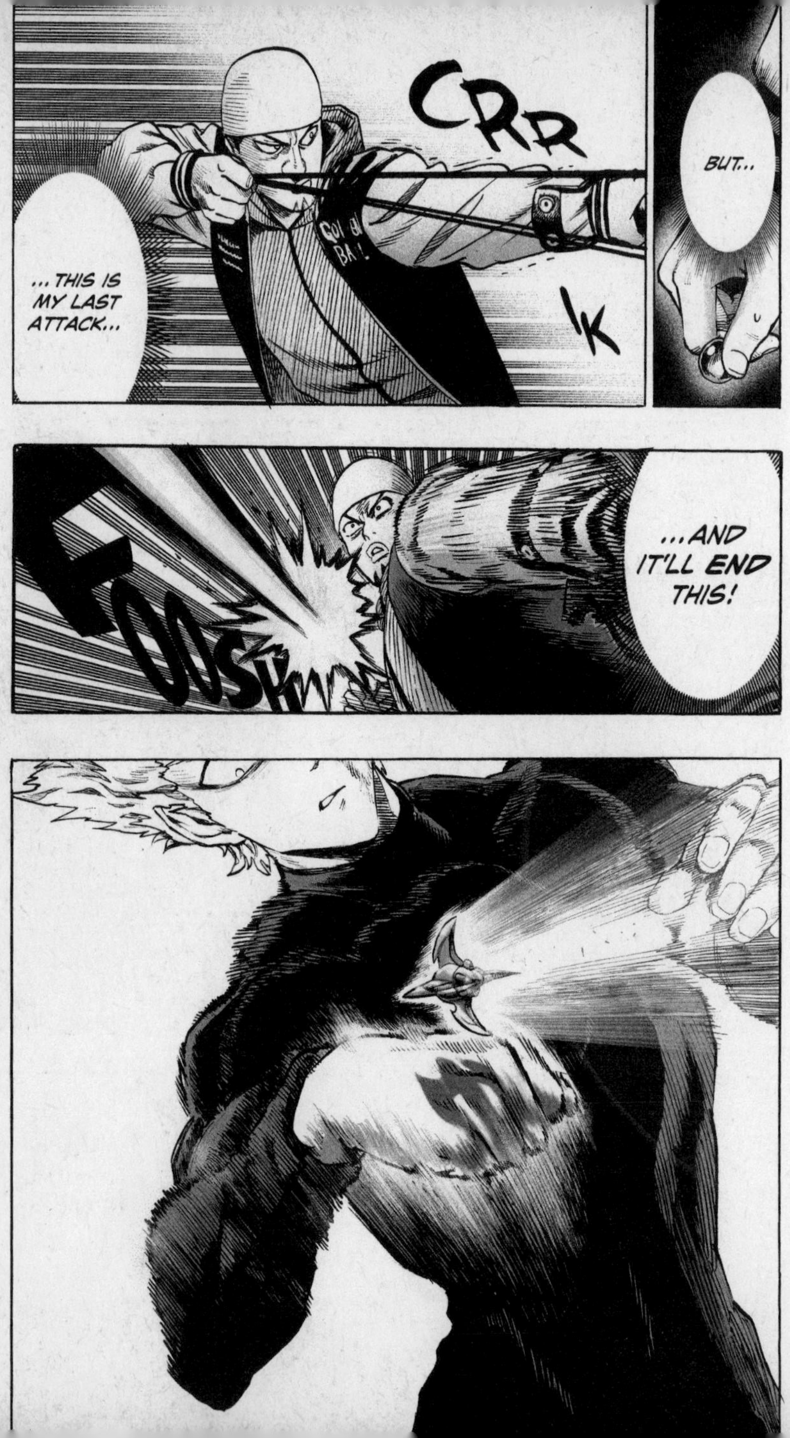
BUT...
CRR
K
...THIS IS MY LAST ATTACK...
...AND IT'LL END THIS!
FOOSH

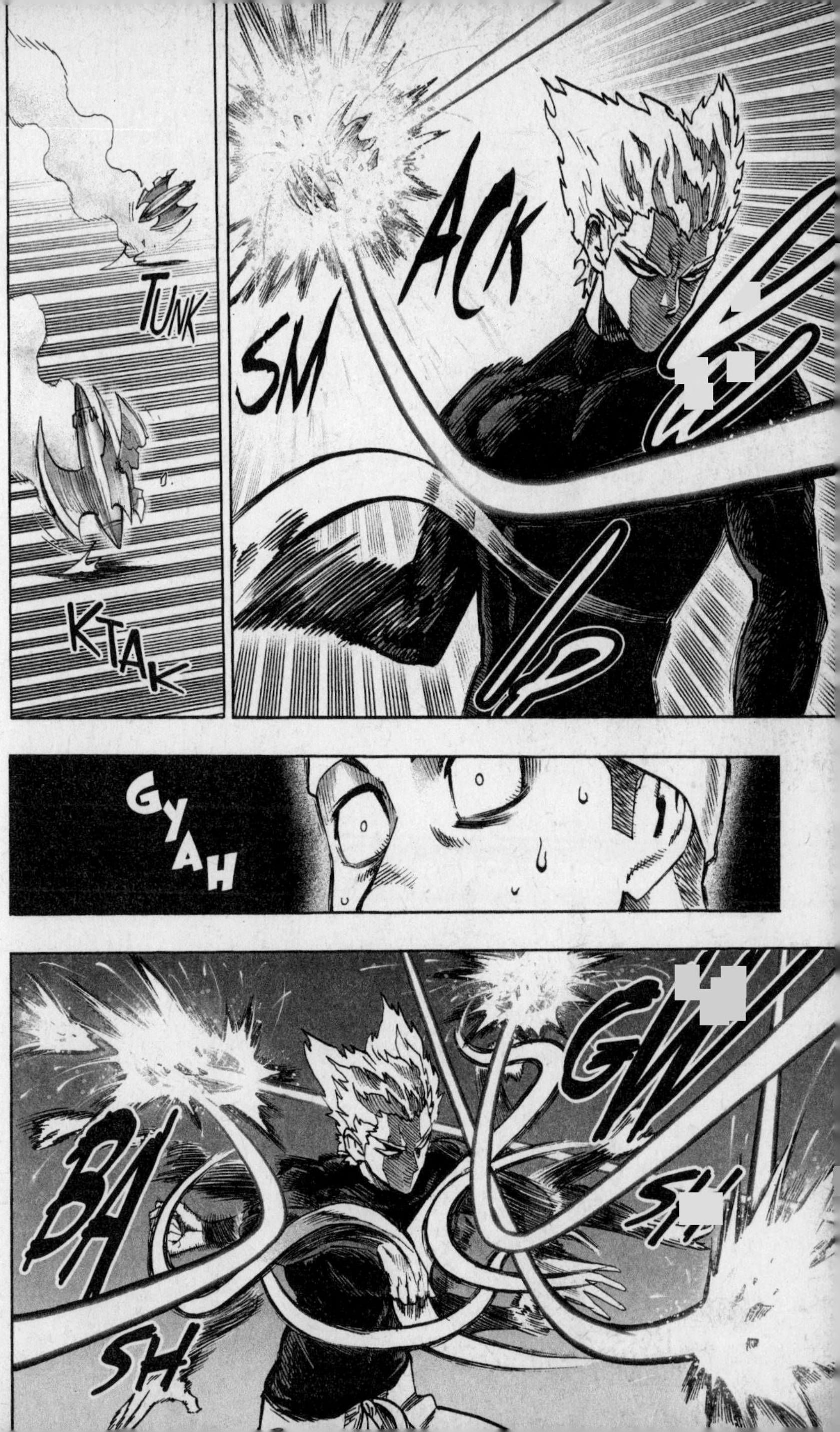
SM
ACK
TUNK
KTAK
GYAH
GW
BA
SH

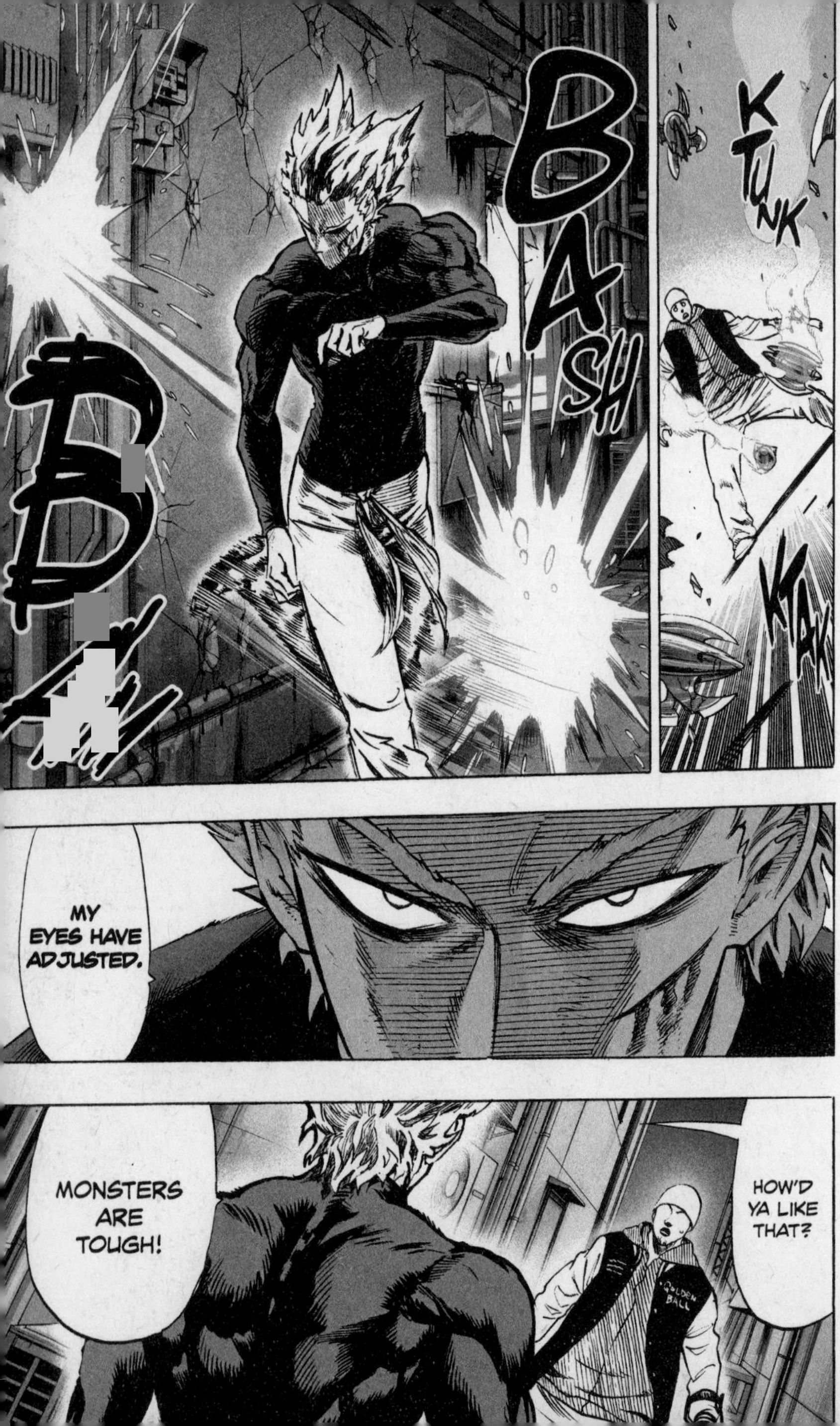
KTUNK
KTAK
BASH
MY EYES HAVE ADJUSTED.
HOW'D YA LIKE THAT?
GOLDEN BALL
MONSTERS ARE TOUGH!

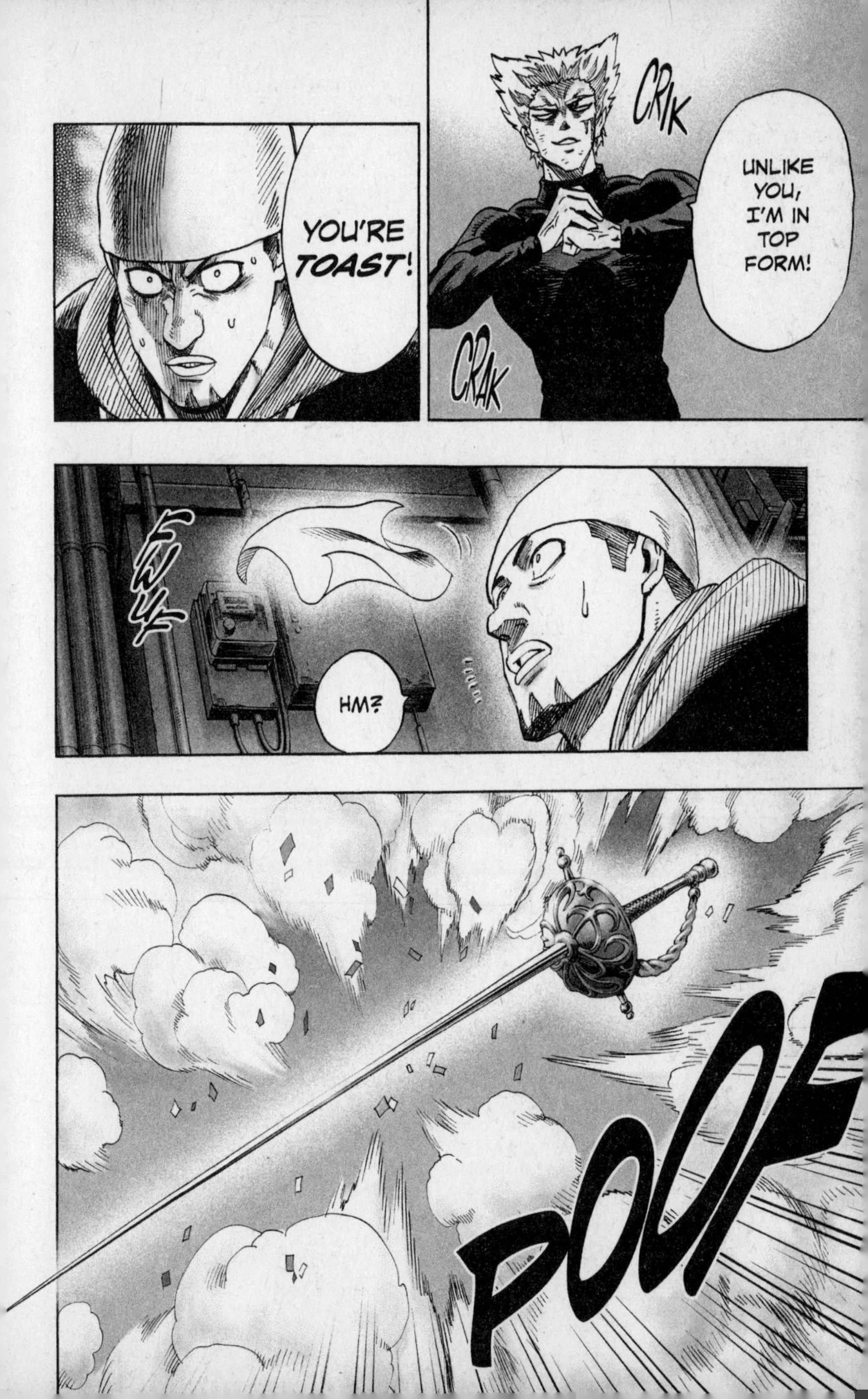
CRIK
UNLIKE YOU, I'M IN TOP FORM!
CRAK
YOU'RE TOAST!
FWUF
HM?
POOF

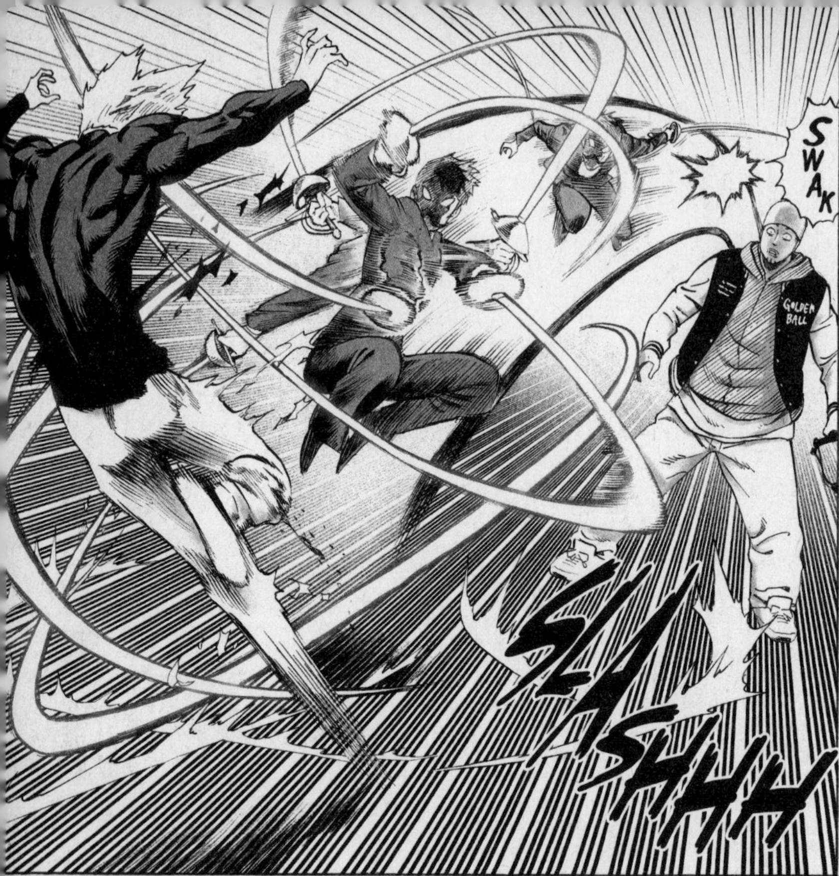
SWAK
GOLDEN BALL
SHHHH

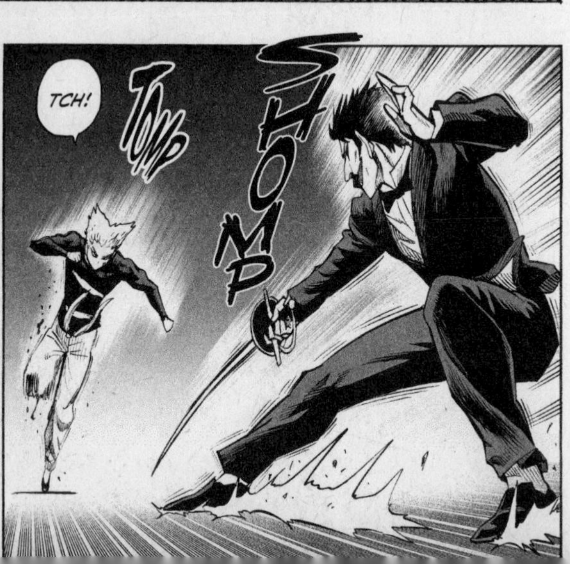
TCH!
TOMP
SHOMP

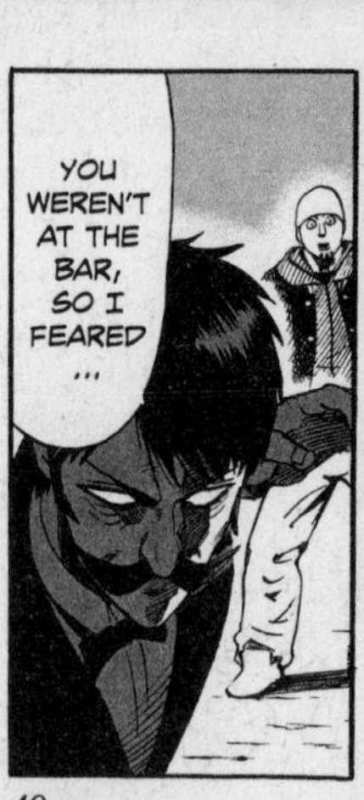
YOU WEREN'T AT THE BAR, SO I FEARED ...

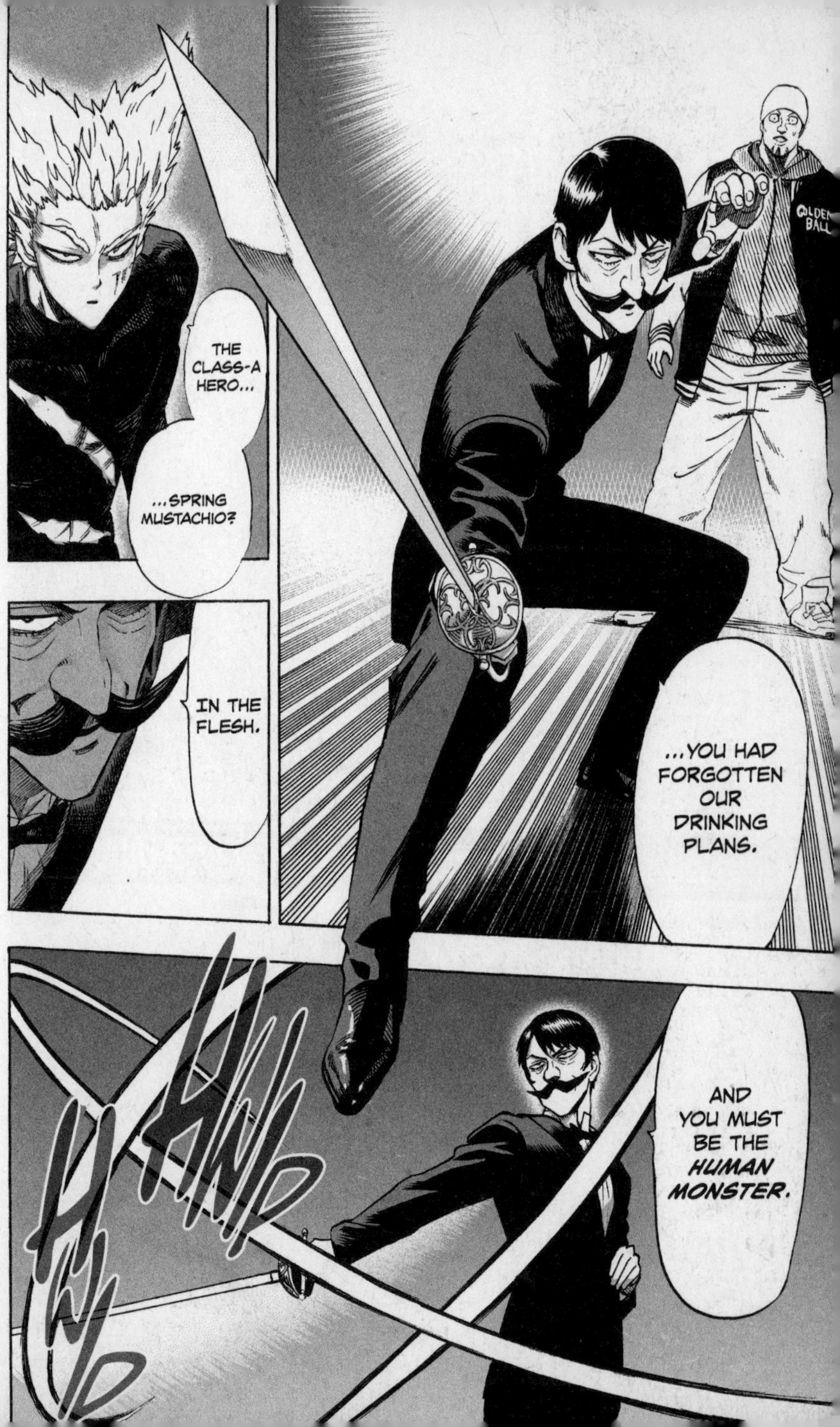
...YOU HAD FORGOTTEN OUR DRINKING PLANS.
THE CLASS-A HERO...
...SPRING MUSTACHIO?
IN THE FLESH.
AND YOU MUST BE THE *HUMAN MONSTER*.

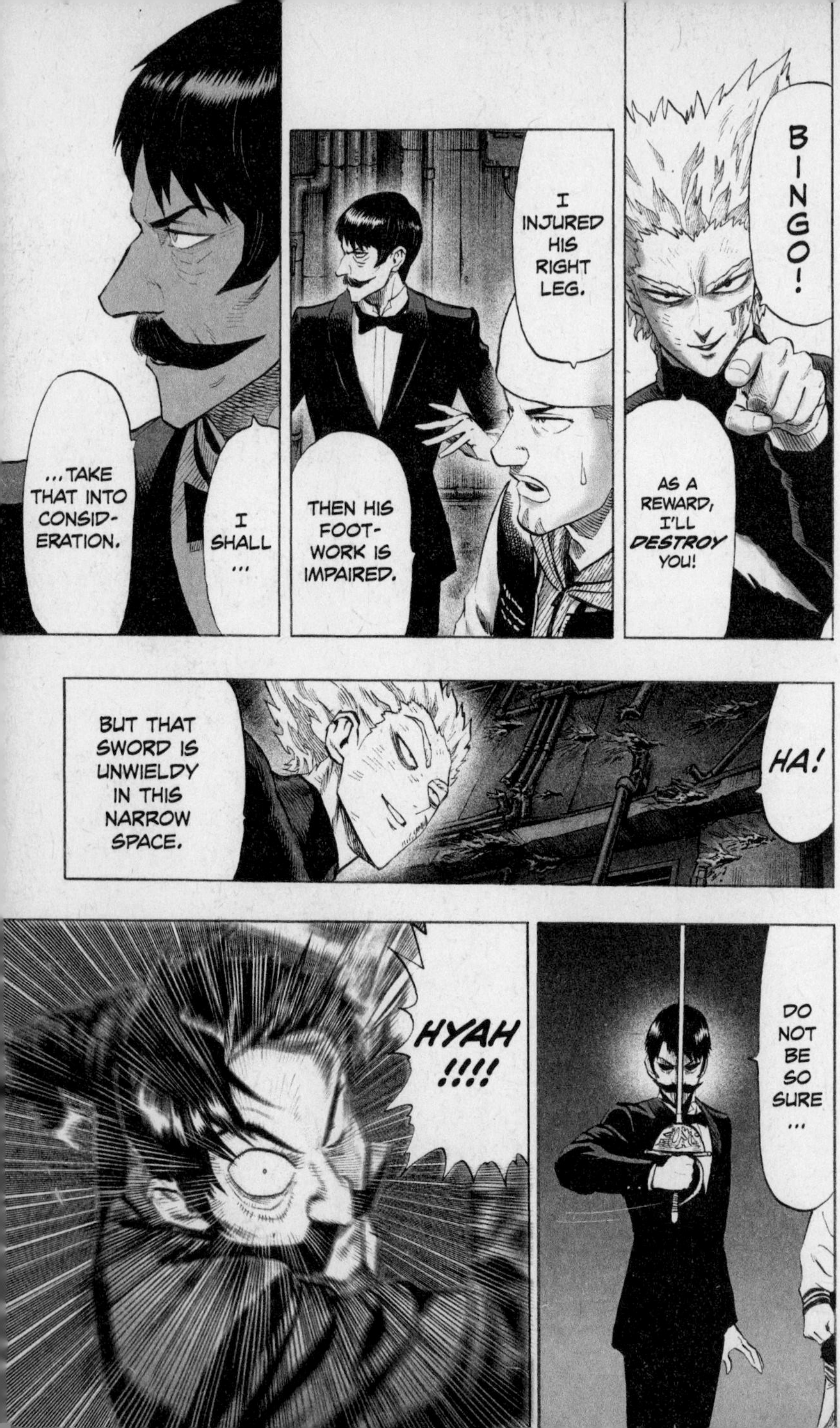
BINGO!
AS A REWARD, I'LL DESTROY YOU!
I INJURED HIS RIGHT LEG.
THEN HIS FOOTWORK IS IMPAIRED.
I SHALL ...
...TAKE THAT INTO CONSIDERATION.
HA!
BUT THAT SWORD IS UNWIELDY IN THIS NARROW SPACE.
DO NOT BE SO SURE ...
HYAH!!!!

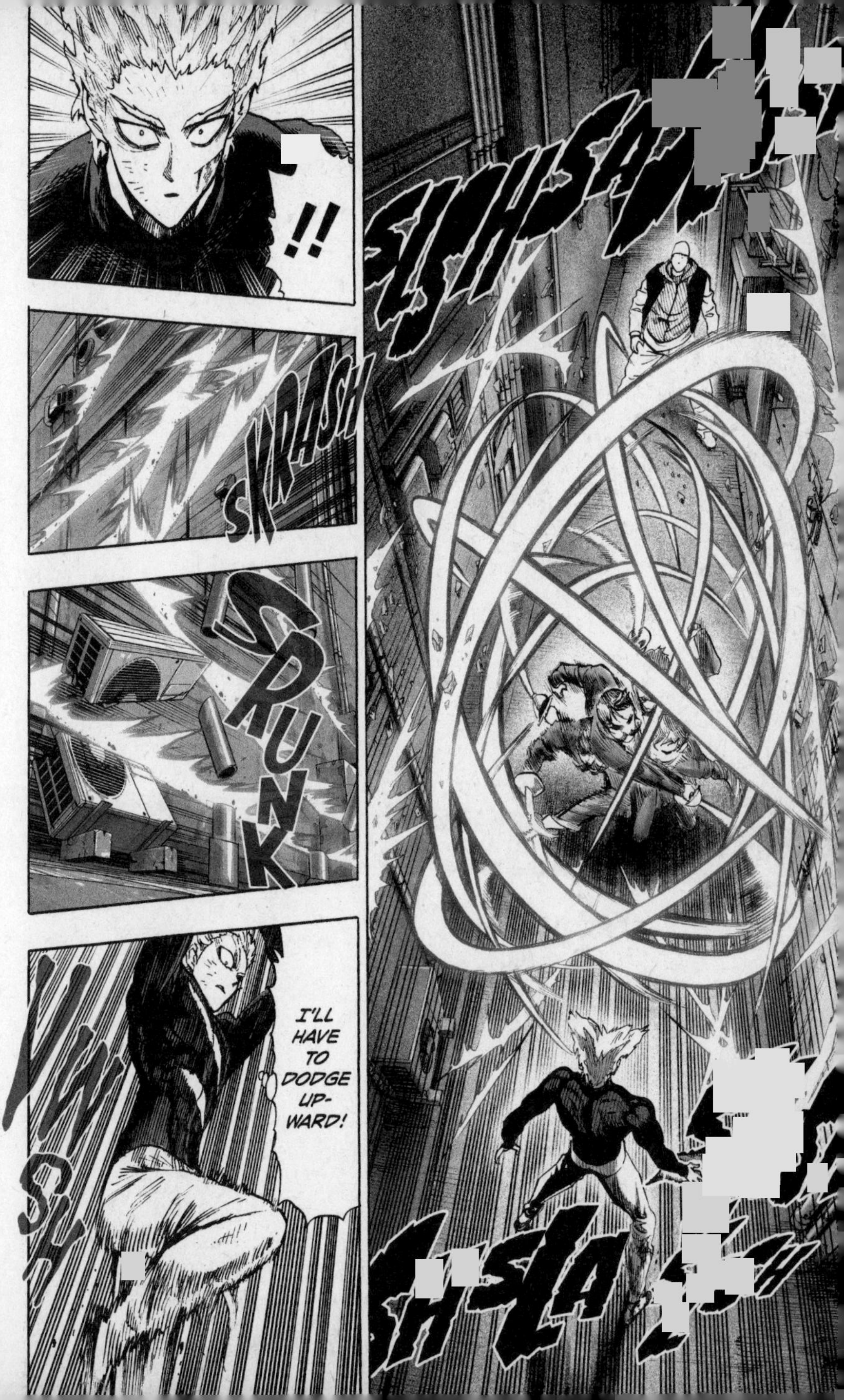
!!
SKRASH
I'LL HAVE TO DODGE UPWARD!

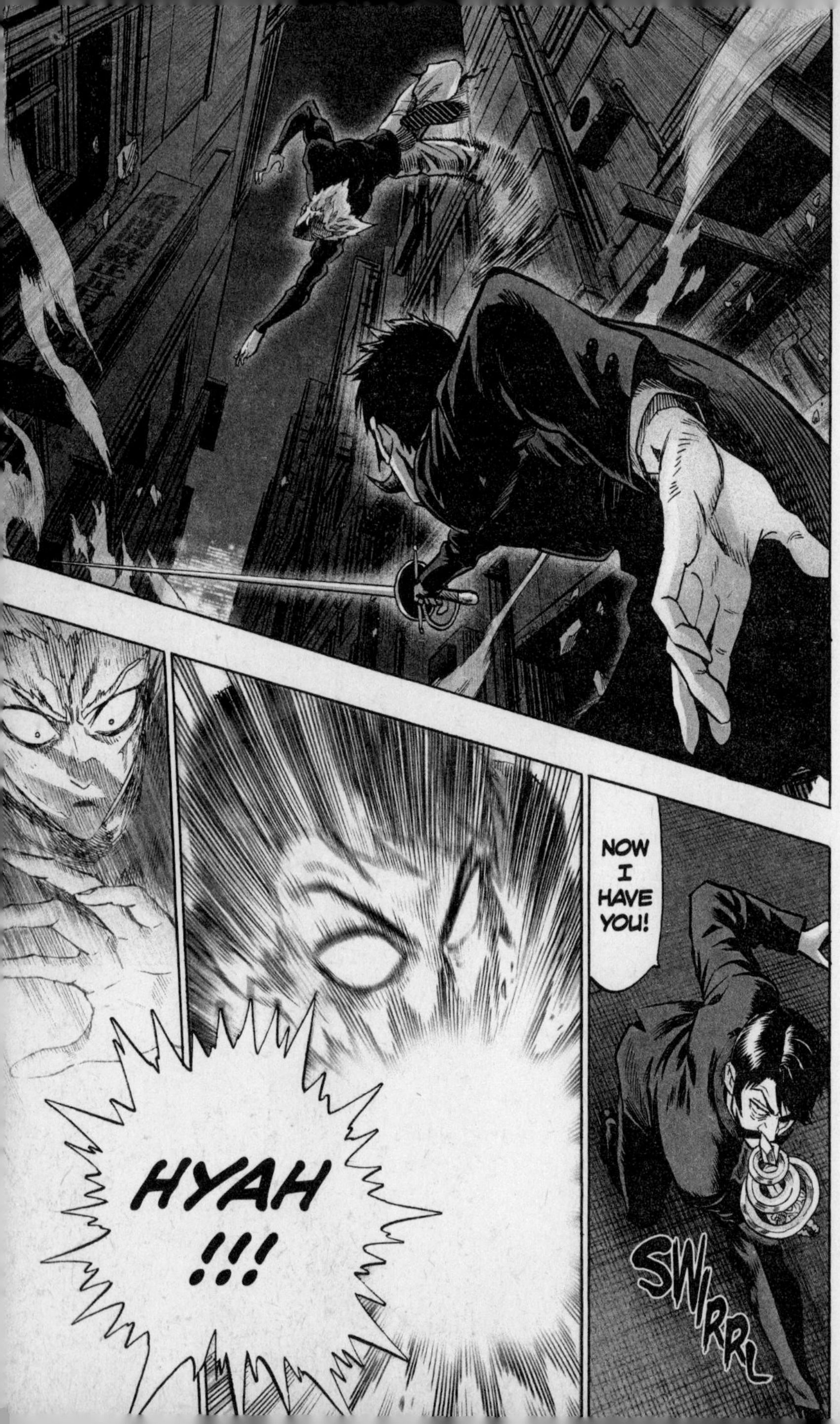
NOW I HAVE YOU!
SWIRRL
HYAH!!!

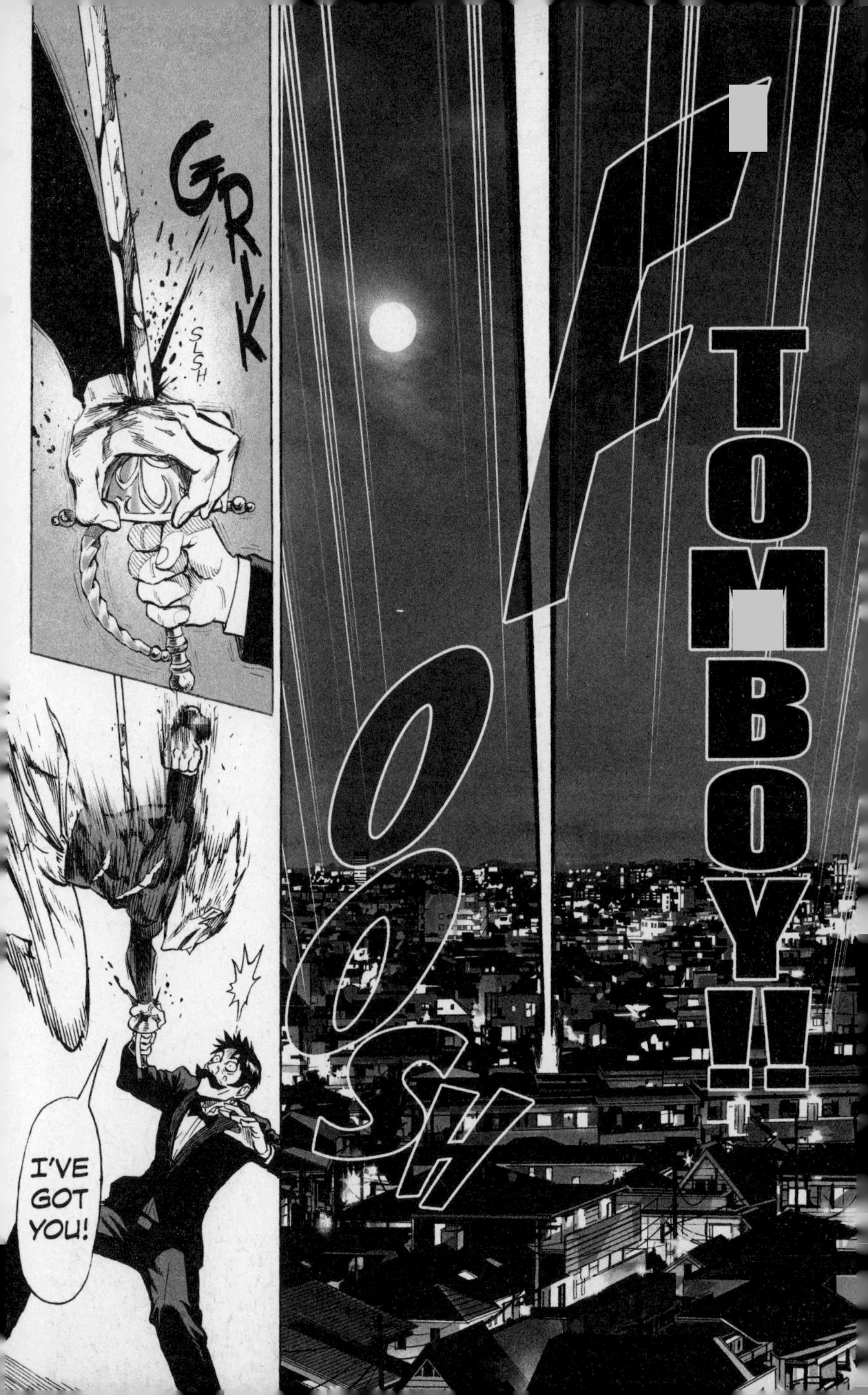
TOMBOY!!
OOSH
GRIK
SLSH
I'VE GOT YOU!

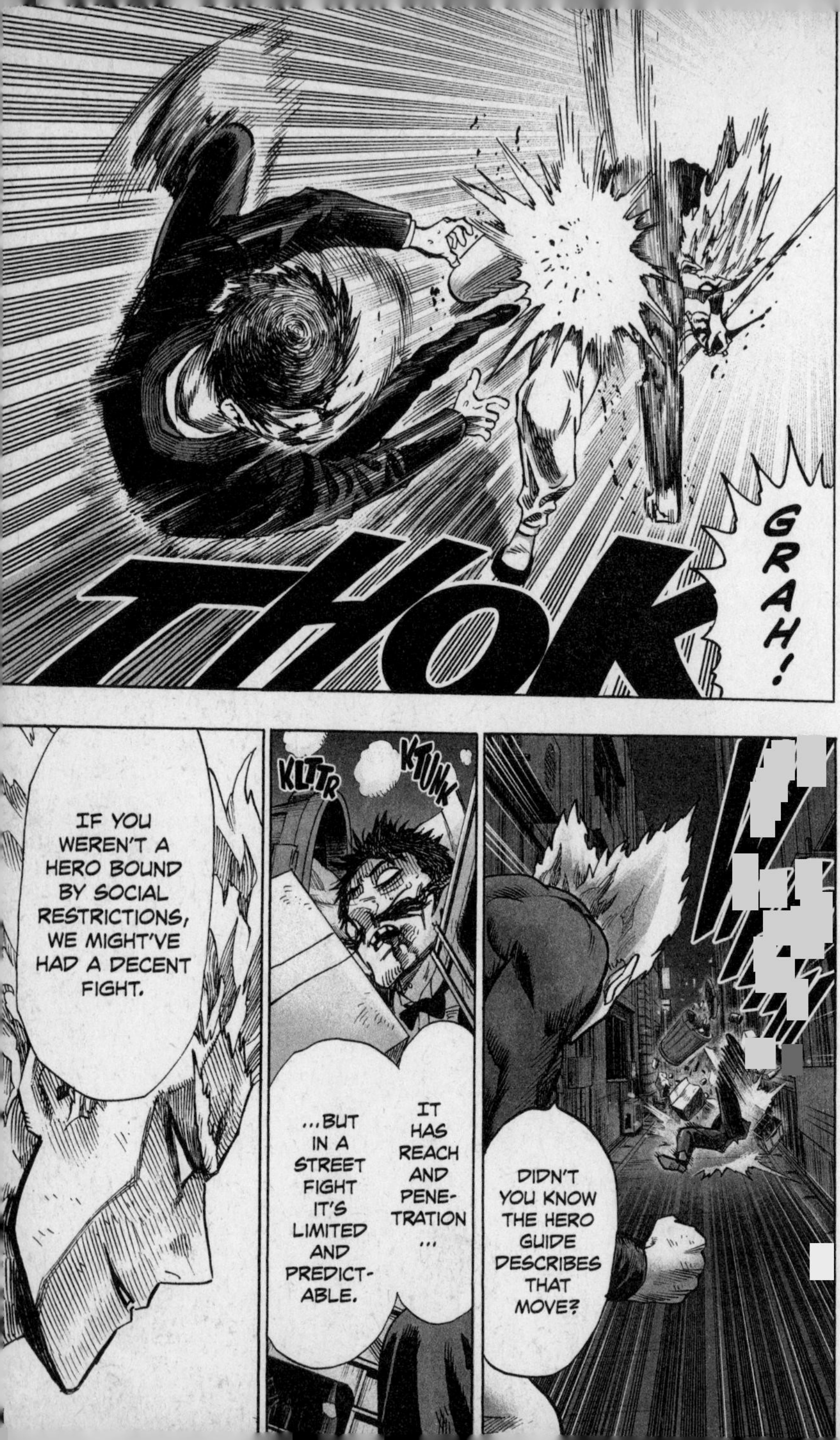
GRAH!
THOK
DIDN'T YOU KNOW THE HERO GUIDE DESCRIBES THAT MOVE?
KTUNK
KLTTR
IT HAS REACH AND PENE-TRATION...
...BUT IN A STREET FIGHT IT'S LIMITED AND PREDICT-ABLE.
IF YOU WEREN'T A HERO BOUND BY SOCIAL RESTRICTIONS, WE MIGHT'VE HAD A DECENT FIGHT.

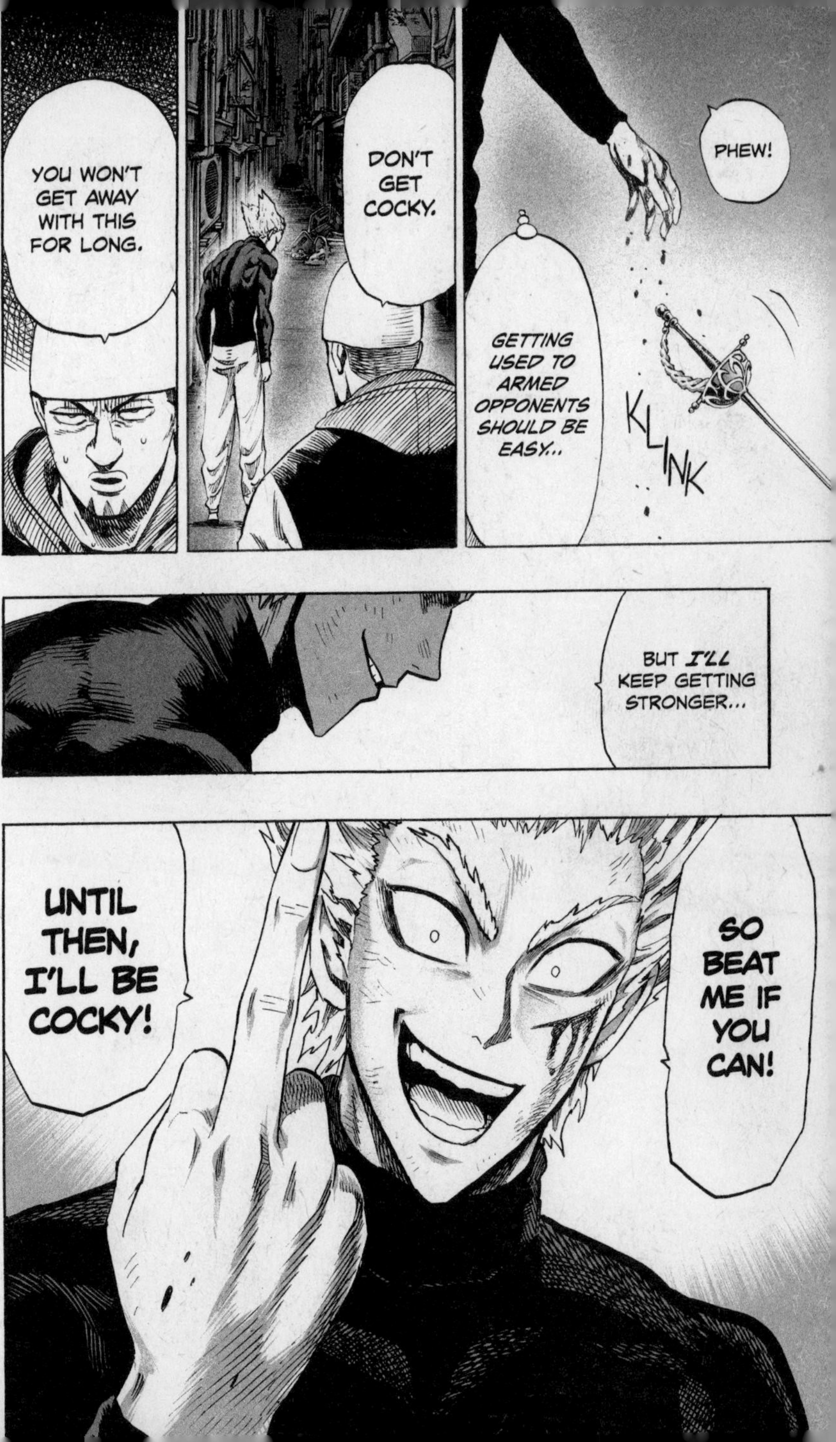
PHEW!
GETTING USED TO ARMED OPPONENTS SHOULD BE EASY...
KLINK
DON'T GET COCKY.
YOU WON'T GET AWAY WITH THIS FOR LONG.
BUT *I'LL* KEEP GETTING STRONGER...
SO BEAT ME IF YOU CAN!
UNTIL THEN, I'LL BE COCKY!

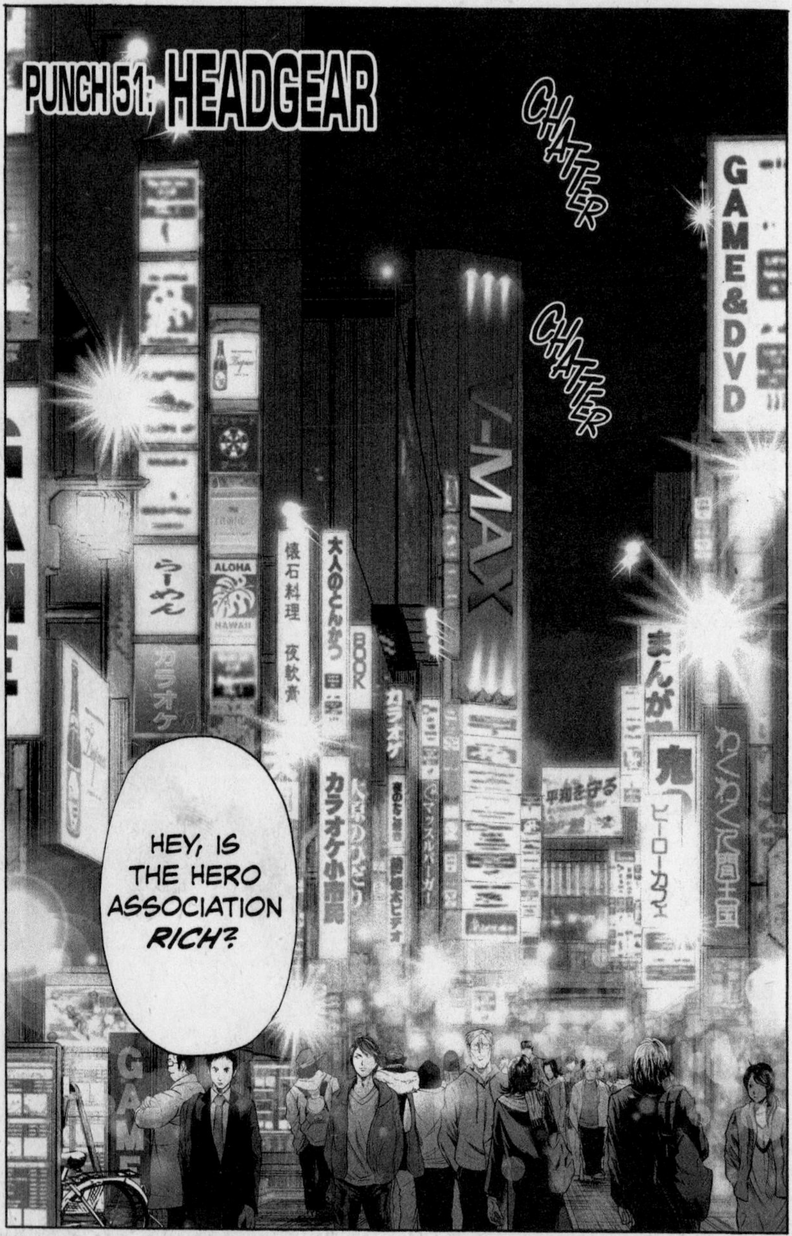
PUNCH 51: HEADGEAR
CHATTER
CHATTER
HEY, IS THE HERO ASSOCIATION *RICH*?

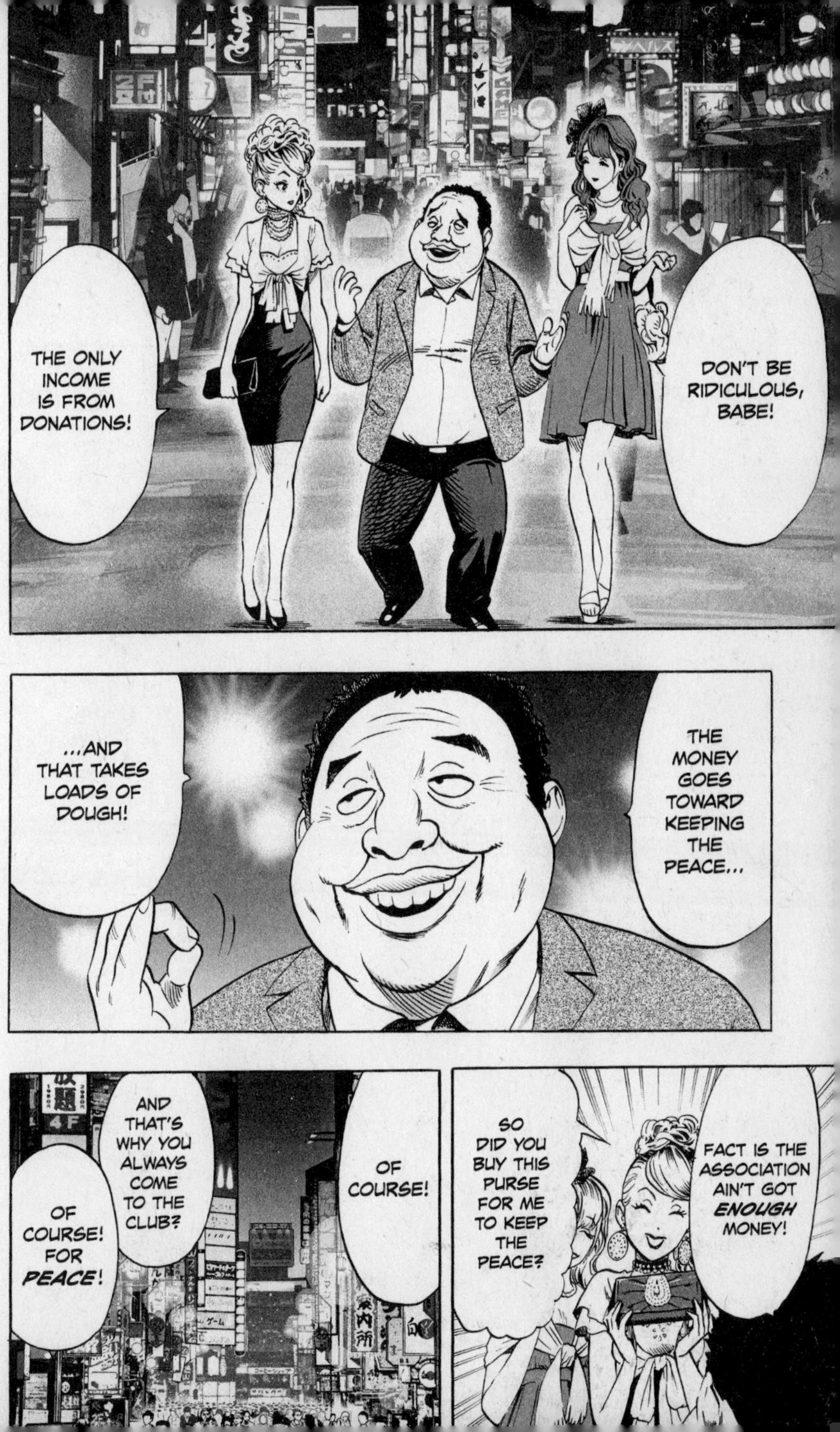
DON'T BE RIDICULOUS, BABE!
THE ONLY INCOME IS FROM DONATIONS!
THE MONEY GOES TOWARD KEEPING THE PEACE...
...AND THAT TAKES LOADS OF DOUGH!
FACT IS THE ASSOCIATION AIN'T GOT *ENOUGH* MONEY!
SO DID YOU BUY THIS PURSE FOR ME TO KEEP THE PEACE?
OF COURSE!
AND THAT'S WHY YOU ALWAYS COME TO THE CLUB?
OF COURSE! FOR *PEACE*!

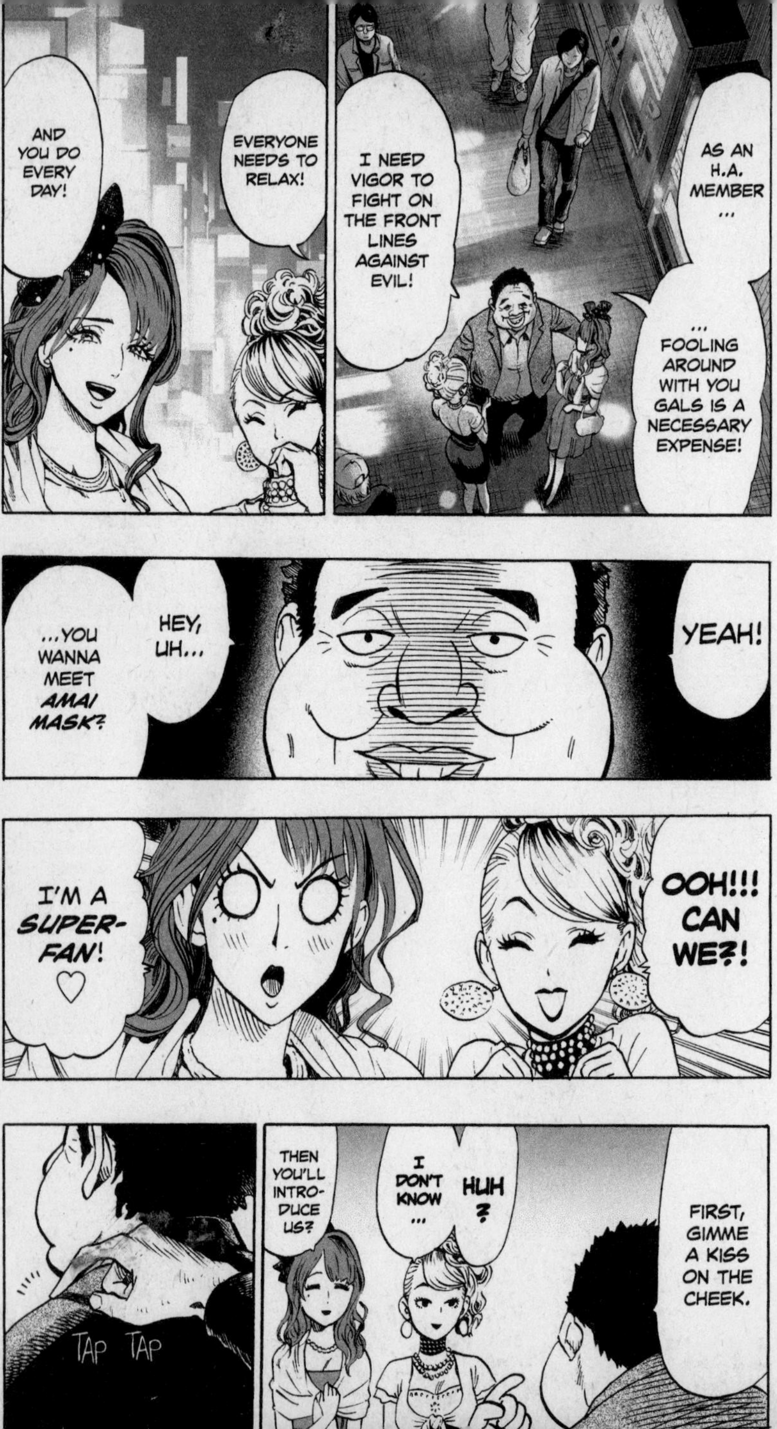
AS AN H.A. MEMBER ...
... FOOLING AROUND WITH YOU GALS IS A NECESSARY EXPENSE!
I NEED VIGOR TO FIGHT ON THE FRONT LINES AGAINST EVIL!
EVERYONE NEEDS TO RELAX!
AND YOU DO EVERY DAY!
YEAH!
HEY, UH...
...YOU WANNA MEET *AMAI MASK*?
OOH!!! CAN WE?!
I'M A *SUPER-FAN*! ♡
FIRST, GIMME A KISS ON THE CHEEK.
HUH?
I DON'T KNOW ...
THEN YOU'LL INTRO-DUCE US?
TAP TAP

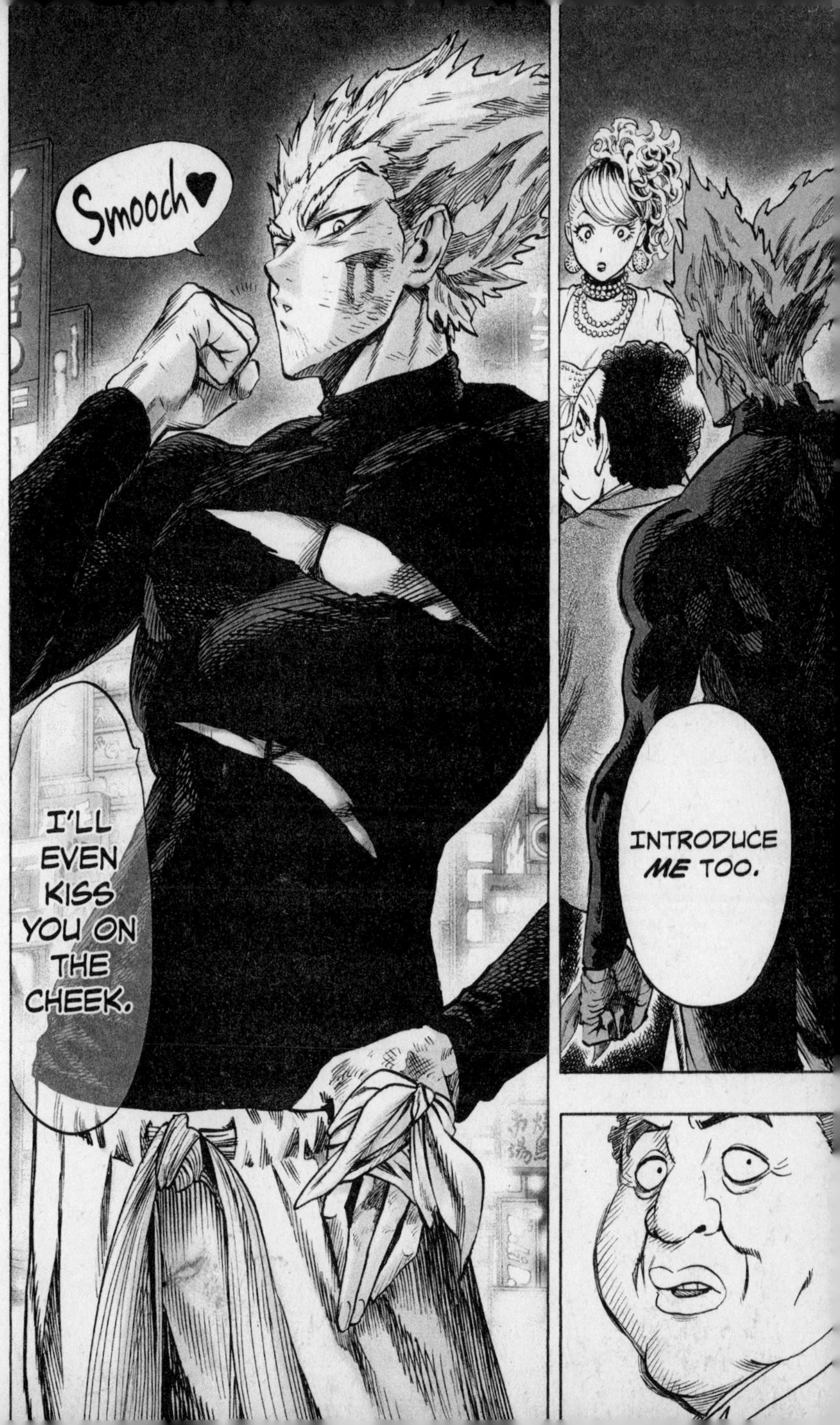
INTRODUCE *ME* TOO.
I'LL EVEN KISS YOU ON THE CHEEK.
Smooch♥

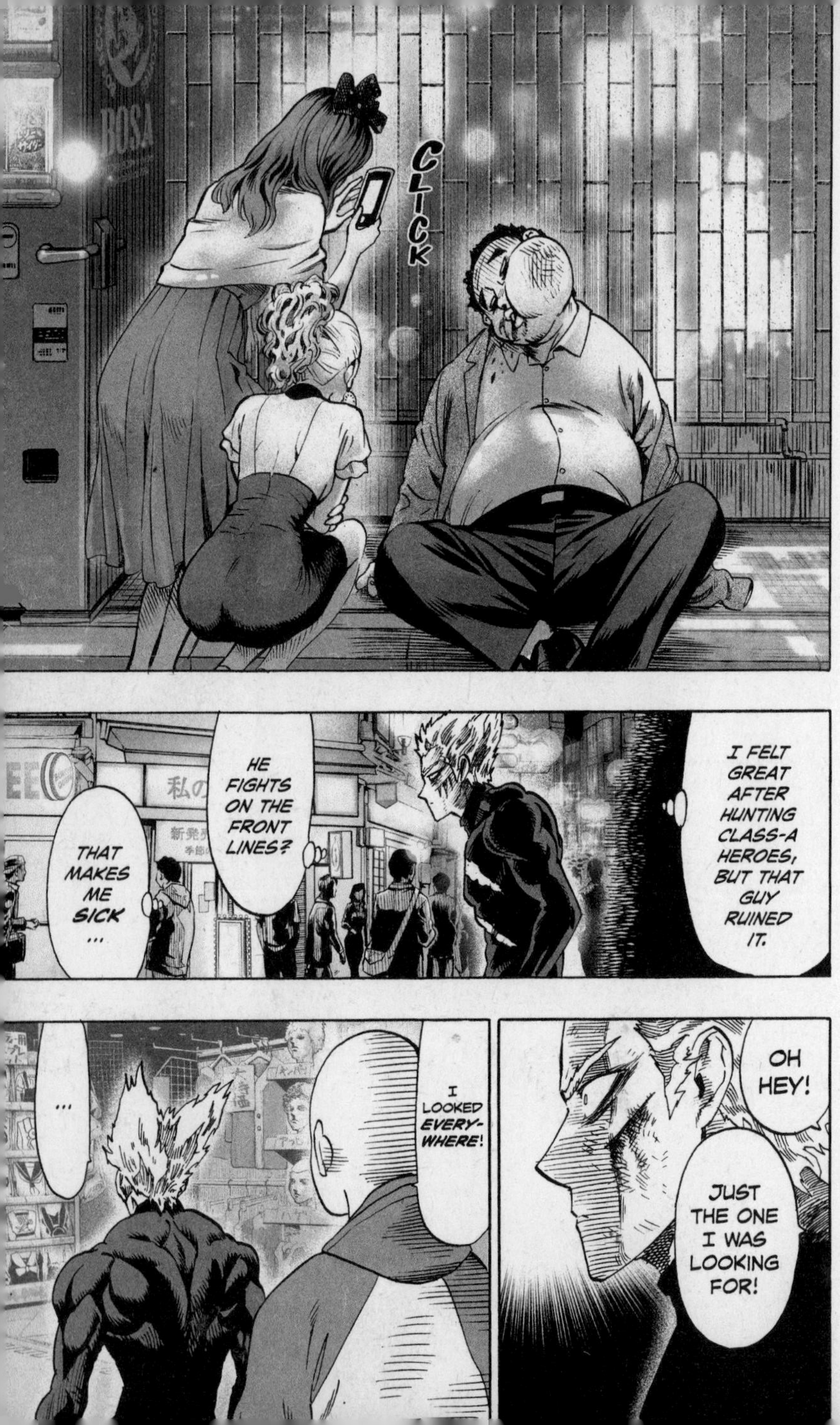
BOSA
CLICK
I FELT GREAT AFTER HUNTING CLASS-A HEROES, BUT THAT GUY RUINED IT.
HE FIGHTS ON THE FRONT LINES?
THAT MAKES ME SICK ...
OH HEY!
JUST THE ONE I WAS LOOKING FOR!
I LOOKED *EVERYWHERE*!
...

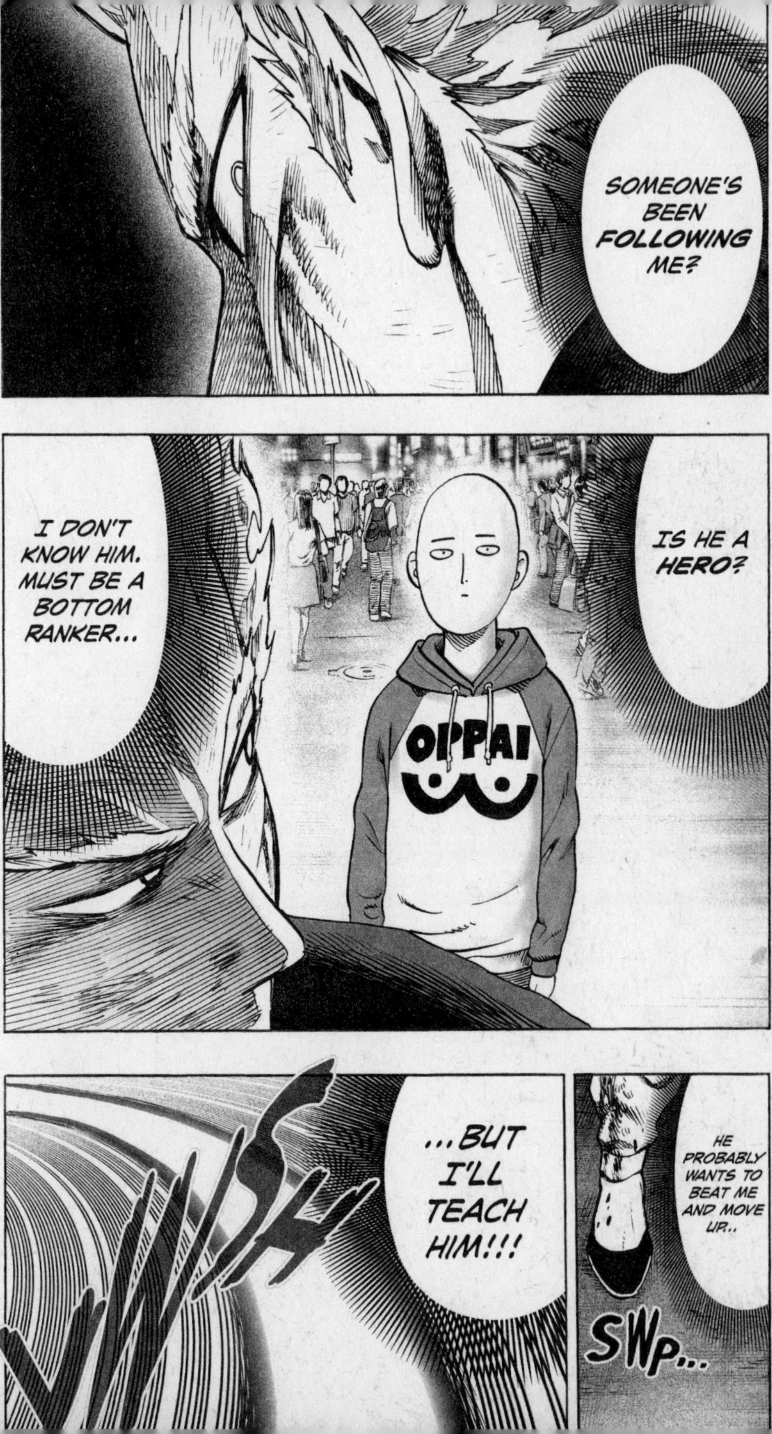
SOMEONE'S BEEN FOLLOWING ME?
IS HE A HERO?
I DON'T KNOW HIM. MUST BE A BOTTOM RANKER...
HE PROBABLY WANTS TO BEAT ME AND MOVE UP...
SWP...
...BUT I'LL TEACH HIM!!!
VWISH

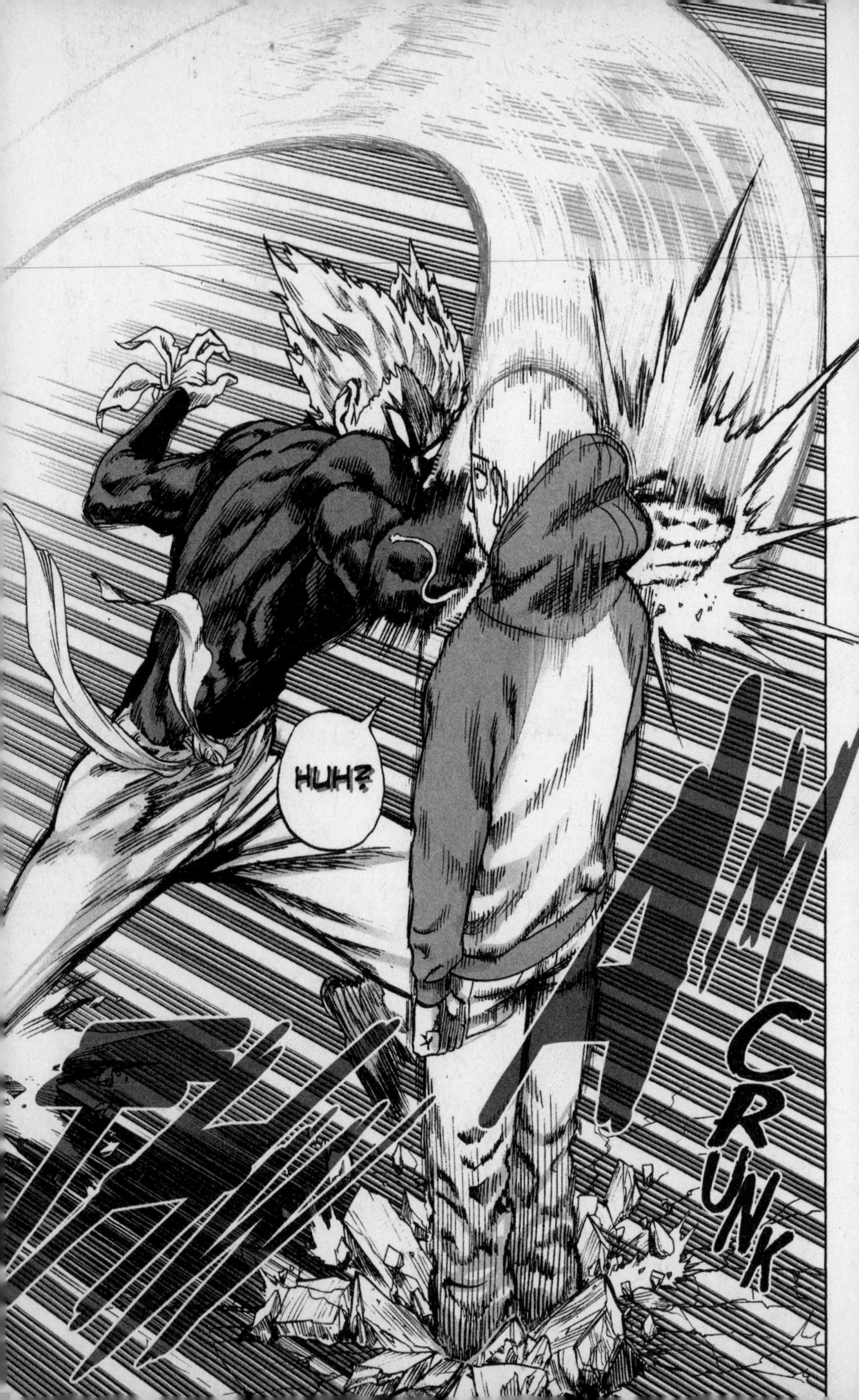
HUH?
CRUNK

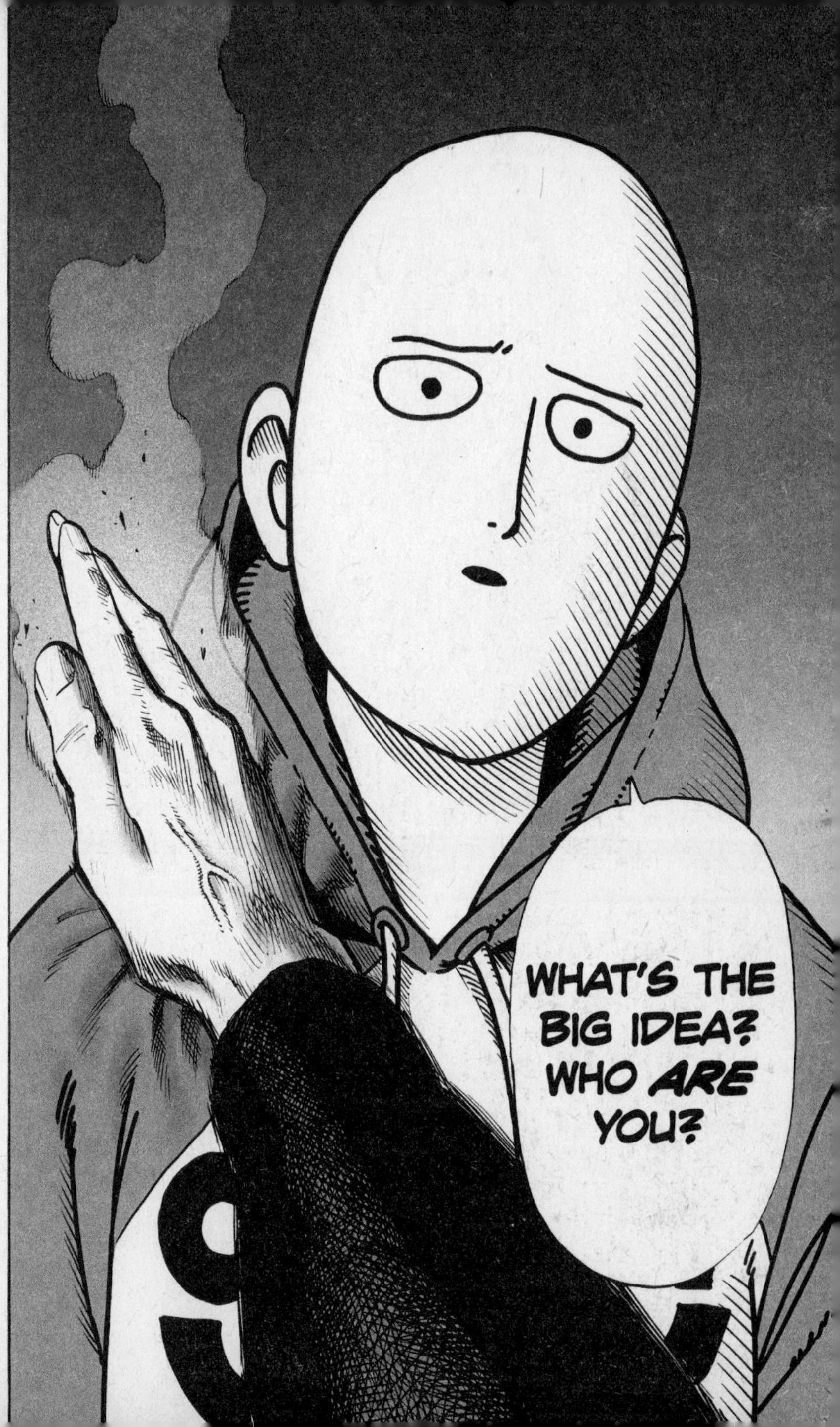
WHAT'S THE BIG IDEA? WHO ARE YOU?

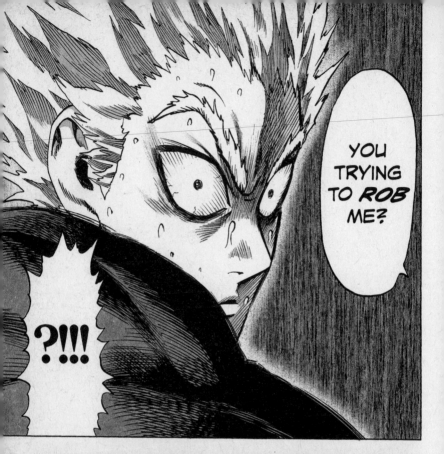

YOU TRYING TO *ROB* ME?

?!!!

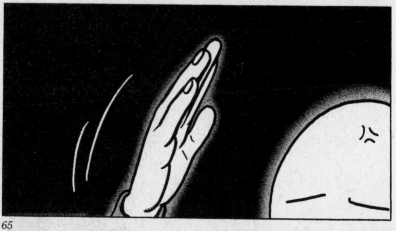

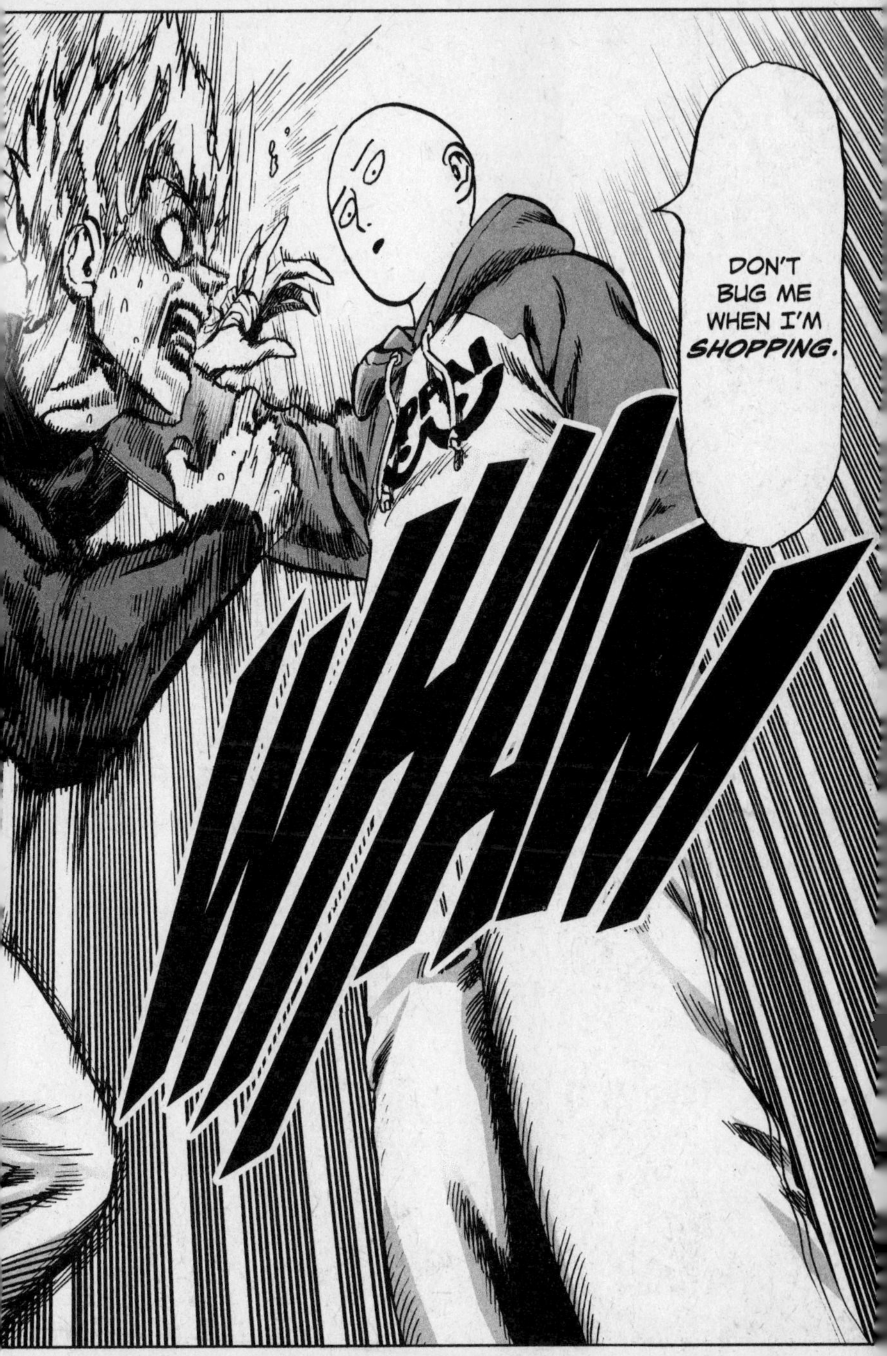
DON'T BUG ME WHEN I'M SHOPPING.
WHAM

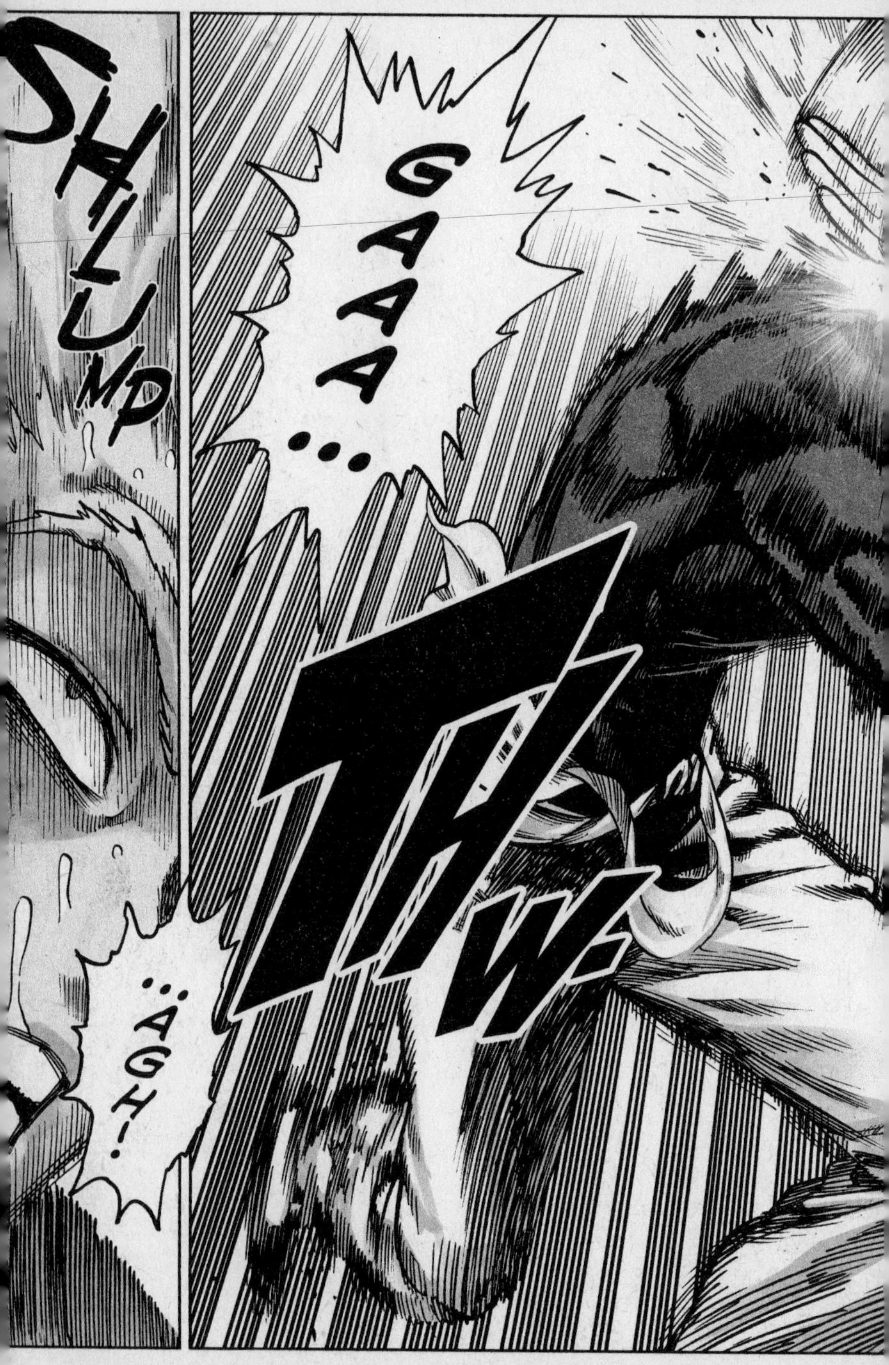
GAAA...
THW
SHLUMP
...AGH!

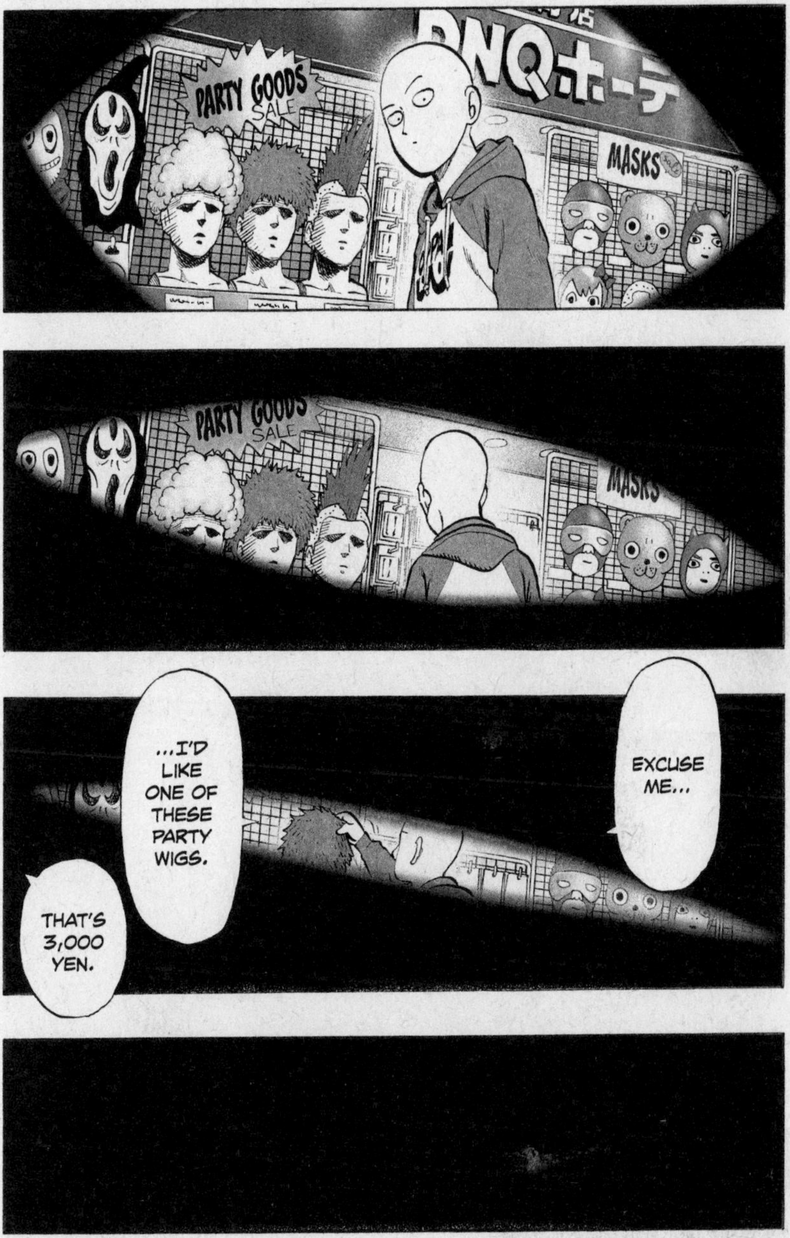
DNQホーテ
PARTY GOODS SALE
MASKS
PARTY GOODS SALE
MASKS
EXCUSE ME...
...I'D LIKE ONE OF THESE PARTY WIGS.
THAT'S 3,000 YEN.

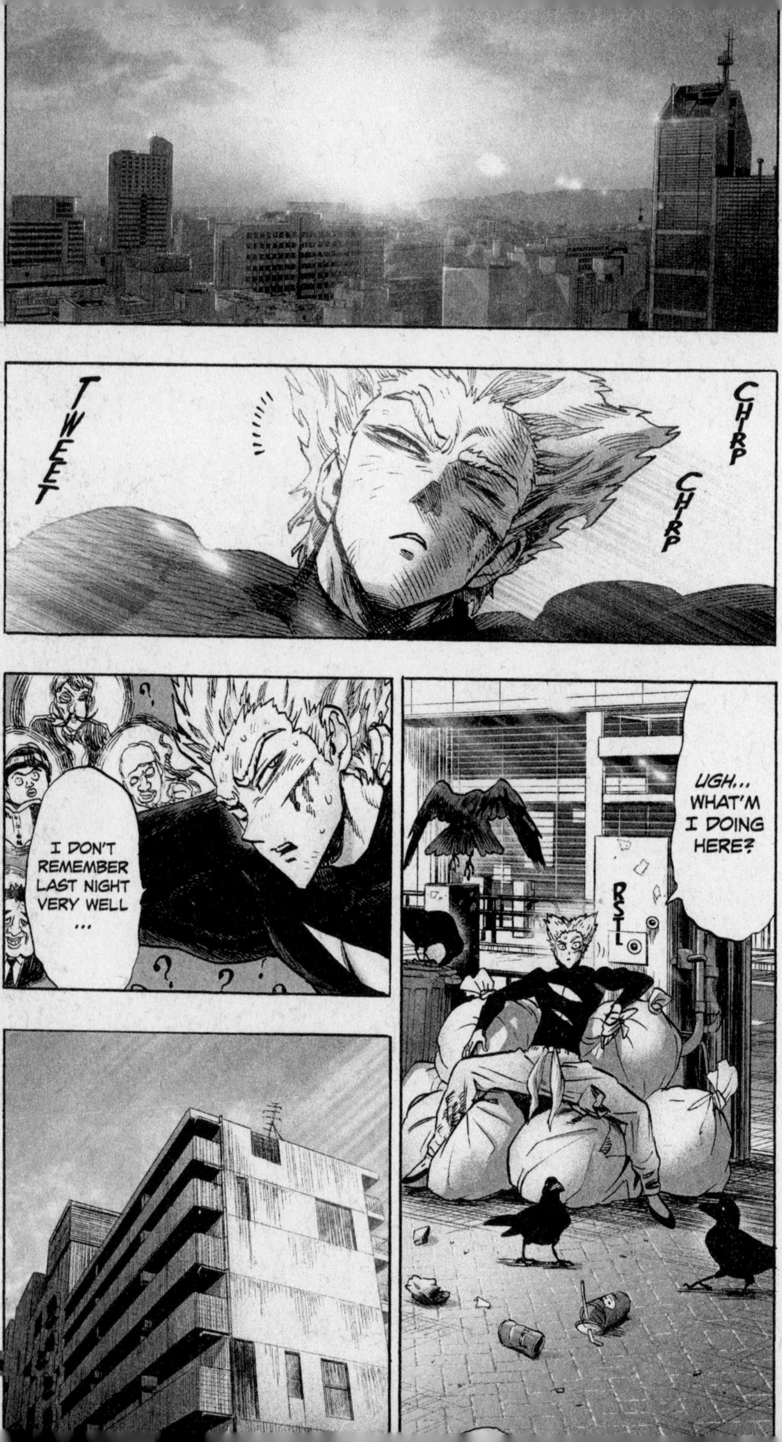
CHIRP
CHIRP
TWEET
UGH... WHAT'M I DOING HERE?
RSTL
I DON'T REMEMBER LAST NIGHT VERY WELL ...

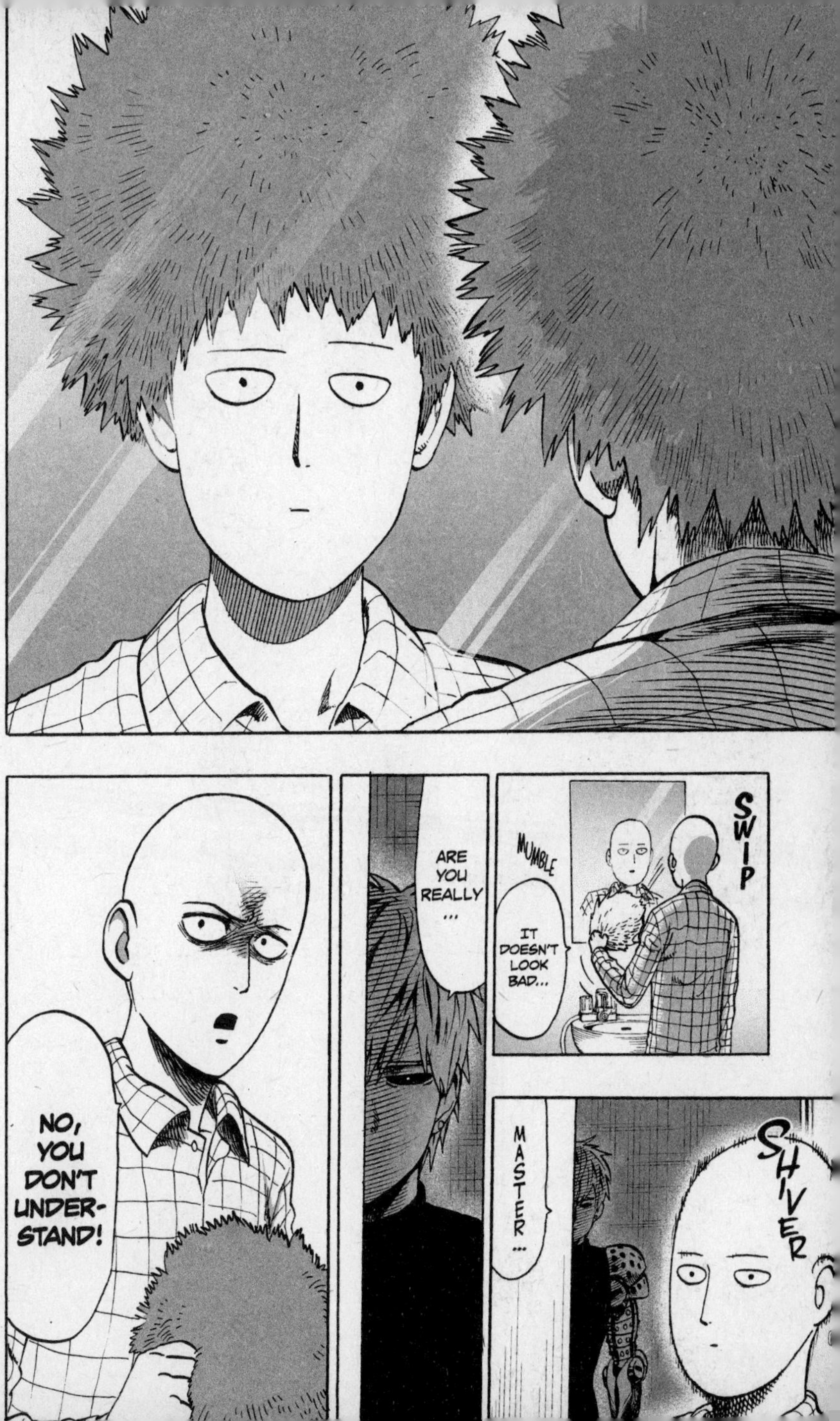
SWIP
MUMBLE
IT DOESN'T LOOK BAD...
SHIVER
MASTER...
ARE YOU REALLY...
NO, YOU DON'T UNDER-STAND!

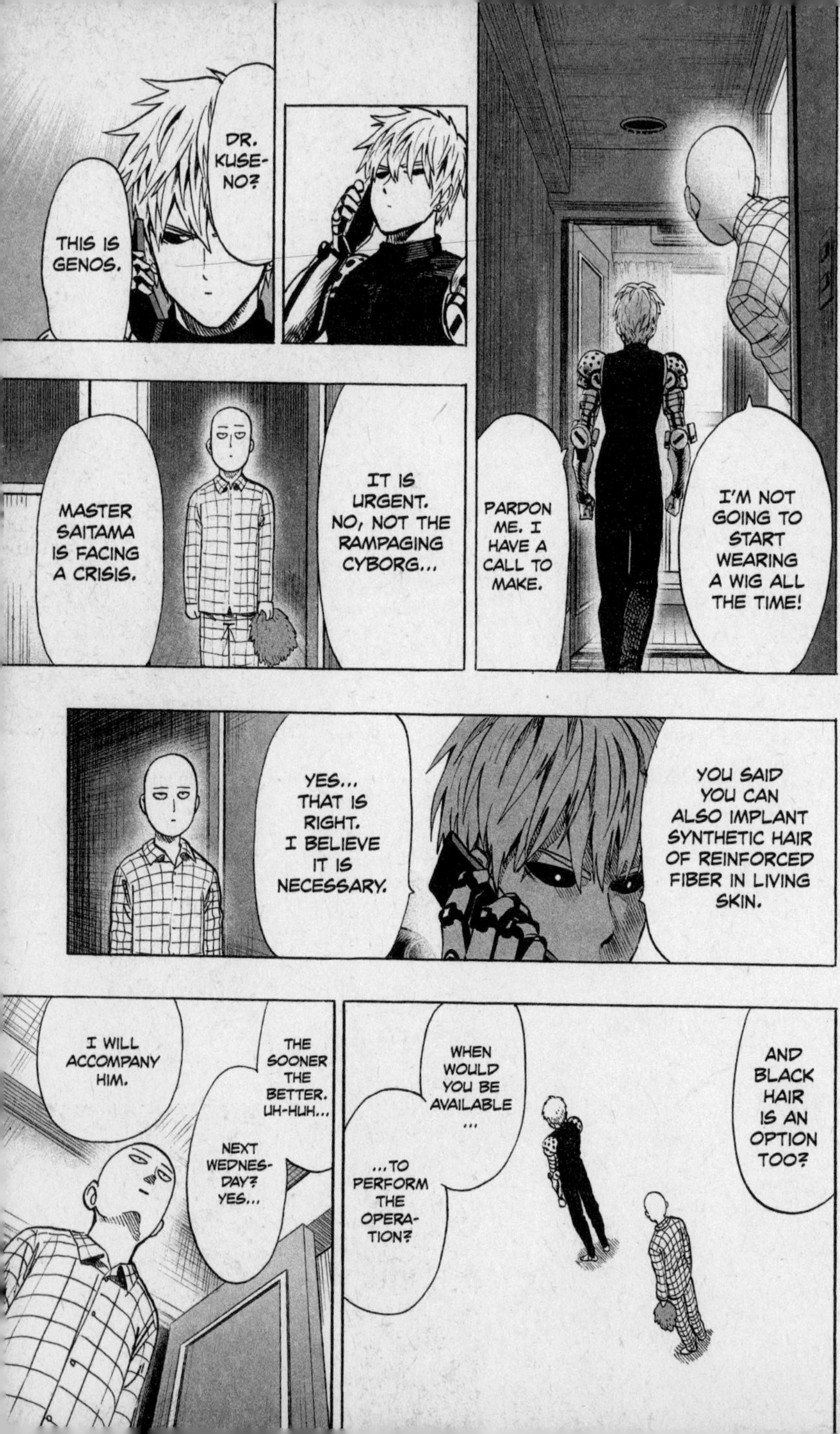
I'M NOT GOING TO START WEARING A WIG ALL THE TIME!
PARDON ME. I HAVE A CALL TO MAKE.
DR. KUSENO?
THIS IS GENOS.
IT IS URGENT. NO, NOT THE RAMPAGING CYBORG...
MASTER SAITAMA IS FACING A CRISIS.
YOU SAID YOU CAN ALSO IMPLANT SYNTHETIC HAIR OF REINFORCED FIBER IN LIVING SKIN.
YES... THAT IS RIGHT. I BELIEVE IT IS NECESSARY.
AND BLACK HAIR IS AN OPTION TOO?
WHEN WOULD YOU BE AVAILABLE...
...TO PERFORM THE OPERATION?
THE SOONER THE BETTER. UH-HUH...
I WILL ACCOMPANY HIM.
NEXT WEDNESDAY? YES...

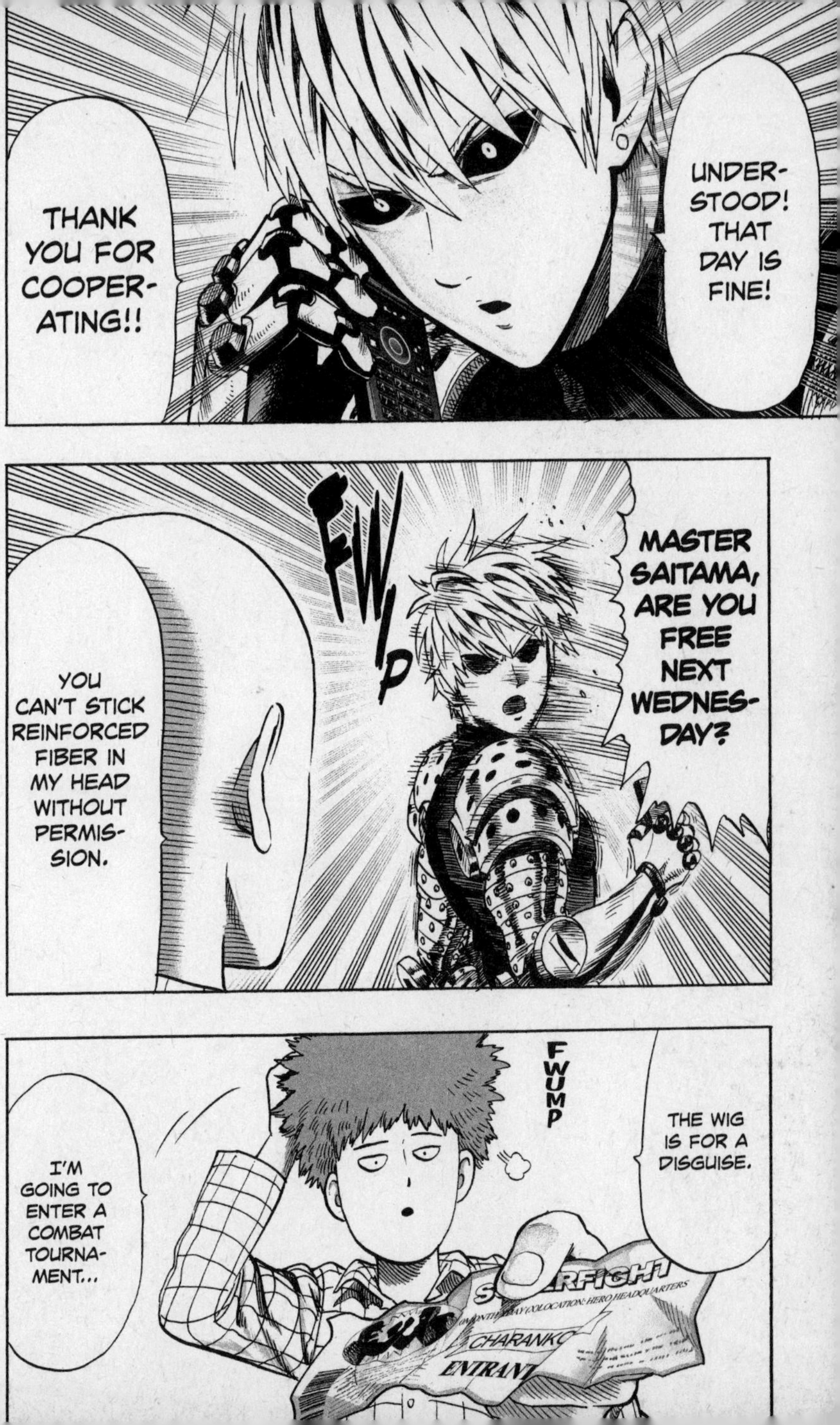
UNDERSTOOD! THAT DAY IS FINE!
THANK YOU FOR COOPERATING!!
FWIP
MASTER SAITAMA, ARE YOU FREE NEXT WEDNESDAY?
YOU CAN'T STICK REINFORCED FIBER IN MY HEAD WITHOUT PERMISSION.
THE WIG IS FOR A DISGUISE.
FWUMP
I'M GOING TO ENTER A COMBAT TOURNAMENT...
LOCATION: HERO HEADQUARTERS
CHARANKO
ENTRANT

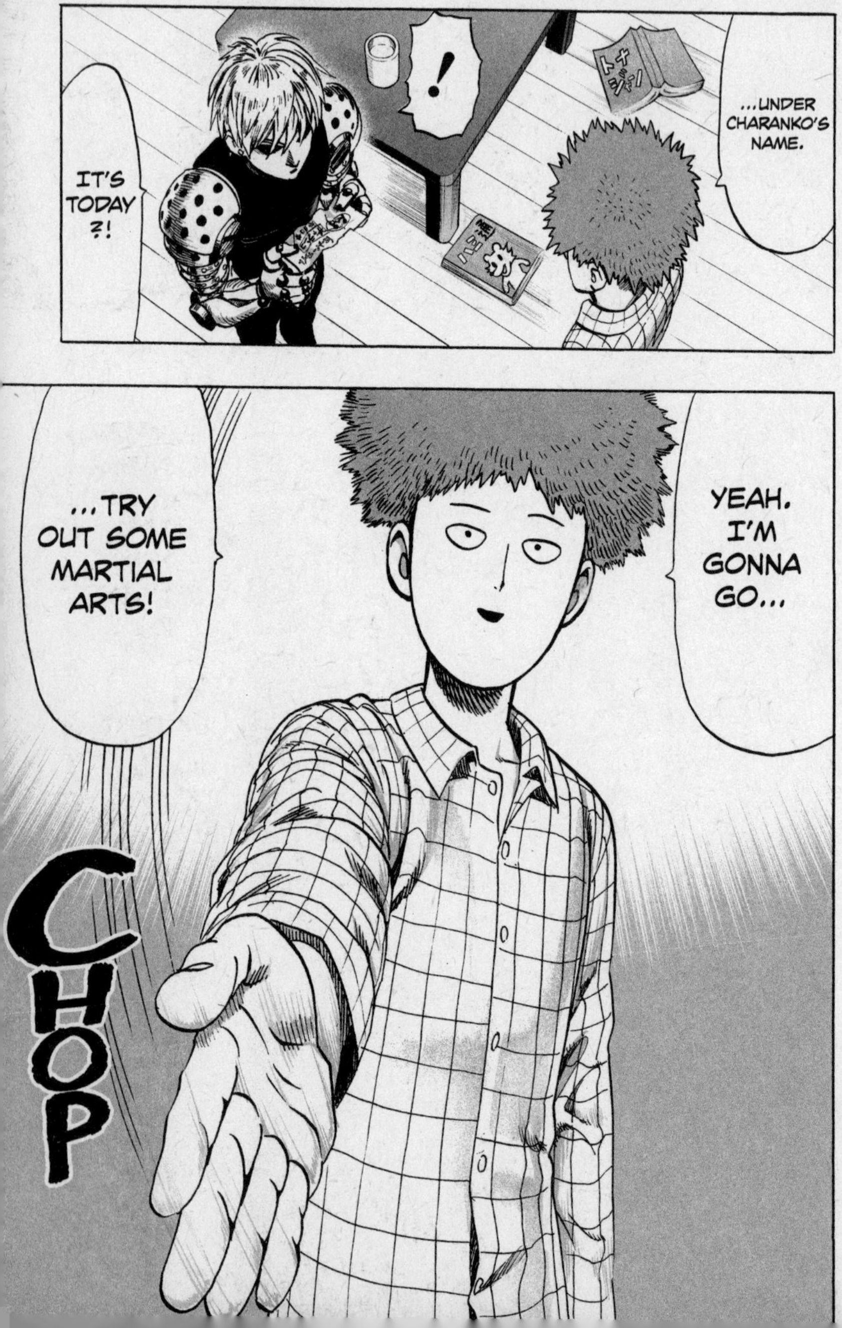
...UNDER CHARANKO'S NAME.
!
IT'S TODAY ?!
YEAH. I'M GONNA GO...
...TRY OUT SOME MARTIAL ARTS!
CHOP

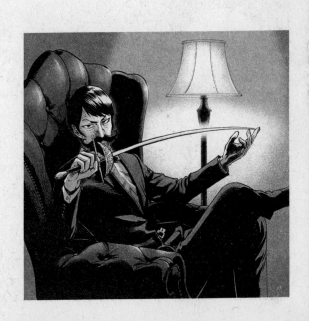

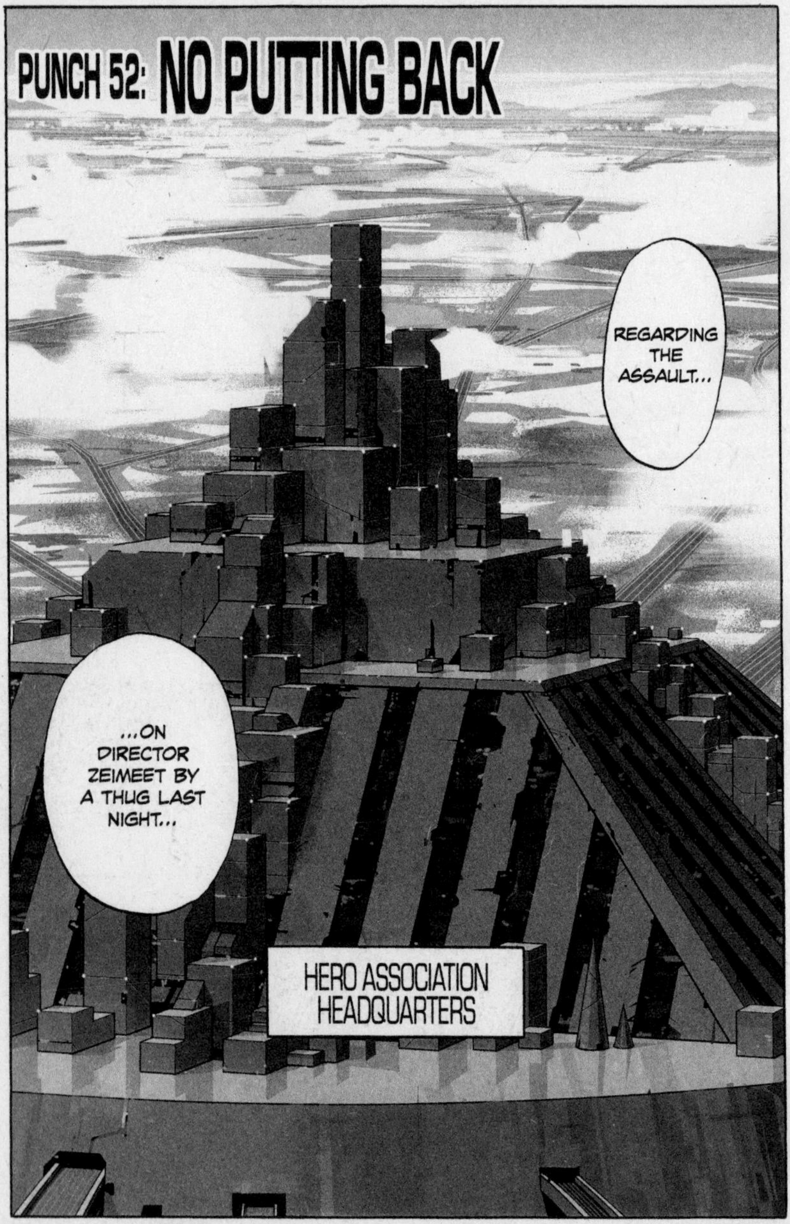
PUNCH 52: NO PUTTING BACK
REGARDING THE ASSAULT...
...ON DIRECTOR ZEIMEET BY A THUG LAST NIGHT...
HERO ASSOCIATION HEADQUARTERS

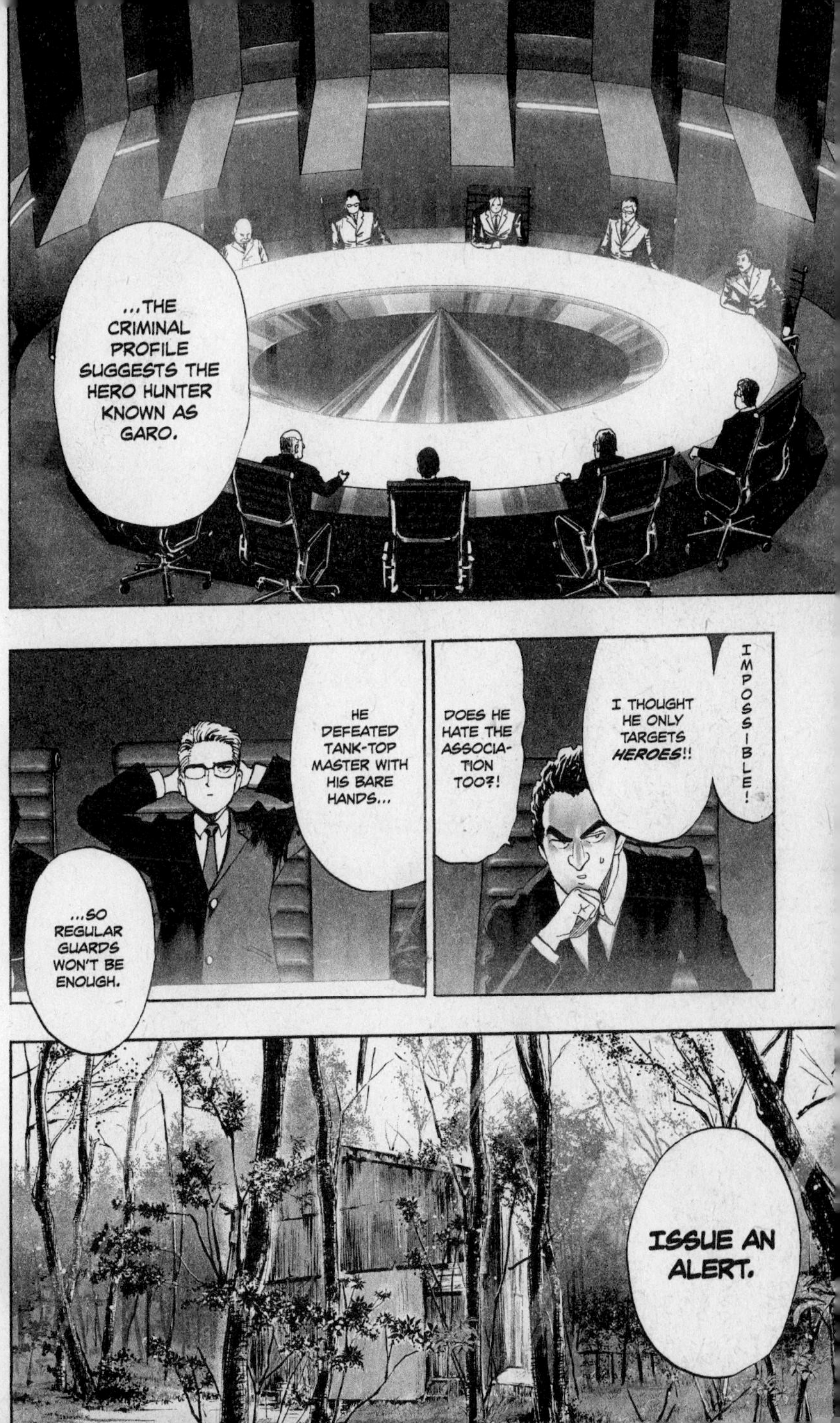
...THE CRIMINAL PROFILE SUGGESTS THE HERO HUNTER KNOWN AS GARO.
IMPOSSIBLE!
I THOUGHT HE ONLY TARGETS *HEROES*!!
DOES HE HATE THE ASSOCIATION TOO?!
HE DEFEATED TANK-TOP MASTER WITH HIS BARE HANDS...
...SO REGULAR GUARDS WON'T BE ENOUGH.
ISSUE AN ALERT.

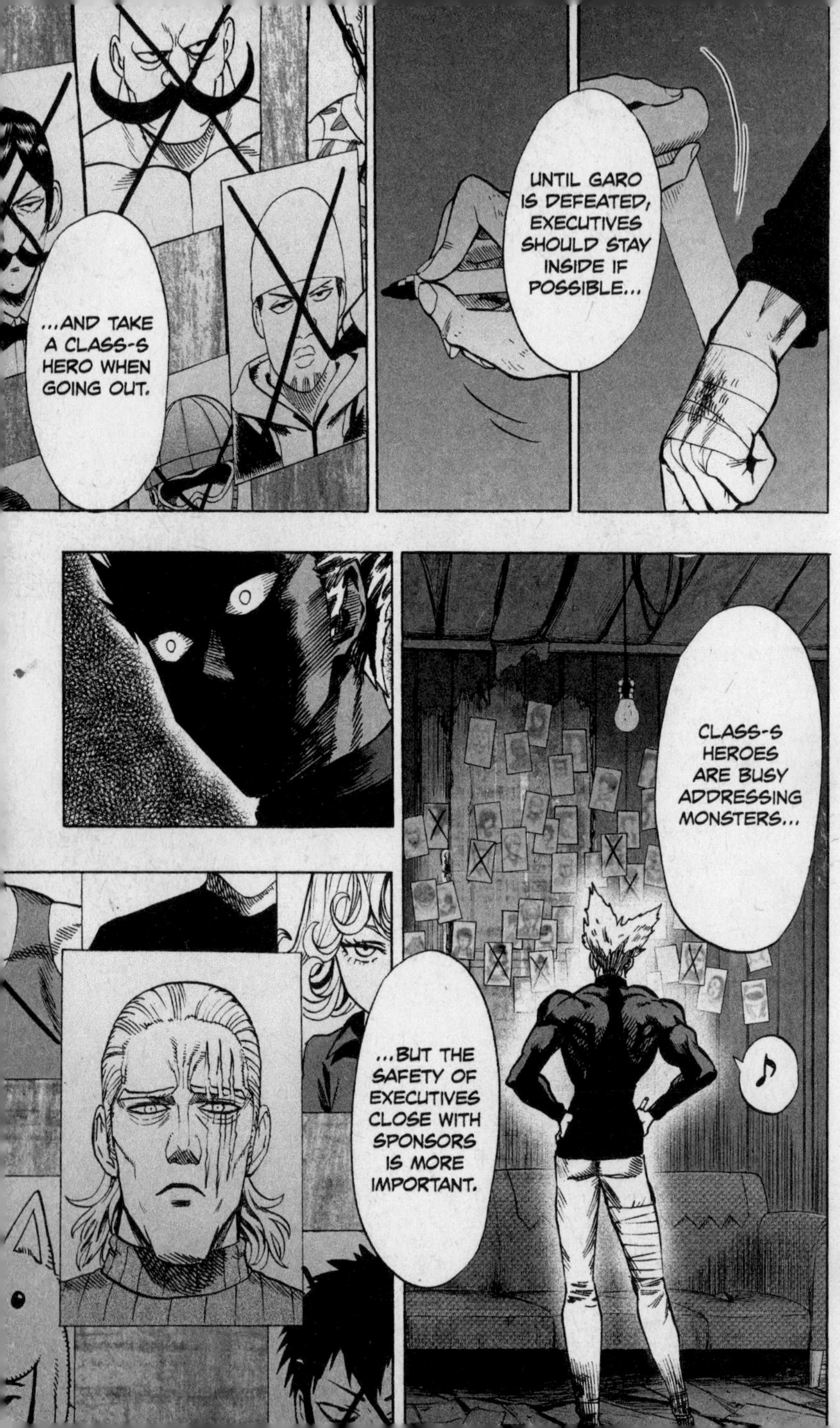
UNTIL GARO IS DEFEATED, EXECUTIVES SHOULD STAY INSIDE IF POSSIBLE...
...AND TAKE A CLASS-S HERO WHEN GOING OUT.
CLASS-S HEROES ARE BUSY ADDRESSING MONSTERS...
♪
...BUT THE SAFETY OF EXECUTIVES CLOSE WITH SPONSORS IS MORE IMPORTANT.

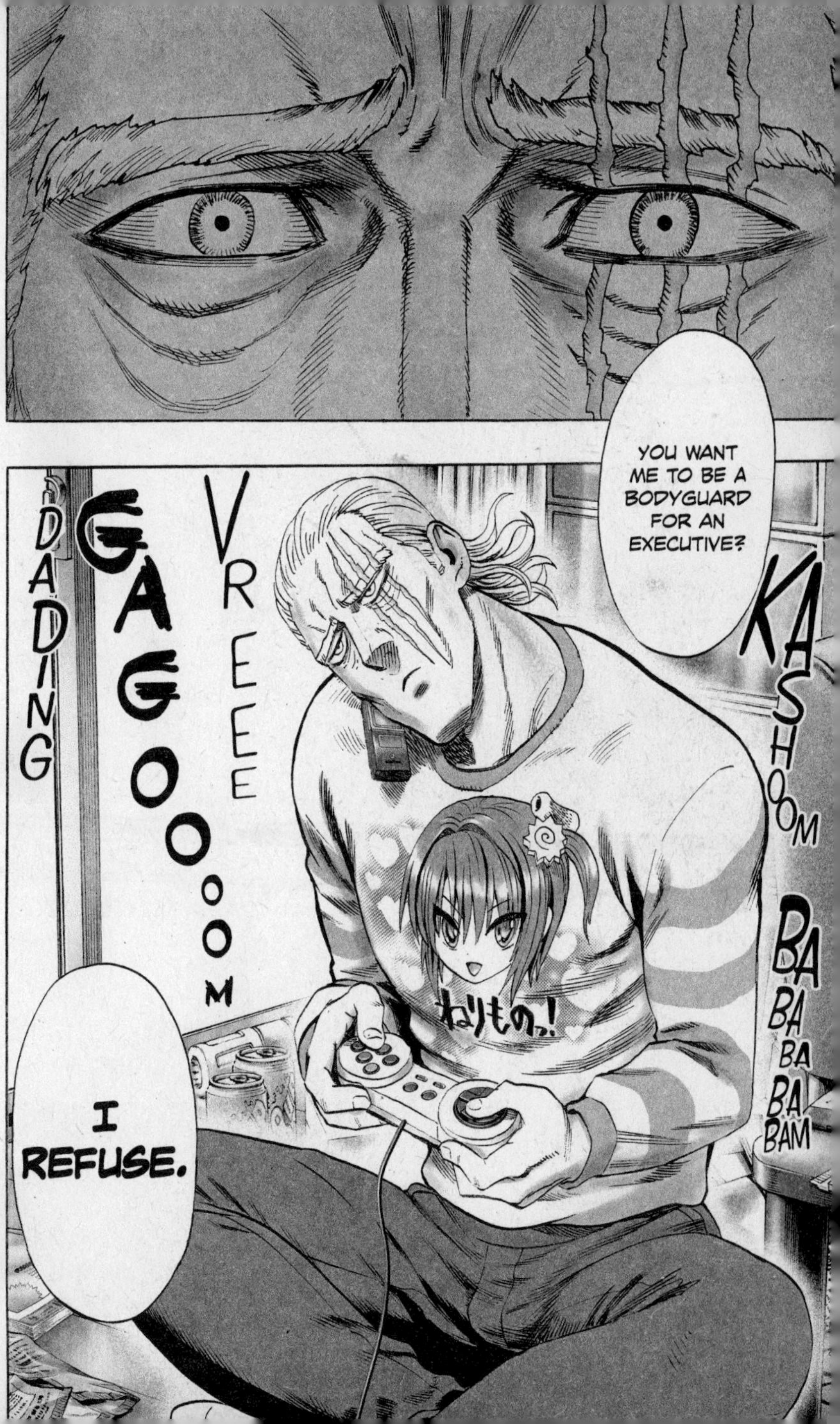
YOU WANT ME TO BE A BODYGUARD FOR AN EXECUTIVE?
KASHOOOM
BABABABABAM
VREEE
GAGOOOOM
DADING
ねりものっ!
I REFUSE.

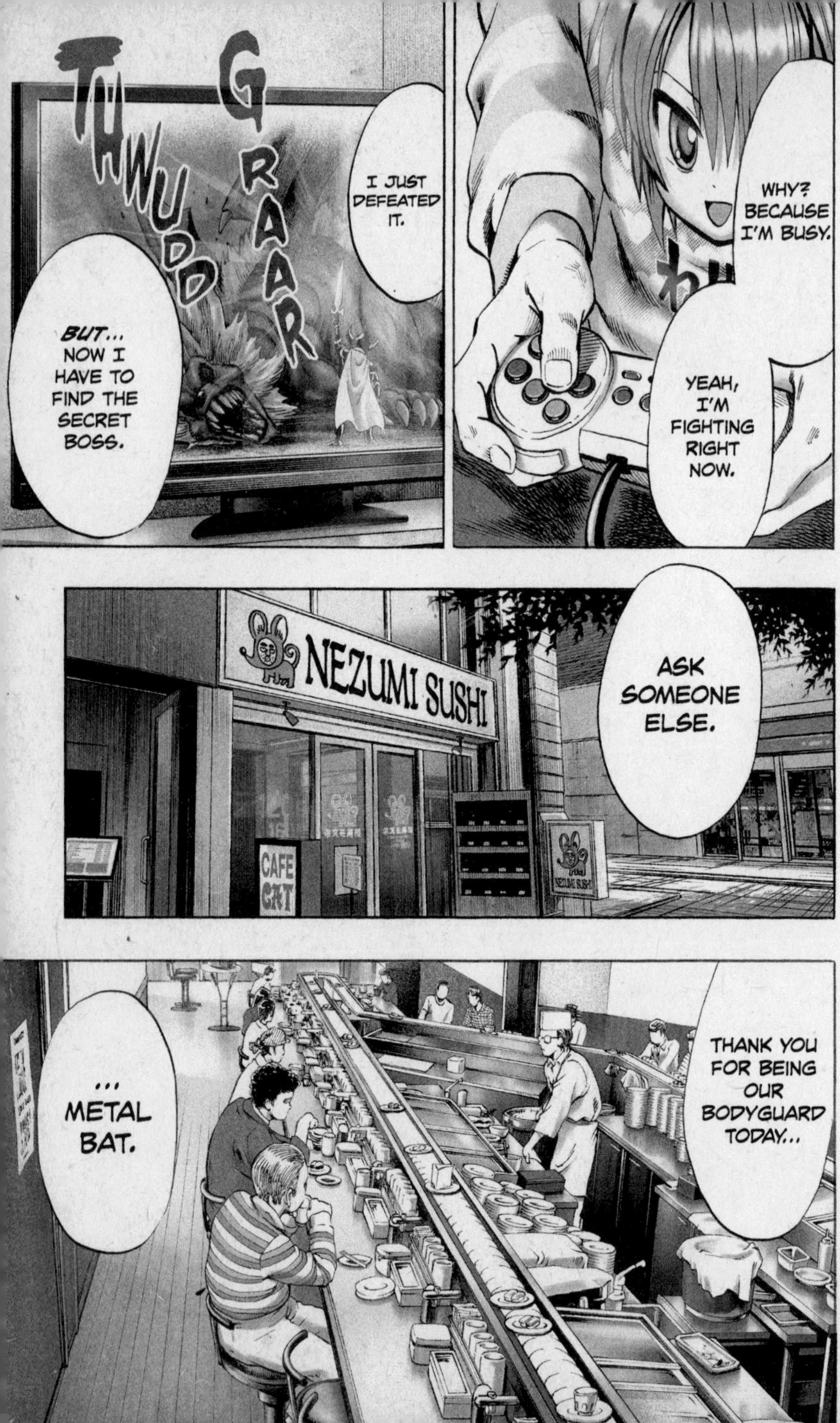
WHY? BECAUSE I'M BUSY.
YEAH, I'M FIGHTING RIGHT NOW.
I JUST DEFEATED IT.
GRAAR
THWUDD
BUT... NOW I HAVE TO FIND THE SECRET BOSS.
ASK SOMEONE ELSE.
NEZUMI SUSHI
CAFE CAT
NEZUMI SUSHI
THANK YOU FOR BEING OUR BODYGUARD TODAY...
... METAL BAT.

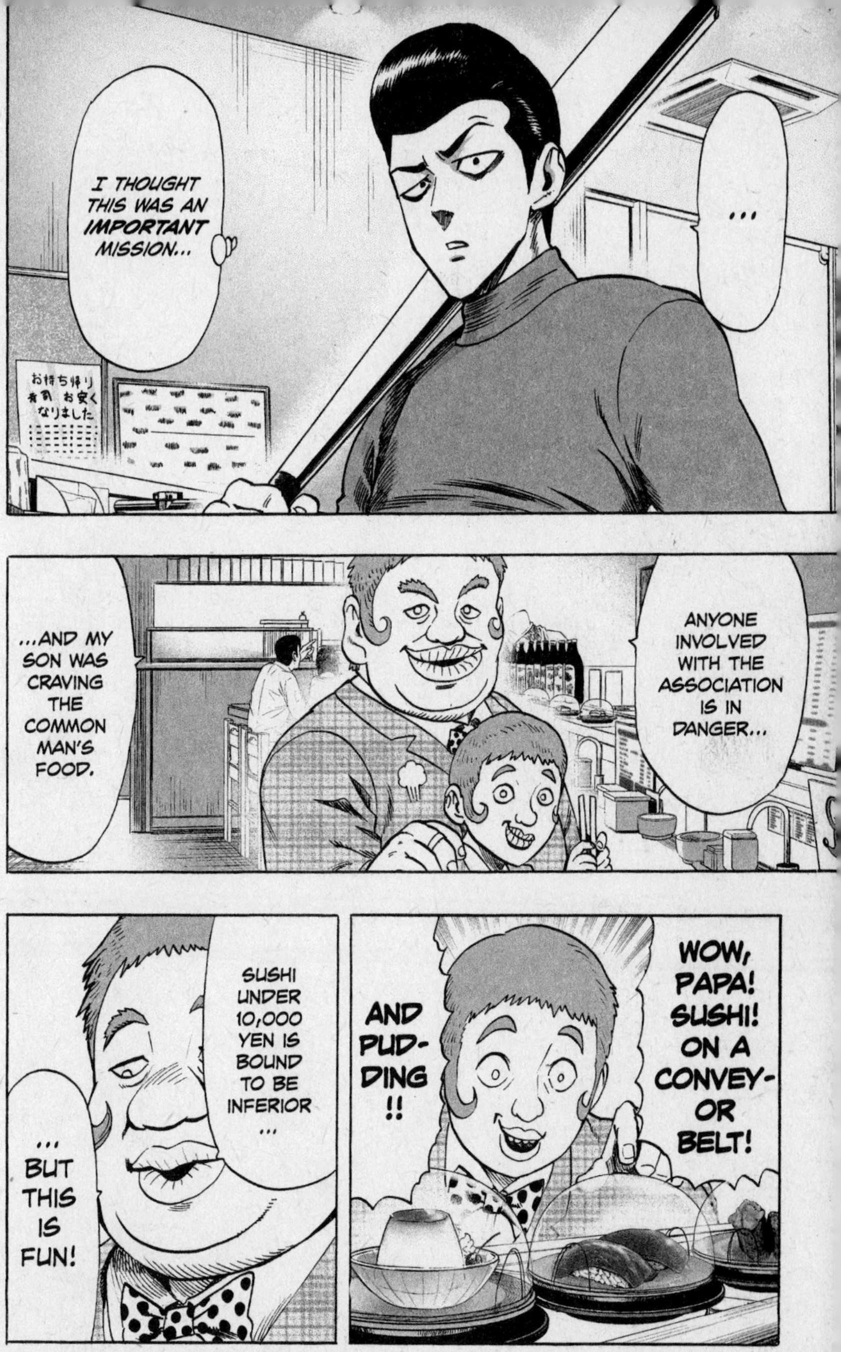
...
I THOUGHT THIS WAS AN *IMPORTANT* MISSION...
お持ち帰り寿司 お安くなりました
ANYONE INVOLVED WITH THE ASSOCIATION IS IN DANGER...
...AND MY SON WAS CRAVING THE COMMON MAN'S FOOD.
WOW, PAPA! SUSHI! ON A CONVEY-OR BELT!
AND PUD-DING!!
SUSHI UNDER 10,000 YEN IS BOUND TO BE INFERIOR...
...BUT THIS IS FUN!

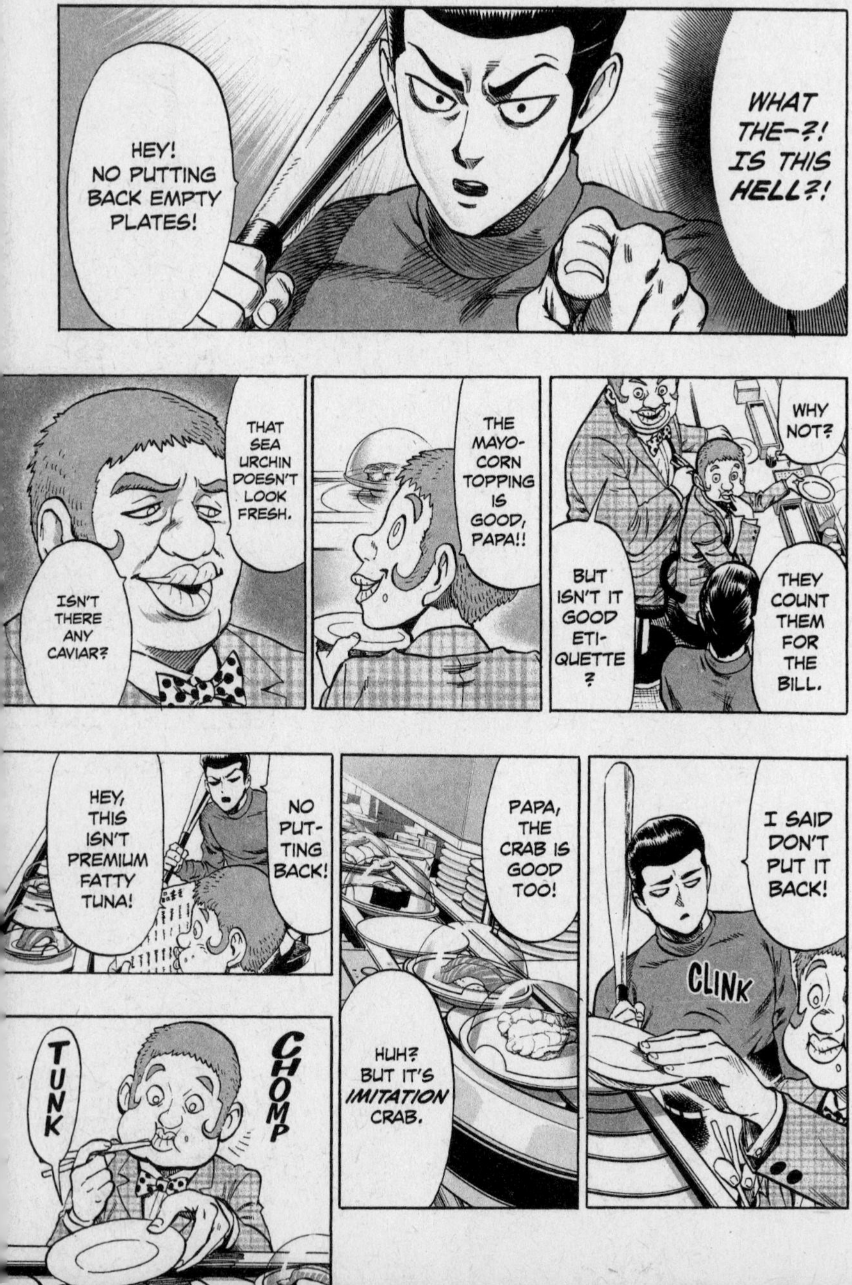
WHAT THE-?! IS THIS HELL?!
HEY! NO PUTTING BACK EMPTY PLATES!
WHY NOT?
THEY COUNT THEM FOR THE BILL.
BUT ISN'T IT GOOD ETIQUETTE?
THE MAYO-CORN TOPPING IS GOOD, PAPA!!
THAT SEA URCHIN DOESN'T LOOK FRESH.
ISN'T THERE ANY CAVIAR?
I SAID DON'T PUT IT BACK!
CLINK
PAPA, THE CRAB IS GOOD TOO!
HUH? BUT IT'S *IMITATION* CRAB.
NO PUT-TING BACK!
HEY, THIS ISN'T PREMIUM FATTY TUNA!
CHOMP
TUNK

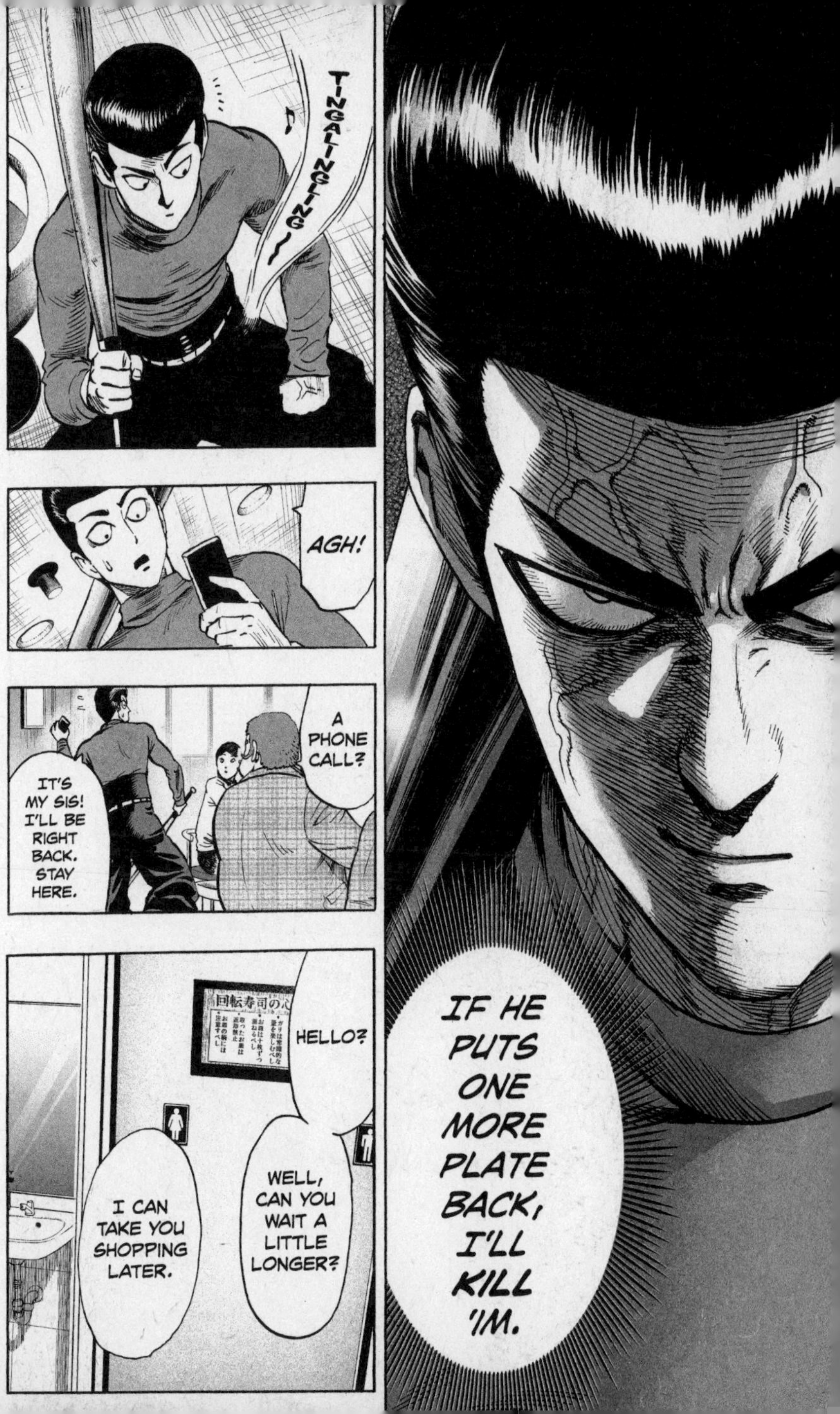
IF HE PUTS ONE MORE PLATE BACK, I'LL KILL 'IM.
TINGALINGLING~
AGH!
A PHONE CALL?
IT'S MY SIS! I'LL BE RIGHT BACK. STAY HERE.
HELLO?
WELL, CAN YOU WAIT A LITTLE LONGER?
I CAN TAKE YOU SHOPPING LATER.

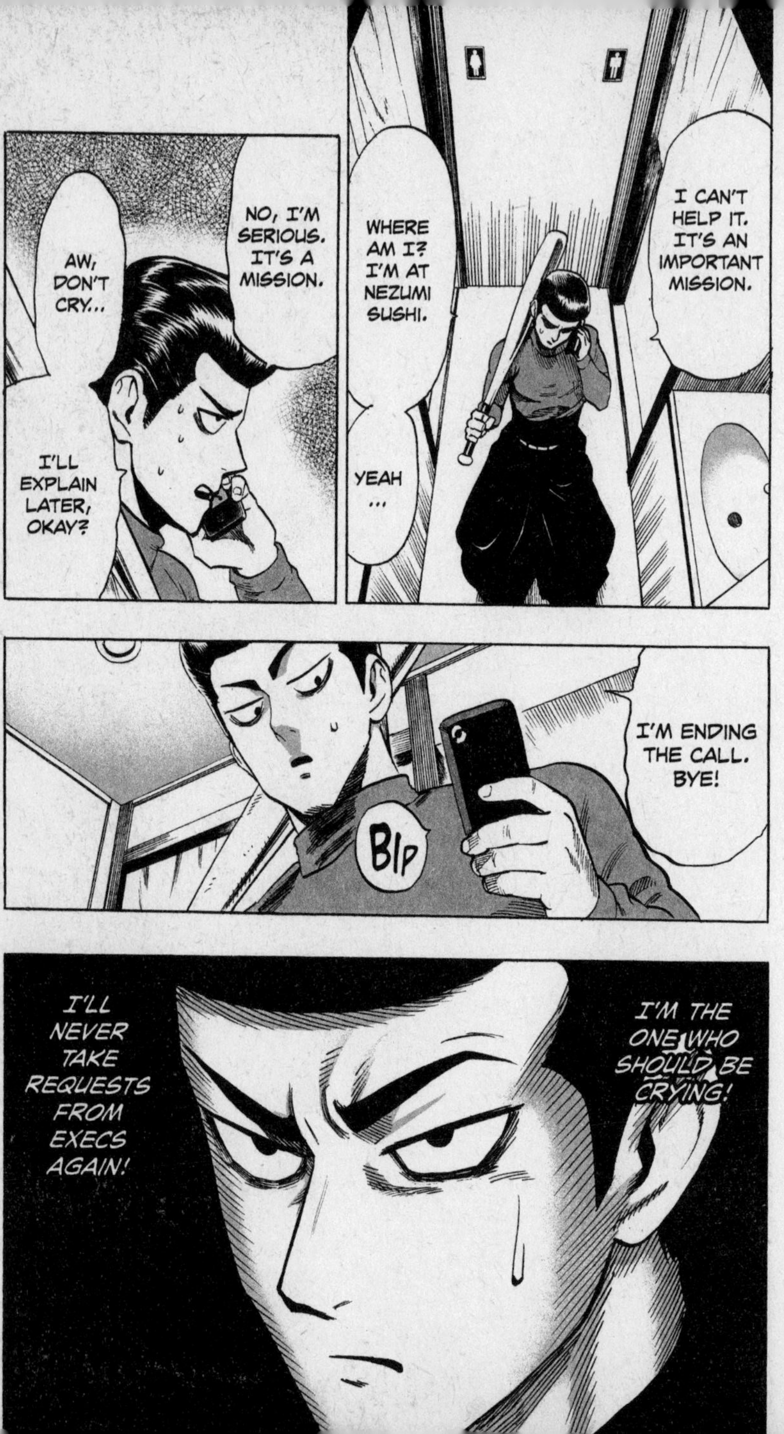
I CAN'T HELP IT. IT'S AN IMPORTANT MISSION.
WHERE AM I? I'M AT NEZUMI SUSHI.
YEAH ...
NO, I'M SERIOUS. IT'S A MISSION.
AW, DON'T CRY...
I'LL EXPLAIN LATER, OKAY?
I'M ENDING THE CALL. BYE!
BIP
I'M THE ONE WHO SHOULD BE CRYING!
I'LL NEVER TAKE REQUESTS FROM EXECS AGAIN!

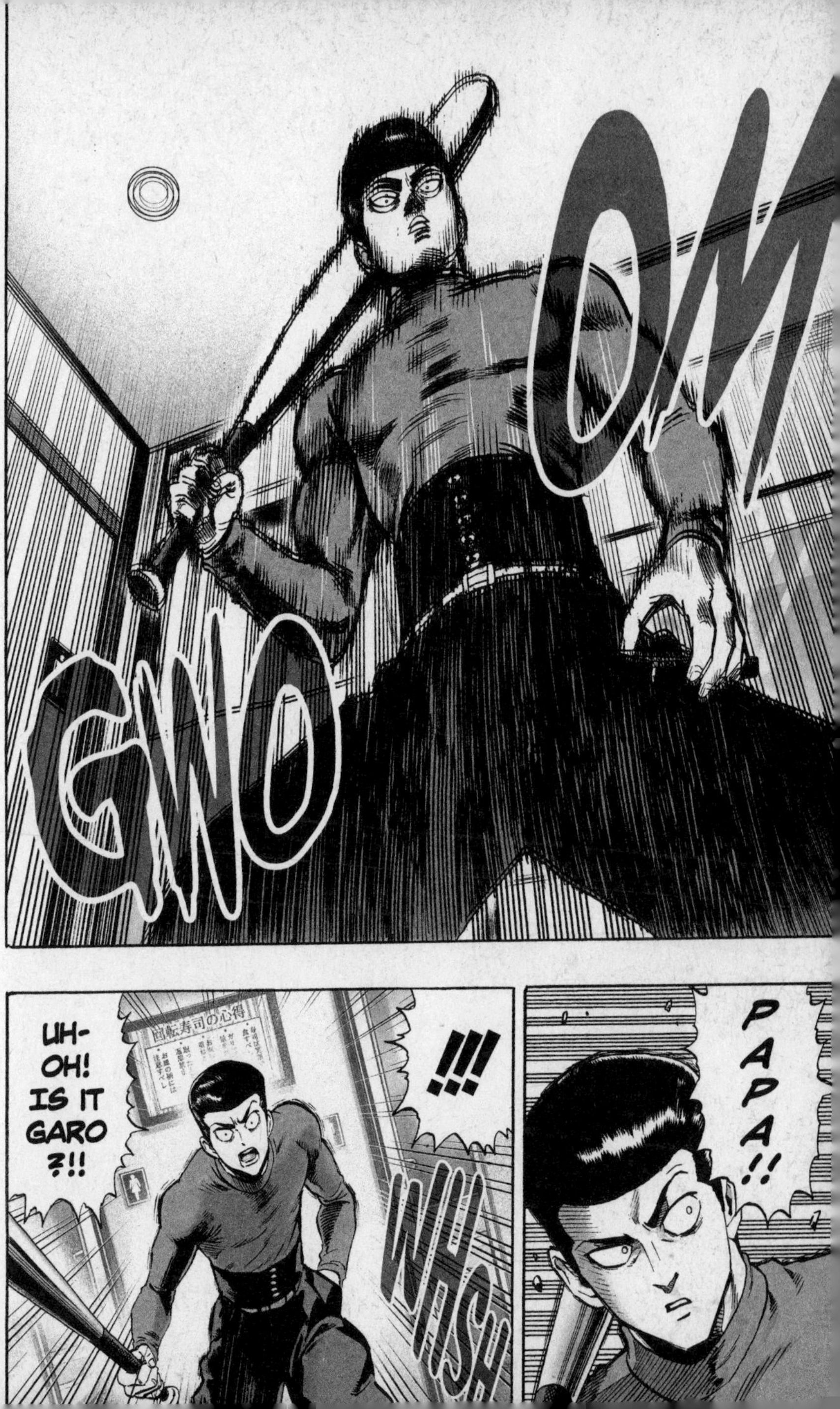

GNO
OM
PAPA!!
!!!
UH-OH! IS IT GARO?!!
回転寿司の心得
WHSH

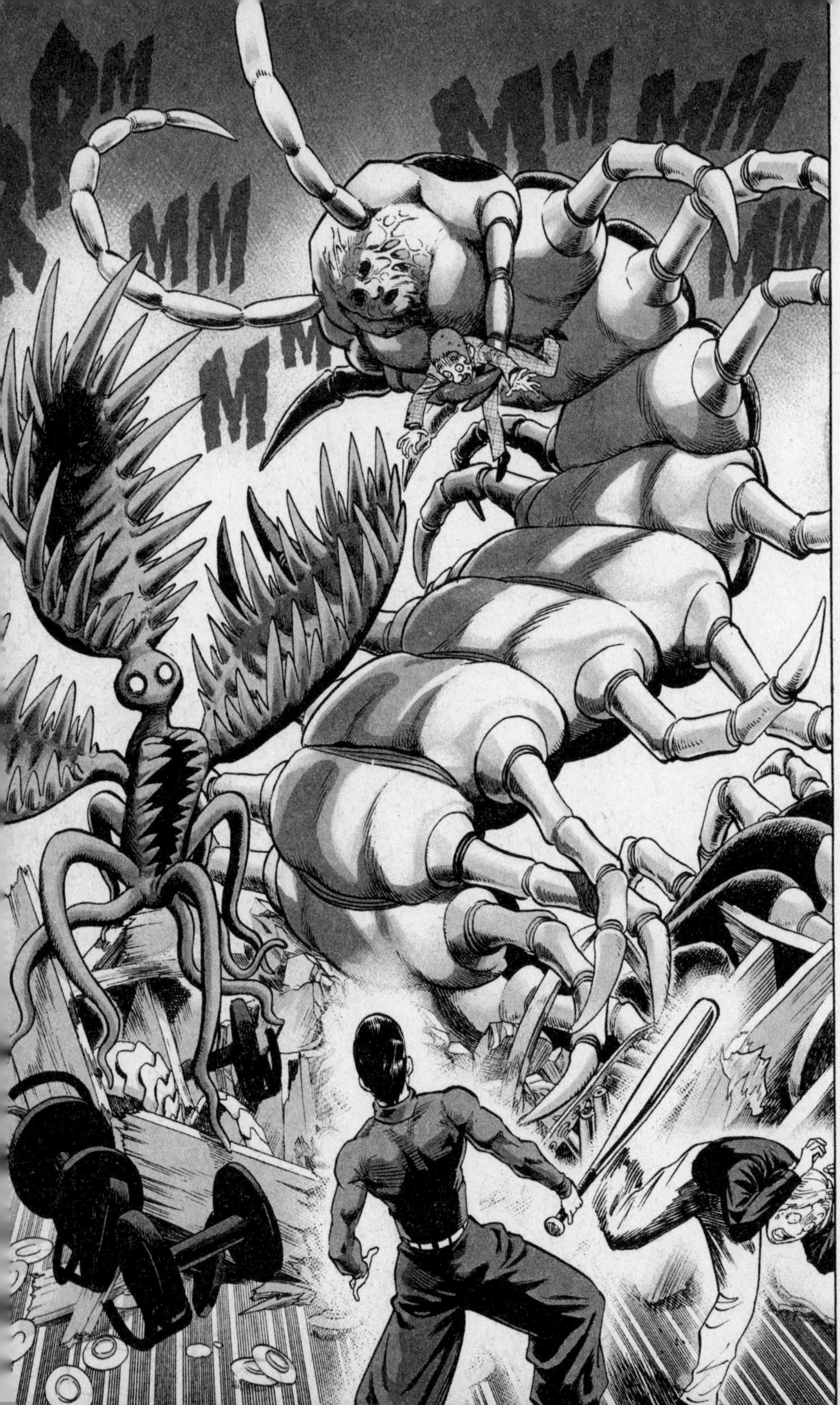
RRM
MM
MMM
MMM MM
MMM

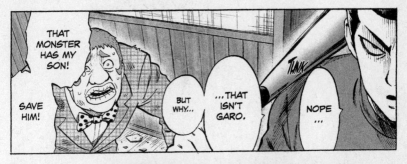

NOPE ...
TUNK
...THAT ISN'T GARO.
BUT WHY...
THAT MONSTER HAS MY SON!
SAVE HIM!
HE MATCHES THE PHOTO ...
...SO HE'S A HERO ASSOCIATION EXECUTIVE.
GOOD THING HE'S WITH HIS KID.
THE BRAT IS MINE.
HOLD ON A SEC!
KLTTR
FWISH
YOU AREN'T LEAVING THIS RESTAU-RANT.

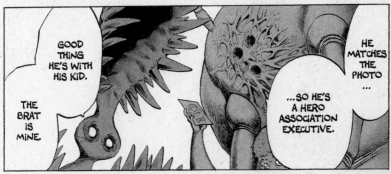

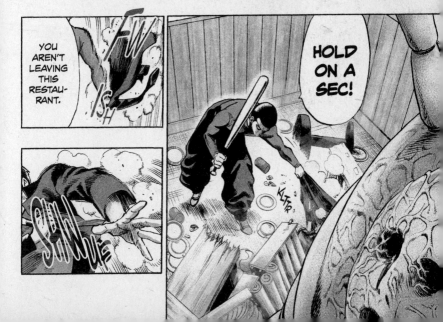

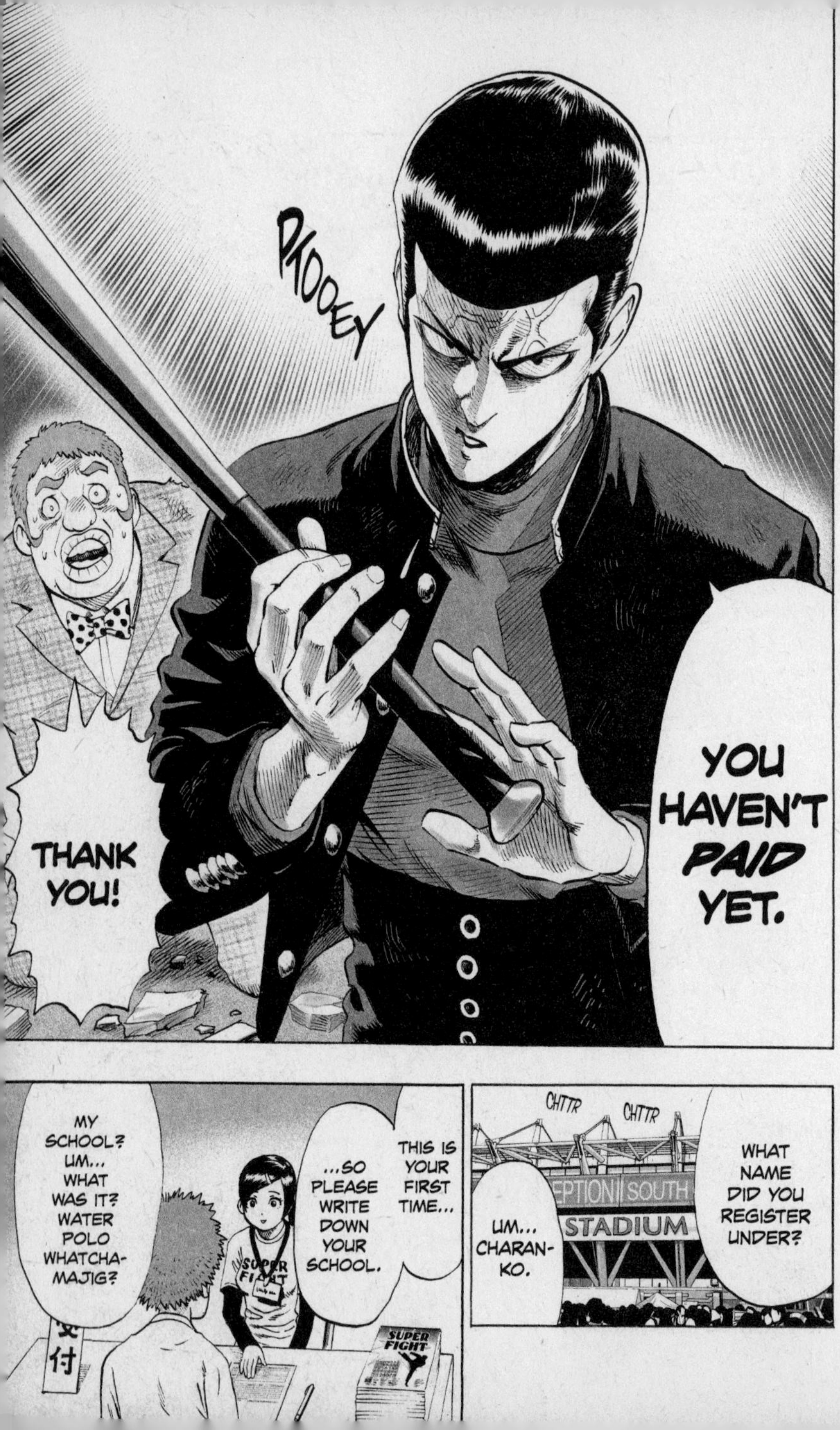
PKOOEY
YOU HAVEN'T PAID YET.
THANK YOU!
CHTTR
CHTTR
WHAT NAME DID YOU REGISTER UNDER?
UM... CHARAN-KO.
SOUTH
STADIUM
THIS IS YOUR FIRST TIME...
...SO PLEASE WRITE DOWN YOUR SCHOOL.
MY SCHOOL? UM... WHAT WAS IT? WATER POLO WHATCHA-MAJIG?
SUPER FIGHT
SUPER FIGHT
付

ONE-PUNCH MAN 10

ONE + YUSUKE MURATA

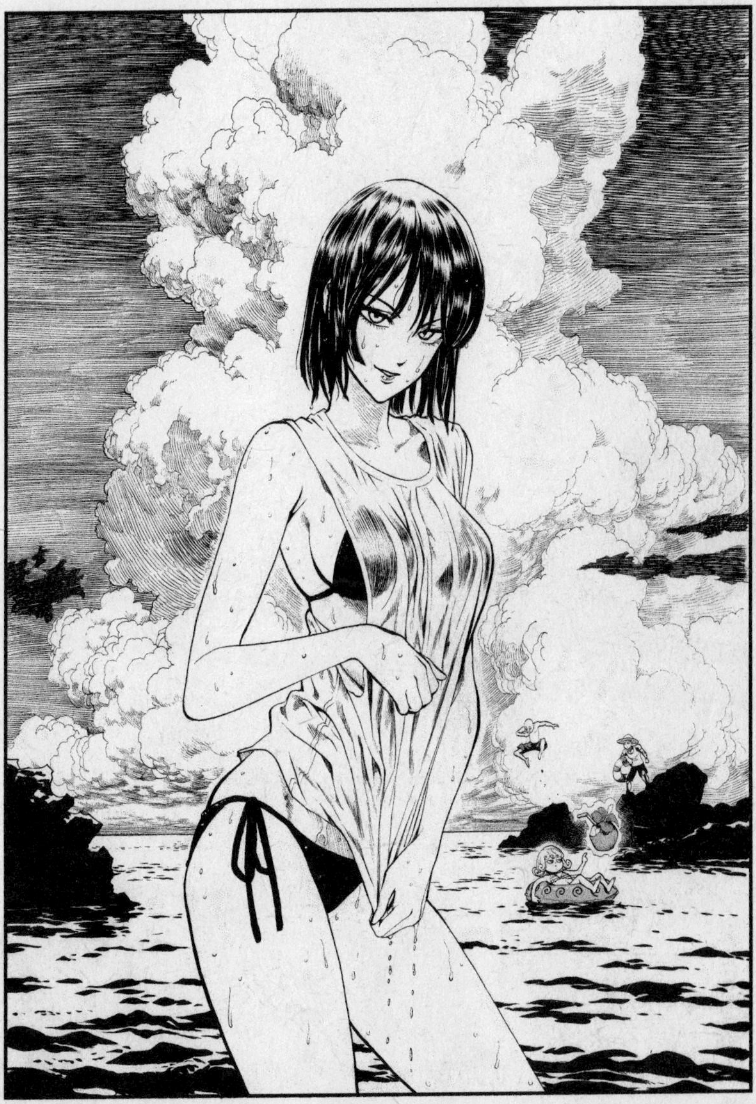

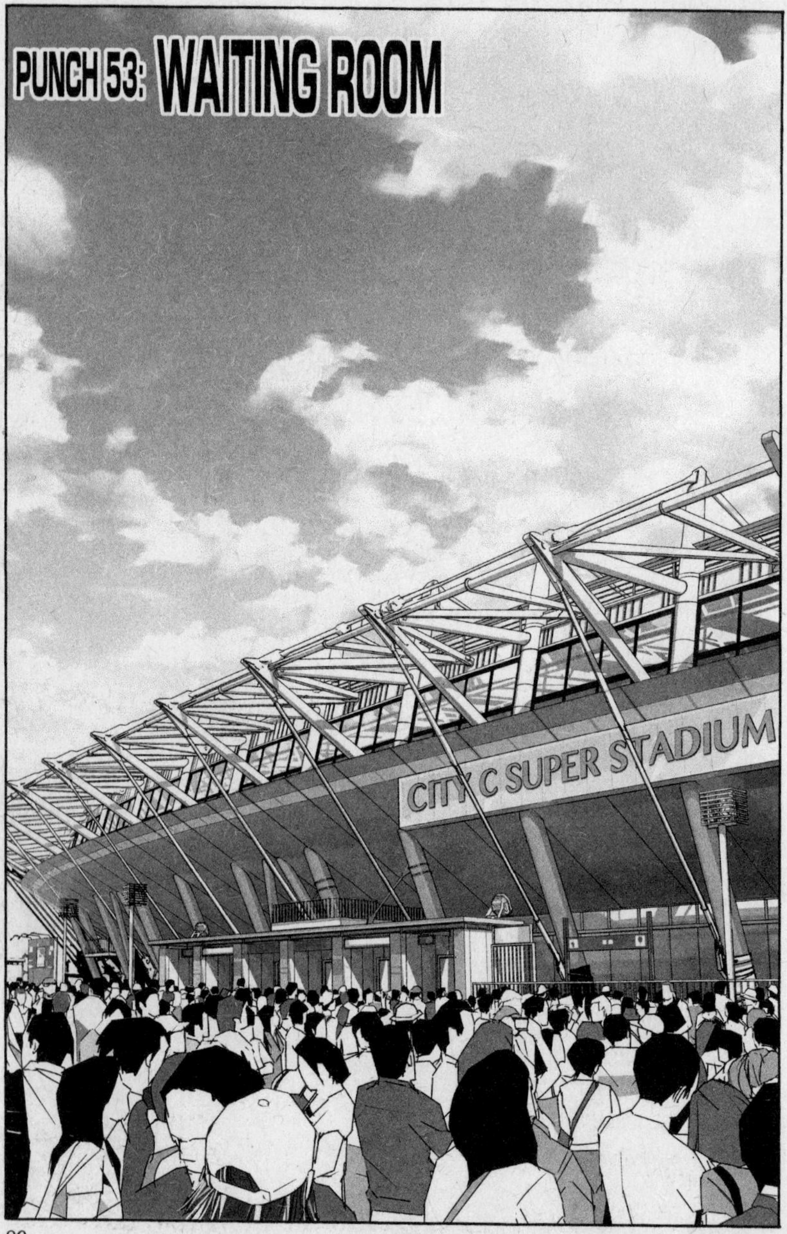
PUNCH 53: WAITING ROOM
CITY C SUPER STADIUM

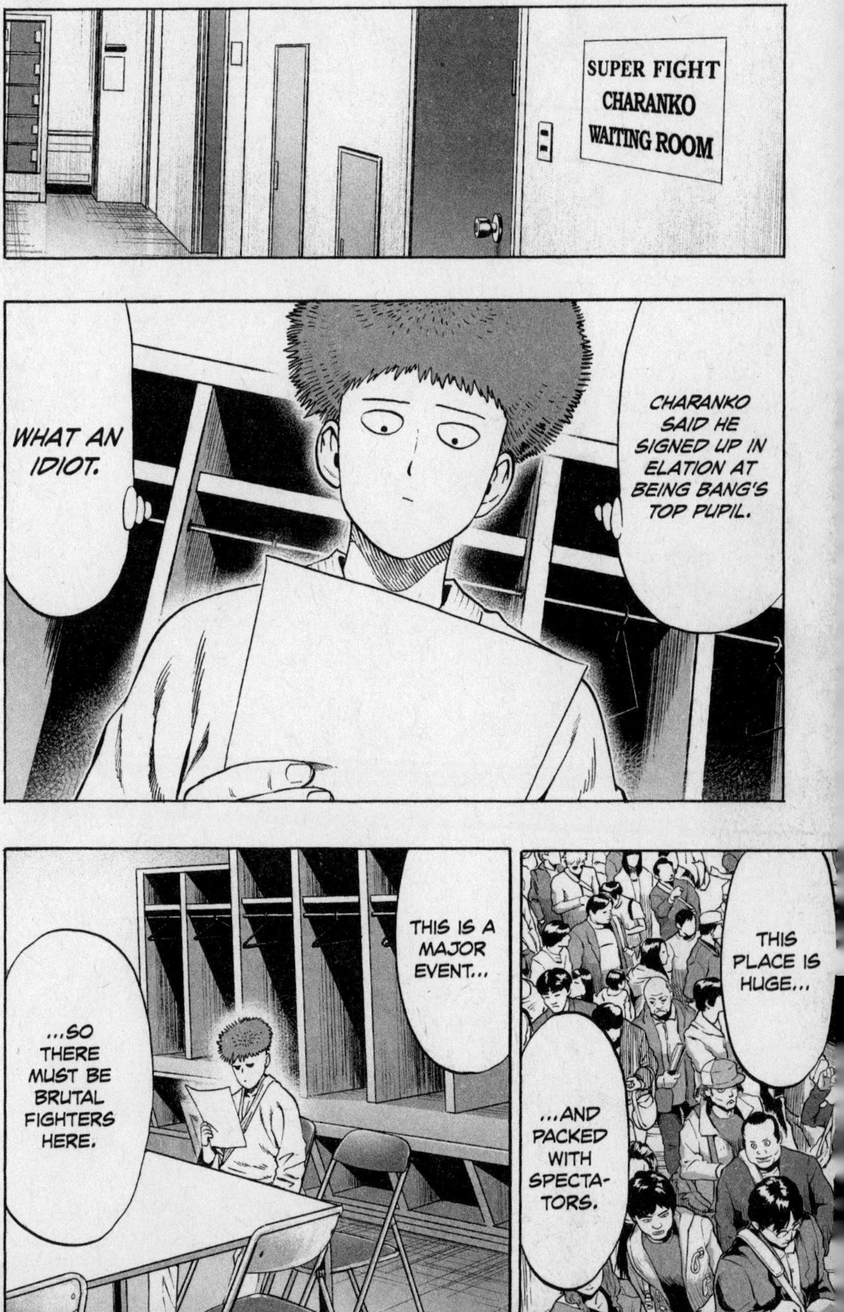
SUPER FIGHT
CHARANKO
WAITING ROOM
CHARANKO SAID HE SIGNED UP IN ELATION AT BEING BANG'S TOP PUPIL.
WHAT AN IDIOT.
THIS PLACE IS HUGE...
...AND PACKED WITH SPECTA-TORS.
THIS IS A MAJOR EVENT...
...SO THERE MUST BE BRUTAL FIGHTERS HERE.

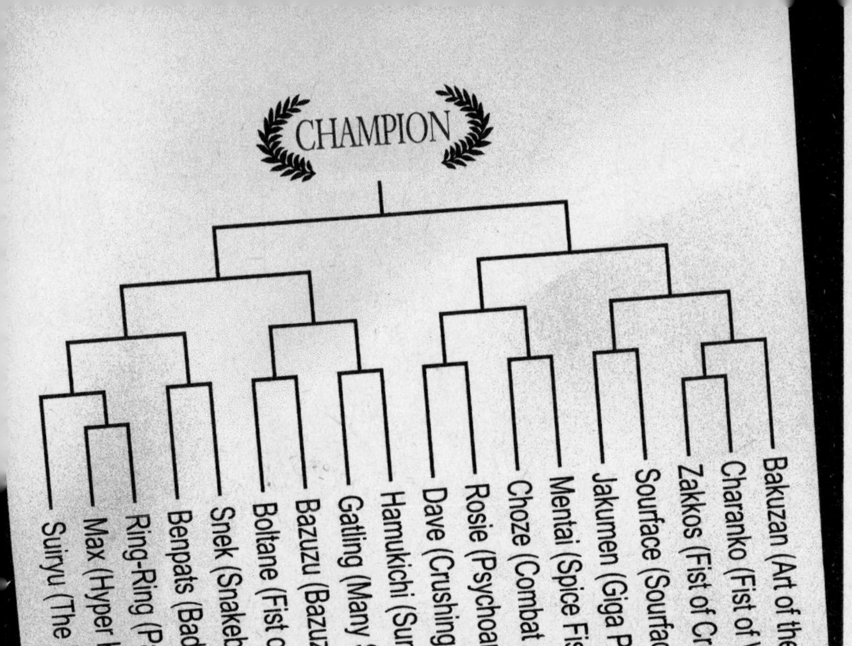
CHAMPION
Bakuzan (Art of the Darkness Hellkill
Charanko (Fist of Water Polo, Carbo
Zakkos (Fist of Crazy Collision, Fierce Truth)
Sourface (Sourface-Style Kempo)
Jakumen (Giga Pro Wrestling)
Mentai (Spice Fist)
Choze (Combat Arts of the Chosen People)
Rosie (Psychoanalytic Martial Arts)
Dave (Crushing Giant Method)
Hamukichi (Sunflower Dojo's Gentle Art of Self-Defense
Gatling (Many Striking Fists)
Bazuzu (Bazuzu's Nuclear Fist)
Boltane (Fist of Thunder and Lightning)
Snek (Snakebite Fist)
Benpats (Bad Roads Martial Arts)
Ring-Ring (Palm Bells Fist)
Max (Hyper Karate)
Suiryu (The Dark Body Art)
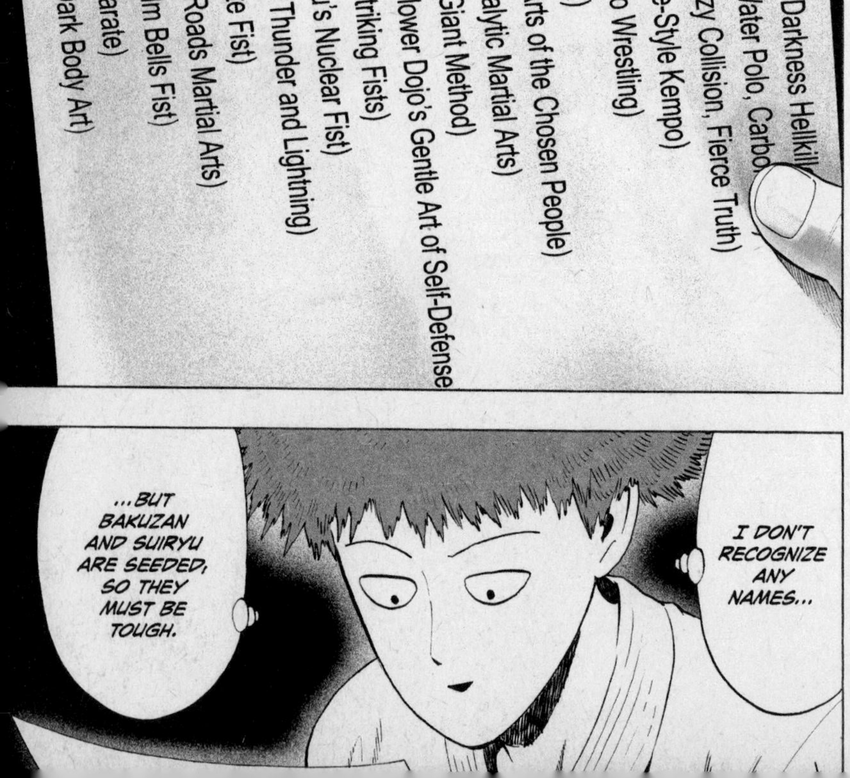
I DON'T RECOGNIZE ANY NAMES...
...BUT BAKUZAN AND SUIRYU ARE SEEDED, SO THEY MUST BE TOUGH.

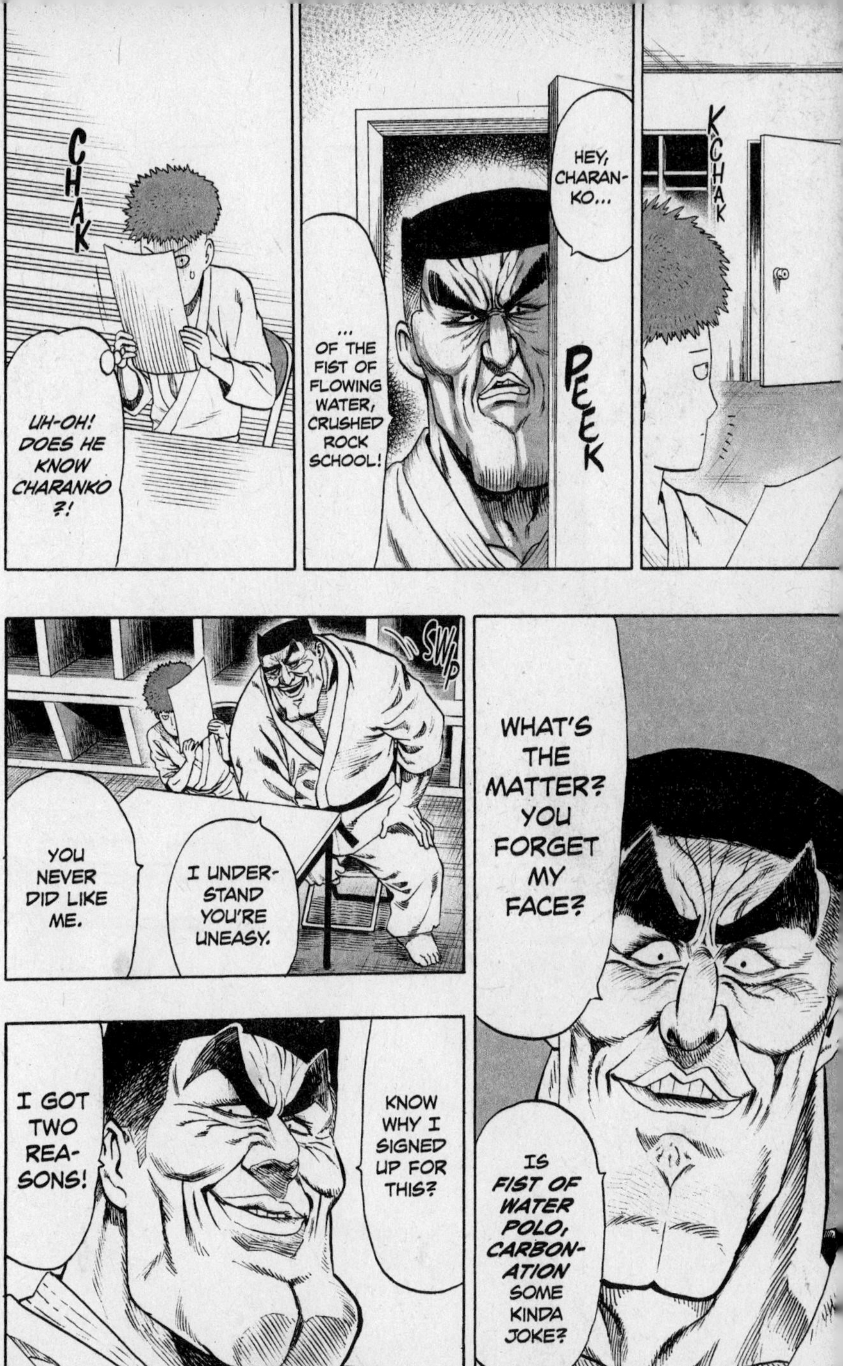
K'CHAK
HEY, CHARAN-KO...
PEEK
...OF THE FIST OF FLOWING WATER, CRUSHED ROCK SCHOOL!
CHAK
UH-OH! DOES HE KNOW CHARANKO ?!
WHAT'S THE MATTER? YOU FORGET MY FACE?
IS *FIST OF WATER POLO, CARBONATION* SOME KINDA JOKE?
SWP
I UNDER-STAND YOU'RE UNEASY.
YOU NEVER DID LIKE ME.
KNOW WHY I SIGNED UP FOR THIS?
I GOT TWO REA-SONS!

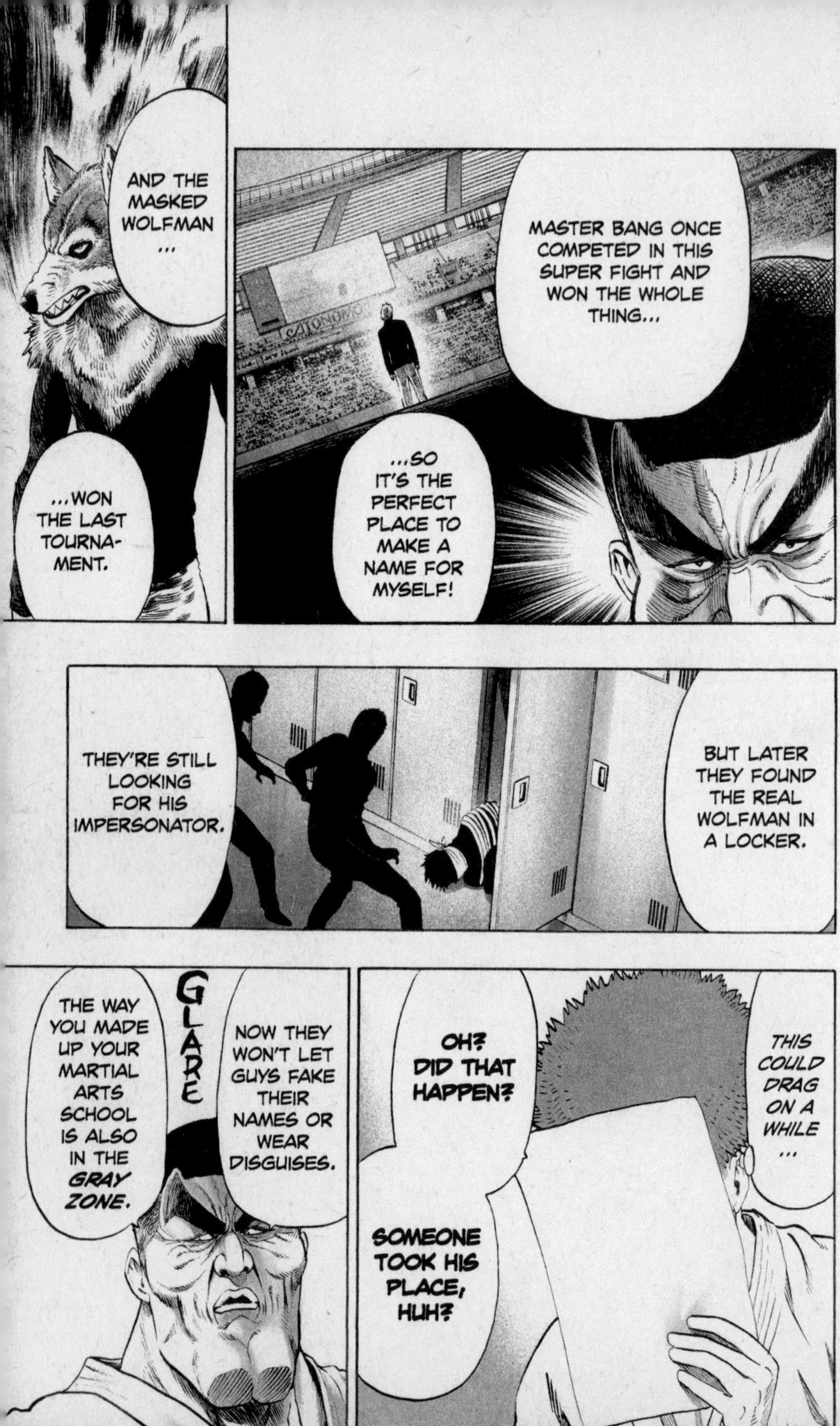
MASTER BANG ONCE COMPETED IN THIS SUPER FIGHT AND WON THE WHOLE THING...
...SO IT'S THE PERFECT PLACE TO MAKE A NAME FOR MYSELF!
AND THE MASKED WOLFMAN ...
...WON THE LAST TOURNA-MENT.
BUT LATER THEY FOUND THE REAL WOLFMAN IN A LOCKER.
THEY'RE STILL LOOKING FOR HIS IMPERSONATOR.
THIS COULD DRAG ON A WHILE ...
OH? DID THAT HAPPEN?
SOMEONE TOOK HIS PLACE, HUH?
NOW THEY WON'T LET GUYS FAKE THEIR NAMES OR WEAR DISGUISES.
GLARE
THE WAY YOU MADE UP YOUR MARTIAL ARTS SCHOOL IS ALSO IN THE *GRAY ZONE*.

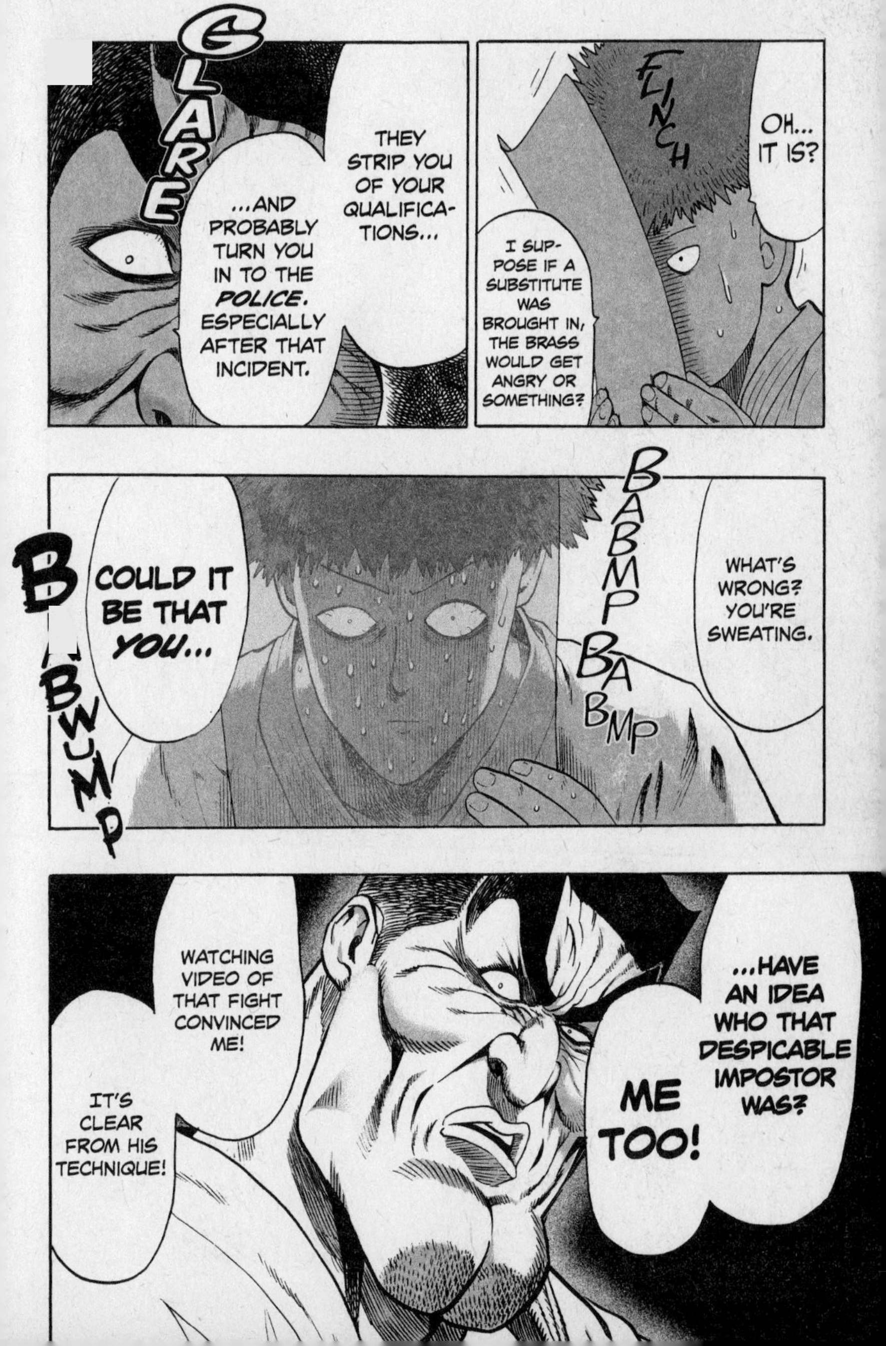
FLINCH
OH... IT IS?
I SUPPOSE IF A SUBSTITUTE WAS BROUGHT IN, THE BRASS WOULD GET ANGRY OR SOMETHING?
LARE
THEY STRIP YOU OF YOUR QUALIFICATIONS...
...AND PROBABLY TURN YOU IN TO THE *POLICE.* ESPECIALLY AFTER THAT INCIDENT.
BABMP BABMP
WHAT'S WRONG? YOU'RE SWEATING.
COULD IT BE THAT *YOU*...
BWUMP
...HAVE AN IDEA WHO THAT DESPICABLE IMPOSTOR WAS?
ME TOO!
WATCHING VIDEO OF THAT FIGHT CONVINCED ME!
IT'S CLEAR FROM HIS TECHNIQUE!

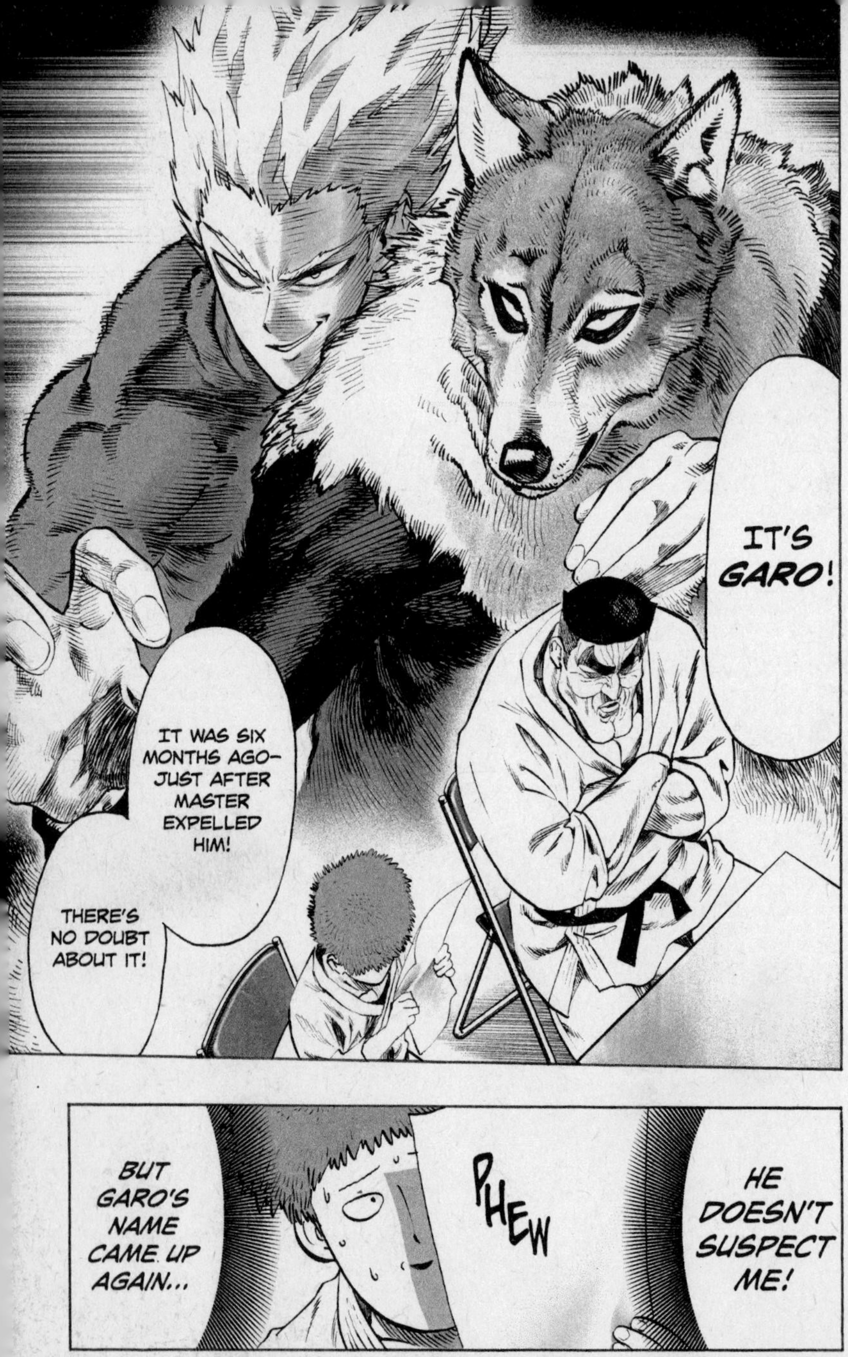
IT'S GARO!
IT WAS SIX MONTHS AGO— JUST AFTER MASTER EXPELLED HIM!
THERE'S NO DOUBT ABOUT IT!
HE DOESN'T SUSPECT ME!
PHEW
BUT GARO'S NAME CAME UP AGAIN...

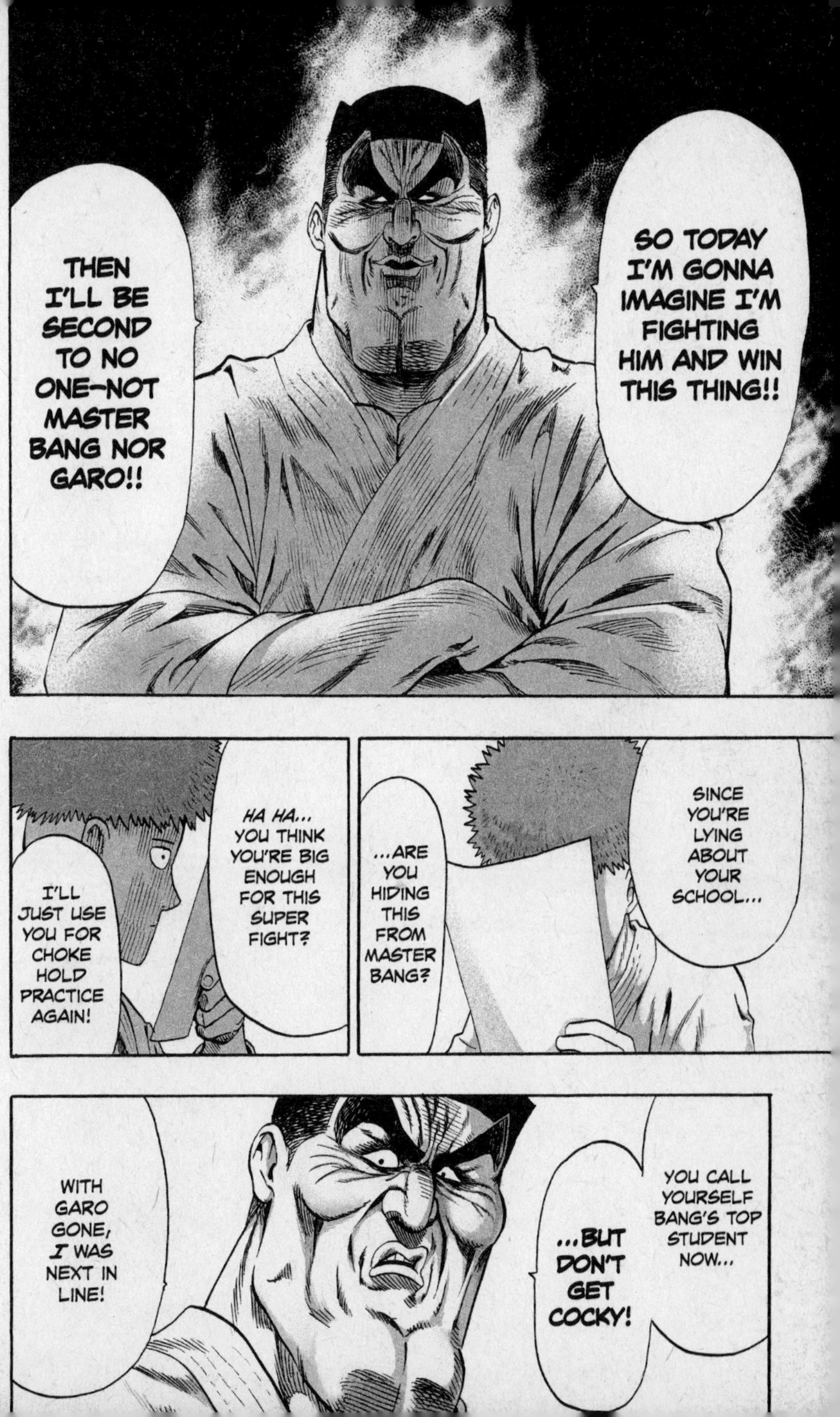
SO TODAY I'M GONNA IMAGINE I'M FIGHTING HIM AND WIN THIS THING!!
THEN I'LL BE SECOND TO NO ONE—NOT MASTER BANG NOR GARO!!
SINCE YOU'RE LYING ABOUT YOUR SCHOOL...
...ARE YOU HIDING THIS FROM MASTER BANG?
HA HA... YOU THINK YOU'RE BIG ENOUGH FOR THIS SUPER FIGHT?
I'LL JUST USE YOU FOR CHOKE HOLD PRACTICE AGAIN!
YOU CALL YOURSELF BANG'S TOP STUDENT NOW...
...BUT DON'T GET COCKY!
WITH GARO GONE, I WAS NEXT IN LINE!

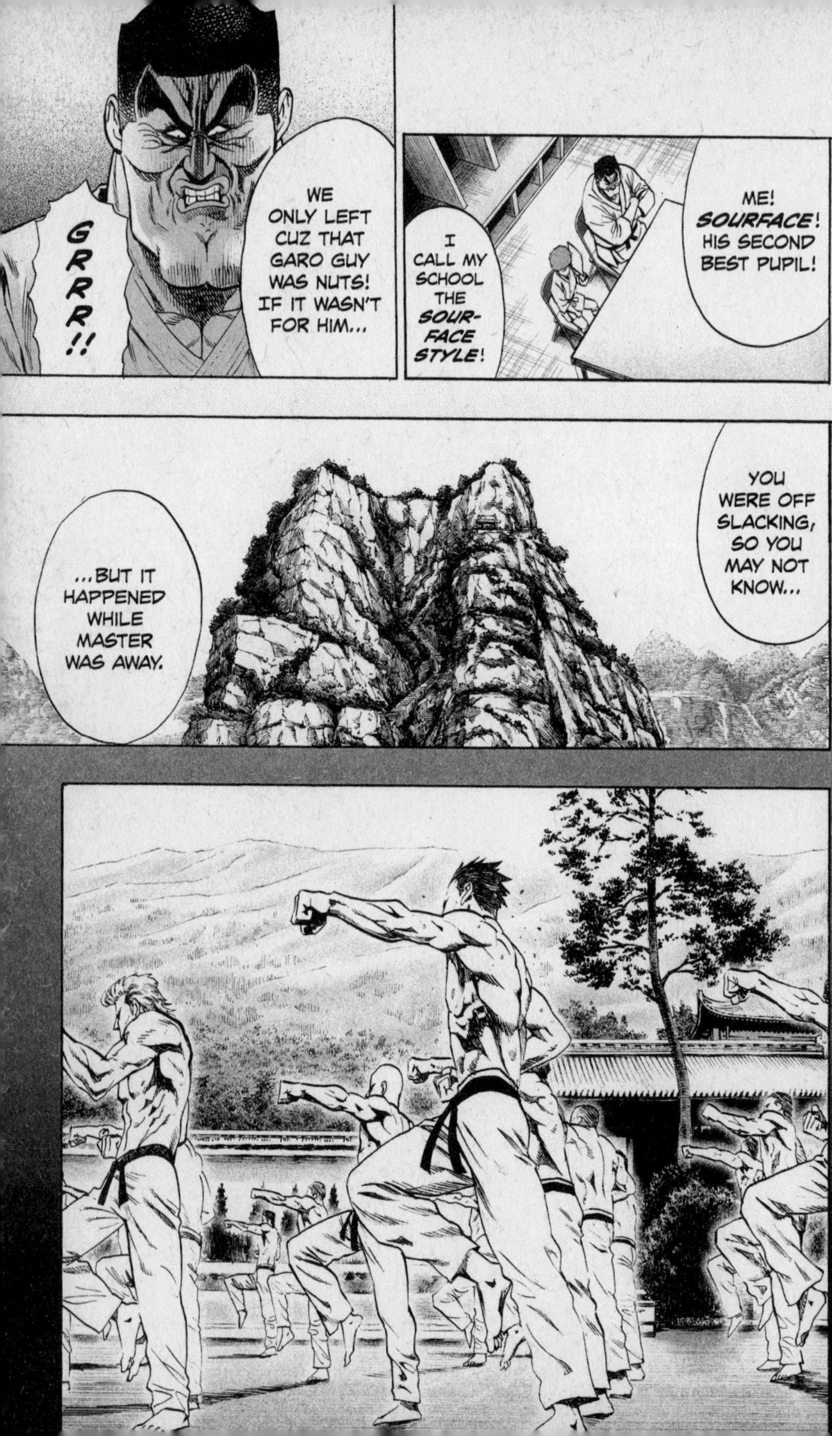
ME! SOURFACE! HIS SECOND BEST PUPIL!
I CALL MY SCHOOL THE SOURFACE STYLE!
WE ONLY LEFT CUZ THAT GARO GUY WAS NUTS! IF IT WASN'T FOR HIM...
GRRR!!
YOU WERE OFF SLACKING, SO YOU MAY NOT KNOW...
...BUT IT HAPPENED WHILE MASTER WAS AWAY.

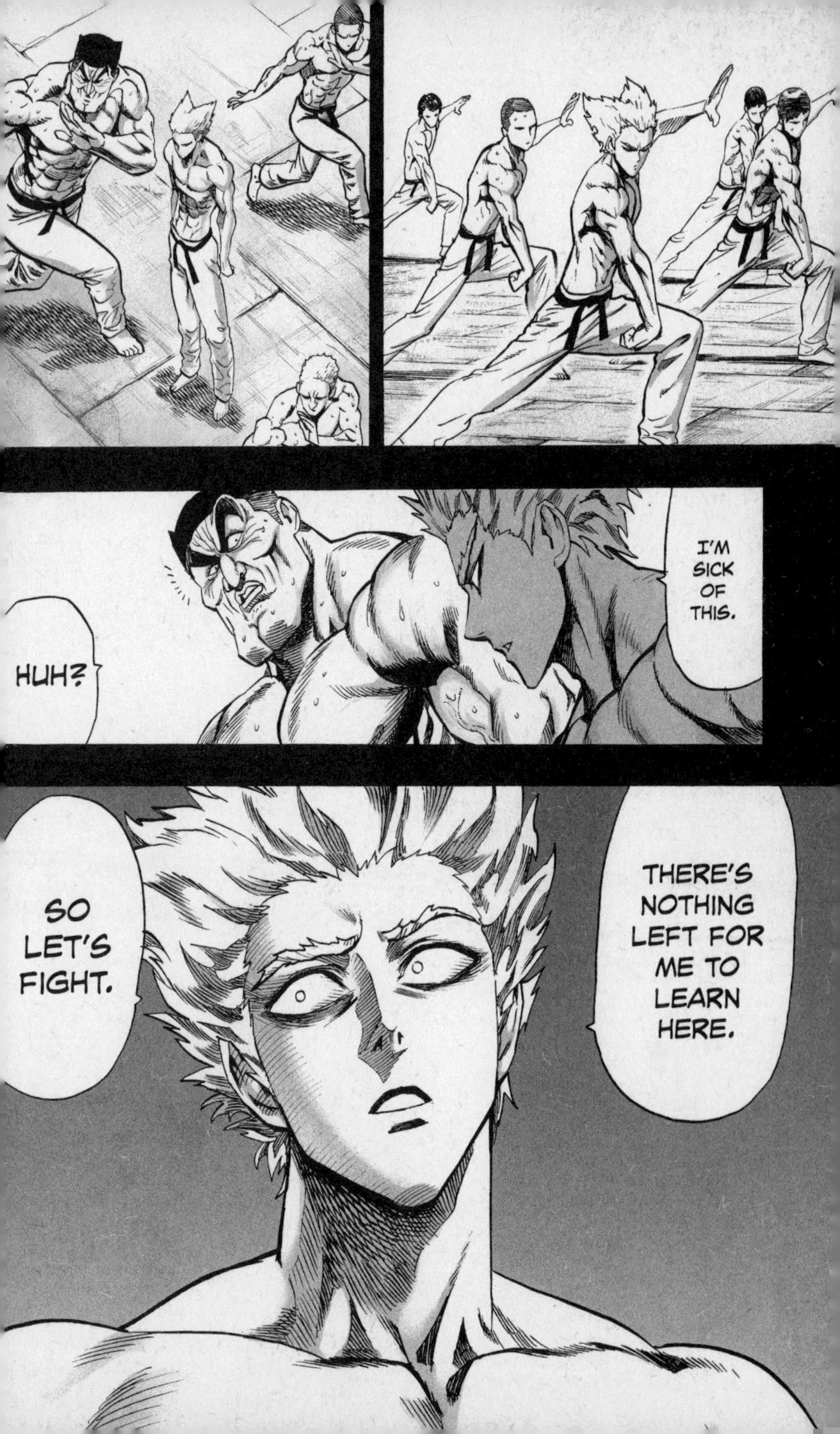
I'M SICK OF THIS.
HUH?
THERE'S NOTHING LEFT FOR ME TO LEARN HERE.
SO LET'S FIGHT.

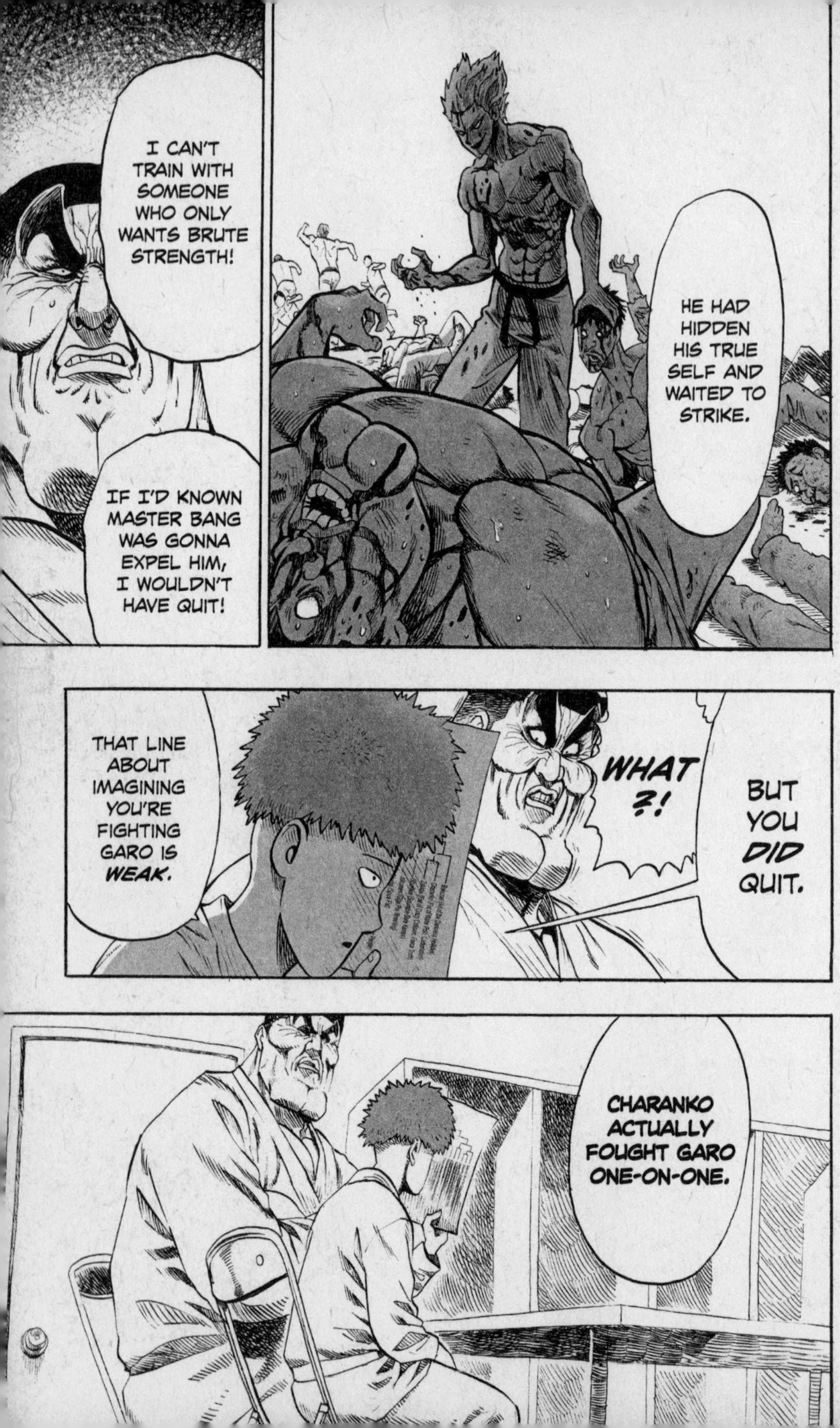
HE HAD HIDDEN HIS TRUE SELF AND WAITED TO STRIKE.
I CAN'T TRAIN WITH SOMEONE WHO ONLY WANTS BRUTE STRENGTH!
IF I'D KNOWN MASTER BANG WAS GONNA EXPEL HIM, I WOULDN'T HAVE QUIT!
BUT YOU *DID* QUIT.
WHAT?!
THAT LINE ABOUT IMAGINING YOU'RE FIGHTING GARO IS *WEAK.*
CHARANKO ACTUALLY FOUGHT GARO ONE-ON-ONE.

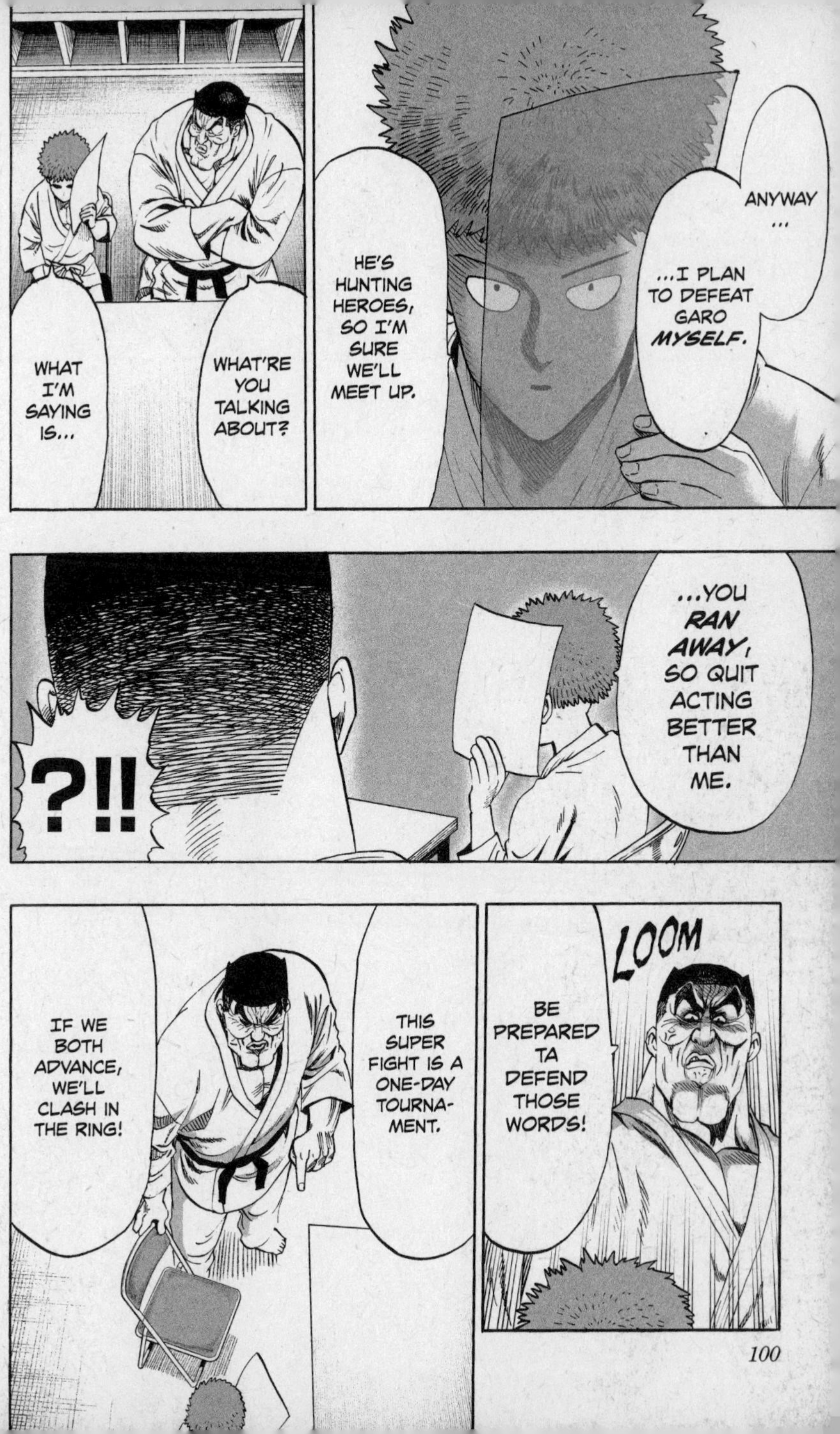
ANYWAY ...
...I PLAN TO DEFEAT GARO MYSELF.
HE'S HUNTING HEROES, SO I'M SURE WE'LL MEET UP.
WHAT'RE YOU TALKING ABOUT?
WHAT I'M SAYING IS...
...YOU RAN AWAY, SO QUIT ACTING BETTER THAN ME.
?!!
LOOM
BE PREPARED TA DEFEND THOSE WORDS!
THIS SUPER FIGHT IS A ONE-DAY TOURNA-MENT.
IF WE BOTH ADVANCE, WE'LL CLASH IN THE RING!

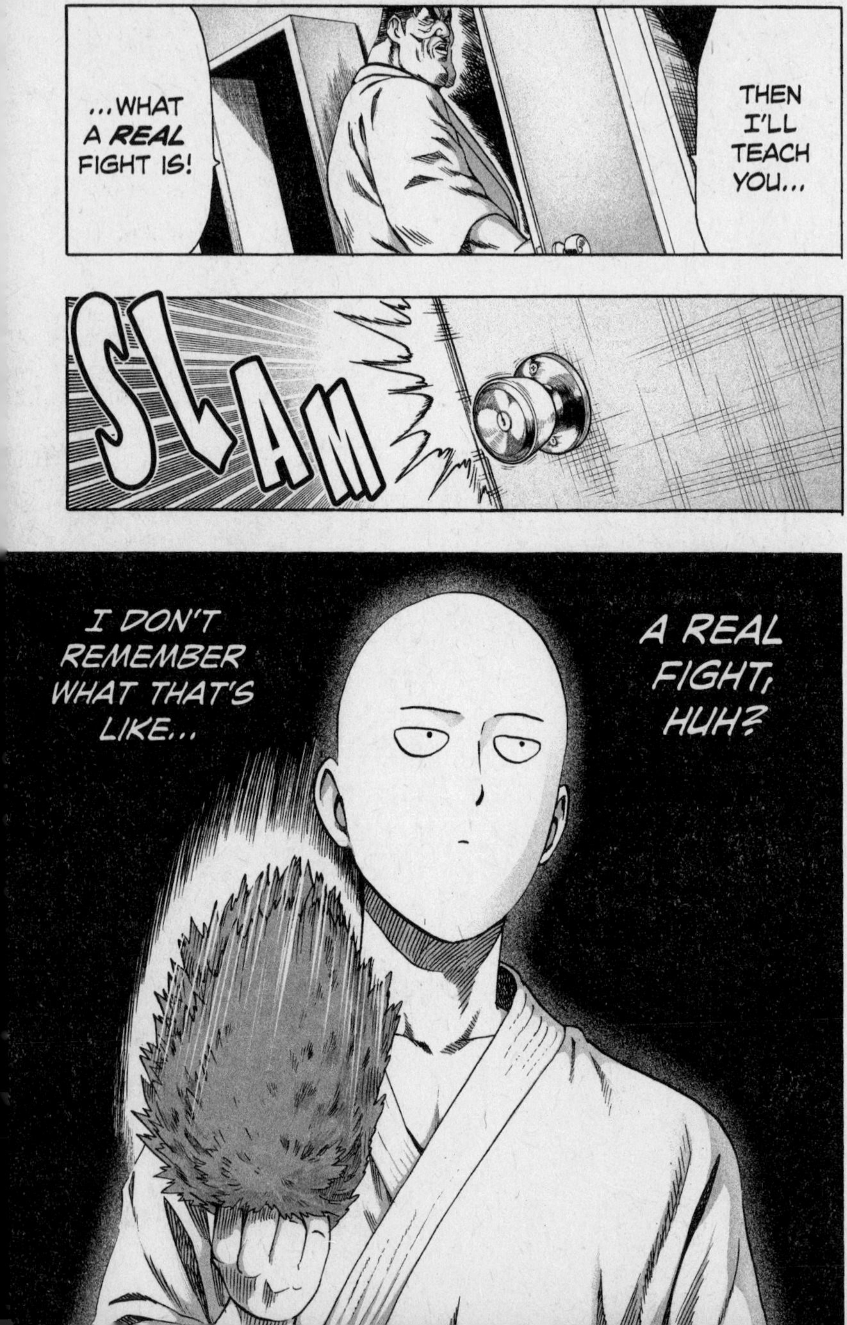
THEN I'LL TEACH YOU...
...WHAT A REAL FIGHT IS!
SLAM
A REAL FIGHT, HUH?
I DON'T REMEMBER WHAT THAT'S LIKE...

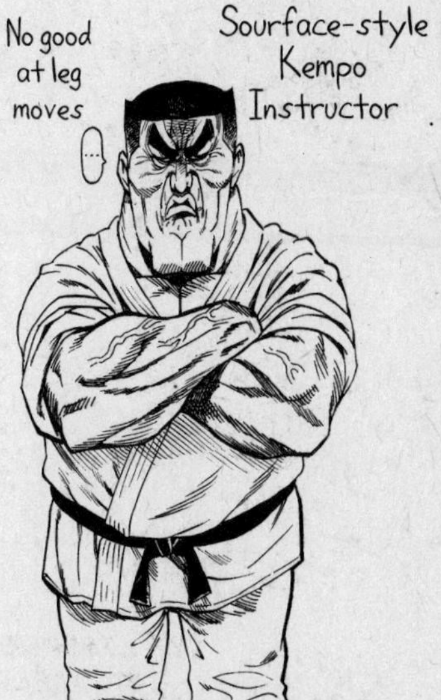
Sourface-style Kempo Instructor
No good at leg moves
...

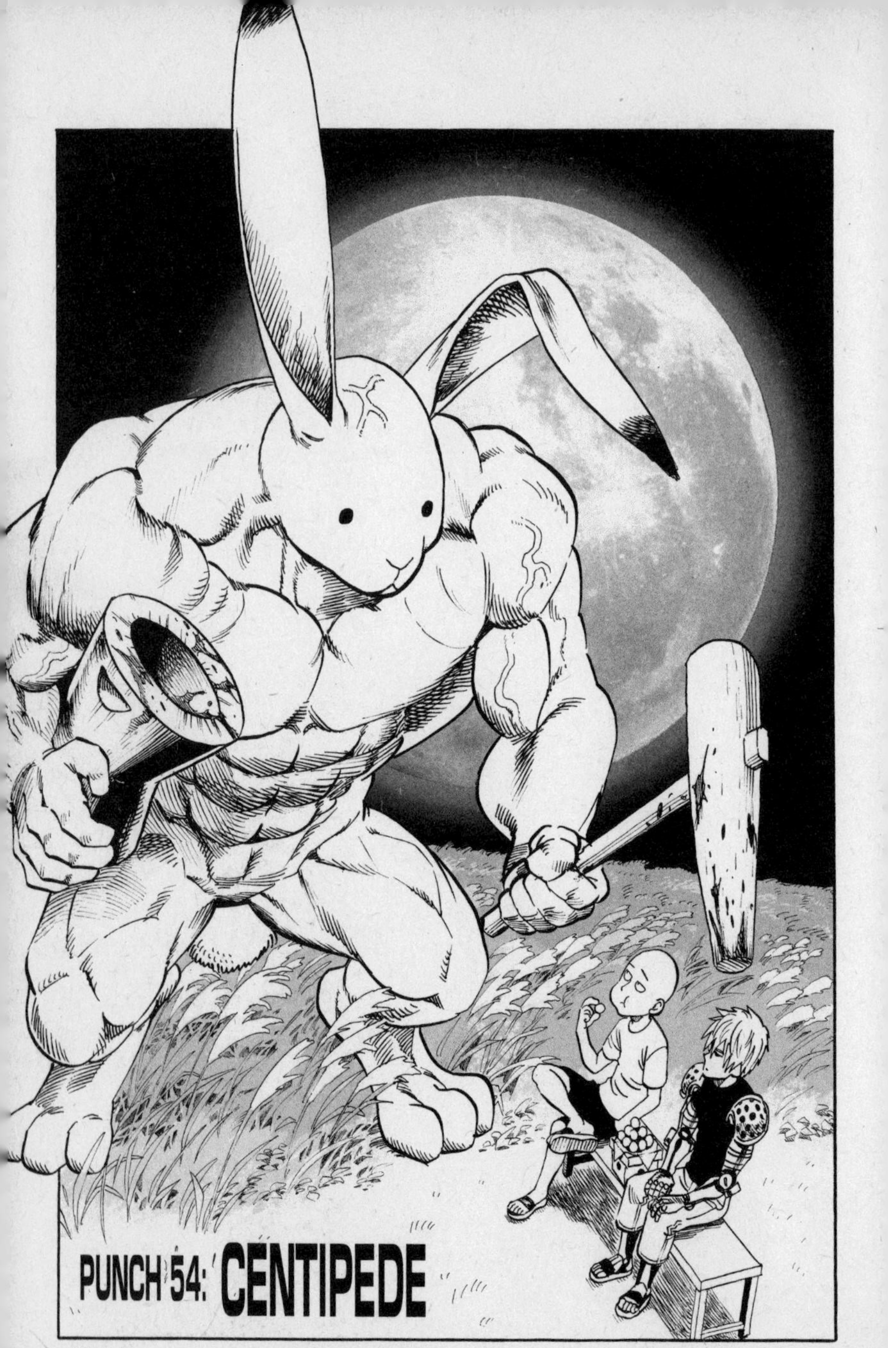
PUNCH 54: CENTIPEDE

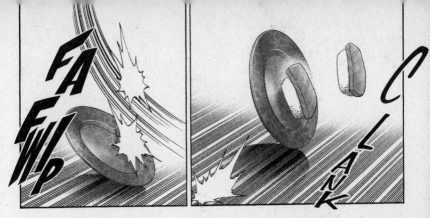

FA FWP

CLANK

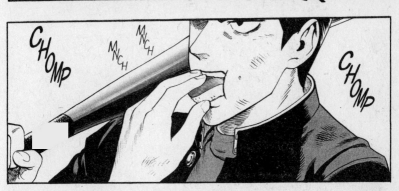

CHOMP

MNCH
MNCH
MNCH

CHOMP

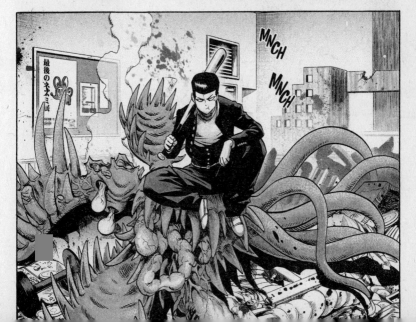

MNCH
MNCH

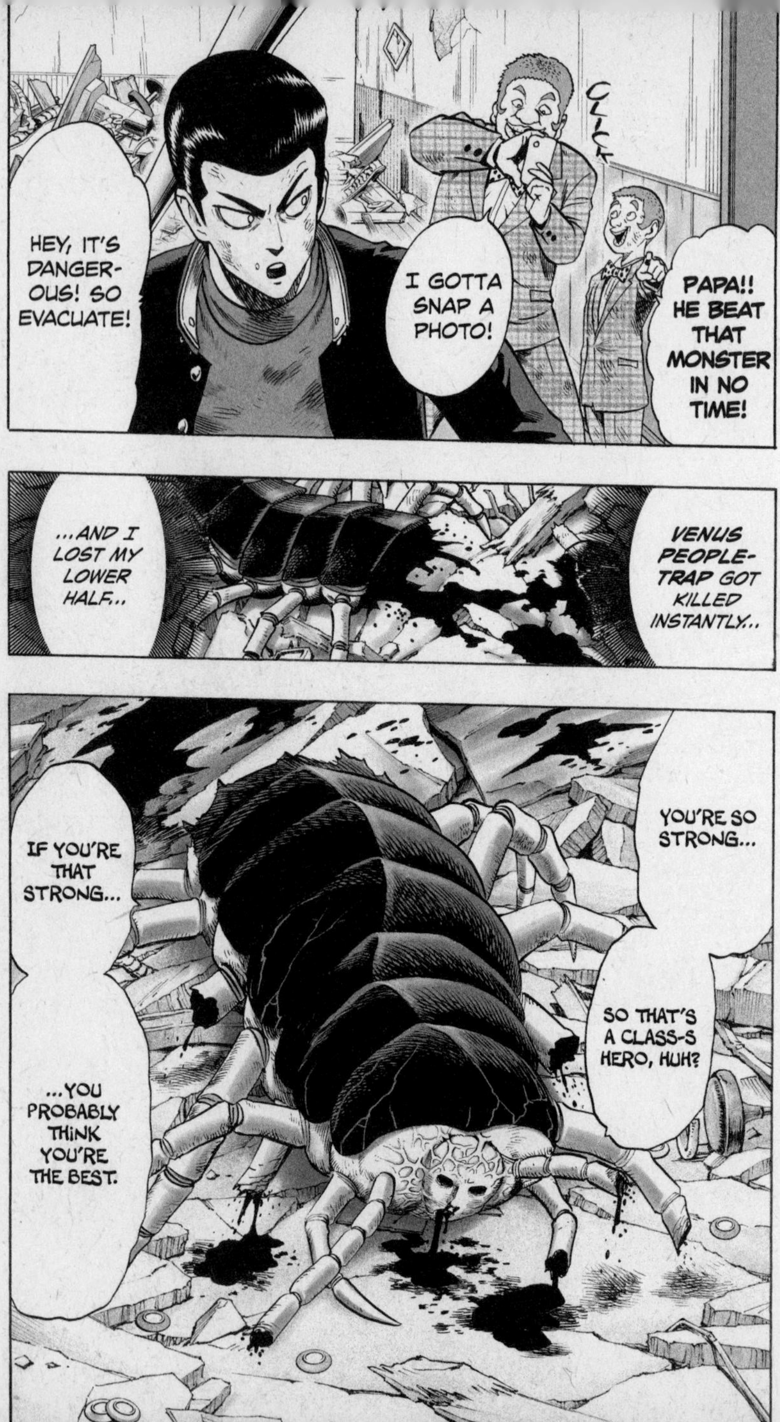
PAPA!! HE BEAT THAT MONSTER IN NO TIME!
CLICK
I GOTTA SNAP A PHOTO!
HEY, IT'S DANGER-OUS! SO EVACUATE!
VENUS PEOPLE-TRAP GOT KILLED INSTANTLY...
...AND I LOST MY LOWER HALF...
YOU'RE SO STRONG...
SO THAT'S A CLASS-S HERO, HUH?
IF YOU'RE THAT STRONG...
...YOU PROBABLY THINK YOU'RE THE BEST.

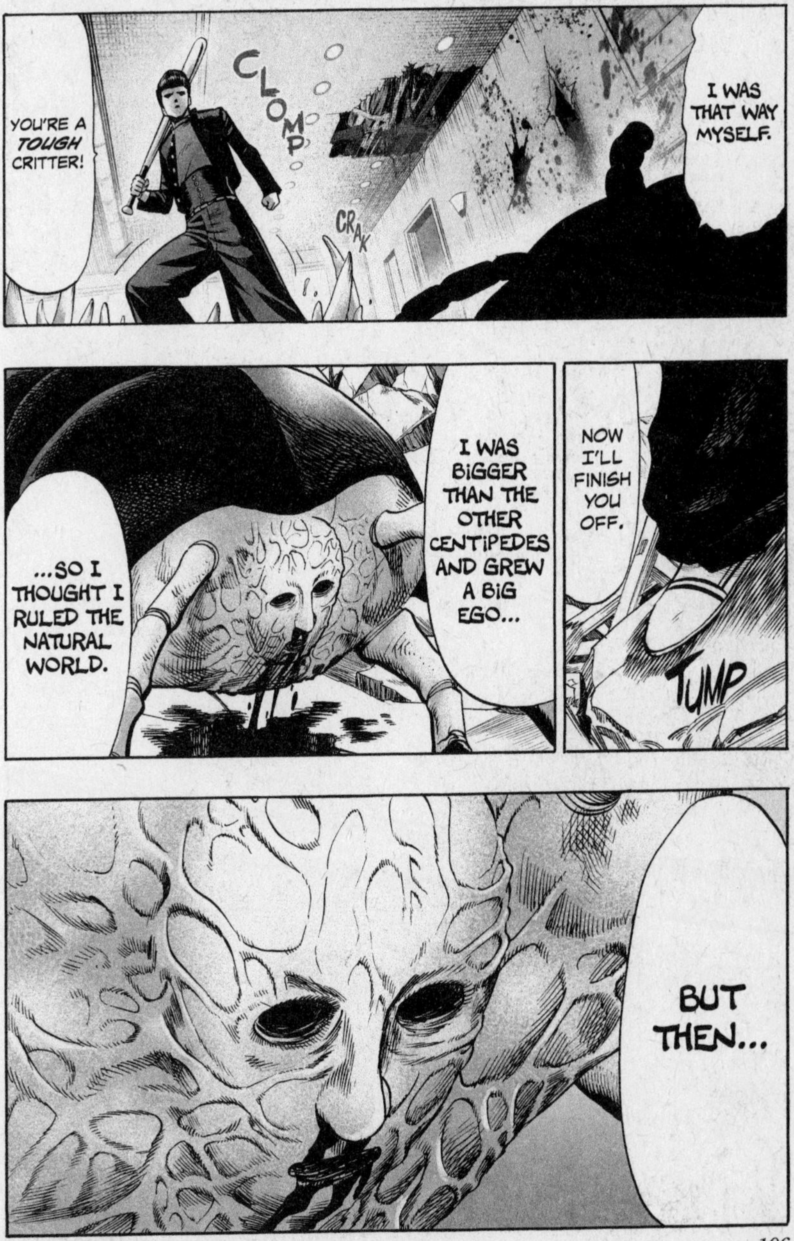
I WAS THAT WAY MYSELF.
CLOMP
CRAK
YOU'RE A *TOUGH* CRITTER!
NOW I'LL FINISH YOU OFF.
TUMP
I WAS BIGGER THAN THE OTHER CENTIPEDES AND GREW A BIG EGO...
...SO I THOUGHT I RULED THE NATURAL WORLD.
BUT THEN...

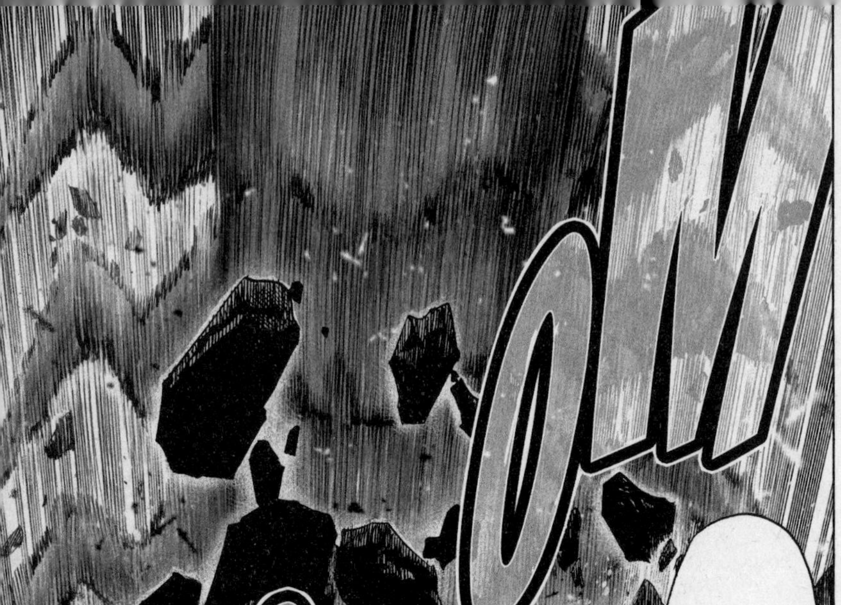
WHOOM
...HE SHOWED UP.

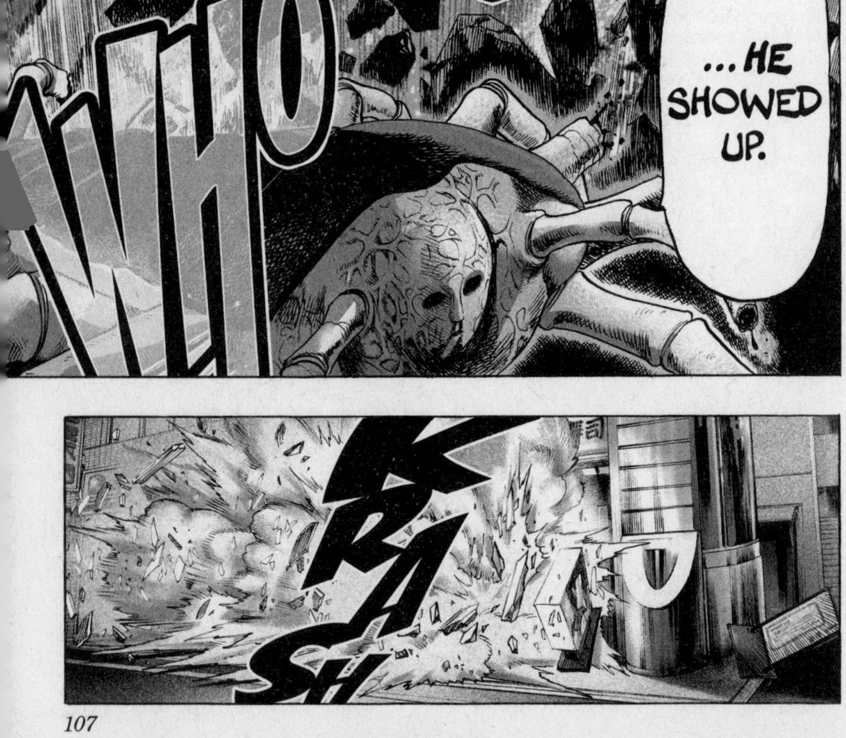
KRASH

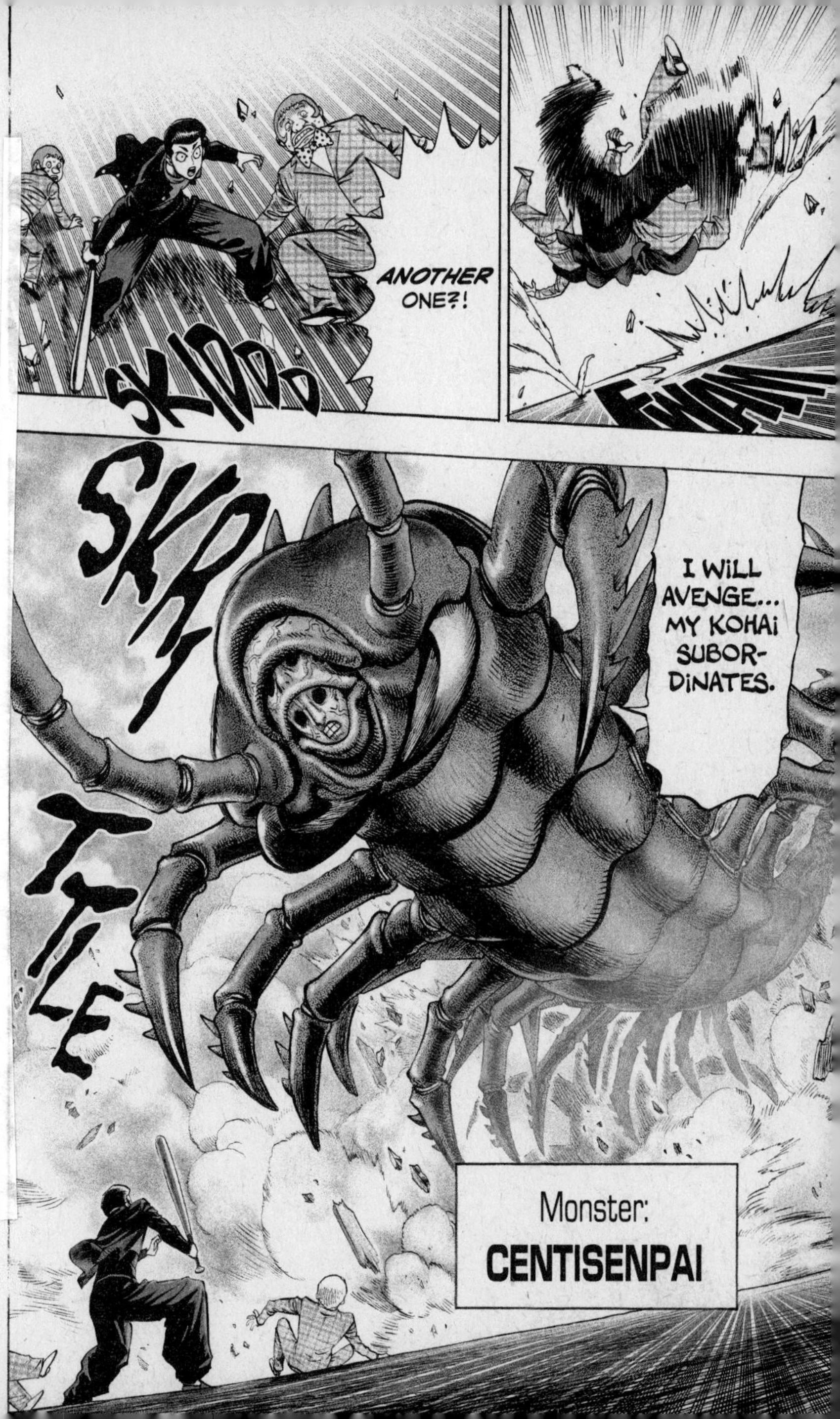
FWAM
ANOTHER ONE?!
SKIDDD
SKRITTLE
I WILL AVENGE... MY KOHAI SUBOR-DINATES.
Monster:
CENTISENPAI

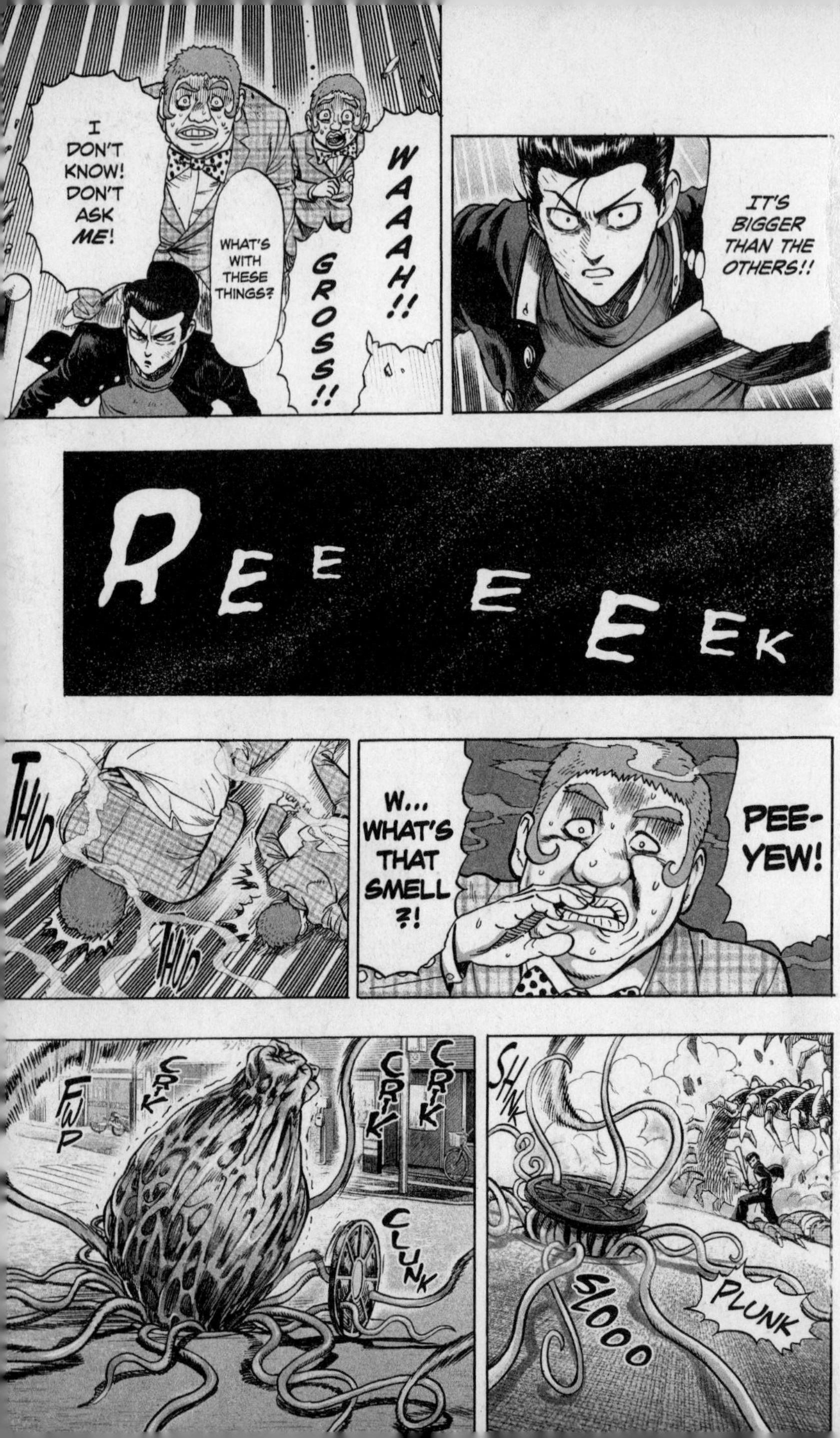
IT'S BIGGER THAN THE OTHERS!!
WAAAAH!!
GROSS!!
WHAT'S WITH THESE THINGS?
I DON'T KNOW! DON'T ASK ME!
REEEEEK
PEE-YEW!
W... WHAT'S THAT SMELL?!
THUD
THUD
SHNK
PLUNK
SLOOO
CRIK
CRIK
CRIK
FWP
CLUNK

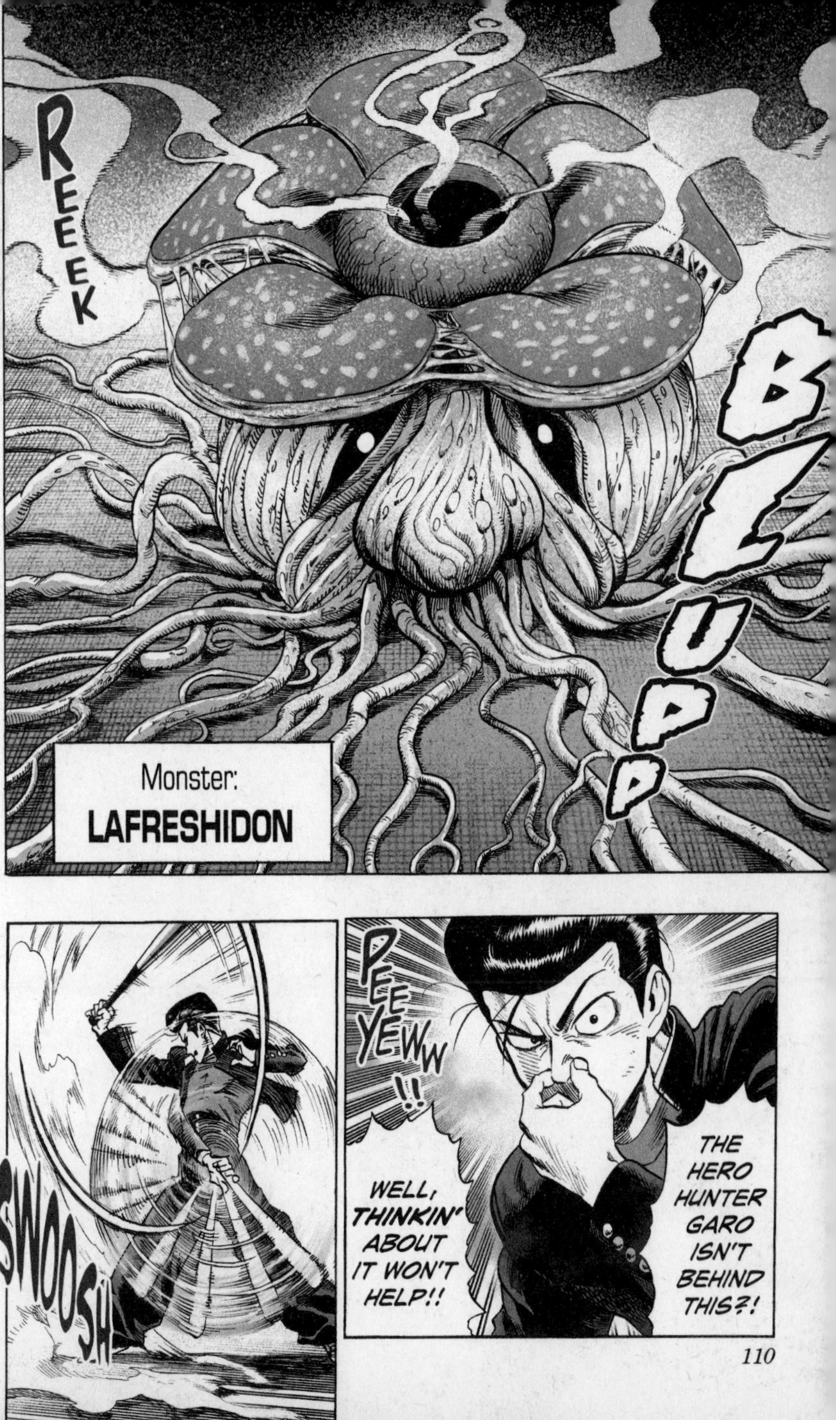
REEEEK
BLUUPP
Monster:
LAFRESHIDON
PEEYEWW!!
THE HERO HUNTER GARO ISN'T BEHIND THIS?!
WELL, THINKIN' ABOUT IT WON'T HELP!!
SWOOSH

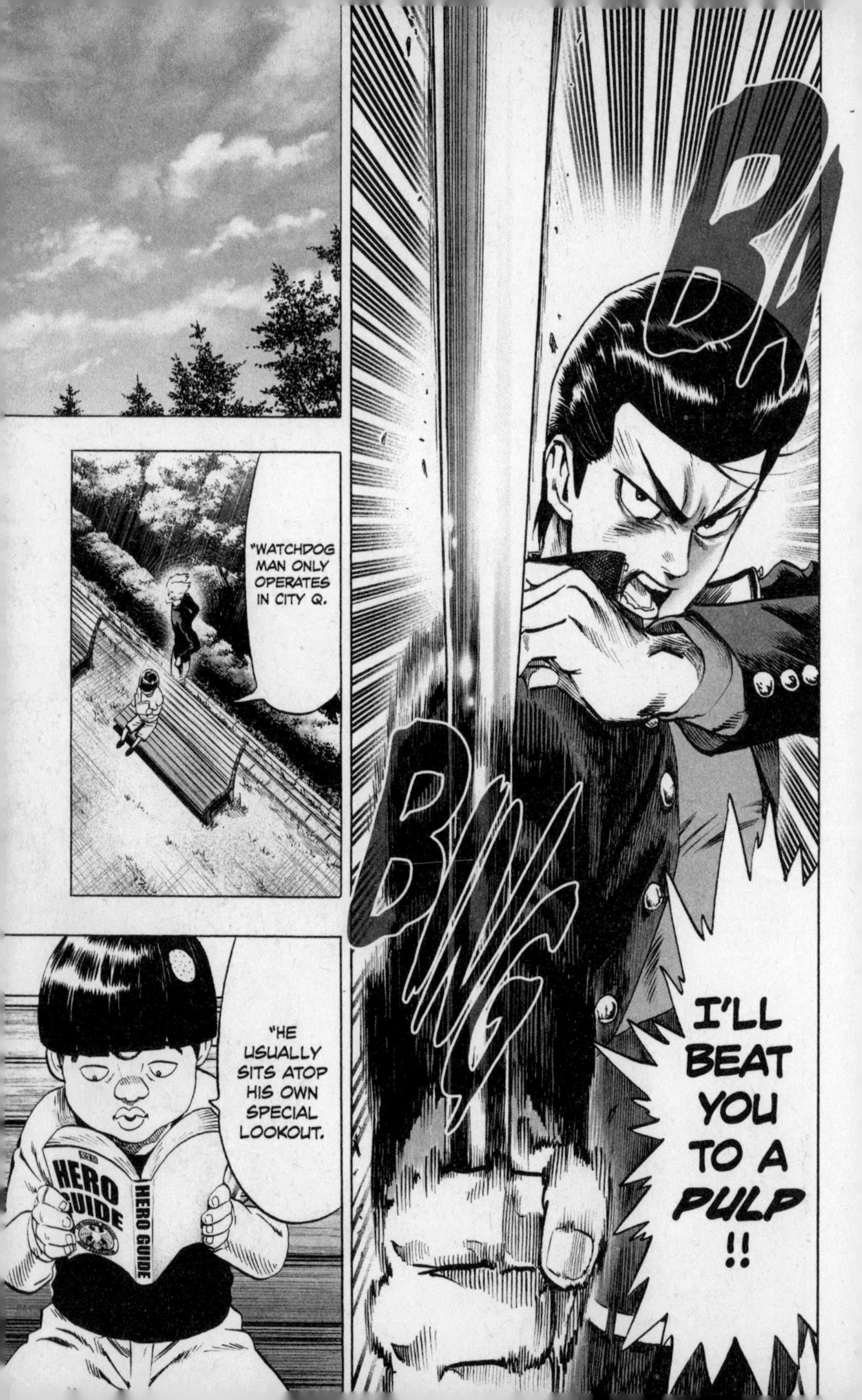
I'LL BEAT YOU TO A PULP !!
"WATCHDOG MAN ONLY OPERATES IN CITY Q.
"HE USUALLY SITS ATOP HIS OWN SPECIAL LOOKOUT.
HERO GUIDE
HERO GUIDE

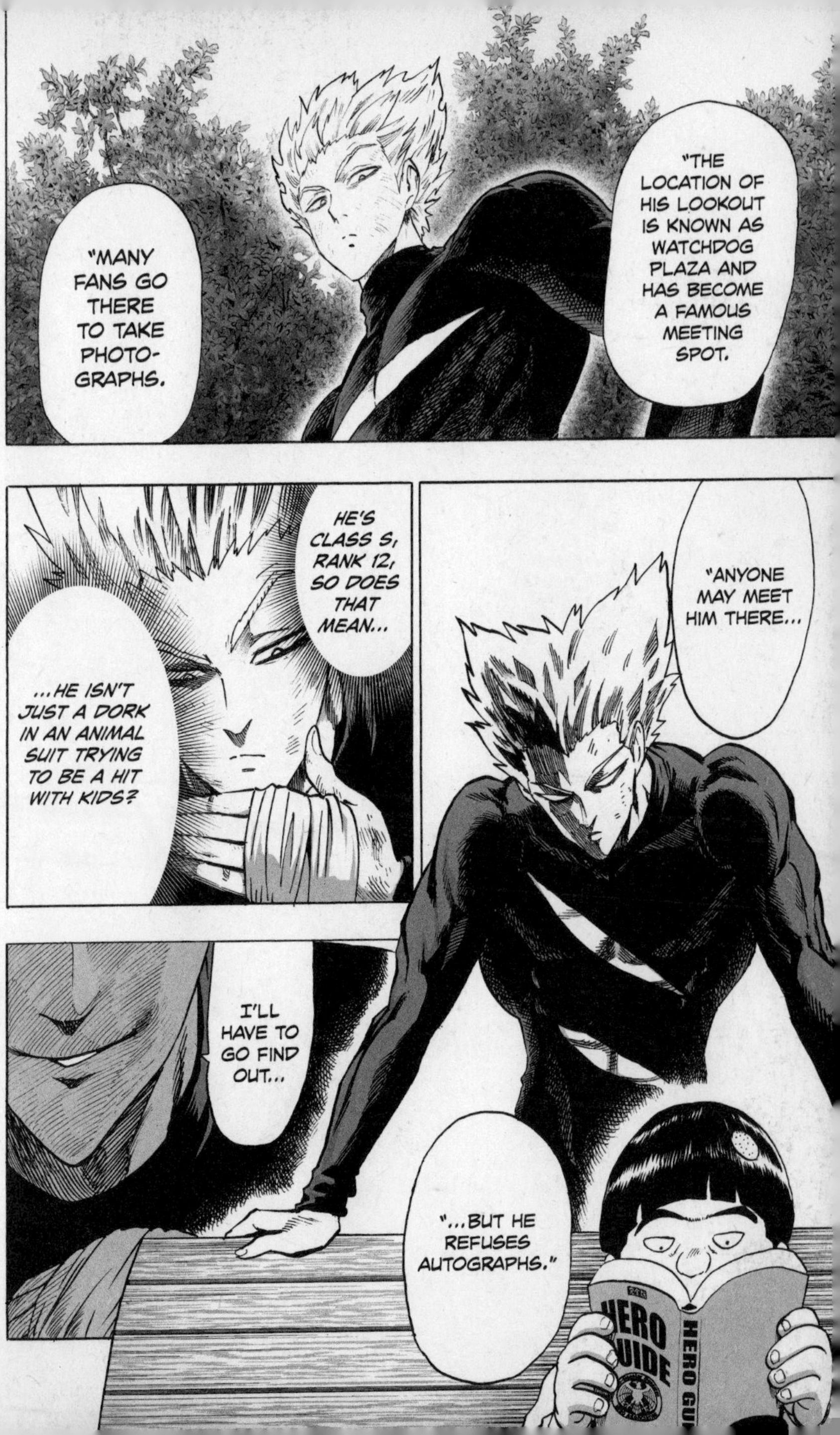
"THE LOCATION OF HIS LOOKOUT IS KNOWN AS WATCHDOG PLAZA AND HAS BECOME A FAMOUS MEETING SPOT.
"MANY FANS GO THERE TO TAKE PHOTO-GRAPHS.
"ANYONE MAY MEET HIM THERE...
"...BUT HE REFUSES AUTOGRAPHS."
HERO GUIDE
HE'S CLASS S, RANK 12, SO DOES THAT MEAN...
...HE ISN'T JUST A DORK IN AN ANIMAL SUIT TRYING TO BE A HIT WITH KIDS?
I'LL HAVE TO GO FIND OUT...

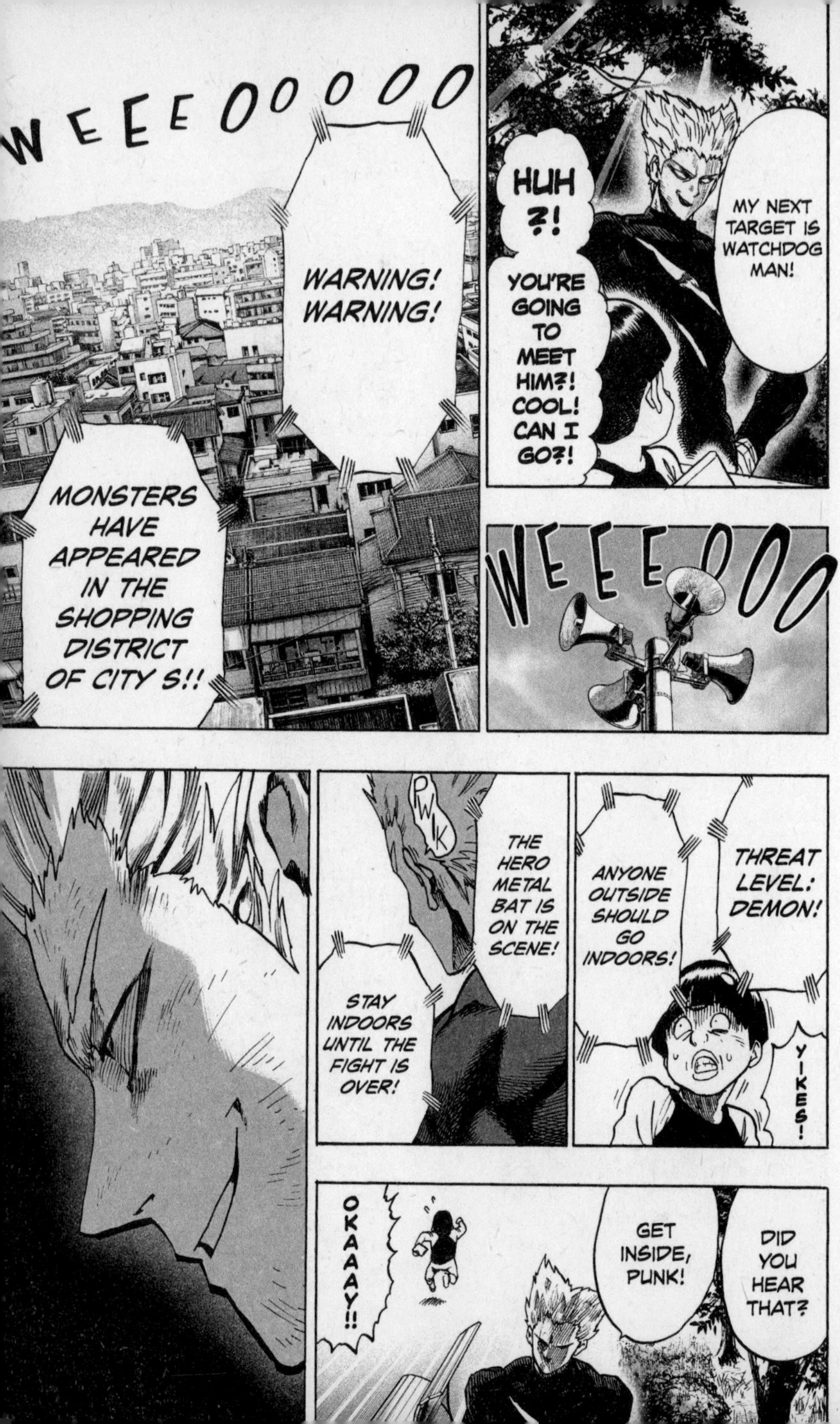
MY NEXT TARGET IS WATCHDOG MAN!
HUH?!
YOU'RE GOING TO MEET HIM?! COOL! CAN I GO?!
WEEEOOO
WEEEOOOOO
WARNING! WARNING!
MONSTERS HAVE APPEARED IN THE SHOPPING DISTRICT OF CITY S!!
THREAT LEVEL: DEMON!
ANYONE OUTSIDE SHOULD GO INDOORS!
YIKES!
PWIK
THE HERO METAL BAT IS ON THE SCENE!
STAY INDOORS UNTIL THE FIGHT IS OVER!
DID YOU HEAR THAT?
GET INSIDE, PUNK!
OKAAAY!!

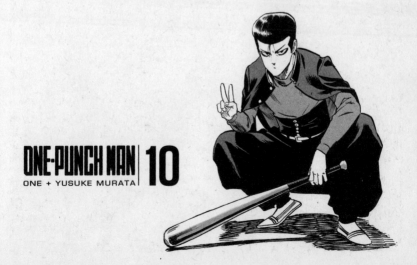

ONE-PUNCH MAN | 10

ONE + YUSUKE MURATA

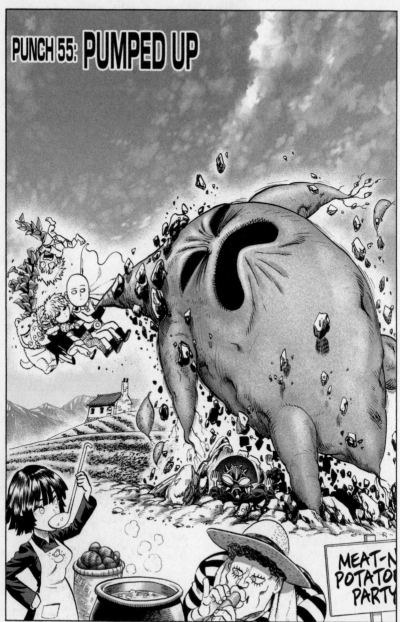

PUNCH 55: PUMPED UP

MEAT-N
POTATO
PARTY

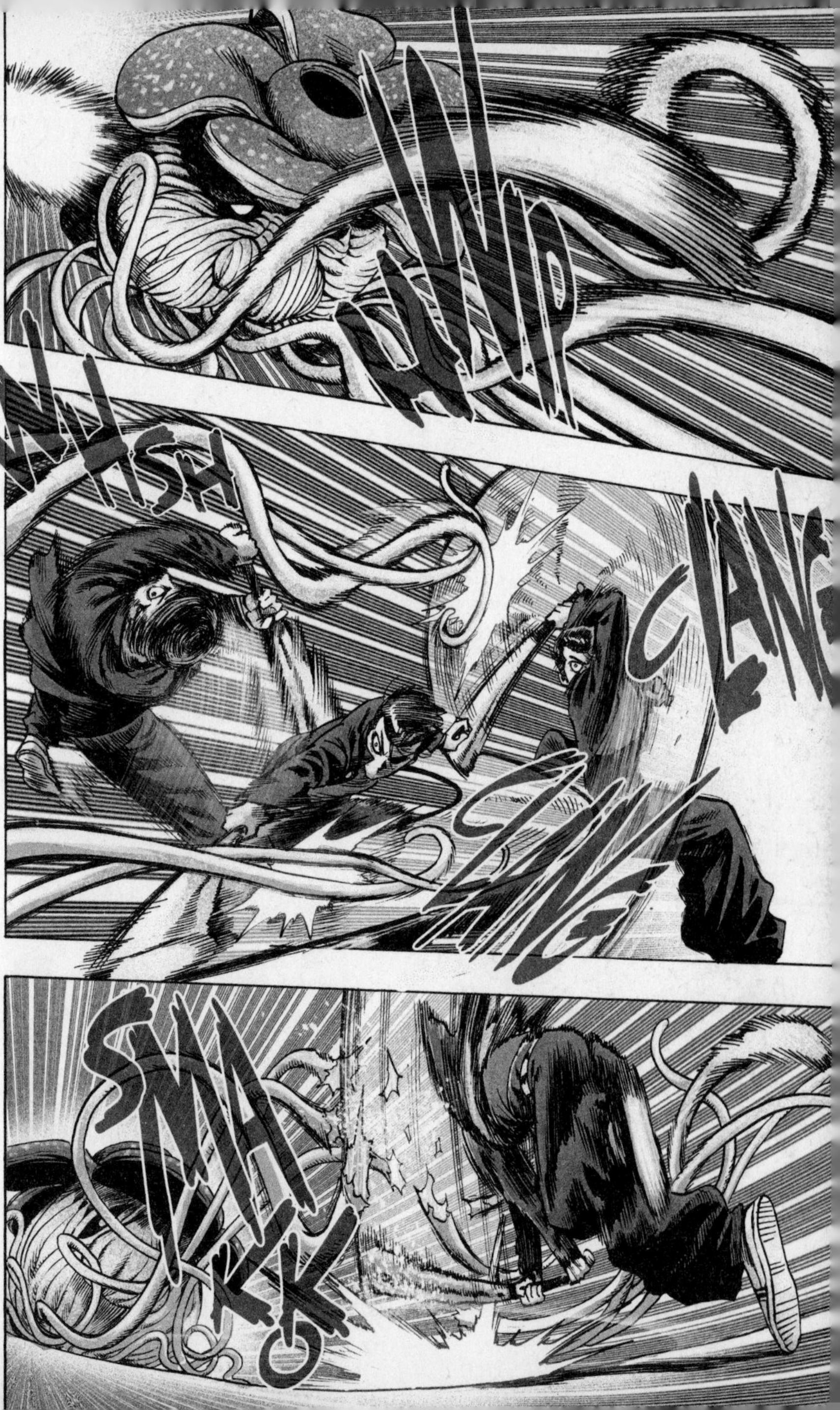
WHAP
CLANG
WHISH
CLANG
SMACK

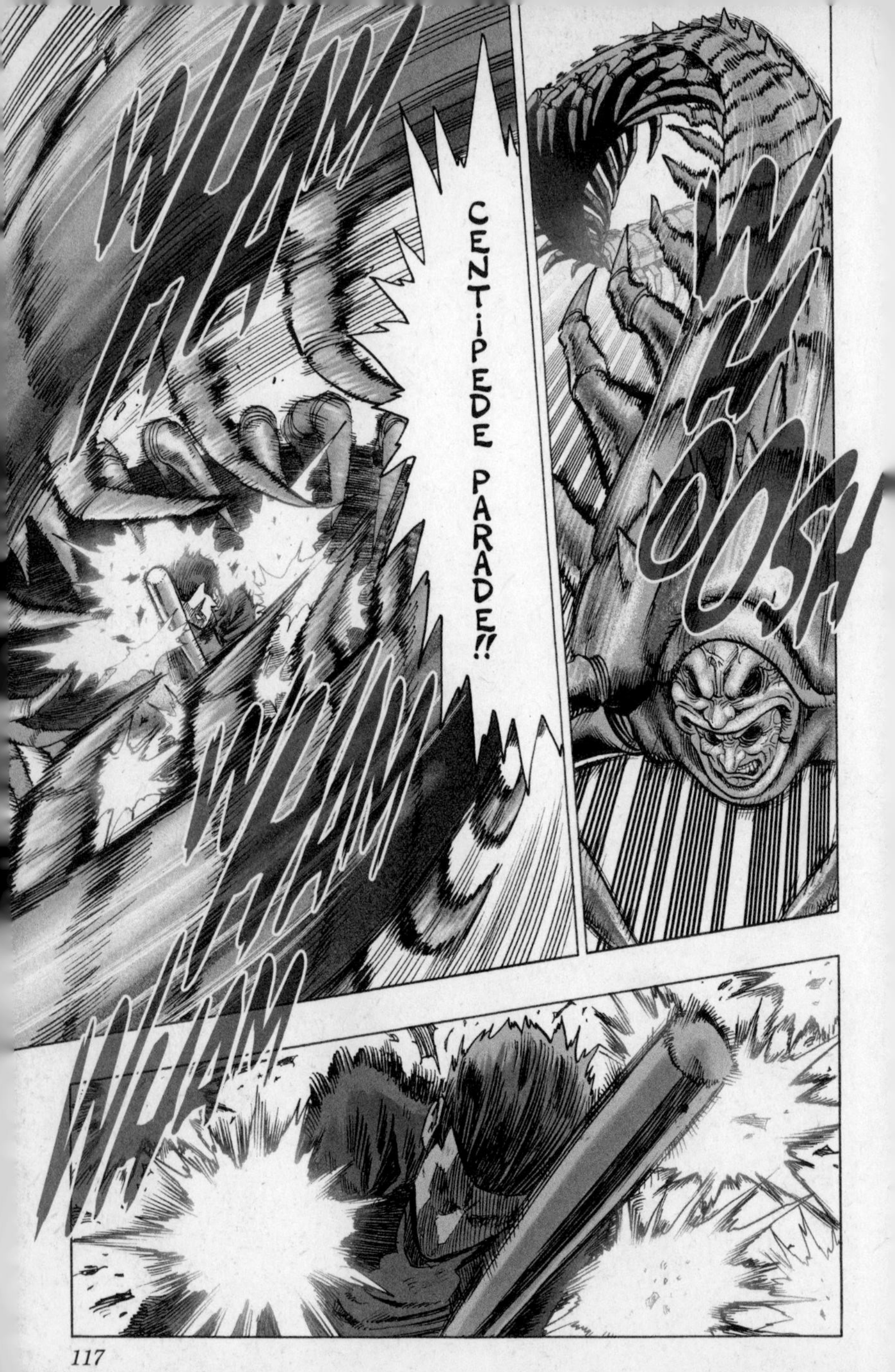
WOOSH
CENTIPEDE PARADE!!
WHAM
WHAM

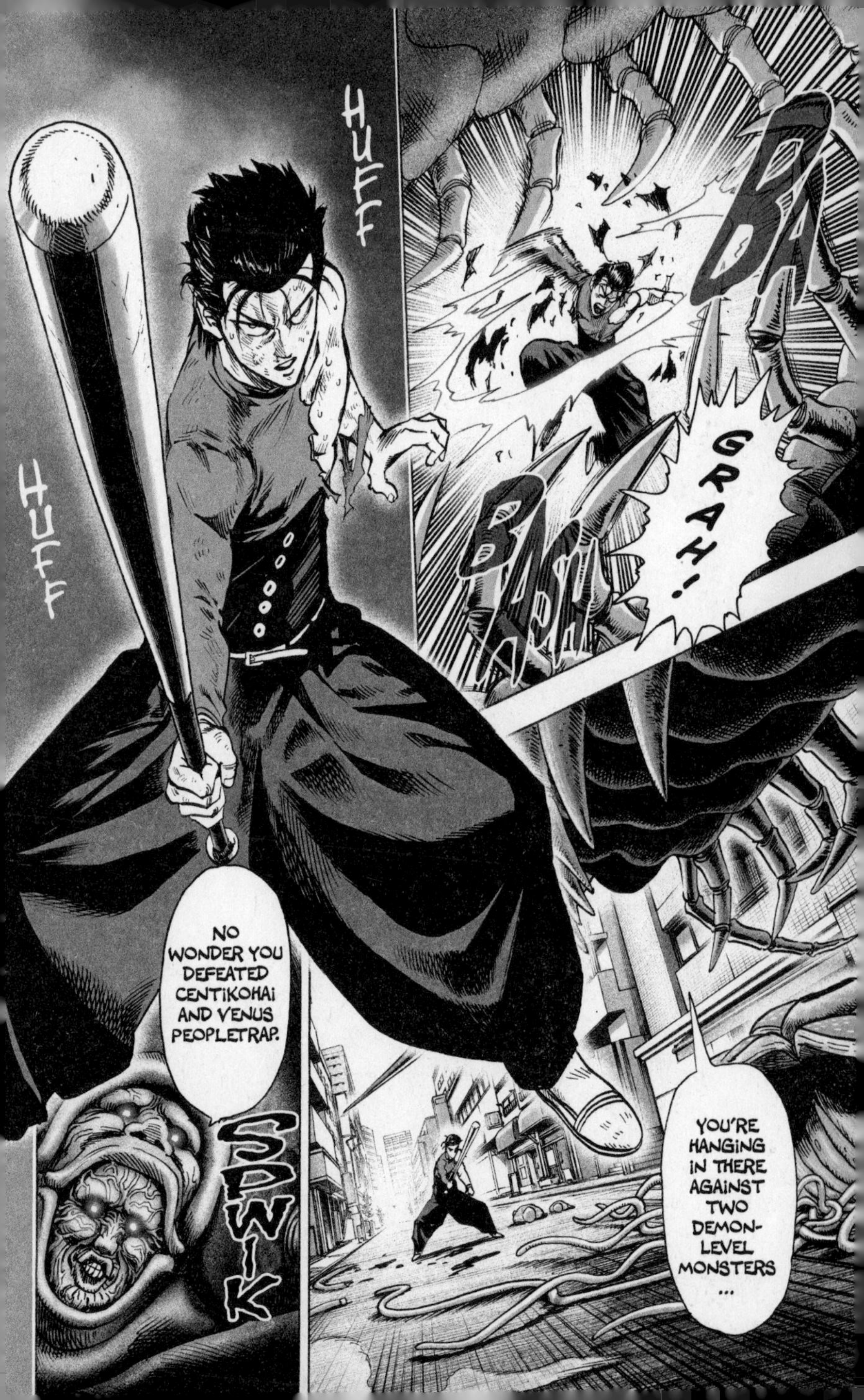
GRAH!!
HUFF
HUFF
YOU'RE HANGING IN THERE AGAINST TWO DEMON-LEVEL MONSTERS...
NO WONDER YOU DEFEATED CENTIKOHAI AND VENUS PEOPLETRAP.
SPWIK

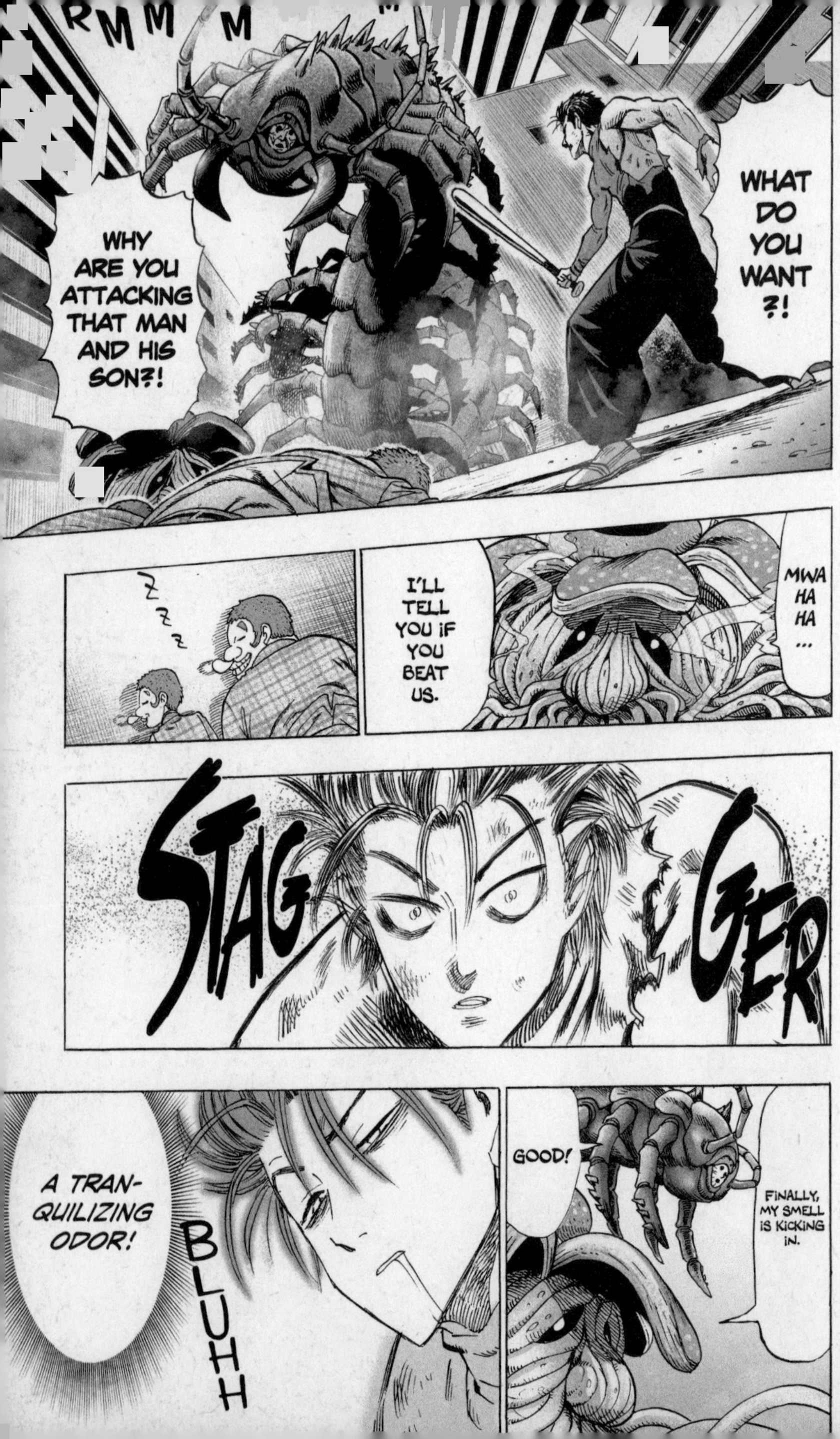
RMMM M
WHAT DO YOU WANT?!
WHY ARE YOU ATTACKING THAT MAN AND HIS SON?!
MWA HA HA...
I'LL TELL YOU IF YOU BEAT US.
Z Z Z
STAGGER
GOOD!
FINALLY, MY SMELL IS KICKING IN.
A TRAN-QUILIZING ODOR!
BLUHH

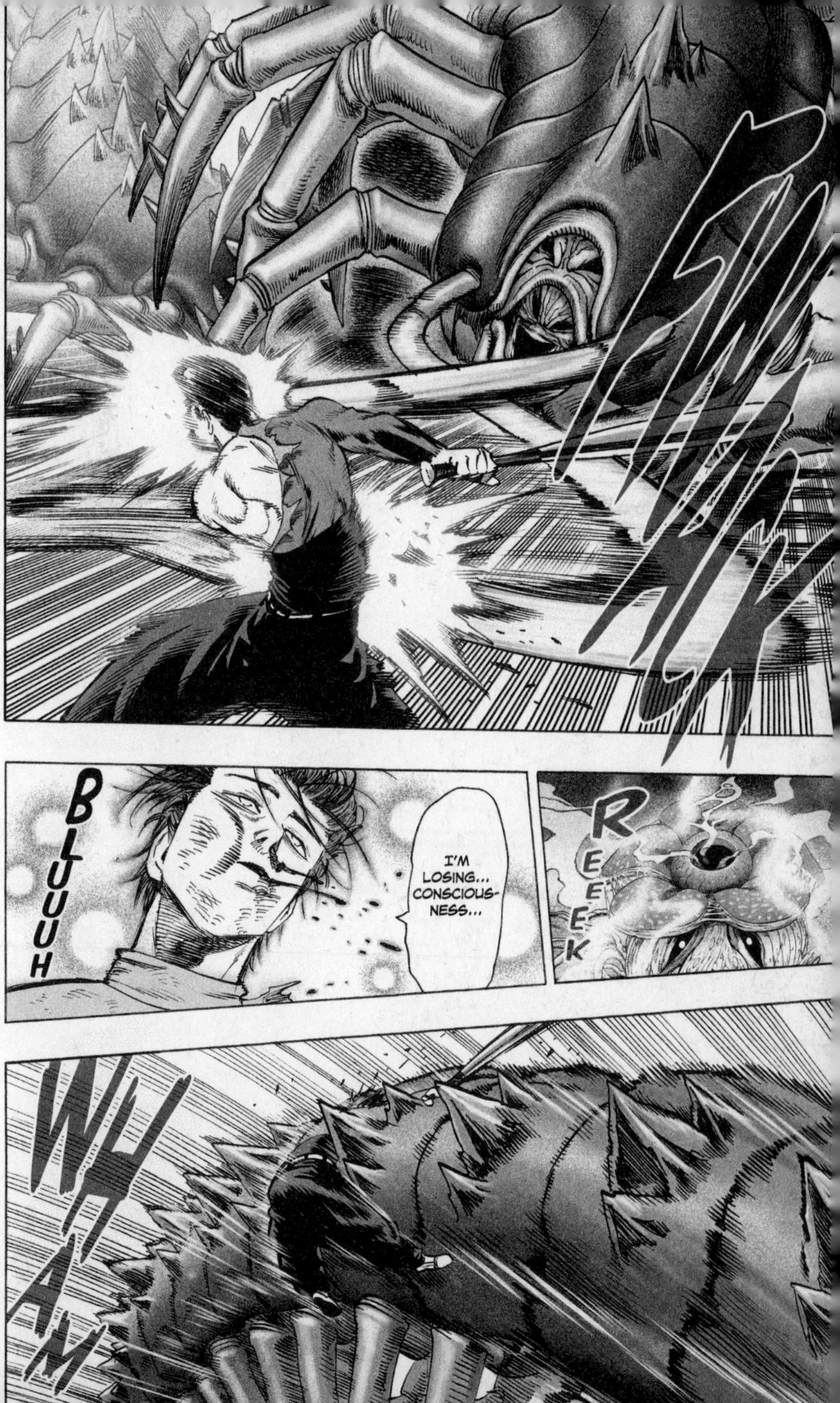
REEEEK
BLUUUUH
I'M LOSING... CONSCIOUSNESS...
WHAM

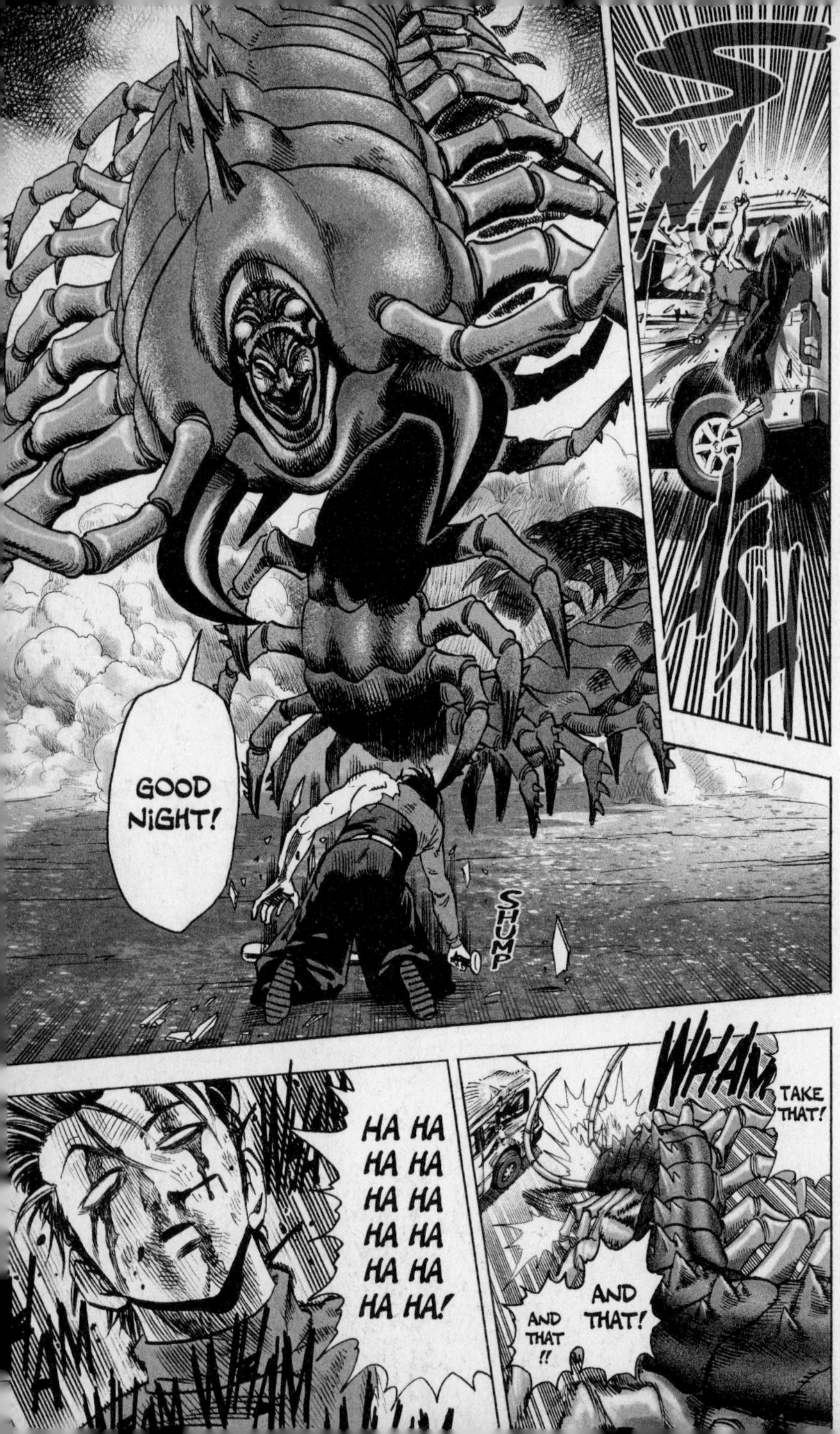
SMASH
GOOD NIGHT!
SHUMP
WHAM
TAKE THAT!
AND THAT!
AND THAT !!
HA HA HA HA HA HA HA HA HA HA HA HA!
WHAM WHAM

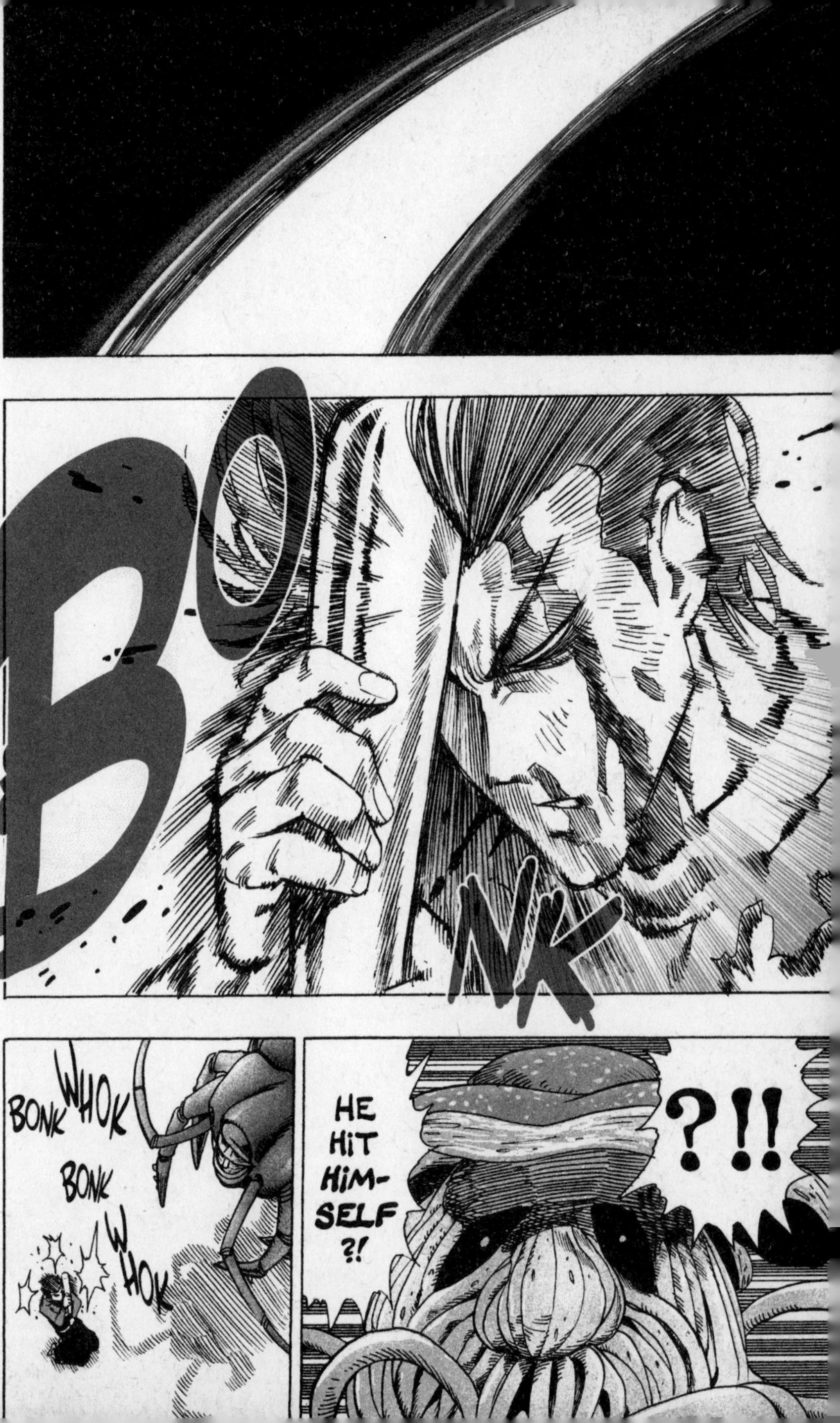
BONK
?!!
HE HIT HIM-SELF ?!
WHOK
BONK
BONK
WHOK

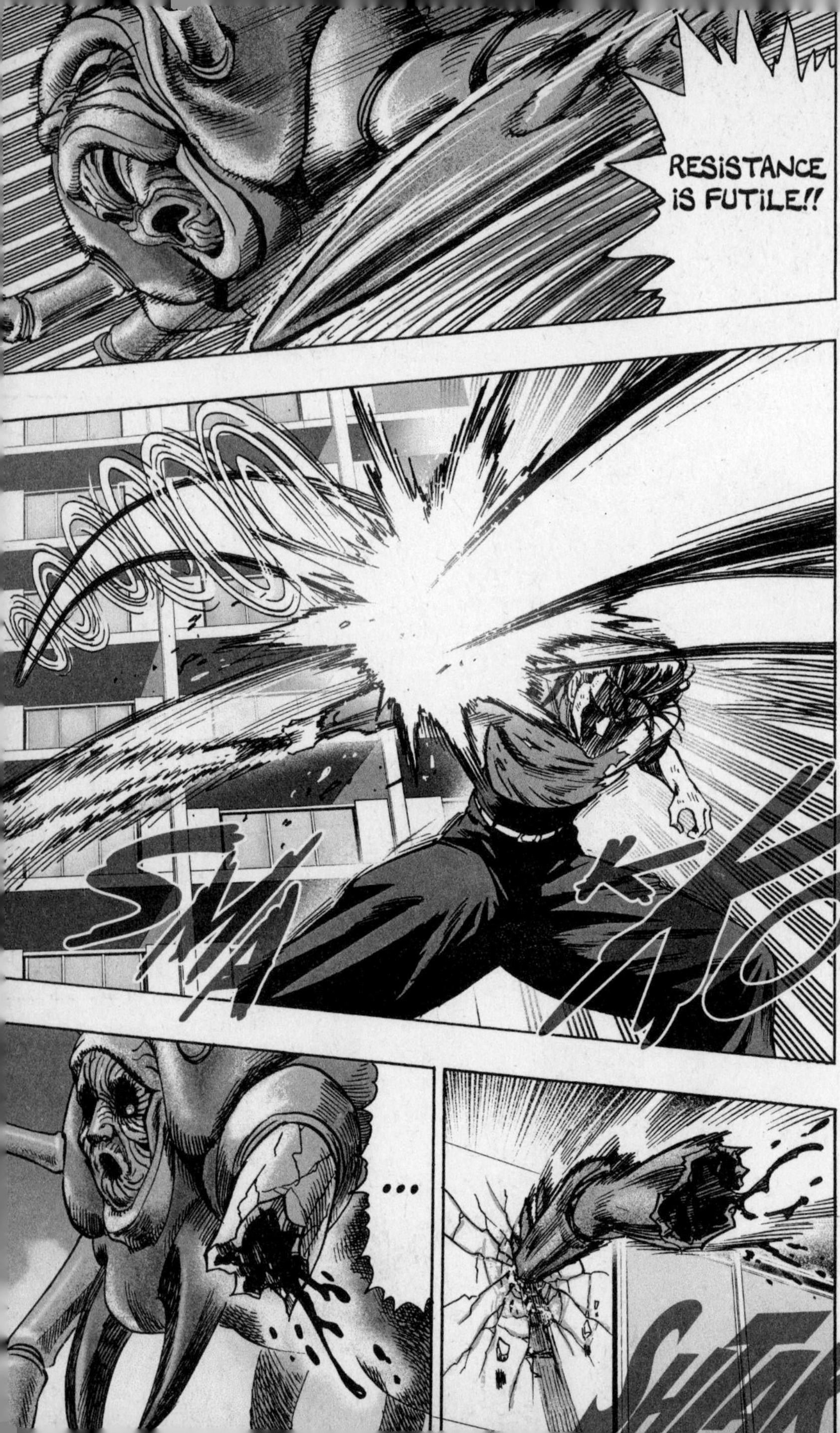
RESISTANCE IS FUTILE!!
SMACK
...
SHTAK

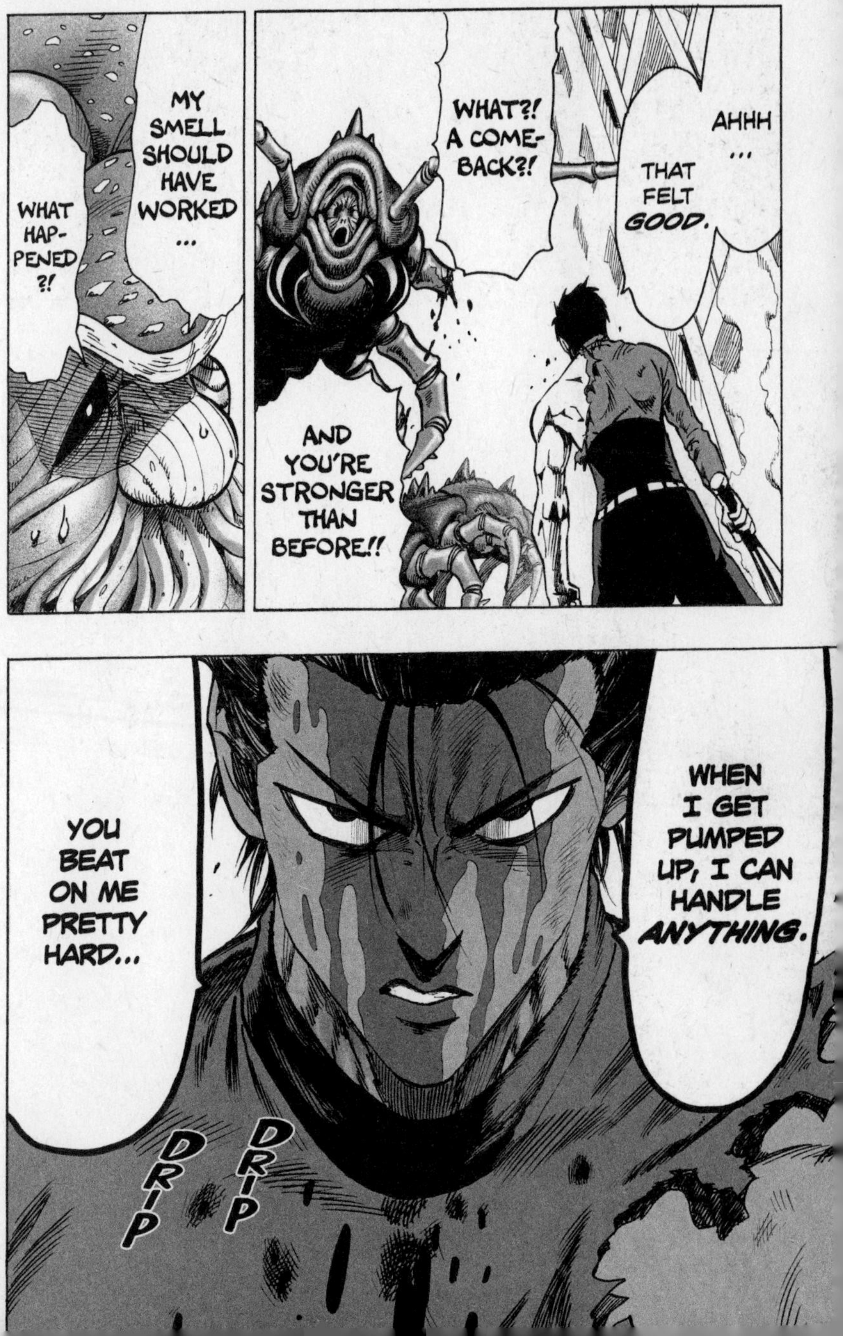
AHHH ... THAT FELT GOOD.
WHAT?! A COME-BACK?!
AND YOU'RE STRONGER THAN BEFORE!!
MY SMELL SHOULD HAVE WORKED ...
WHAT HAP-PENED ?!
WHEN I GET PUMPED UP, I CAN HANDLE ANYTHING.
YOU BEAT ON ME PRETTY HARD...
DRIP
DRIP

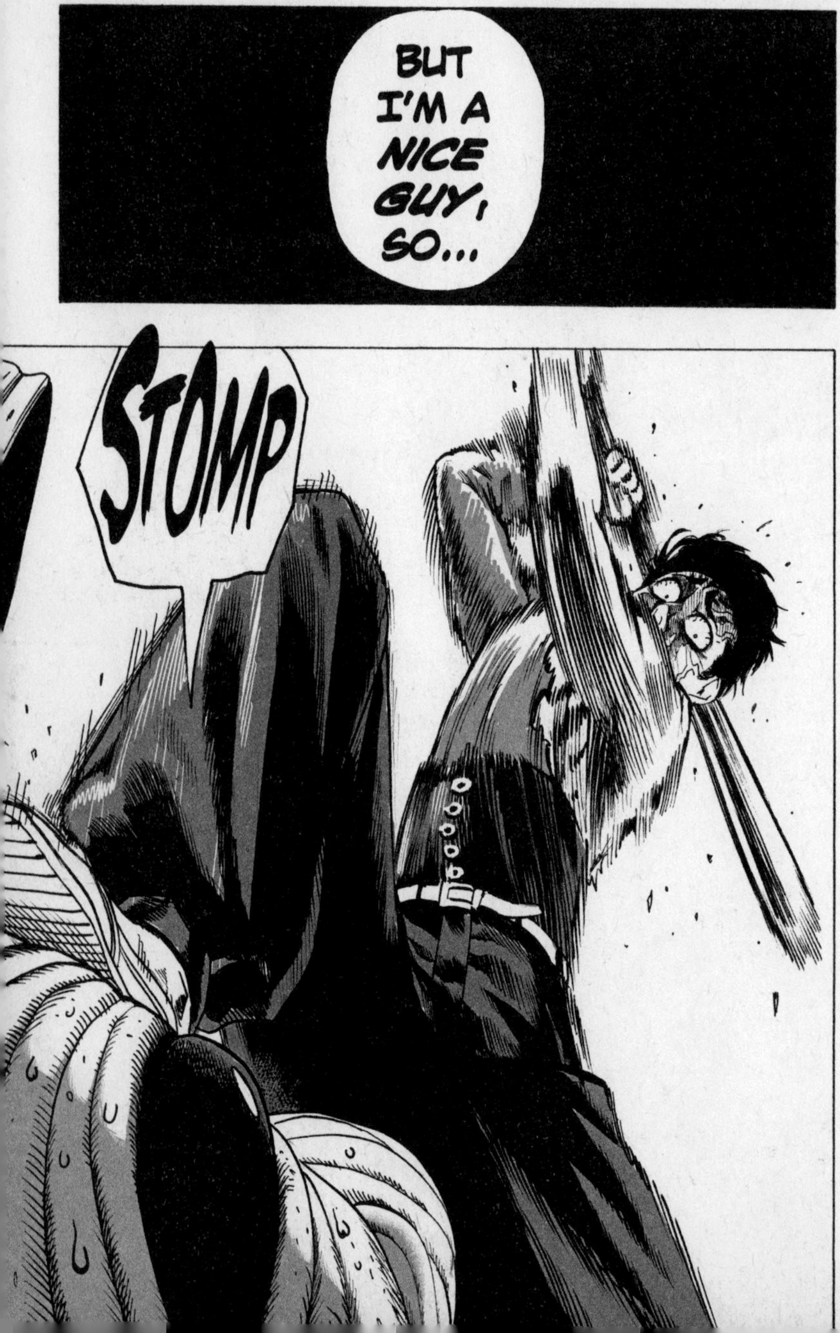
BUT I'M A NICE GUY, SO...
STOMP

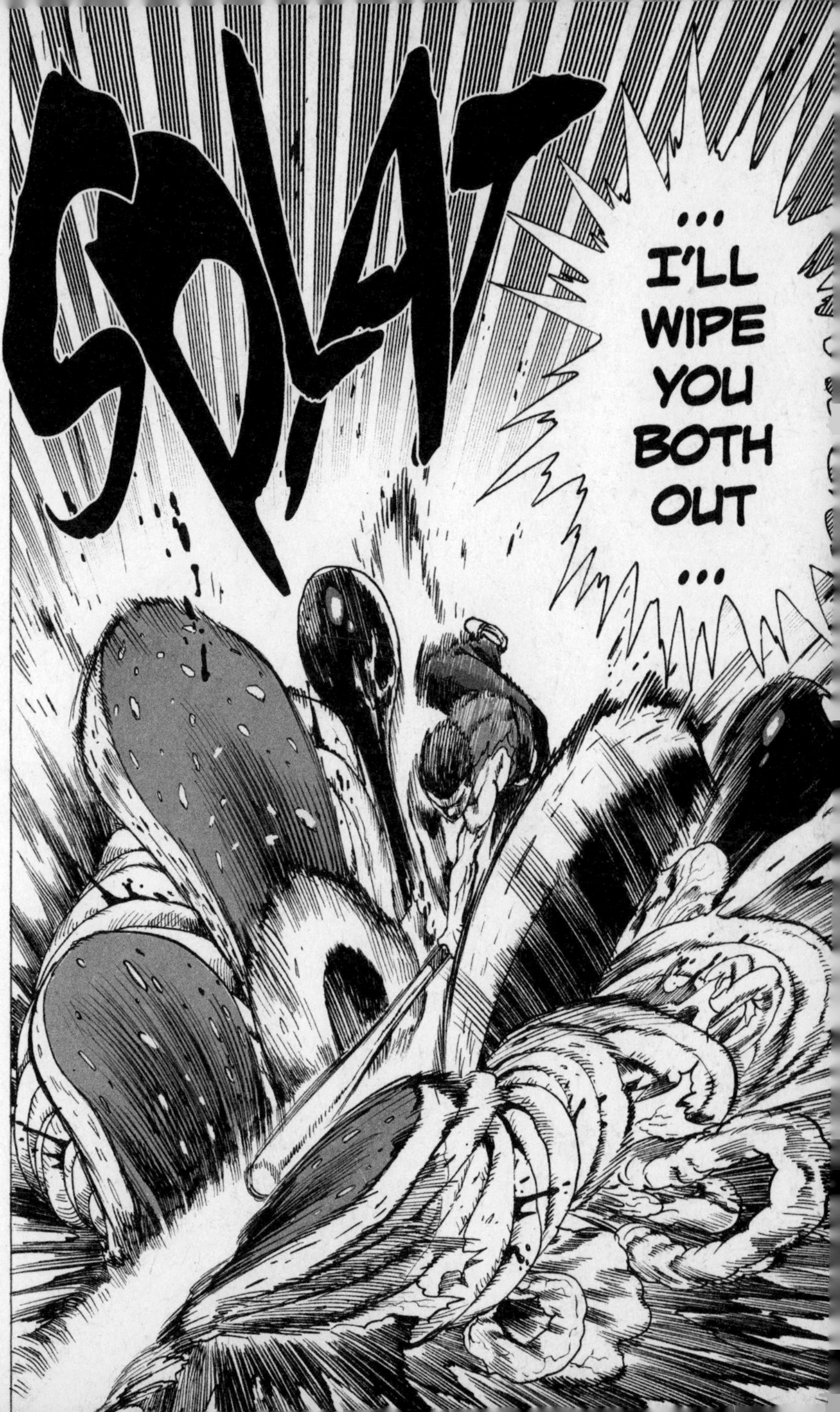
SPLAT
... I'LL WIPE YOU BOTH OUT ...

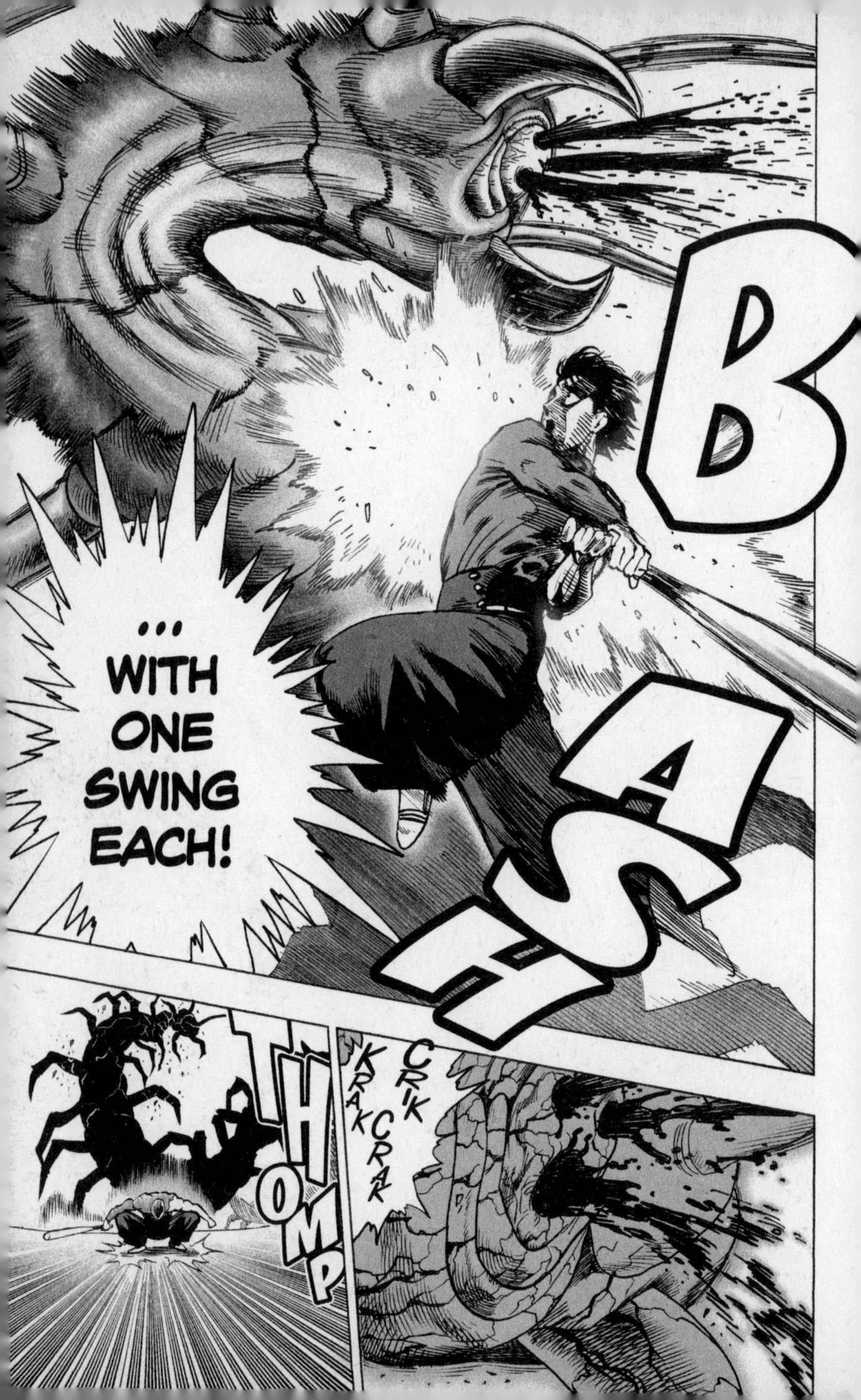
...WITH ONE SWING EACH!
BASH
CRIK
CRAK
KRAK
THOMP

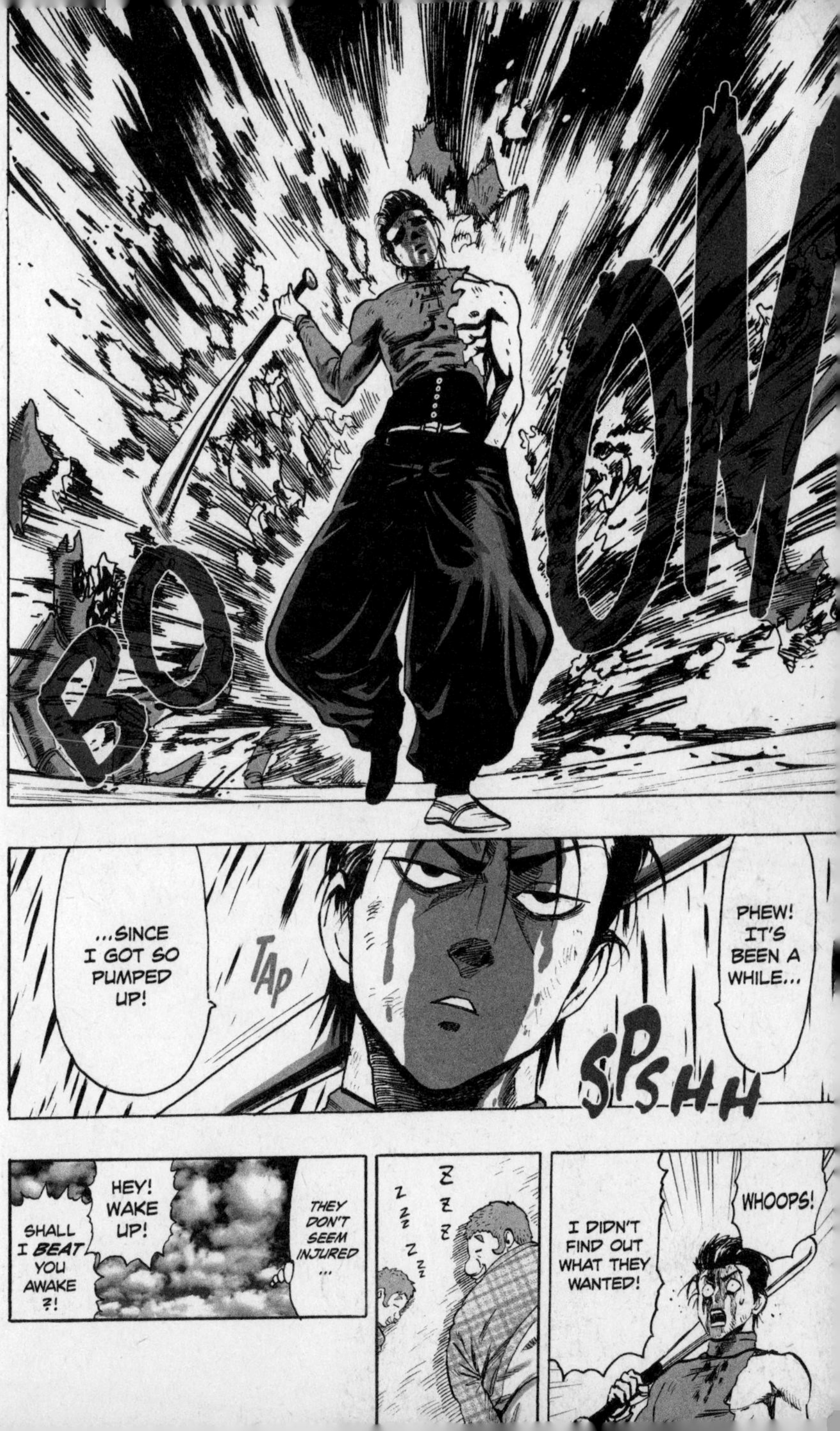
BOOM
PHEW! IT'S BEEN A WHILE...
SPSHH
TAP
...SINCE I GOT SO PUMPED UP!
WHOOPS!
I DIDN'T FIND OUT WHAT THEY WANTED!
Z Z Z
THEY DON'T SEEM INJURED...
HEY! WAKE UP!
SHALL I *BEAT* YOU AWAKE?!

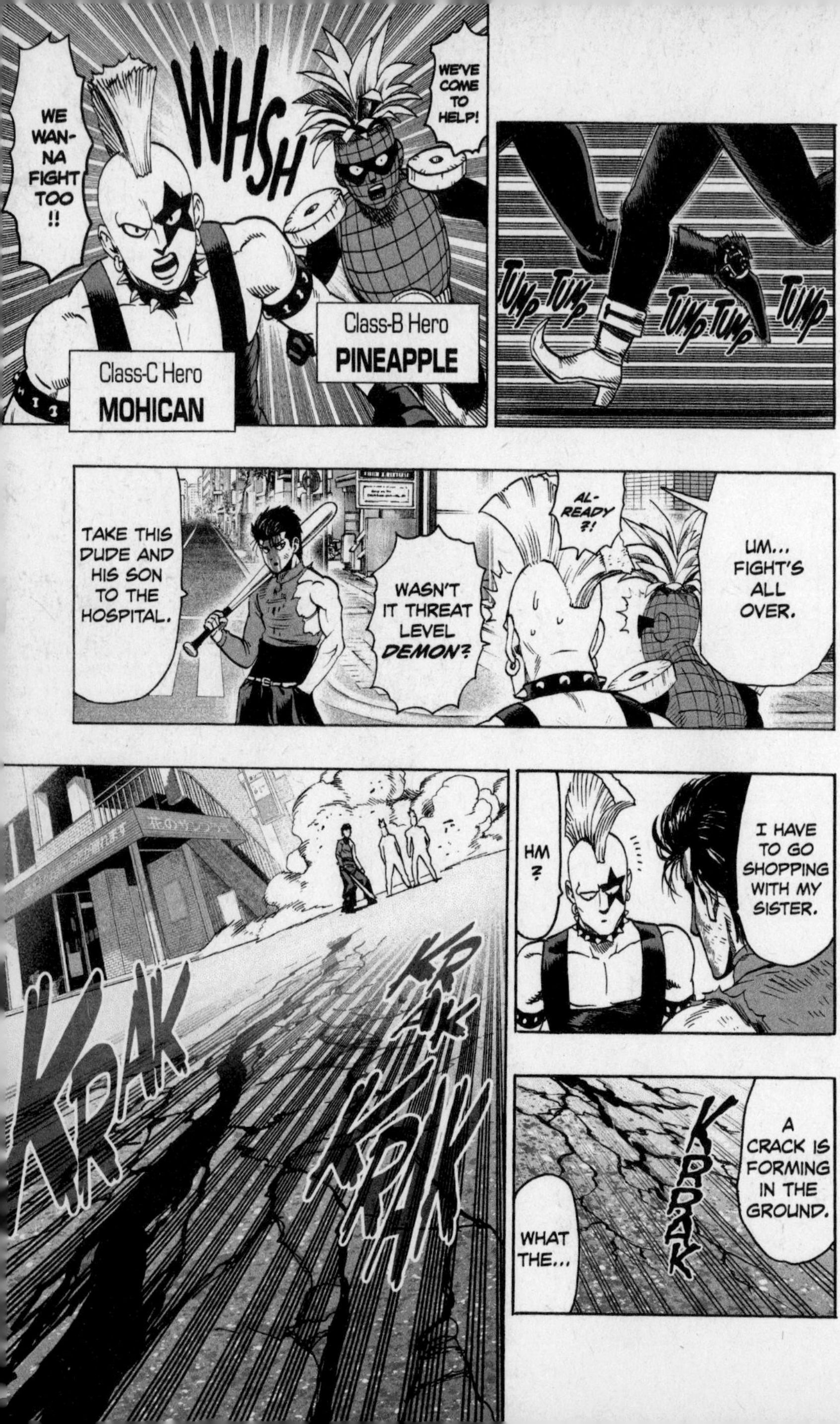
TUMP TUMP
TUMP TUMP TUMP
WE'VE COME TO HELP!
WHSH
WE WAN-NA FIGHT TOO!!
Class-B Hero
PINEAPPLE
Class-C Hero
MOHICAN
UM... FIGHT'S ALL OVER.
AL-READY?!
WASN'T IT THREAT LEVEL *DEMON*?
TAKE THIS DUDE AND HIS SON TO THE HOSPITAL.
I HAVE TO GO SHOPPING WITH MY SISTER.
HM?
A CRACK IS FORMING IN THE GROUND.
KRDAK
WHAT THE...
KRAK
KRAK
KRAK

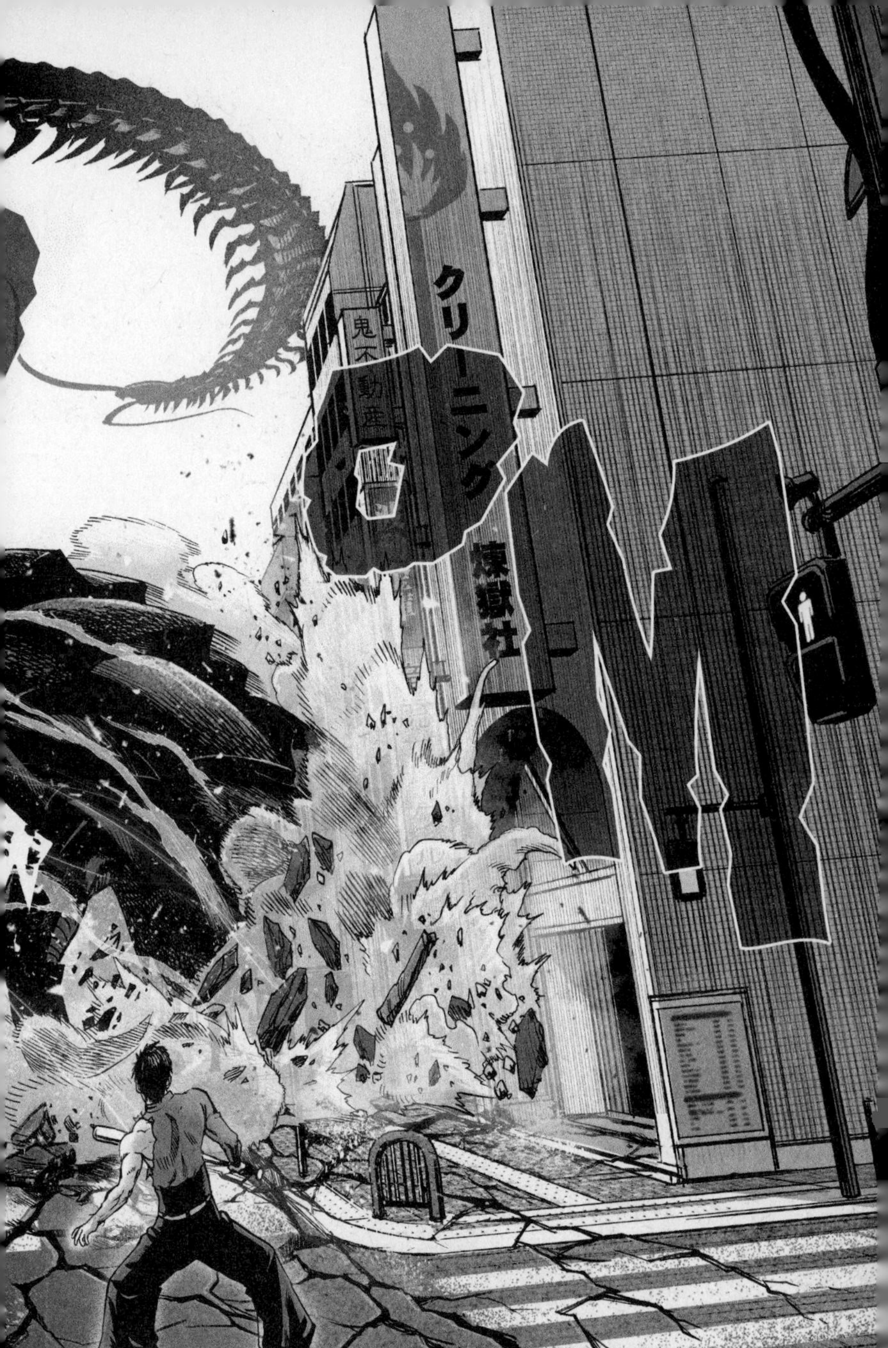
クリーニング
鬼不動産
煉獄社

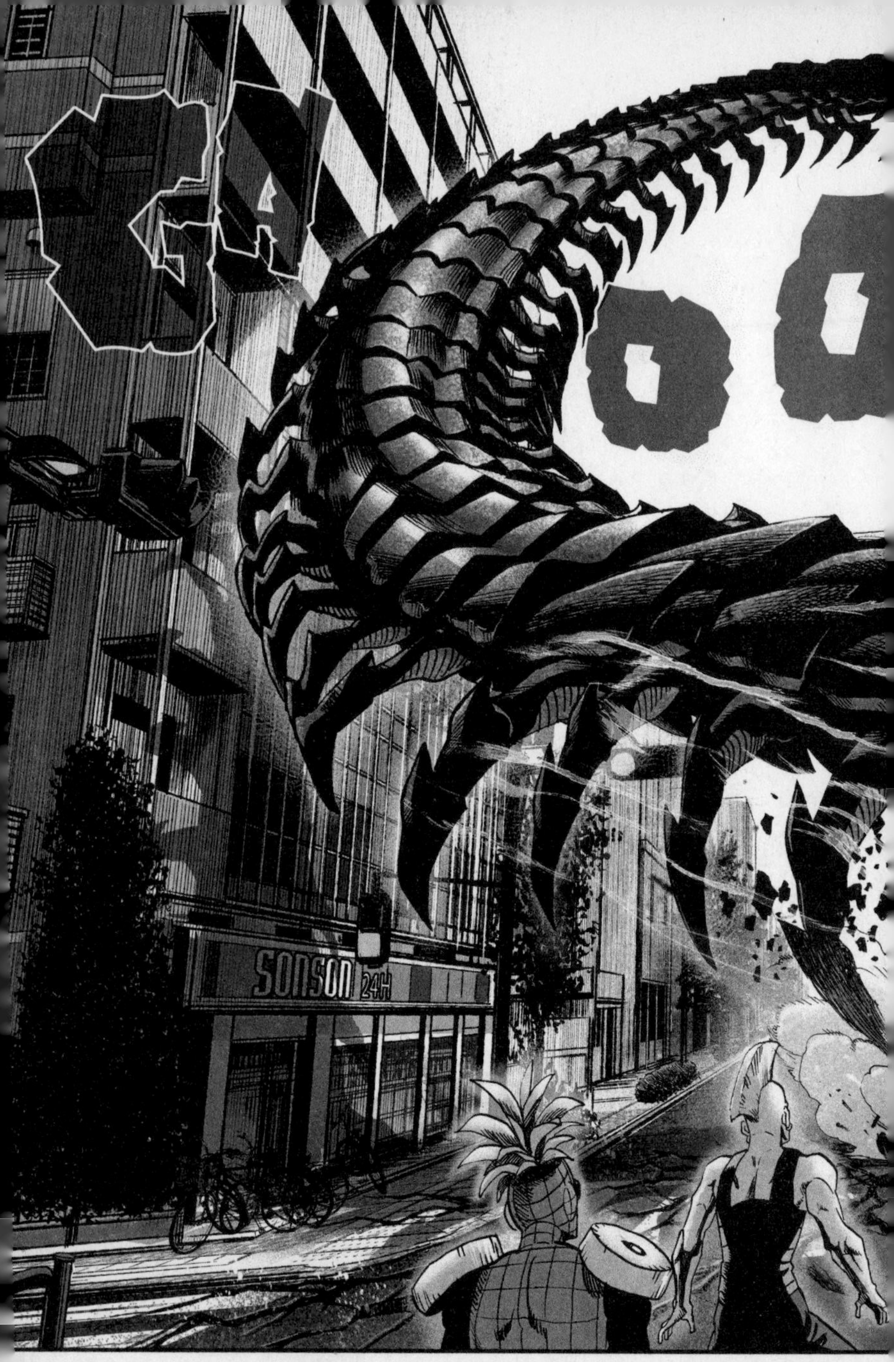
SONSON 24H

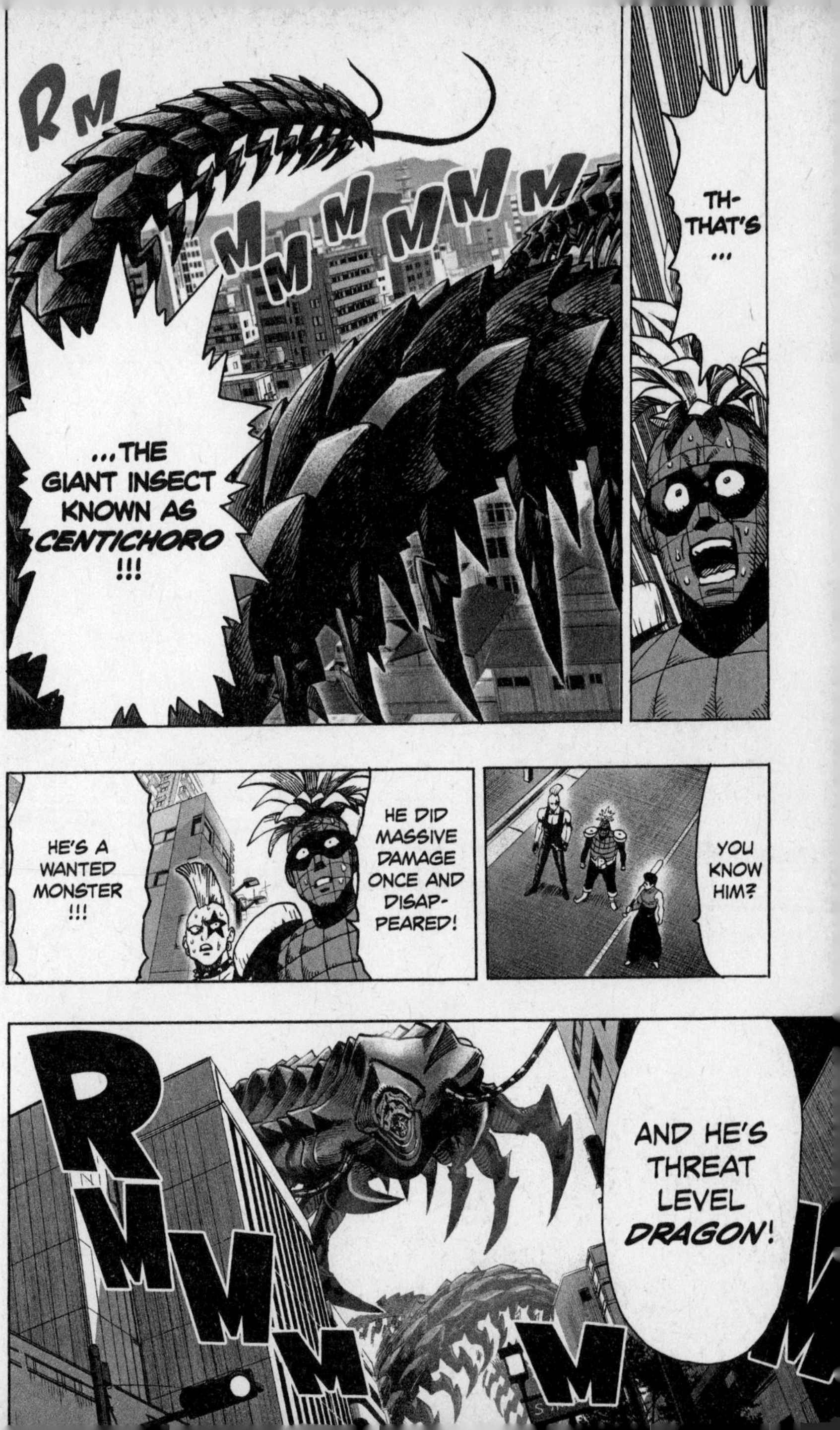
TH- THAT'S ...
RMMMMMMMMMM
...THE GIANT INSECT KNOWN AS *CENTICHORO* !!!
YOU KNOW HIM?
HE DID MASSIVE DAMAGE ONCE AND DISAP-PEARED!
HE'S A WANTED MONSTER !!!
AND HE'S THREAT LEVEL *DRAGON*!
RMMMMMMM

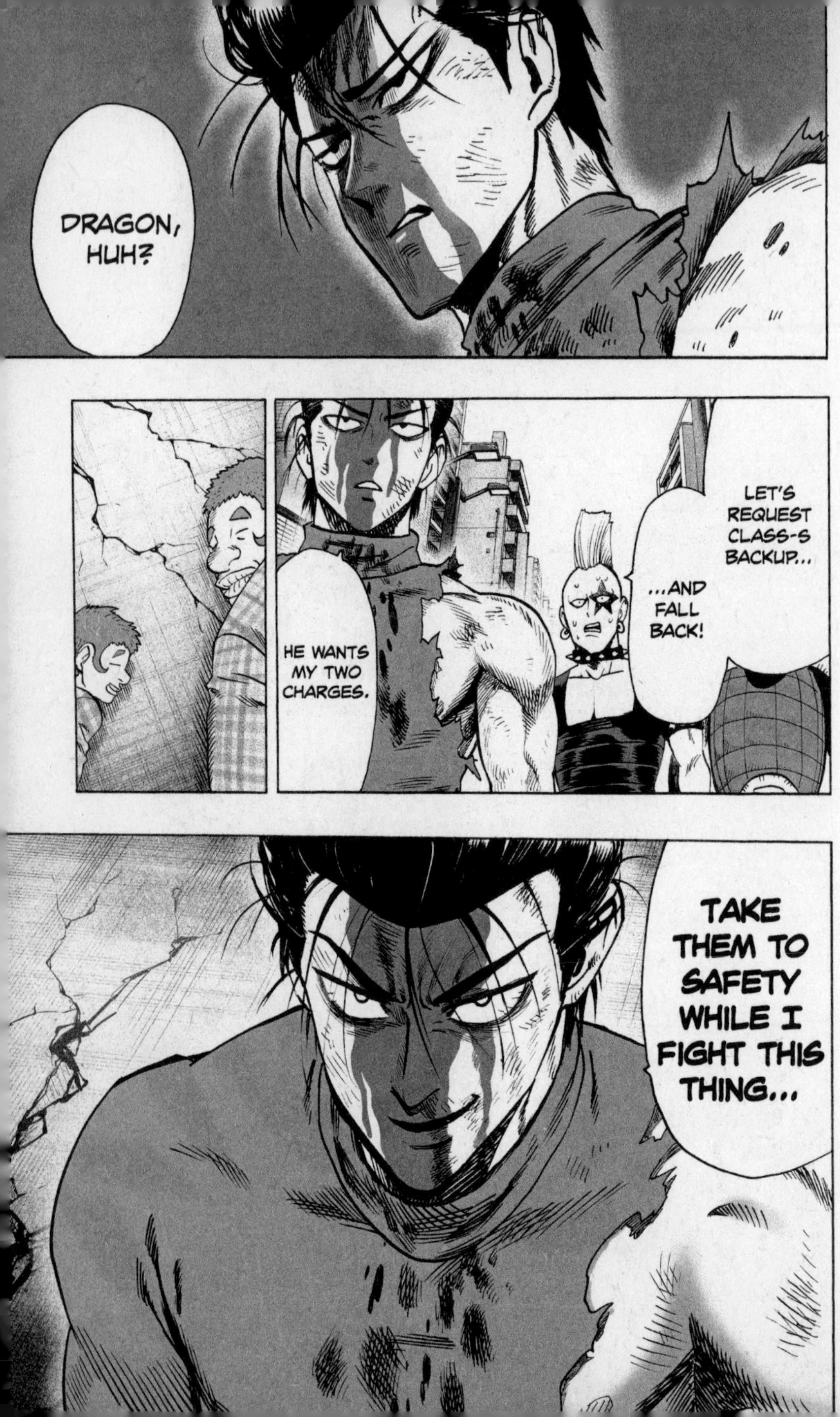
DRAGON, HUH?
LET'S REQUEST CLASS-S BACKUP...
...AND FALL BACK!
HE WANTS MY TWO CHARGES.
TAKE THEM TO SAFETY WHILE I FIGHT THIS THING...

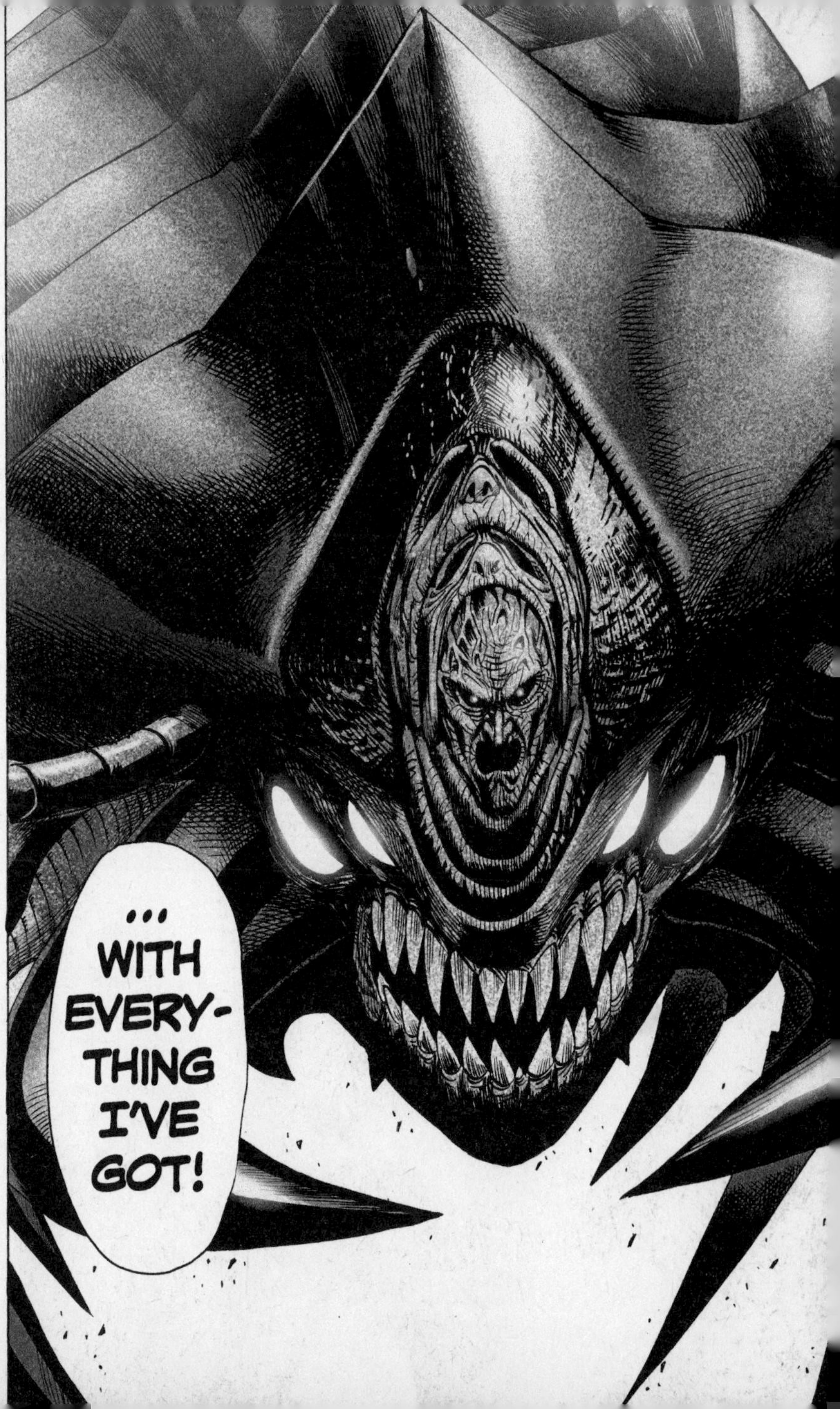
...WITH EVERY-THING I'VE GOT!

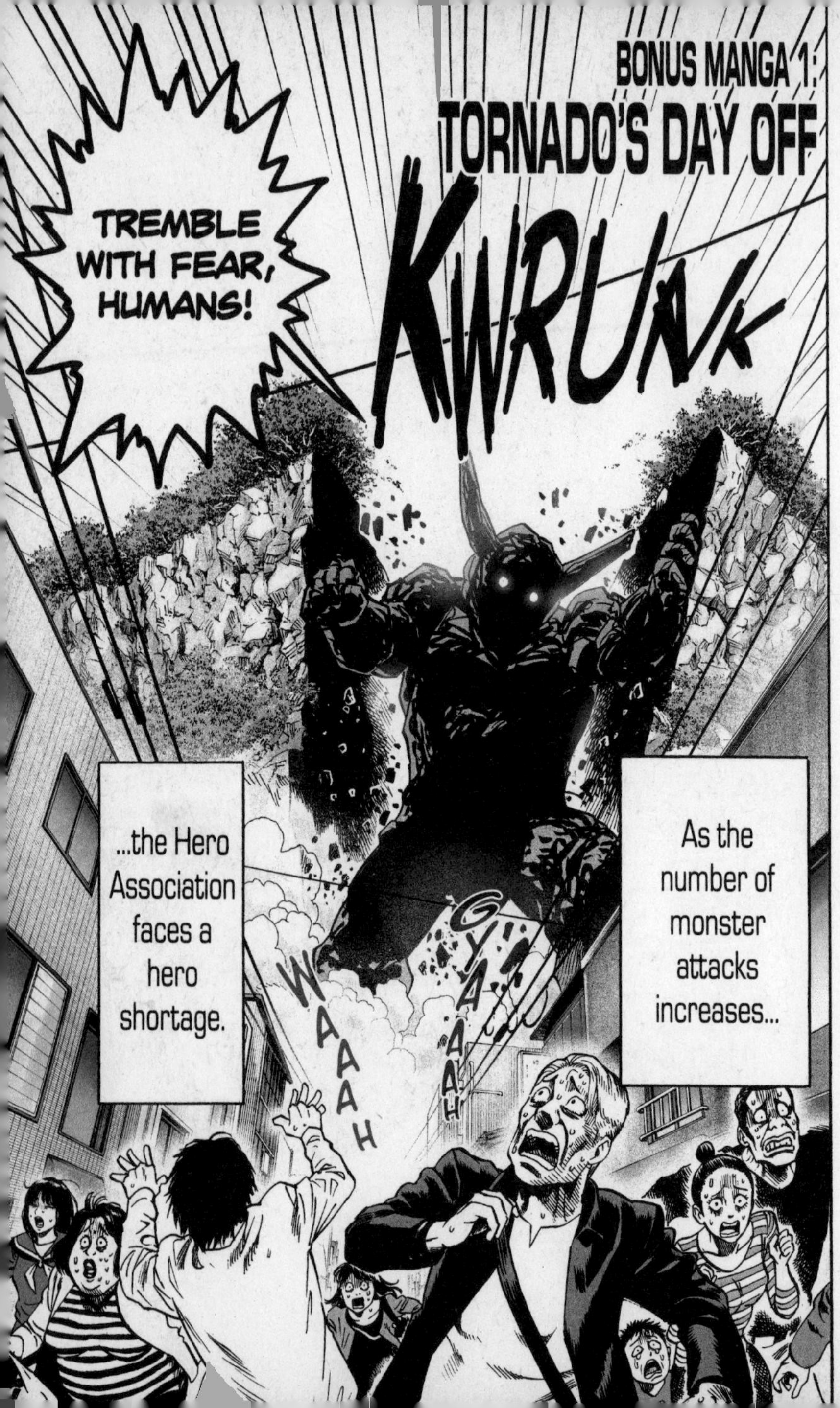
BONUS MANGA 1:
TORNADO'S DAY OFF
KWRUNK
TREMBLE WITH FEAR, HUMANS!
As the number of monster attacks increases...
...the Hero Association faces a hero shortage.
GYAAAAH
WAAAAH

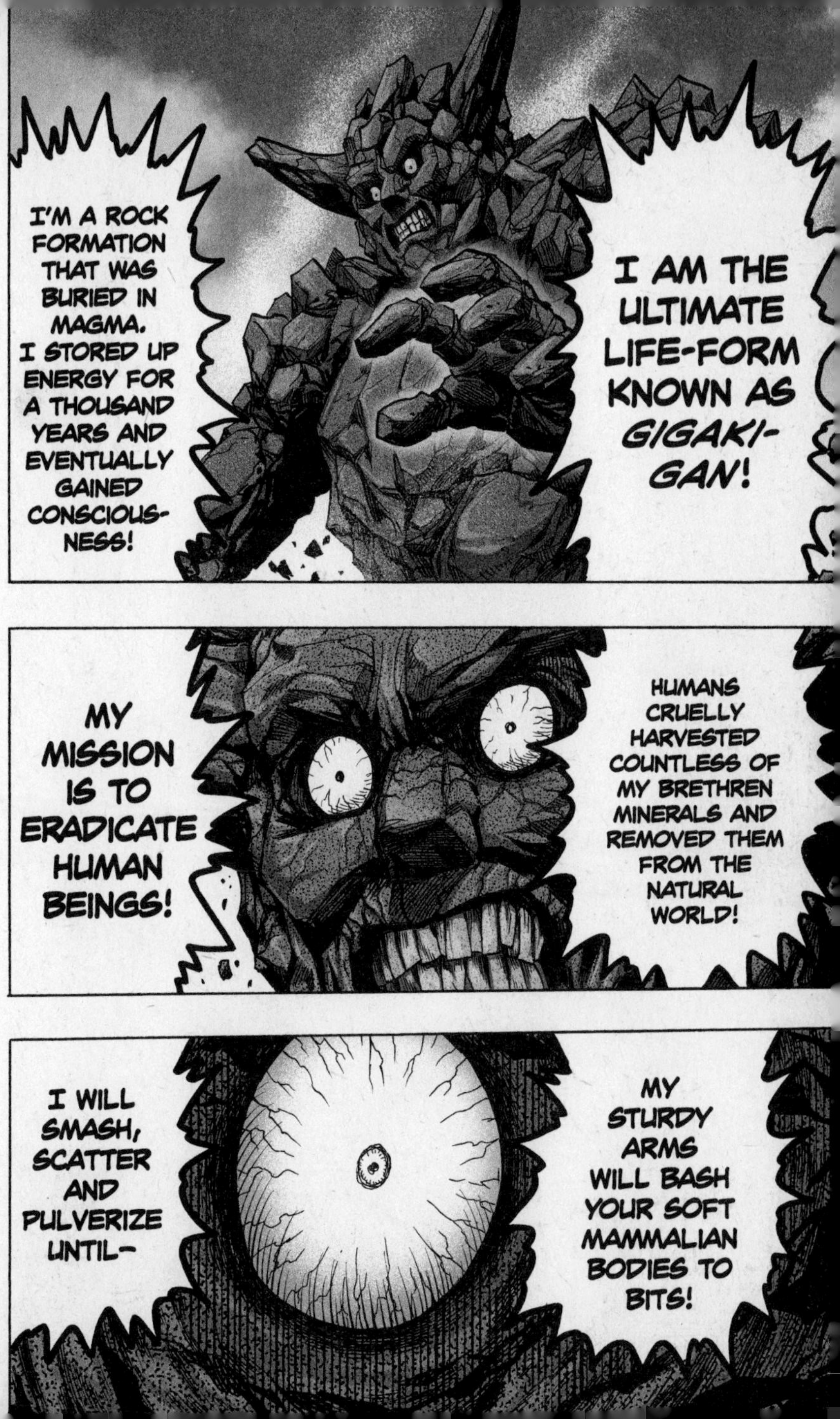
I AM THE ULTIMATE LIFE-FORM KNOWN AS *GIGAKI-GAN*!
I'M A ROCK FORMATION THAT WAS BURIED IN MAGMA. I STORED UP ENERGY FOR A THOUSAND YEARS AND EVENTUALLY GAINED CONSCIOUS-NESS!
HUMANS CRUELLY HARVESTED COUNTLESS OF MY BRETHREN MINERALS AND REMOVED THEM FROM THE NATURAL WORLD!
MY MISSION IS TO ERADICATE HUMAN BEINGS!
MY STURDY ARMS WILL BASH YOUR SOFT MAMMALIAN BODIES TO BITS!
I WILL SMASH, SCATTER AND PULVERIZE UNTIL-

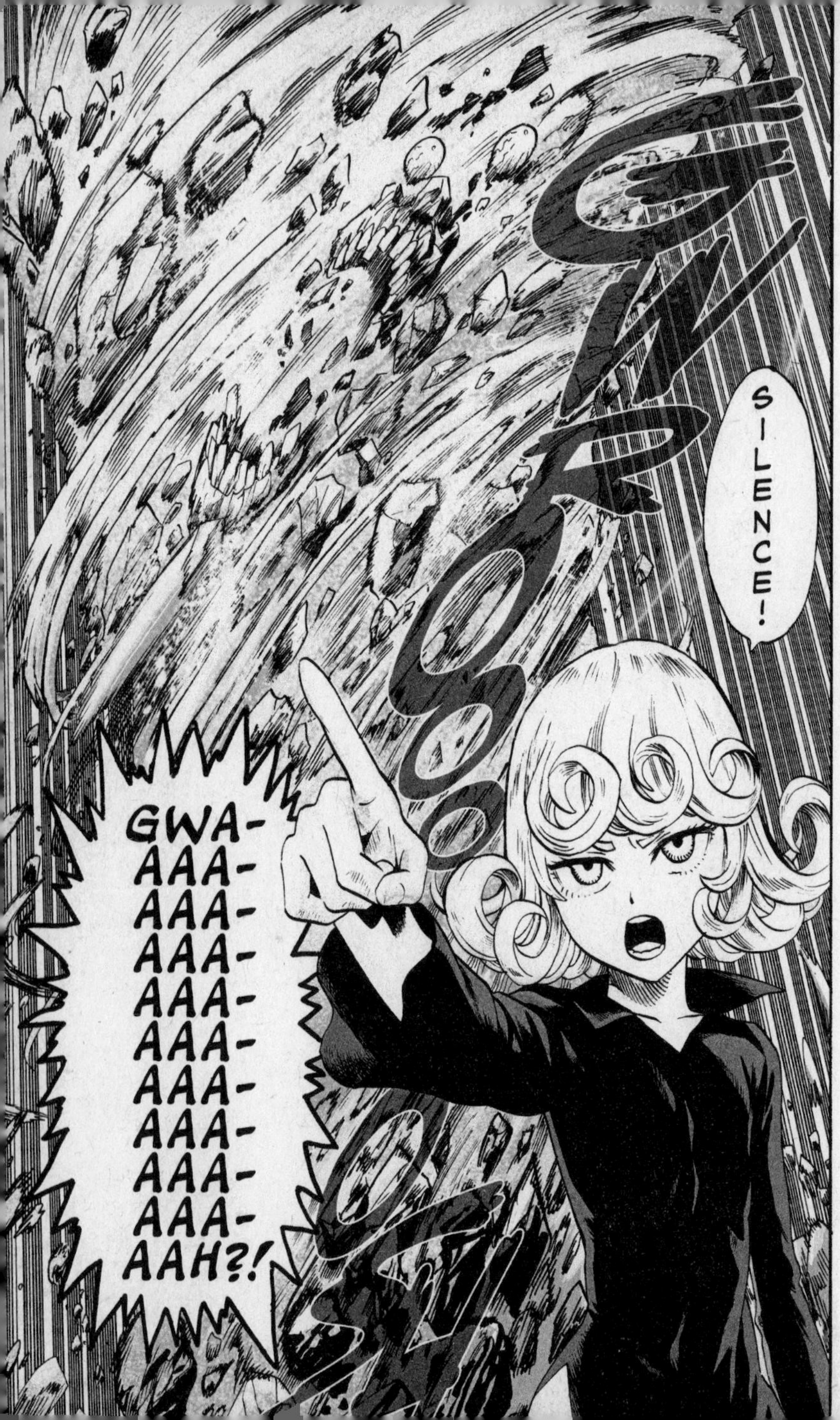
SILENCE!
GWA-AAA-AAA-AAA-AAA-AAA-AAA-AAA-AAA-AAA-AAA-AAH?!

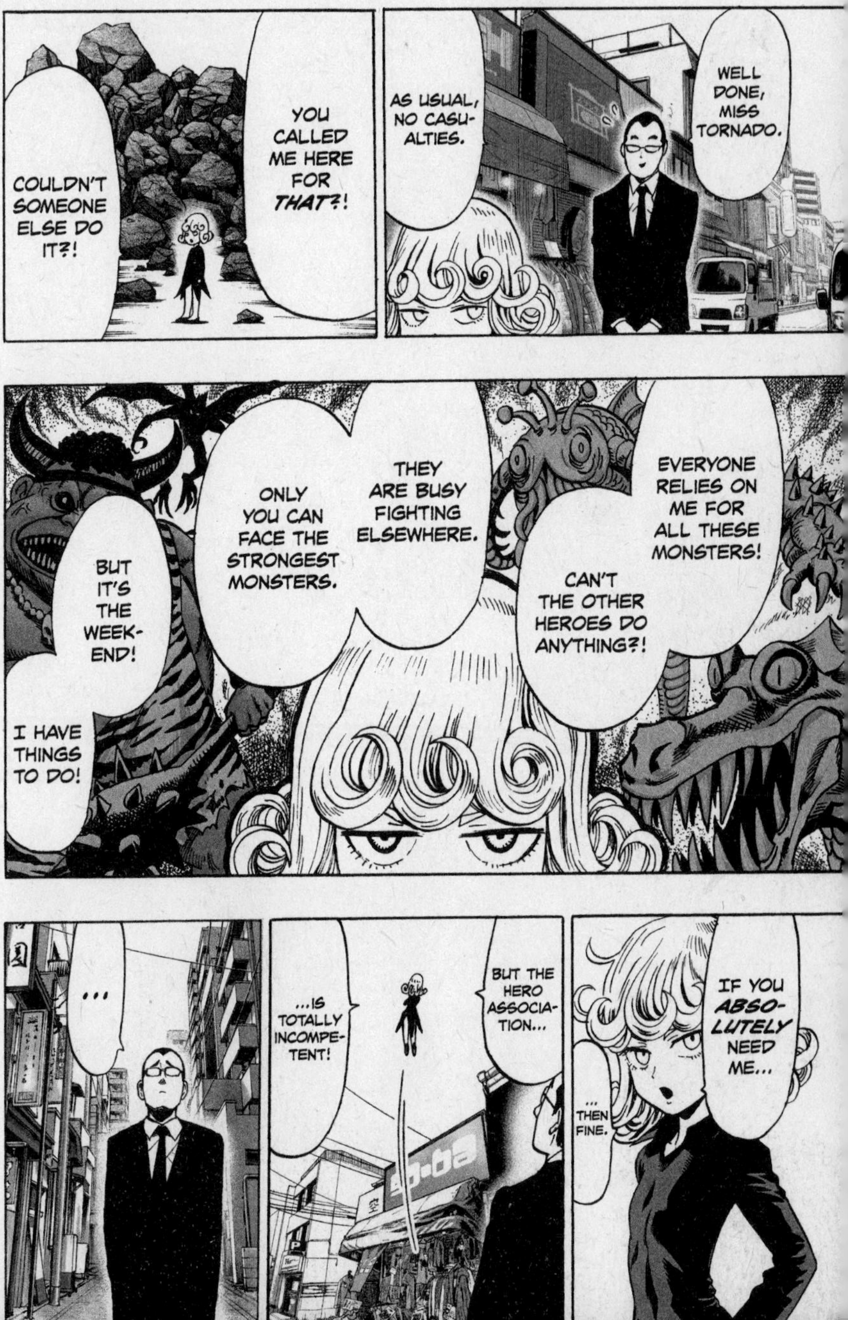
WELL DONE, MISS TORNADO.
AS USUAL, NO CASUALTIES.
YOU CALLED ME HERE FOR *THAT*?!
COULDN'T SOMEONE ELSE DO IT?!
EVERYONE RELIES ON ME FOR ALL THESE MONSTERS!
CAN'T THE OTHER HEROES DO ANYTHING?!
THEY ARE BUSY FIGHTING ELSEWHERE.
ONLY YOU CAN FACE THE STRONGEST MONSTERS.
BUT IT'S THE WEEKEND!
I HAVE THINGS TO DO!
IF YOU *ABSOLUTELY* NEED ME...
...THEN FINE.
BUT THE HERO ASSOCIATION...
...IS TOTALLY INCOMPETENT!
...

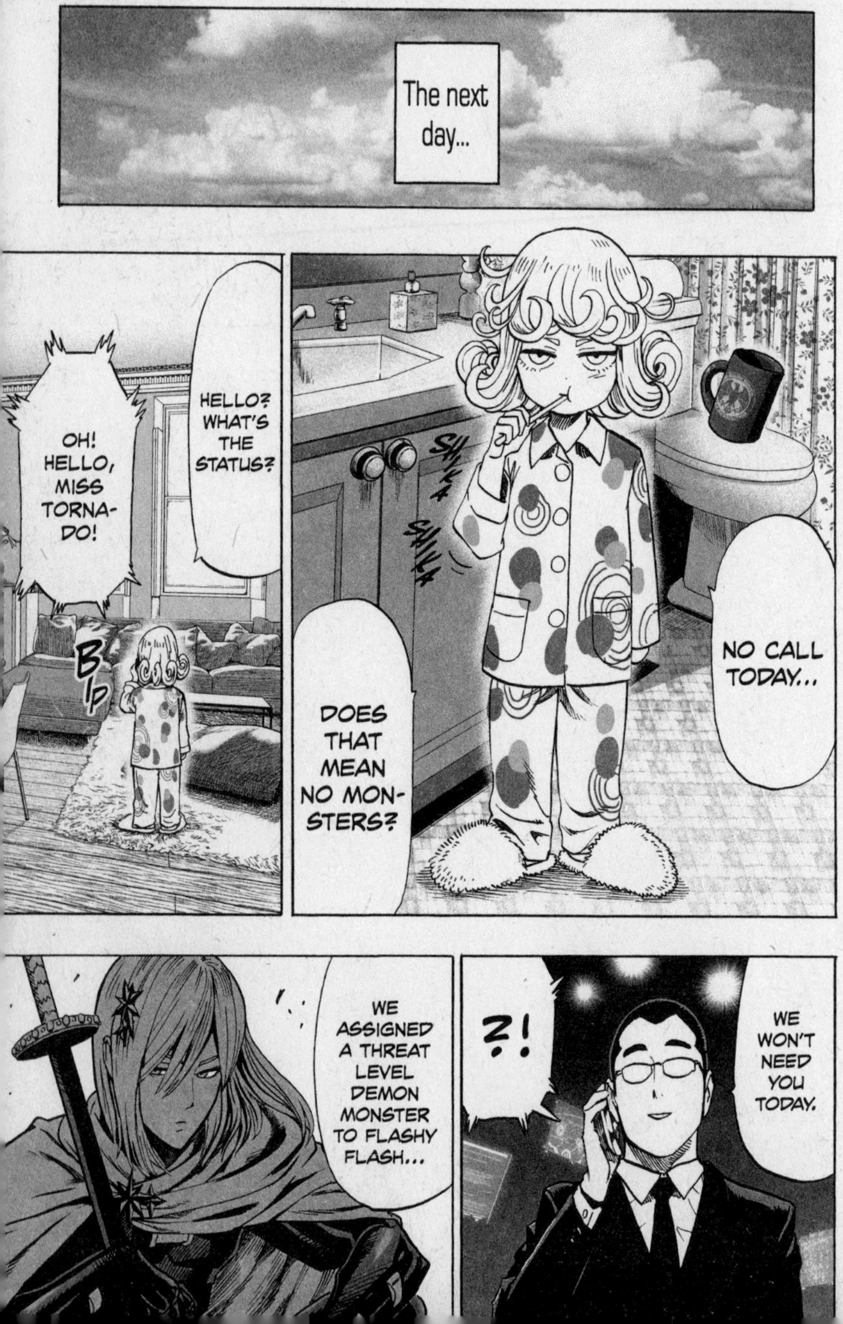
The next day...
NO CALL TODAY...
DOES THAT MEAN NO MONSTERS?
HELLO? WHAT'S THE STATUS?
OH! HELLO, MISS TORNA-DO!
BIP
WE WON'T NEED YOU TODAY.
?!
WE ASSIGNED A THREAT LEVEL DEMON MONSTER TO FLASHY FLASH...
...

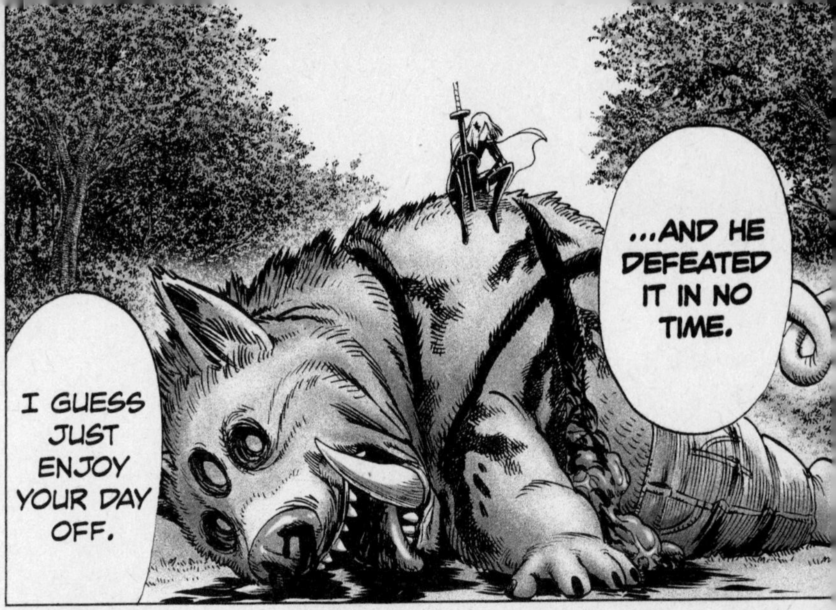
...AND HE DEFEATED IT IN NO TIME.
I GUESS JUST ENJOY YOUR DAY OFF.
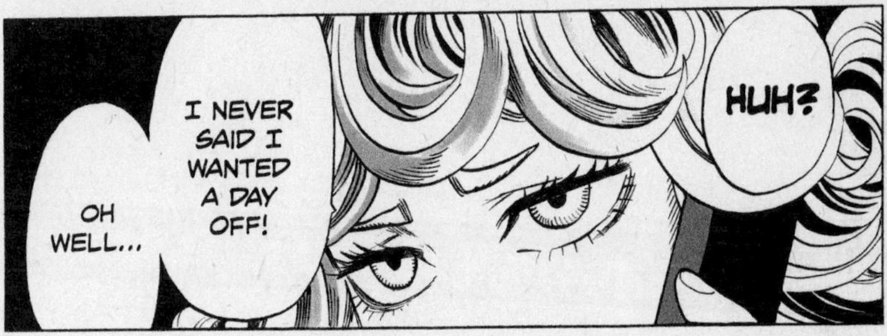
HUH?
I NEVER SAID I WANTED A DAY OFF!
OH WELL...
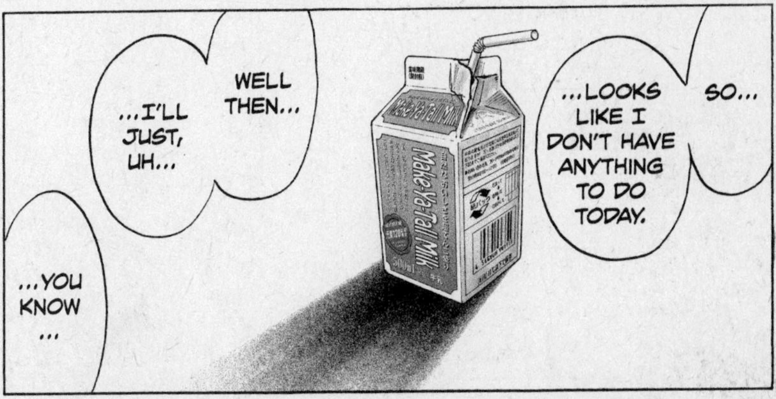
SO...
...LOOKS LIKE I DON'T HAVE ANYTHING TO DO TODAY.
Make Ya-Tall Milk
WELL THEN...
...I'LL JUST, UH...
...YOU KNOW ...

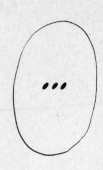

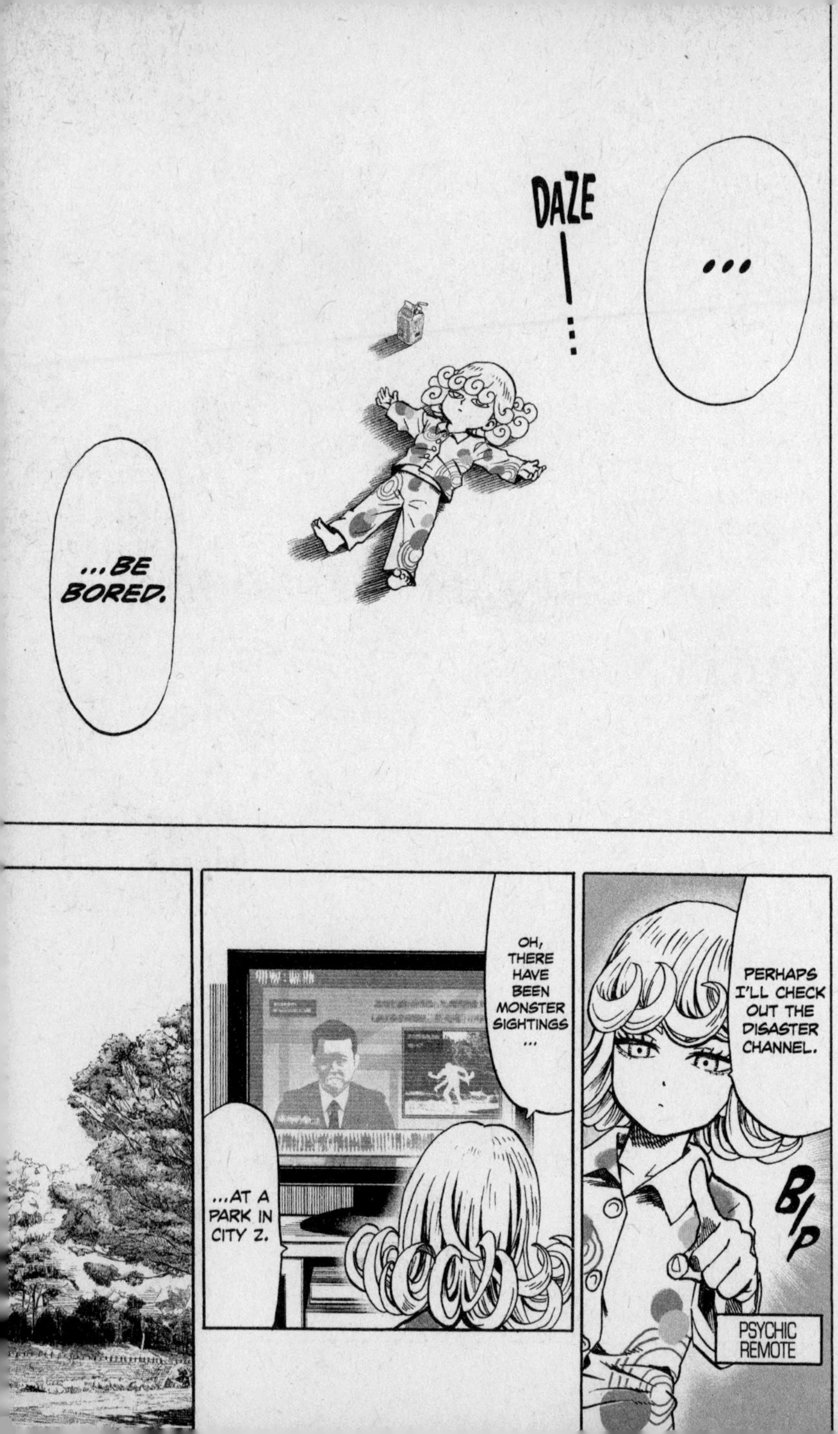
...
DAZE
...BE BORED.
PERHAPS I'LL CHECK OUT THE DISASTER CHANNEL.
B/P
PSYCHIC REMOTE
OH, THERE HAVE BEEN MONSTER SIGHTINGS...
...AT A PARK IN CITY Z.

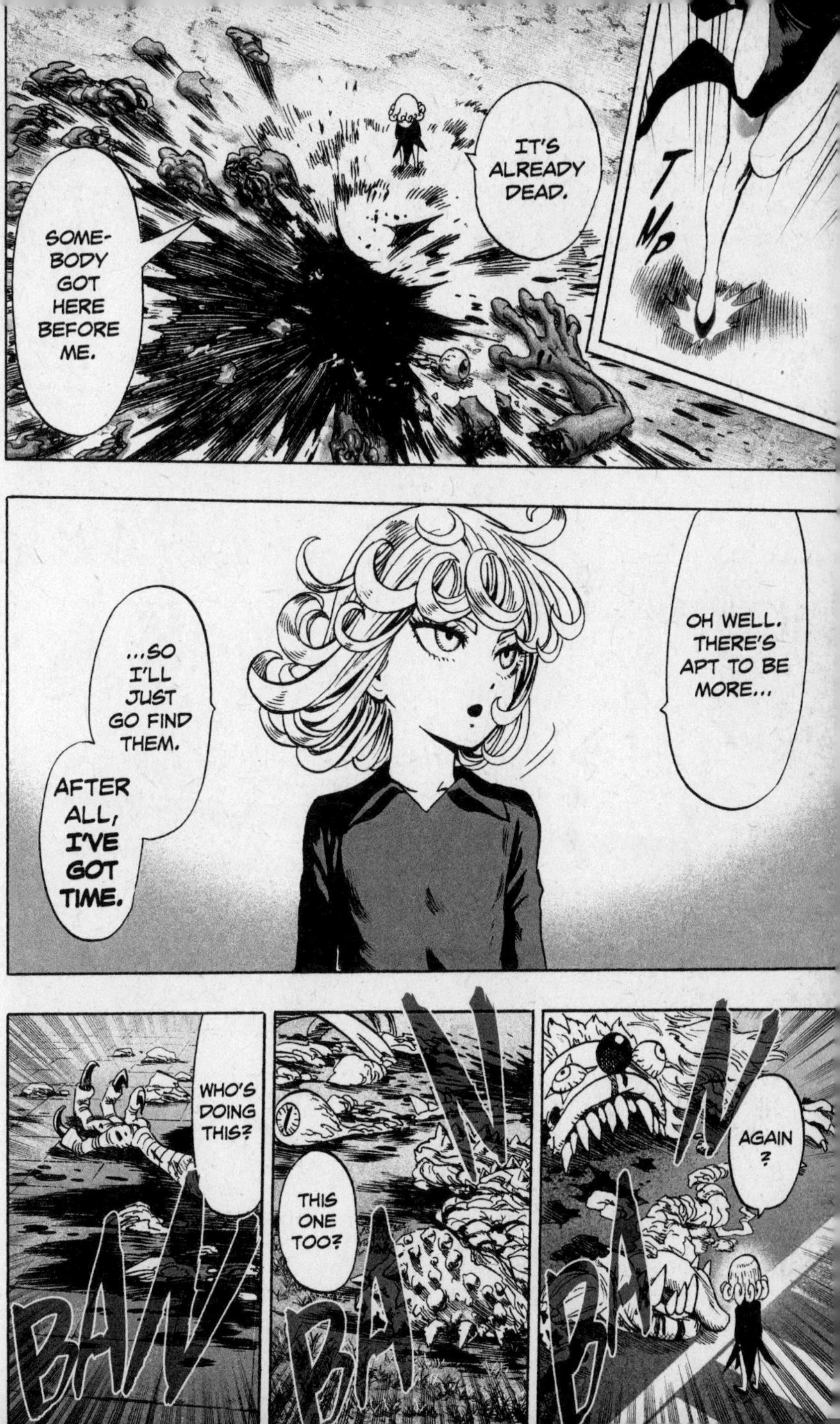
TMP
IT'S ALREADY DEAD.
SOME-BODY GOT HERE BEFORE ME.
OH WELL. THERE'S APT TO BE MORE...
...SO I'LL JUST GO FIND THEM.
AFTER ALL, **I'VE GOT TIME.**
AGAIN?
BAN
THIS ONE TOO?
BAN
WHO'S DOING THIS?
BAN

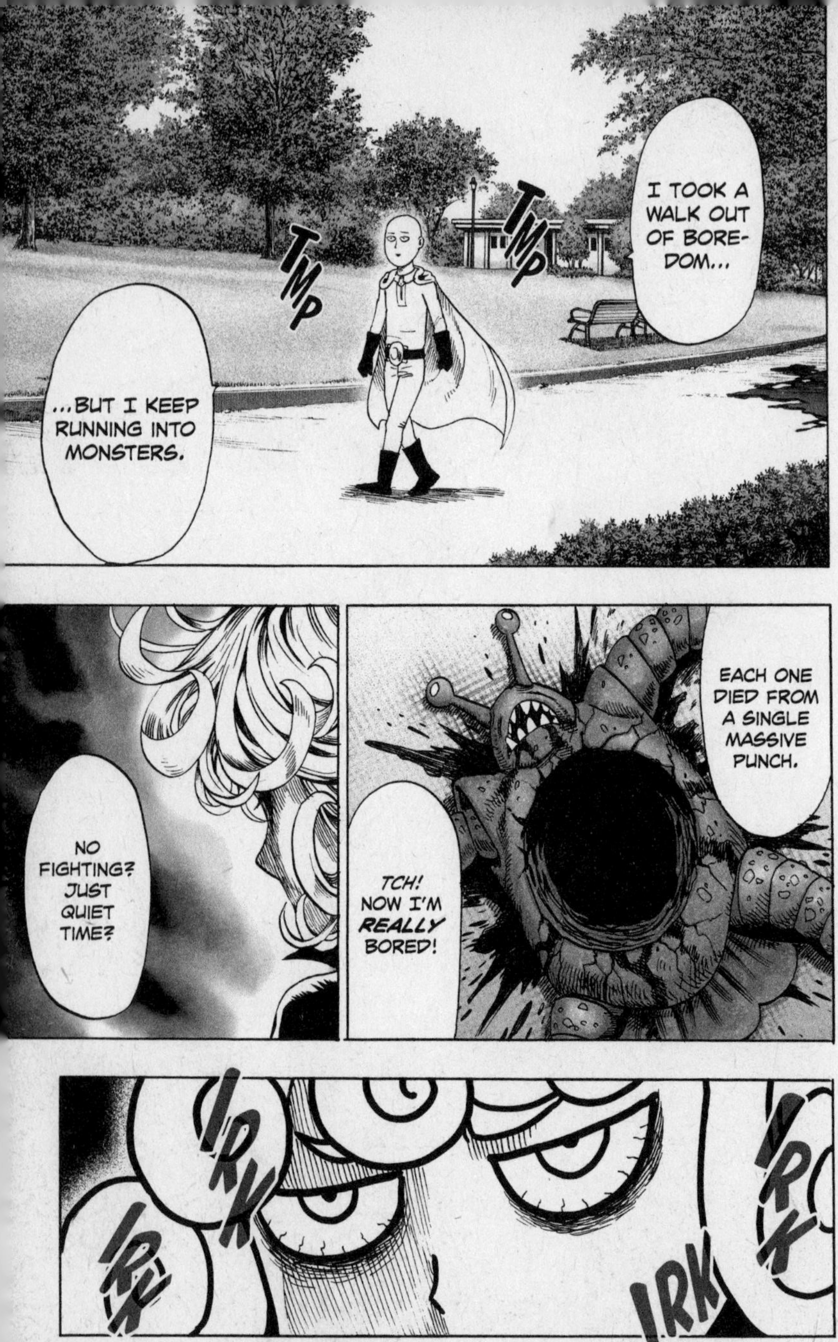
I TOOK A WALK OUT OF BORE-DOM...
TMP
TMP
...BUT I KEEP RUNNING INTO MONSTERS.
EACH ONE DIED FROM A SINGLE MASSIVE PUNCH.
TCH! NOW I'M REALLY BORED!
NO FIGHTING? JUST QUIET TIME?
IRK
IRK
IRK
IRK

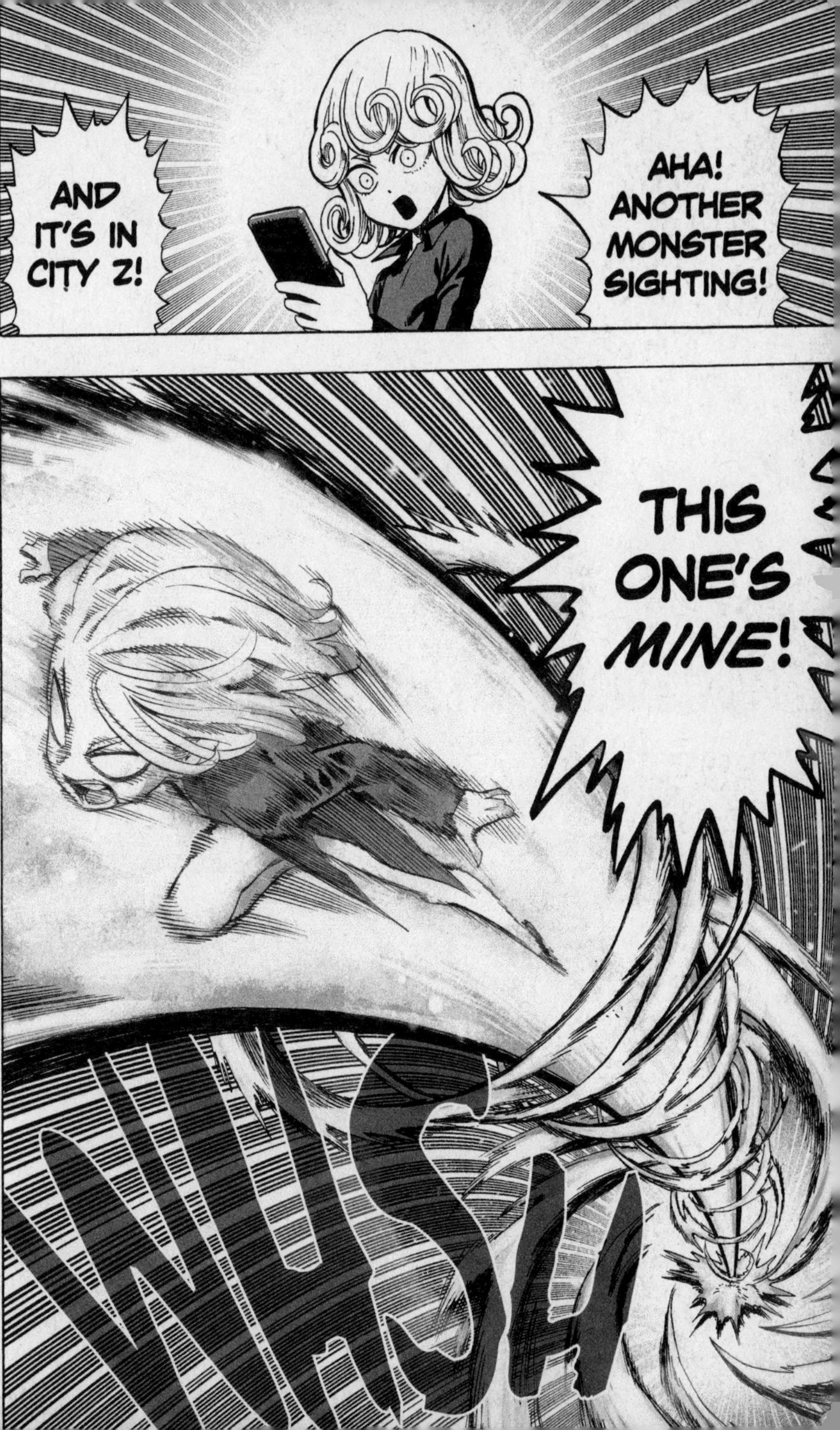
AHA! ANOTHER MONSTER SIGHTING!
AND IT'S IN CITY Z!
THIS ONE'S MINE!

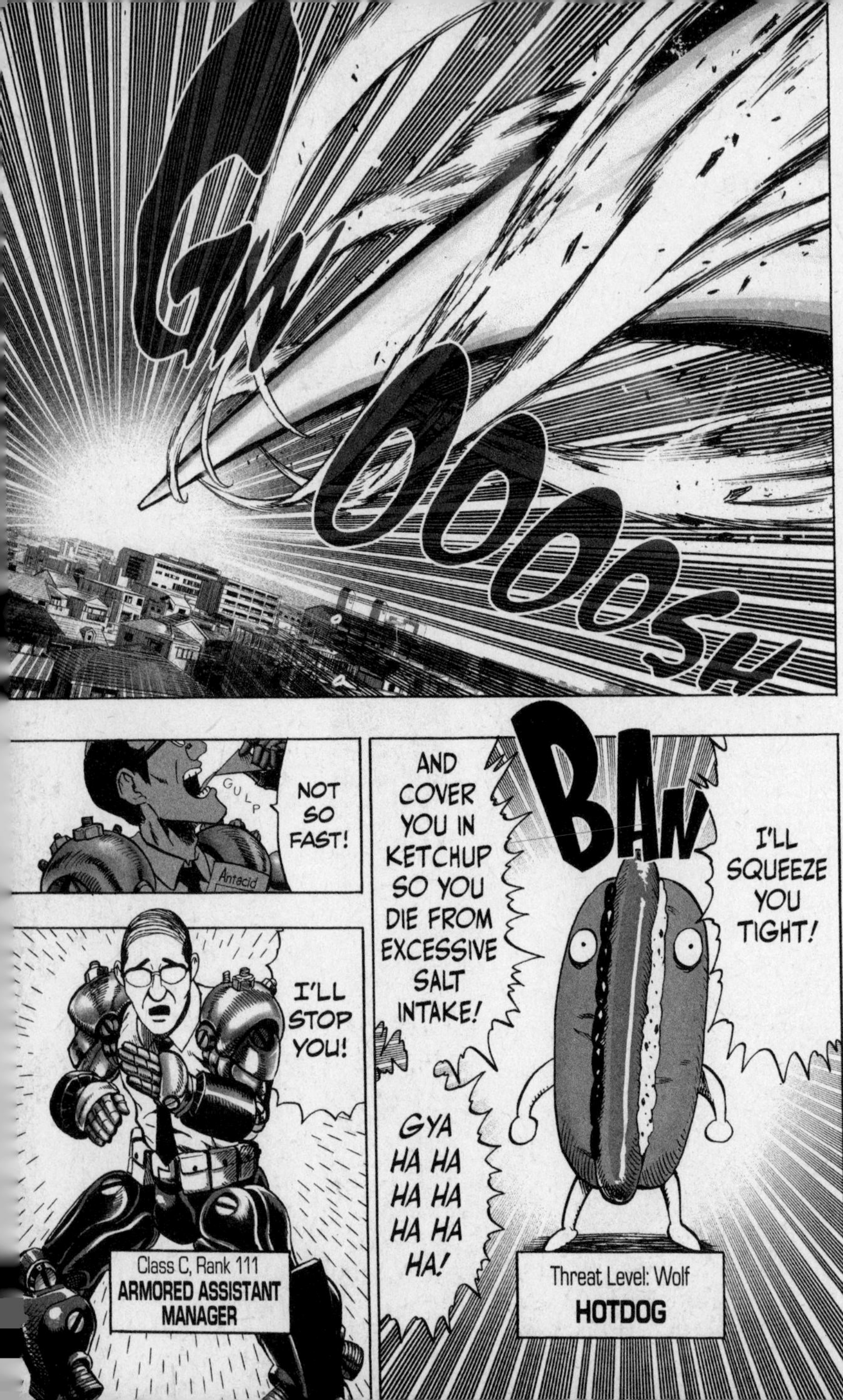
GWOOOOOSH
BAN
I'LL SQUEEZE YOU TIGHT!
AND COVER YOU IN KETCHUP SO YOU DIE FROM EXCESSIVE SALT INTAKE!
GYA HA HA HA HA HA HA HA!
Threat Level: Wolf
HOTDOG
NOT SO FAST!
GULP
Antacid
I'LL STOP YOU!
Class C, Rank 111
ARMORED ASSISTANT MANAGER

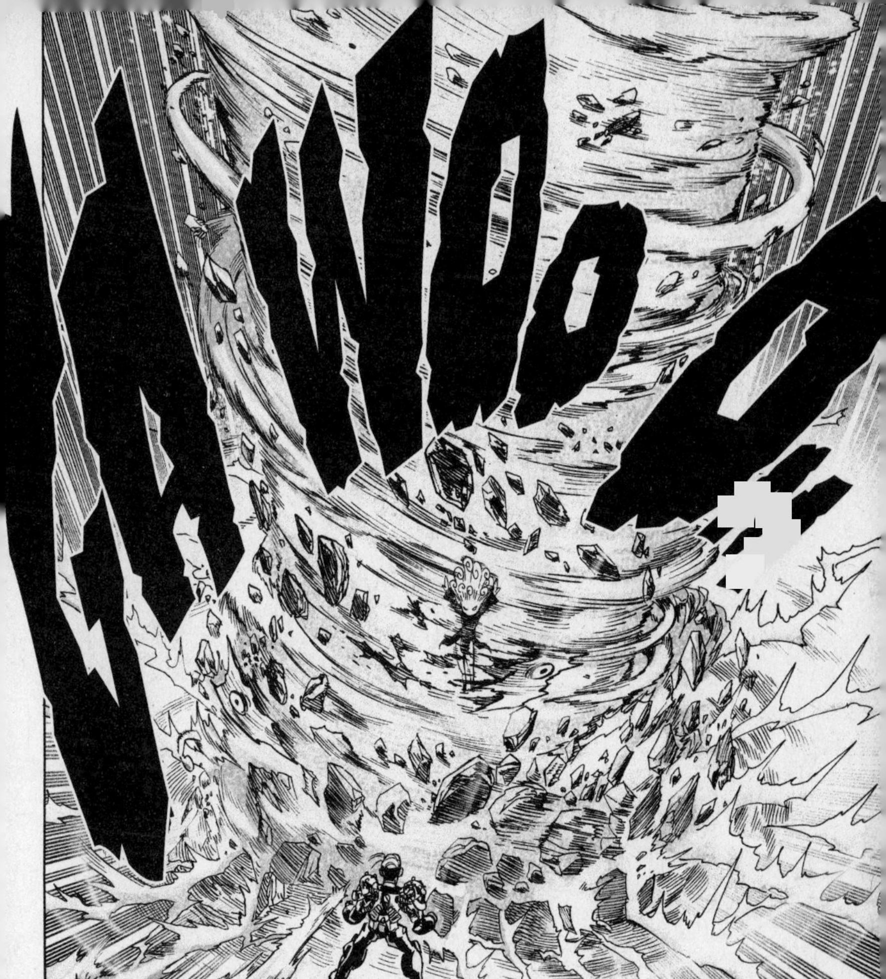

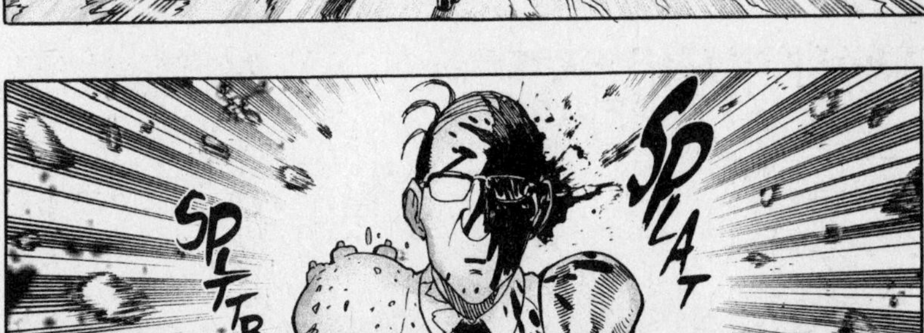
SPLAT
SPLTTR

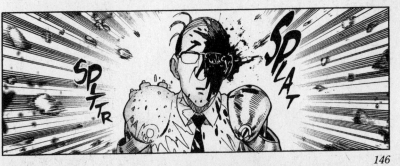

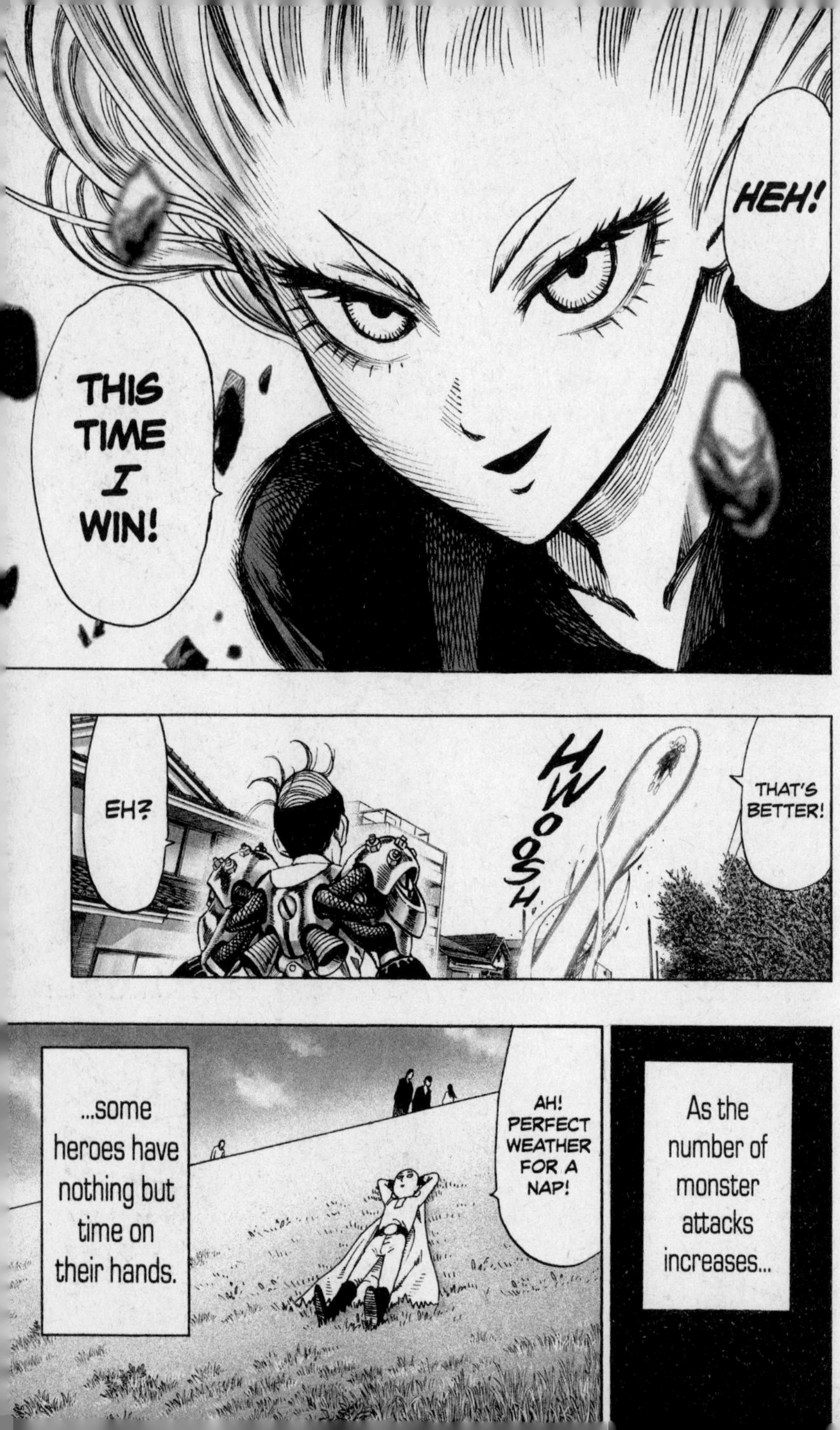
HEH!
THIS TIME I WIN!
THAT'S BETTER!
HWOOOSH
EH?
As the number of monster attacks increases...
AH! PERFECT WEATHER FOR A NAP!
...some heroes have nothing but time on their hands.

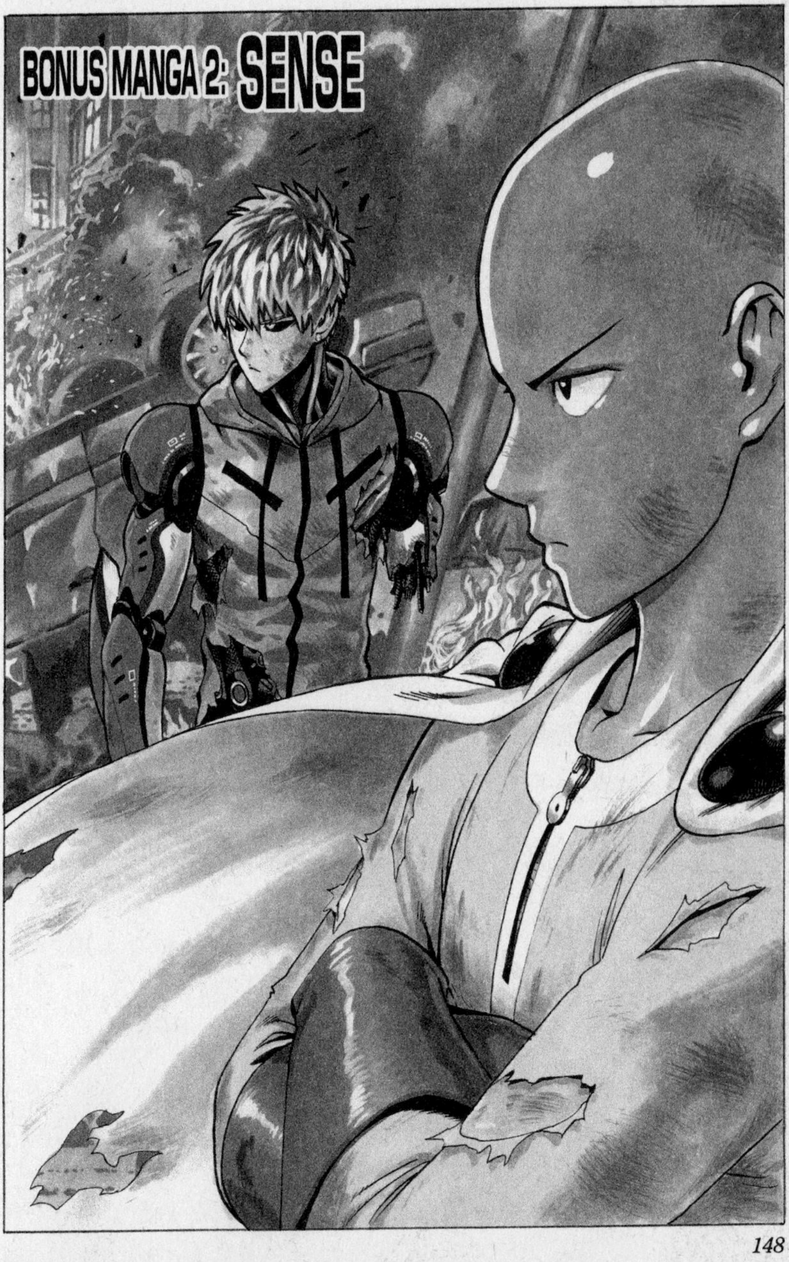
BONUS MANGA 2: SENSE

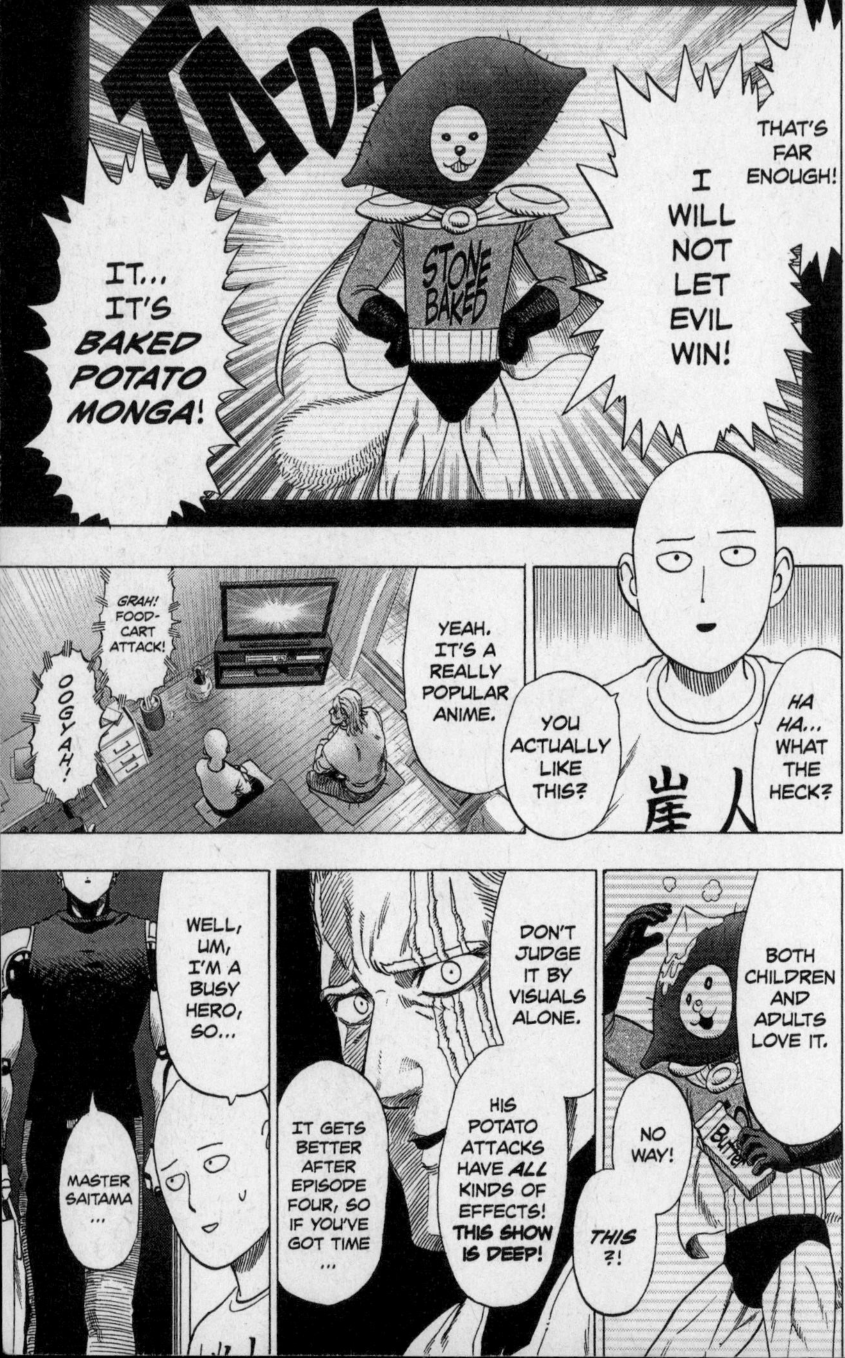
TA-DA
THAT'S FAR ENOUGH!
I WILL NOT LET EVIL WIN!
STONE BAKED
IT... IT'S *BAKED POTATO MONGA*!
HA HA... WHAT THE HECK?
YOU ACTUALLY LIKE THIS?
YEAH. IT'S A REALLY POPULAR ANIME.
GRAH! FOOD-CART ATTACK!
OOGYAH!
BOTH CHILDREN AND ADULTS LOVE IT.
NO WAY!
THIS ?!
Butter
DON'T JUDGE IT BY VISUALS ALONE.
HIS POTATO ATTACKS HAVE *ALL* KINDS OF EFFECTS! **THIS SHOW IS DEEP!**
IT GETS BETTER AFTER EPISODE FOUR, SO IF YOU'VE GOT TIME...
WELL, UM, I'M A BUSY HERO, SO...
MASTER SAITAMA...

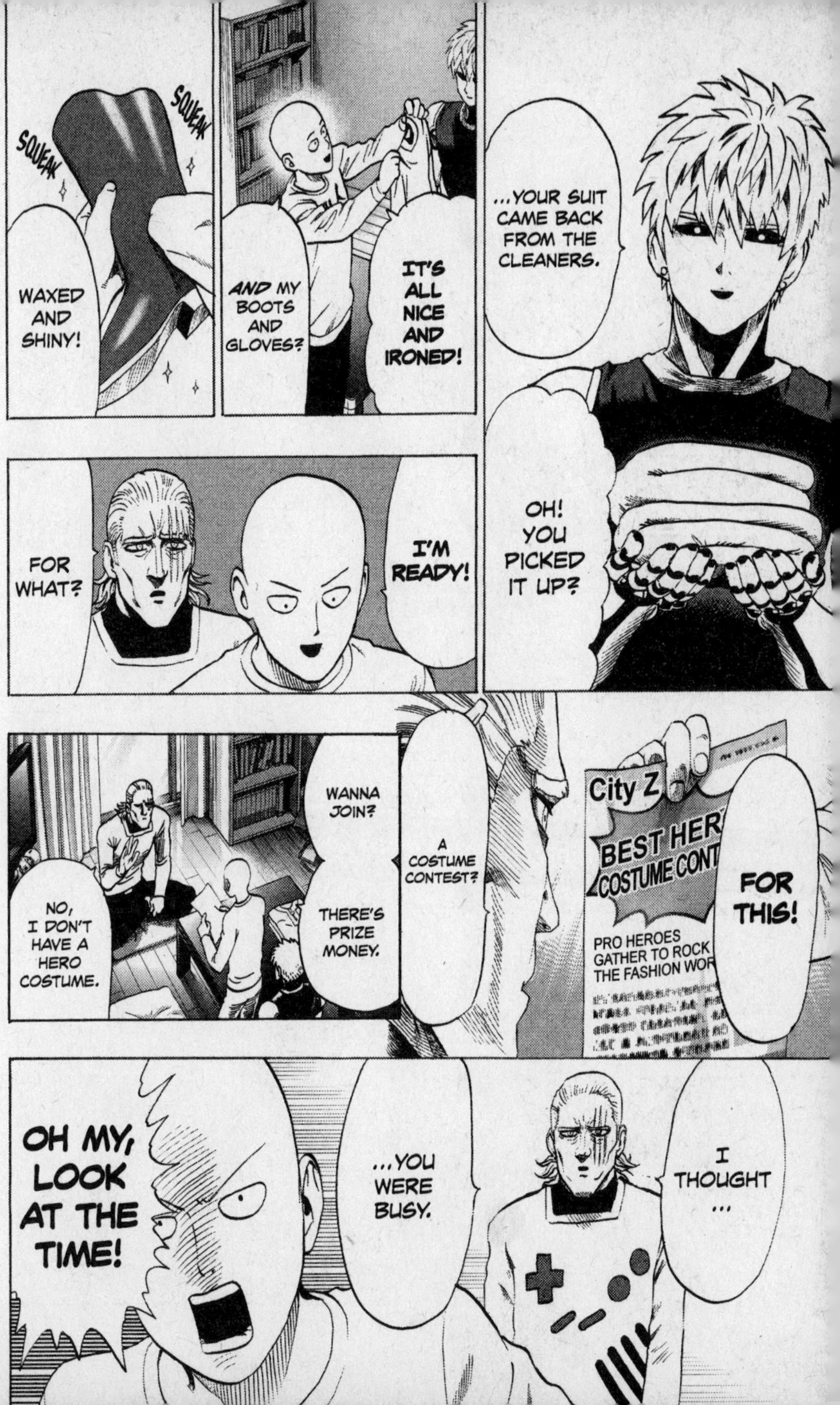
...YOUR SUIT CAME BACK FROM THE CLEANERS.
OH! YOU PICKED IT UP?
IT'S ALL NICE AND IRONED!
AND MY BOOTS AND GLOVES?
SQUEAK
SQUEAK
WAXED AND SHINY!
I'M READY!
FOR WHAT?
FOR THIS!
City Z
BEST HER
COSTUME CONT
PRO HEROES GATHER TO ROCK THE FASHION WOR
A COSTUME CONTEST?
WANNA JOIN?
THERE'S PRIZE MONEY.
NO, I DON'T HAVE A HERO COSTUME.
I THOUGHT ...
...YOU WERE BUSY.
OH MY, LOOK AT THE TIME!

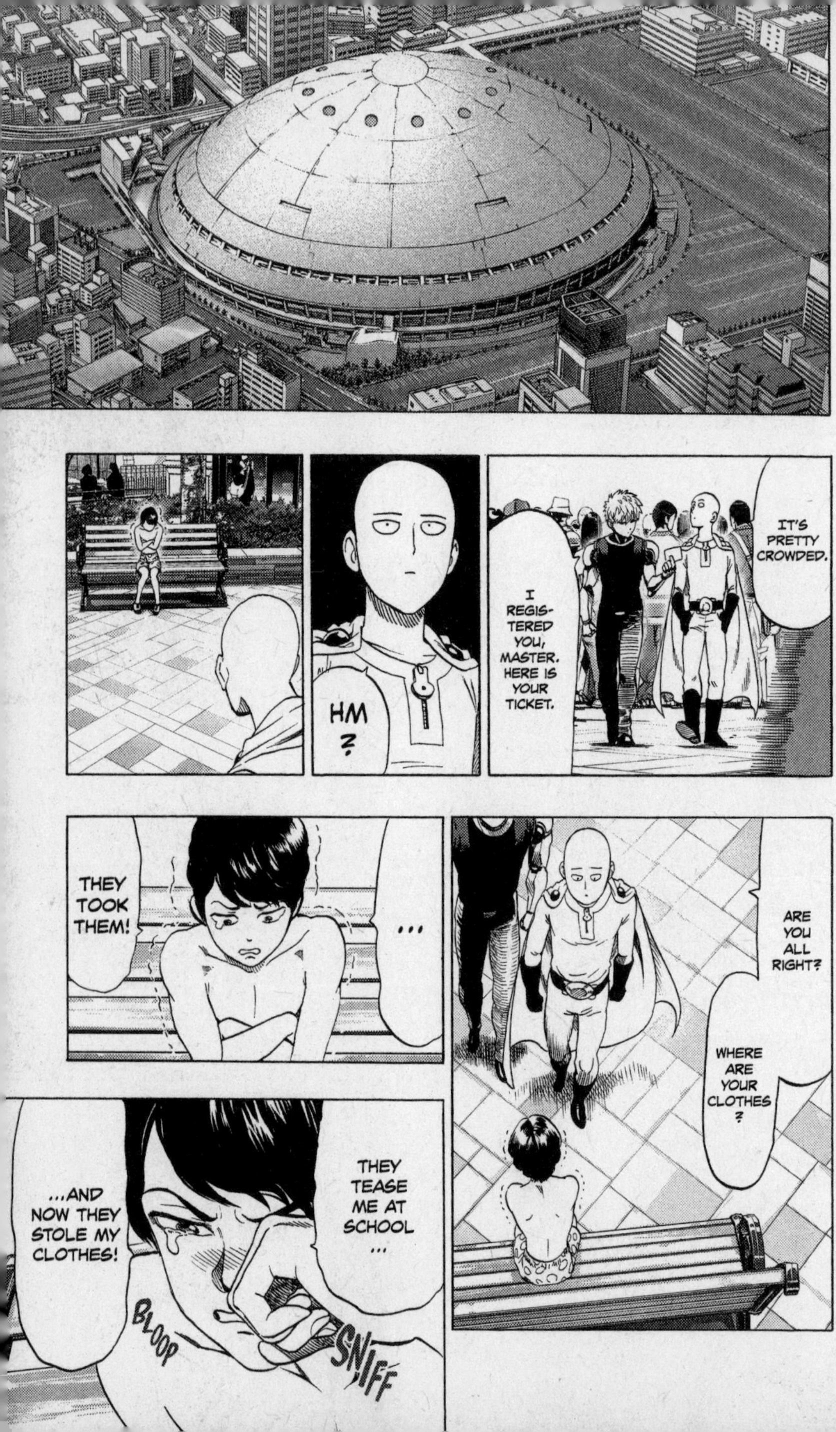
IT'S PRETTY CROWDED.
I REGISTERED YOU, MASTER. HERE IS YOUR TICKET.
HM?
ARE YOU ALL RIGHT?
WHERE ARE YOUR CLOTHES?
...
THEY TOOK THEM!
THEY TEASE ME AT SCHOOL...
...AND NOW THEY STOLE MY CLOTHES!
SNIFF
BLOOP

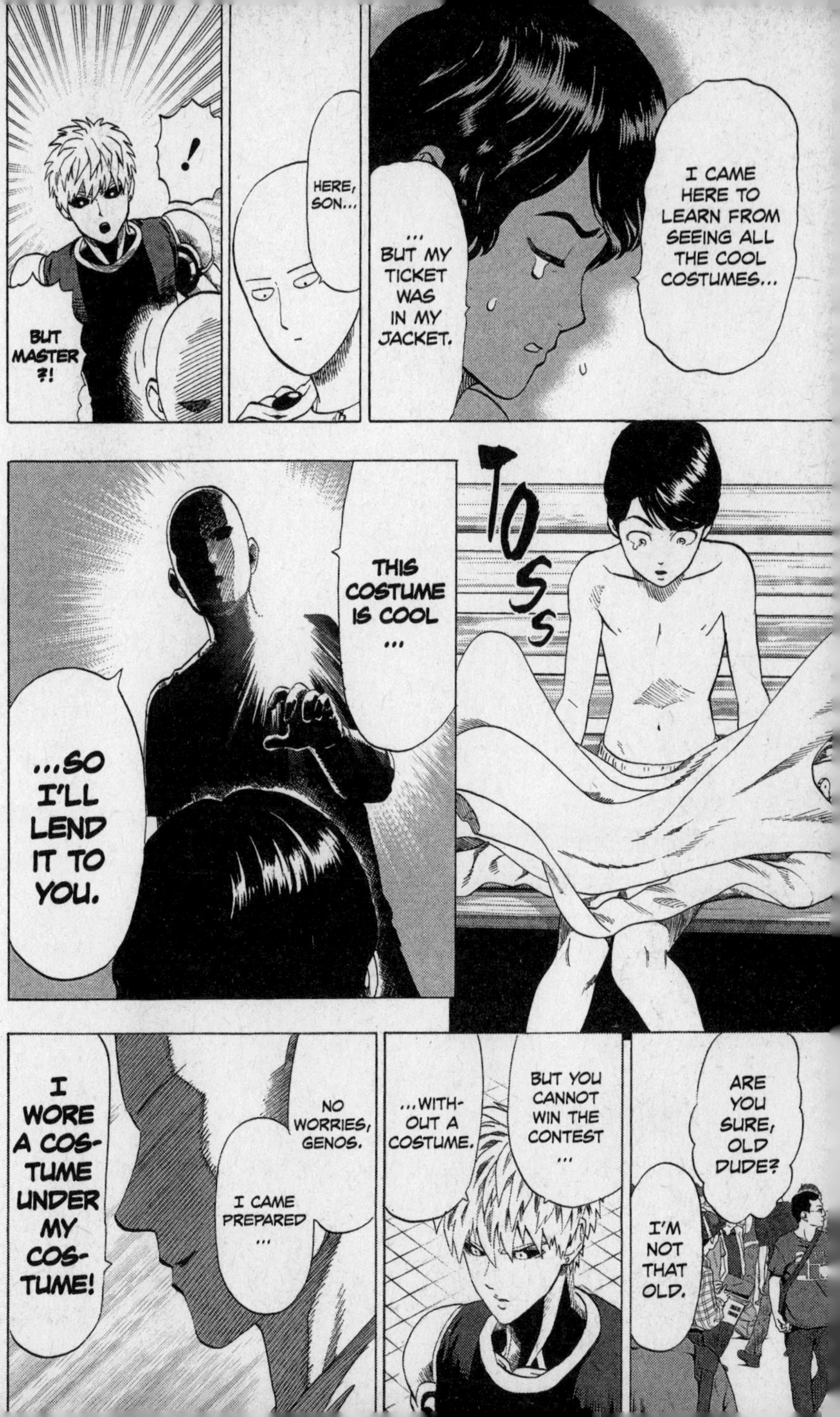
I CAME HERE TO LEARN FROM SEEING ALL THE COOL COSTUMES...
... BUT MY TICKET WAS IN MY JACKET.
HERE, SON...
!
BUT MASTER?!
TOSS
THIS COSTUME IS COOL ...
...SO I'LL LEND IT TO YOU.
ARE YOU SURE, OLD DUDE?
I'M NOT THAT OLD.
BUT YOU CANNOT WIN THE CONTEST ...
...WITHOUT A COSTUME.
NO WORRIES, GENOS.
I CAME PREPARED ...
I WORE A COSTUME UNDER MY COSTUME!

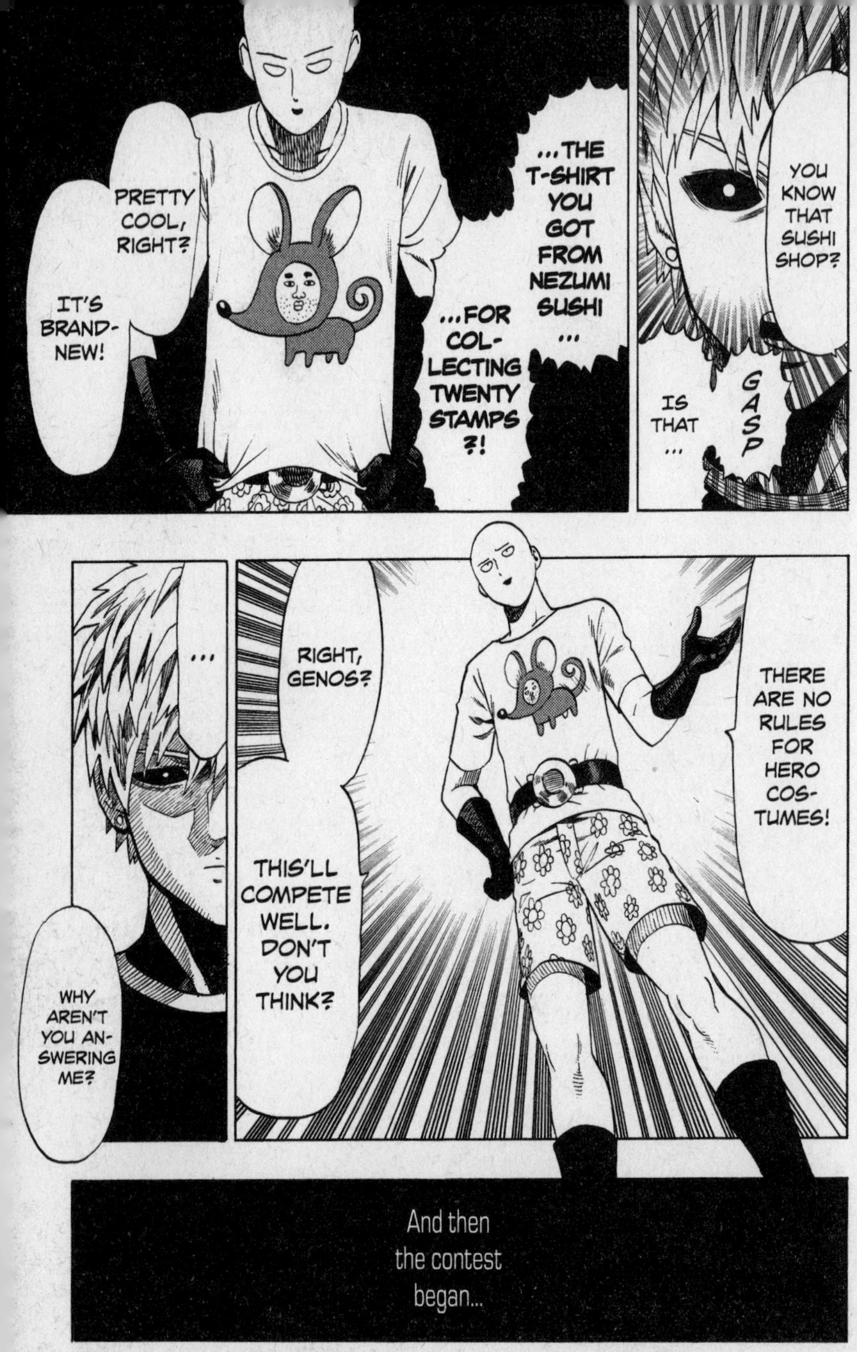
YOU KNOW THAT SUSHI SHOP?
GASP
IS THAT ...
...THE T-SHIRT YOU GOT FROM NEZUMI SUSHI ...
...FOR COL-LECTING TWENTY STAMPS?!
PRETTY COOL, RIGHT?
IT'S BRAND-NEW!
THERE ARE NO RULES FOR HERO COS-TUMES!
RIGHT, GENOS?
THIS'LL COMPETE WELL. DON'T YOU THINK?
...
WHY AREN'T YOU AN-SWERING ME?
And then the contest began...

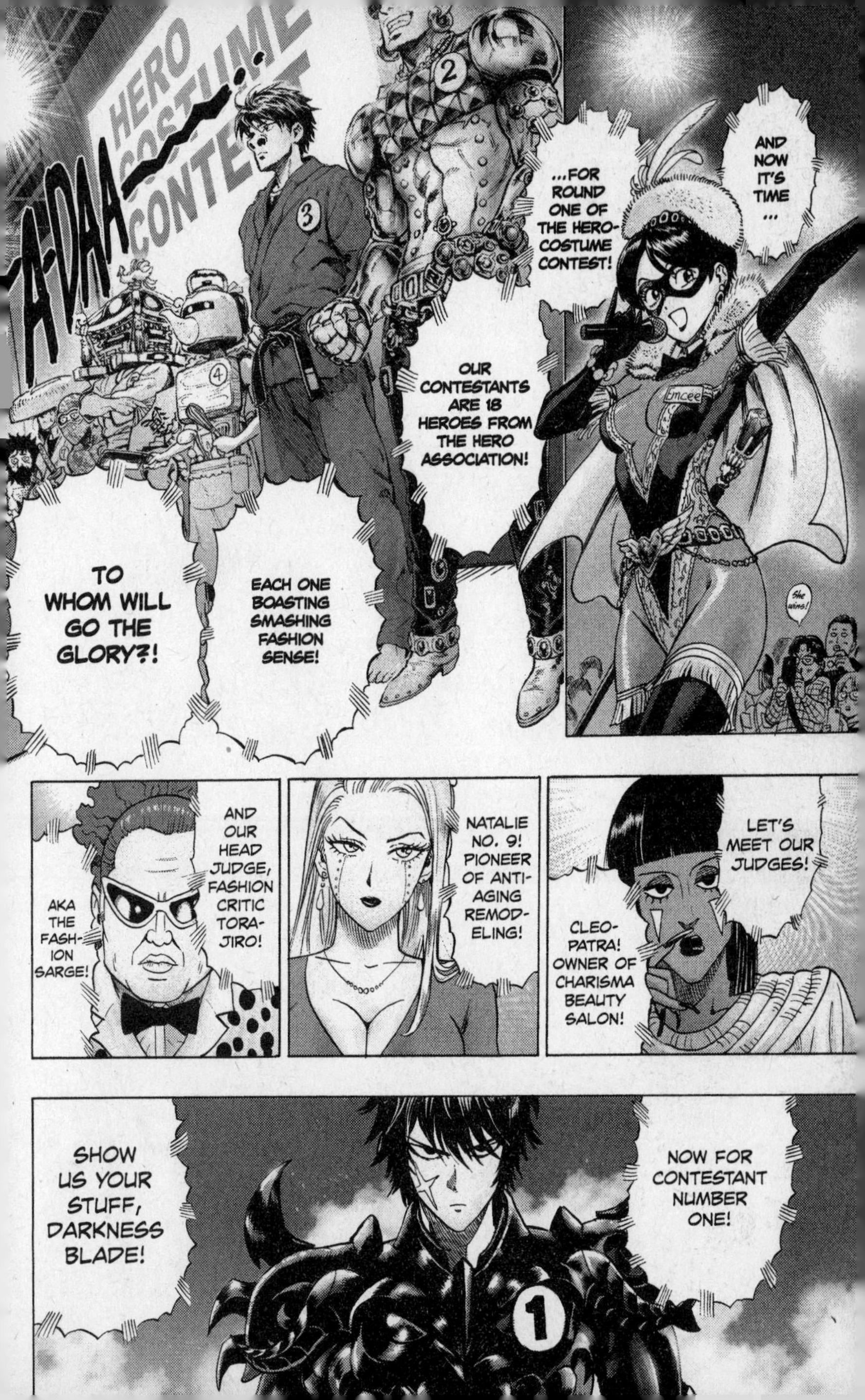
AND NOW IT'S TIME...
...FOR ROUND ONE OF THE HERO-COSTUME CONTEST!
HERO COSTUME CONTEST
TA-DAA—
OUR CONTESTANTS ARE 18 HEROES FROM THE HERO ASSOCIATION!
Emcee
She wins!
EACH ONE BOASTING SMASHING FASHION SENSE!
TO WHOM WILL GO THE GLORY?!
LET'S MEET OUR JUDGES!
CLEOPATRA! OWNER OF CHARISMA BEAUTY SALON!
NATALIE NO. 9! PIONEER OF ANTI-AGING REMODELING!
AND OUR HEAD JUDGE, FASHION CRITIC TORAJIRO!
AKA THE FASHION SARGE!
NOW FOR CONTESTANT NUMBER ONE!
SHOW US YOUR STUFF, DARKNESS BLADE!

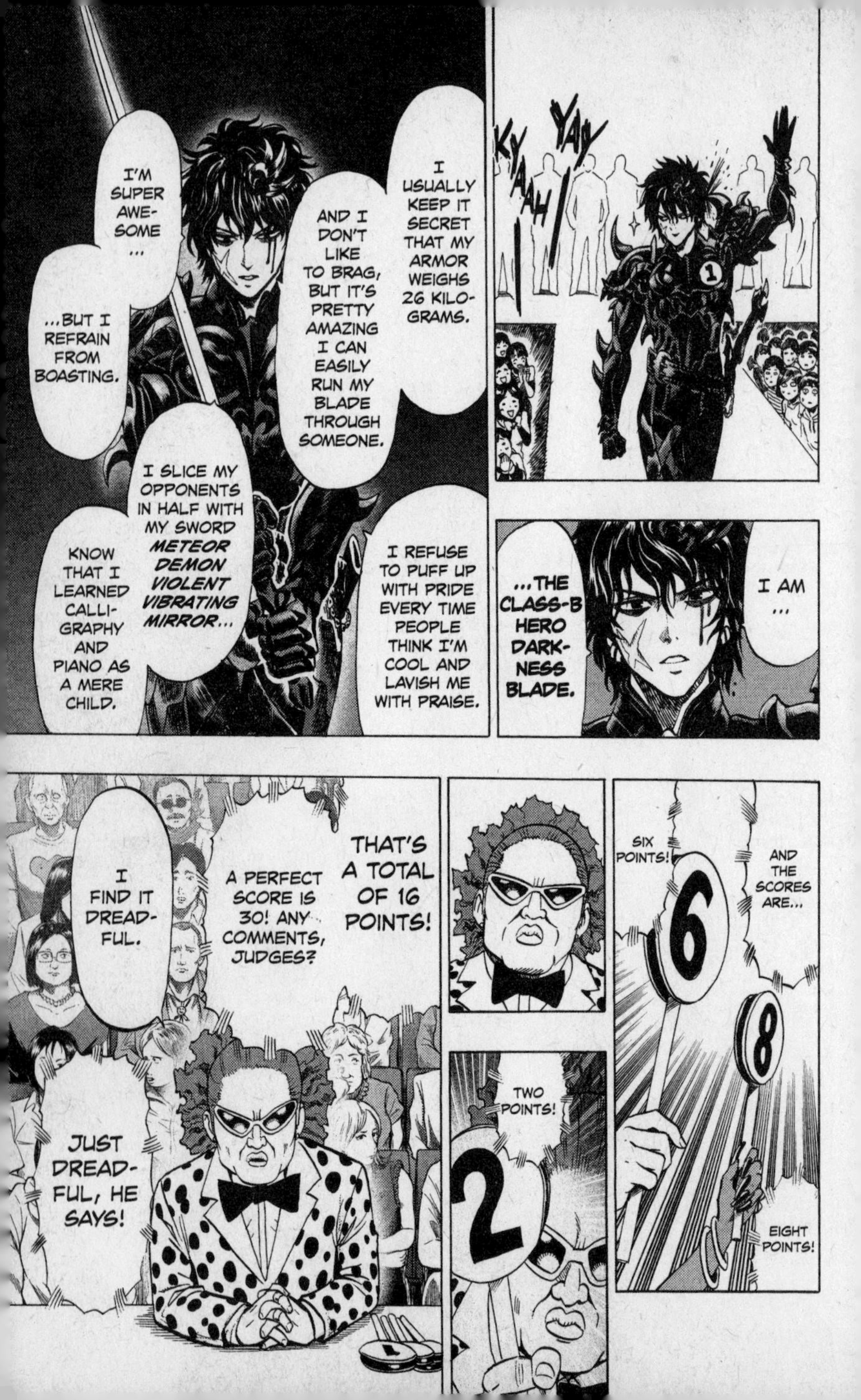
KYAAAH!
YAY
I AM...
...THE CLASS-B HERO DARKNESS BLADE.
I USUALLY KEEP IT SECRET THAT MY ARMOR WEIGHS 26 KILOGRAMS.
AND I DON'T LIKE TO BRAG, BUT IT'S PRETTY AMAZING I CAN EASILY RUN MY BLADE THROUGH SOMEONE.
I'M SUPER AWESOME...
...BUT I REFRAIN FROM BOASTING.
I REFUSE TO PUFF UP WITH PRIDE EVERY TIME PEOPLE THINK I'M COOL AND LAVISH ME WITH PRAISE.
I SLICE MY OPPONENTS IN HALF WITH MY SWORD *METEOR DEMON VIOLENT VIBRATING MIRROR*...
KNOW THAT I LEARNED CALLIGRAPHY AND PIANO AS A MERE CHILD.
AND THE SCORES ARE...
SIX POINTS!
6
8
EIGHT POINTS!
TWO POINTS!
2
THAT'S A TOTAL OF 16 POINTS!
A PERFECT SCORE IS 30! ANY COMMENTS, JUDGES?
I FIND IT DREADFUL.
JUST DREADFUL, HE SAYS!

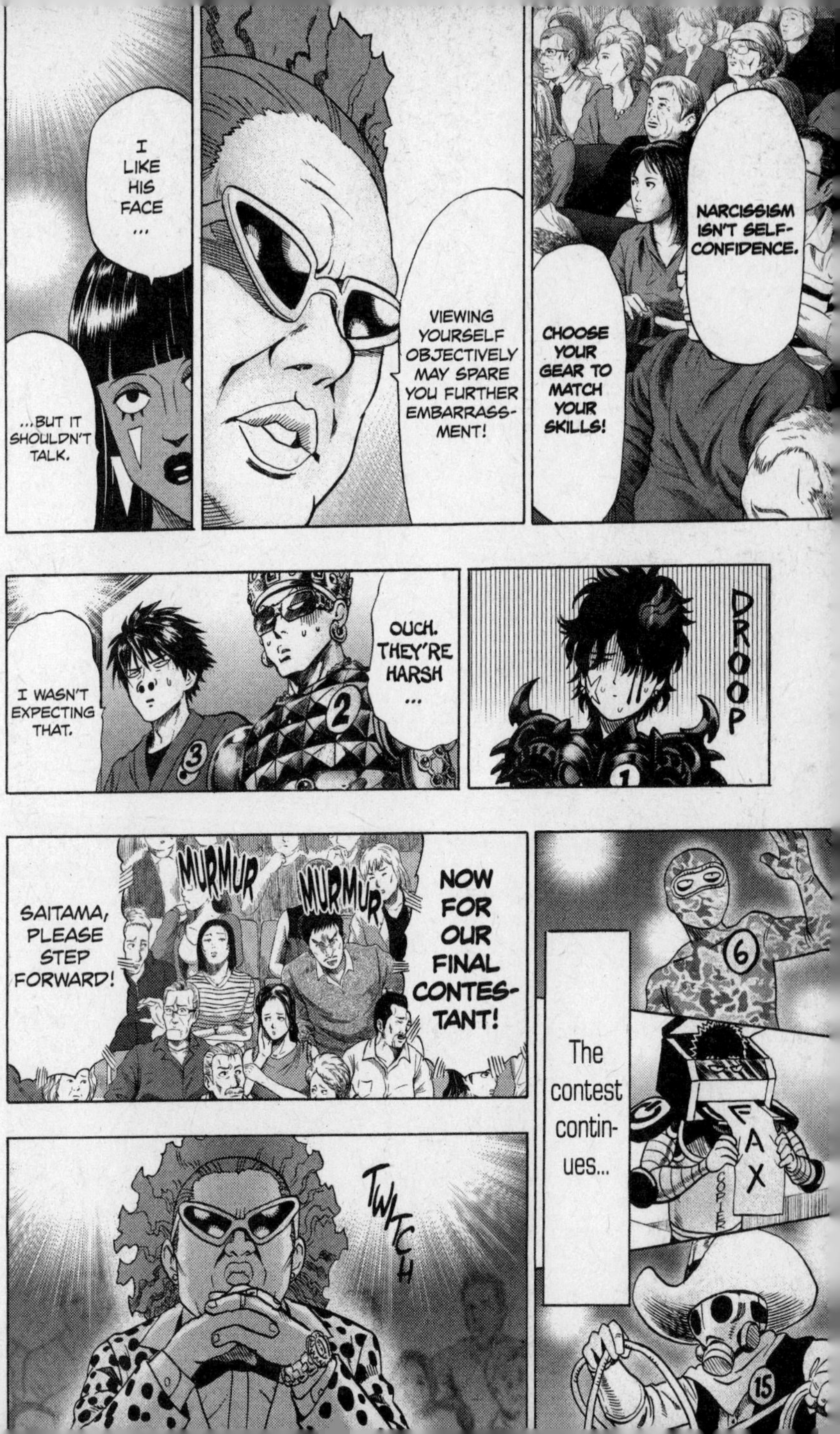
NARCISSISM ISN'T SELF-CONFIDENCE.
CHOOSE YOUR GEAR TO MATCH YOUR SKILLS!
VIEWING YOURSELF OBJECTIVELY MAY SPARE YOU FURTHER EMBARRASS-MENT!
I LIKE HIS FACE...
...BUT IT SHOULDN'T TALK.
DROOP
OUCH. THEY'RE HARSH...
I WASN'T EXPECTING THAT.
FAX
COPIER
The contest contin-ues...
NOW FOR OUR FINAL CONTES-TANT!
MURMUR
MURMUR
SAITAMA, PLEASE STEP FORWARD!
TWITCH

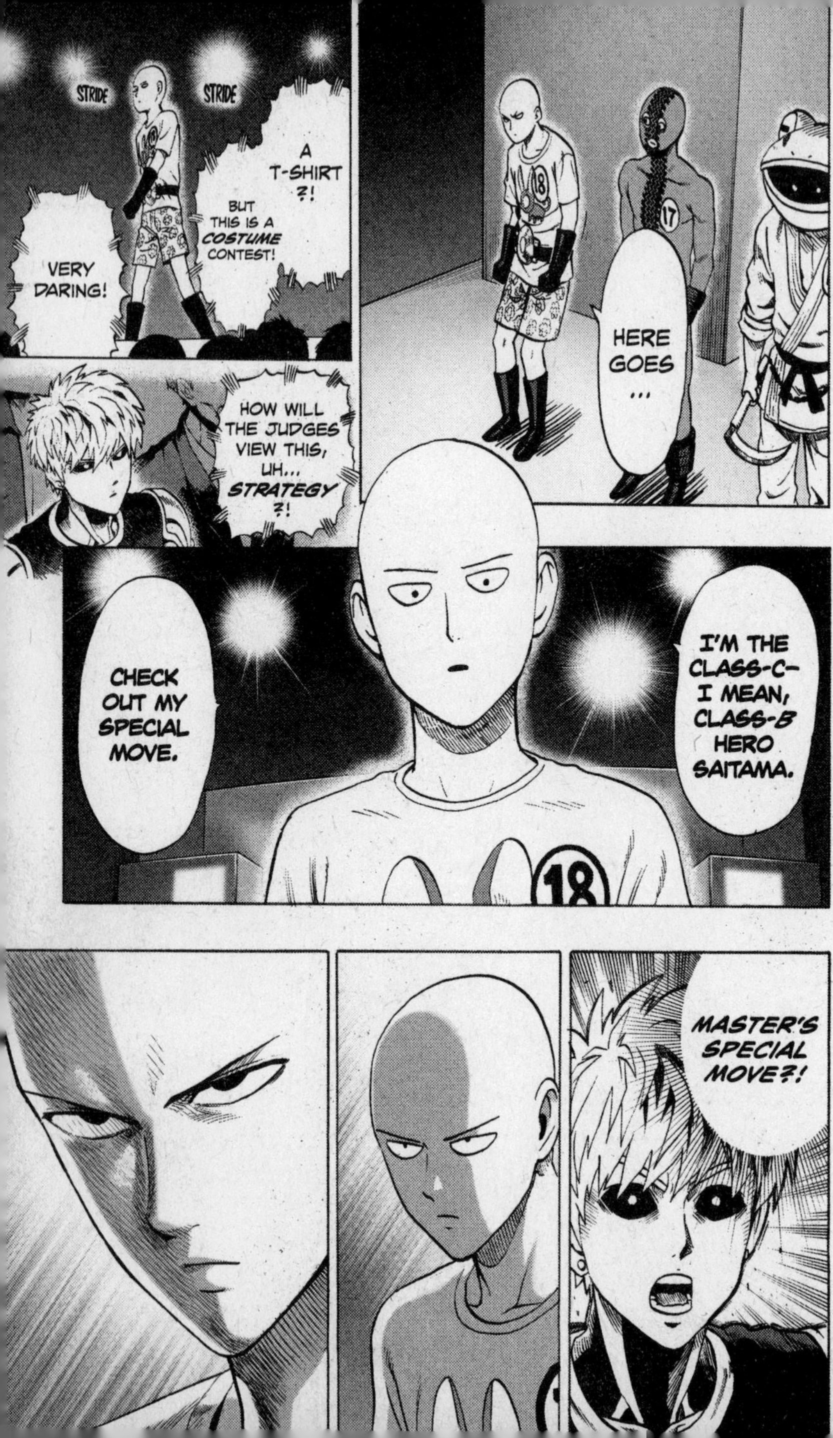
HERE GOES...
STRIDE
STRIDE
A T-SHIRT?!
BUT THIS IS A COSTUME CONTEST!
VERY DARING!
HOW WILL THE JUDGES VIEW THIS, UH... STRATEGY?!
I'M THE CLASS-C— I MEAN, CLASS-B HERO SAITAMA.
CHECK OUT MY SPECIAL MOVE.
MASTER'S SPECIAL MOVE?!

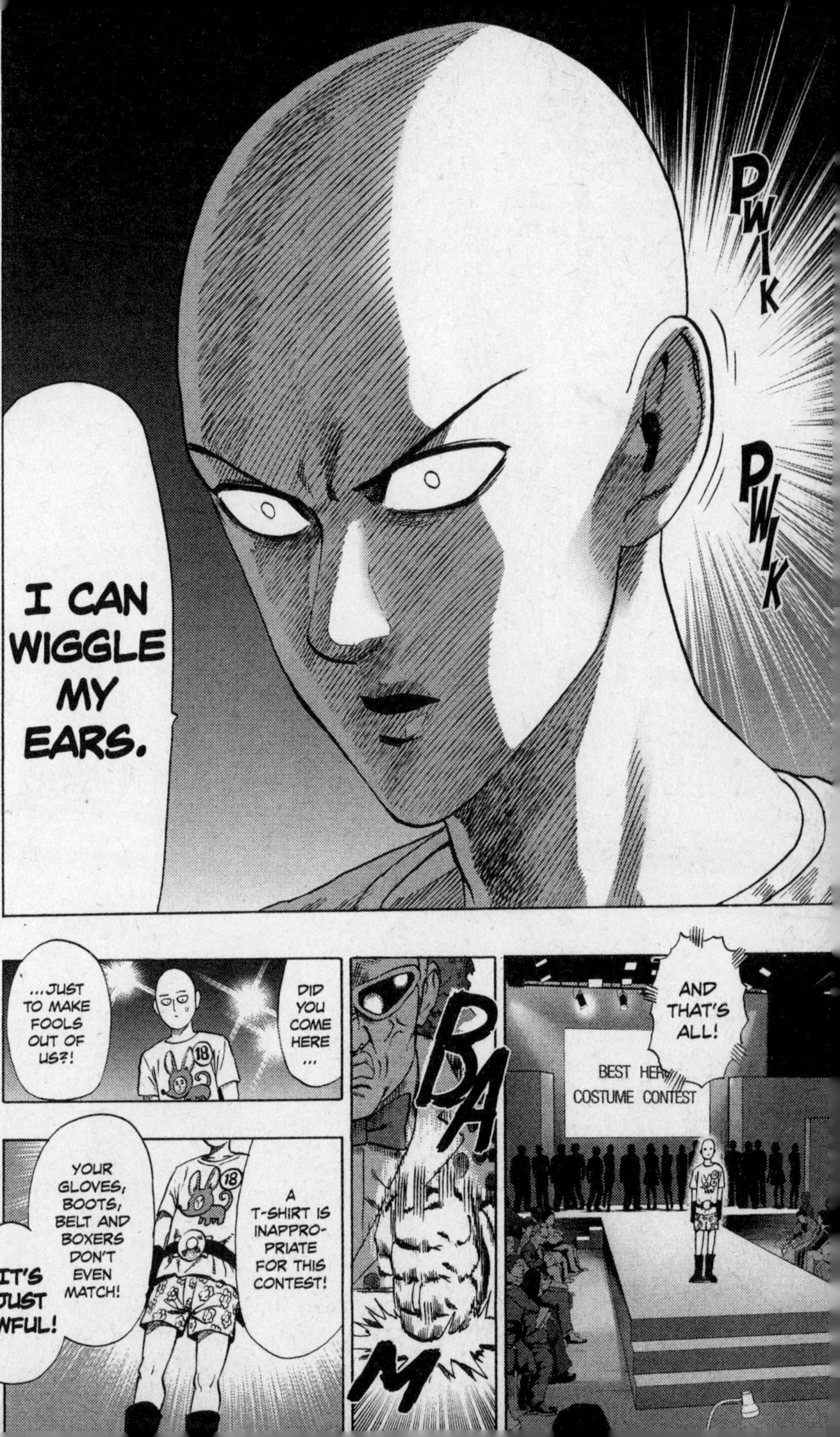
PWIK
PWIK
I CAN WIGGLE MY EARS.
AND THAT'S ALL!
BEST HER
COSTUME CONTEST
BAM
DID YOU COME HERE ...
...JUST TO MAKE FOOLS OUT OF US?!
A T-SHIRT IS INAPPRO-PRIATE FOR THIS CONTEST!
YOUR GLOVES, BOOTS, BELT AND BOXERS DON'T EVEN MATCH!
IT'S JUST AWFUL!

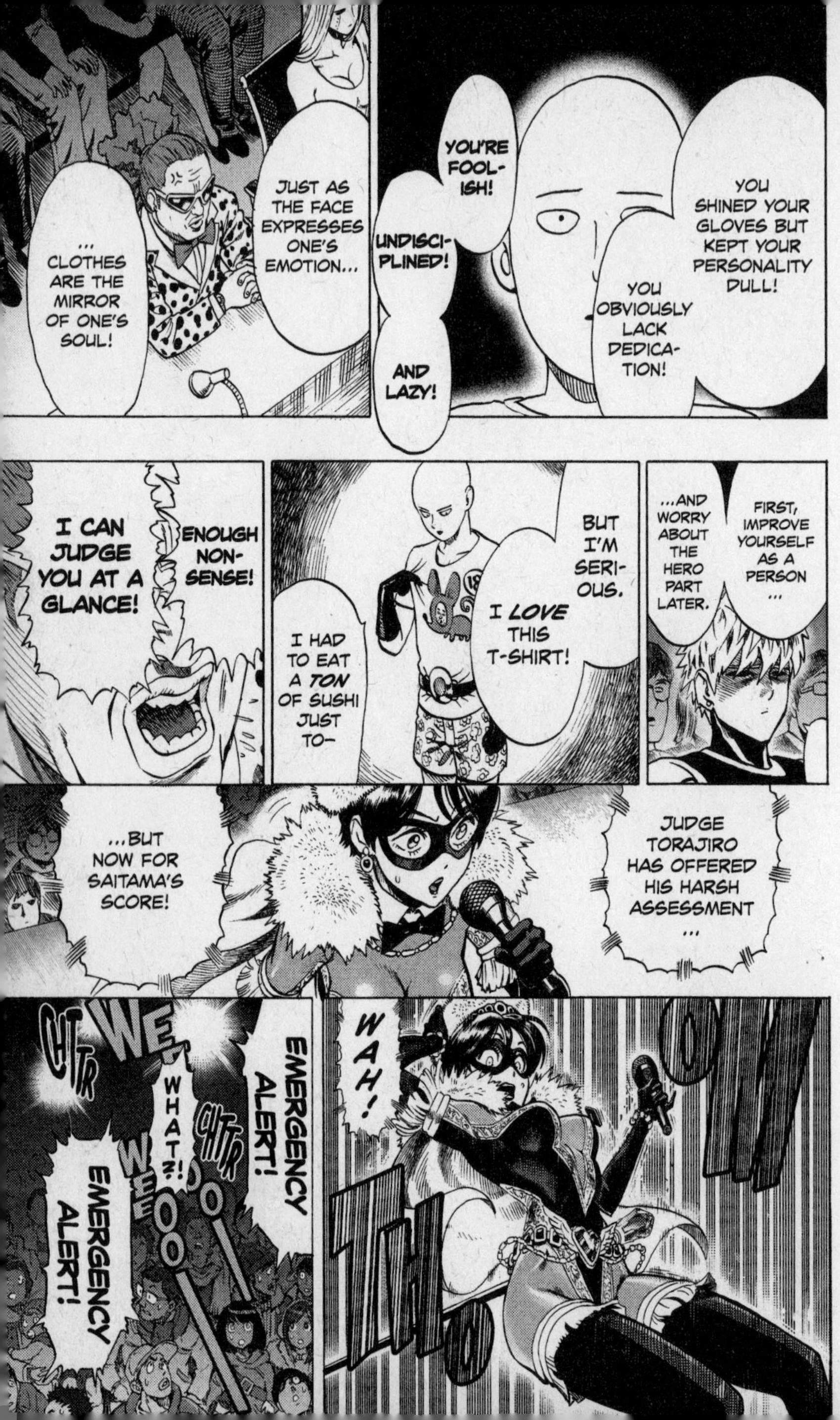
YOU SHINED YOUR GLOVES BUT KEPT YOUR PERSONALITY DULL!
YOU OBVIOUSLY LACK DEDICATION!
YOU'RE FOOLISH!
UNDISCIPLINED!
AND LAZY!
JUST AS THE FACE EXPRESSES ONE'S EMOTION...
...CLOTHES ARE THE MIRROR OF ONE'S SOUL!
FIRST, IMPROVE YOURSELF AS A PERSON ...
...AND WORRY ABOUT THE HERO PART LATER.
BUT I'M SERIOUS.
I *LOVE* THIS T-SHIRT!
I HAD TO EAT A *TON* OF SUSHI JUST TO–
ENOUGH NONSENSE!
I CAN JUDGE YOU AT A GLANCE!
JUDGE TORAJIRO HAS OFFERED HIS HARSH ASSESSMENT ...
...BUT NOW FOR SAITAMA'S SCORE!
WAH!
EMERGENCY ALERT!
WHAT?!
EMERGENCY ALERT!
CHTTR
CHTTR

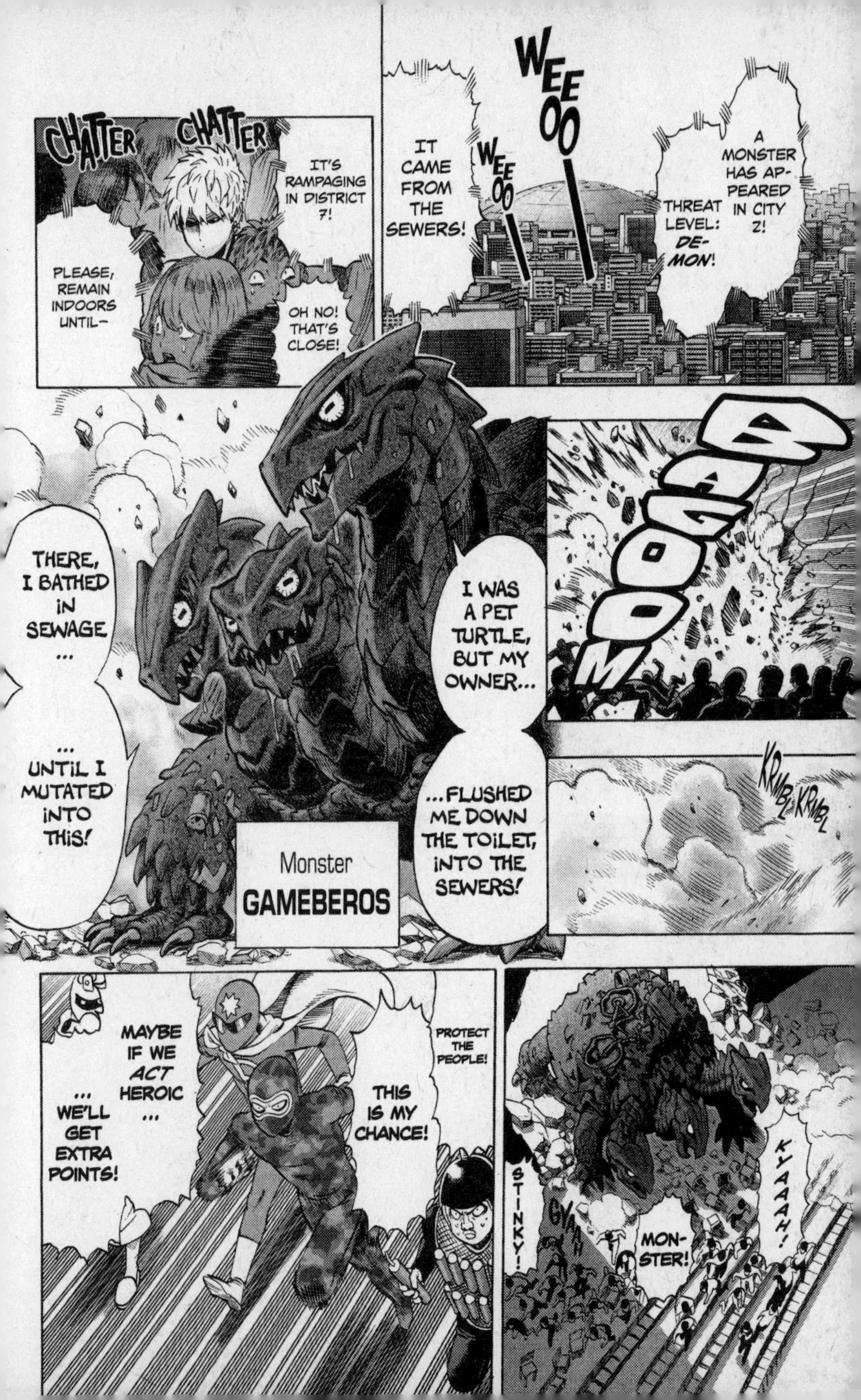
A MONSTER HAS APPEARED IN CITY Z!
THREAT LEVEL: *DEMON*!
WEEOO
WEEOO
IT CAME FROM THE SEWERS!
CHATTER CHATTER
IT'S RAMPAGING IN DISTRICT 7!
OH NO! THAT'S CLOSE!
PLEASE, REMAIN INDOORS UNTIL-
BAGOOM
KRMBL KRMBL
I WAS A PET TURTLE, BUT MY OWNER...
...FLUSHED ME DOWN THE TOILET, INTO THE SEWERS!
THERE, I BATHED IN SEWAGE ...
... UNTIL I MUTATED INTO THIS!
Monster
GAMEBEROS
KYAAAH!
MONSTER!
GYAAH
STINKY!
PROTECT THE PEOPLE!
THIS IS MY CHANCE!
MAYBE IF WE *ACT* HEROIC ...
... WE'LL GET EXTRA POINTS!

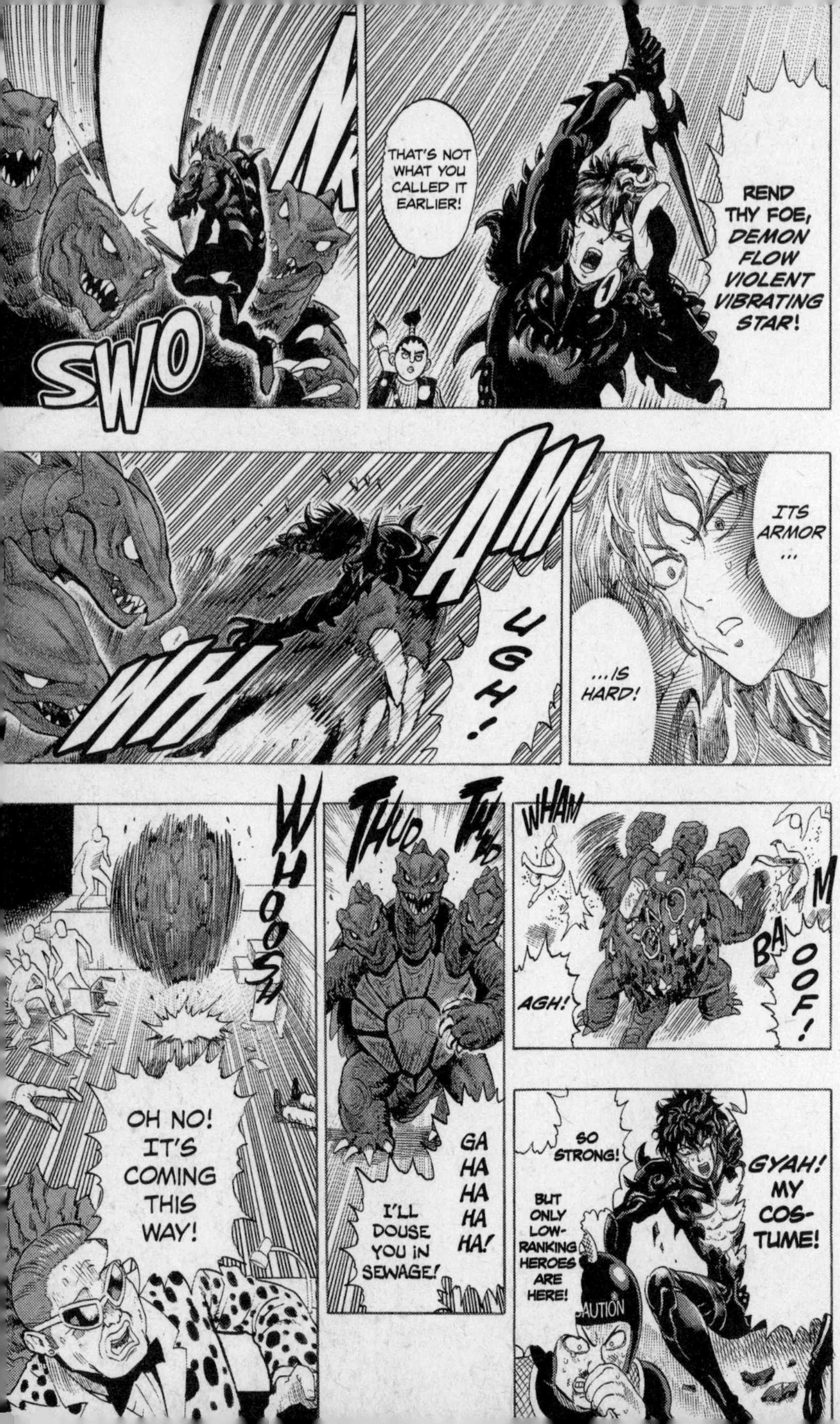
REND THY FOE, DEMON FLOW VIOLENT VIBRATING STAR!
THAT'S NOT WHAT YOU CALLED IT EARLIER!
SWO
ITS ARMOR ...
...IS HARD!
UGH!
WH
AM
WHAM
BAM
AGH!
OOF!
GYAH! MY COS-TUME!
SO STRONG!
BUT ONLY LOW-RANKING HEROES ARE HERE!
THUD
THUD
GA HA HA HA HA HA!
I'LL DOUSE YOU IN SEWAGE!
WHOOSH
OH NO! IT'S COMING THIS WAY!

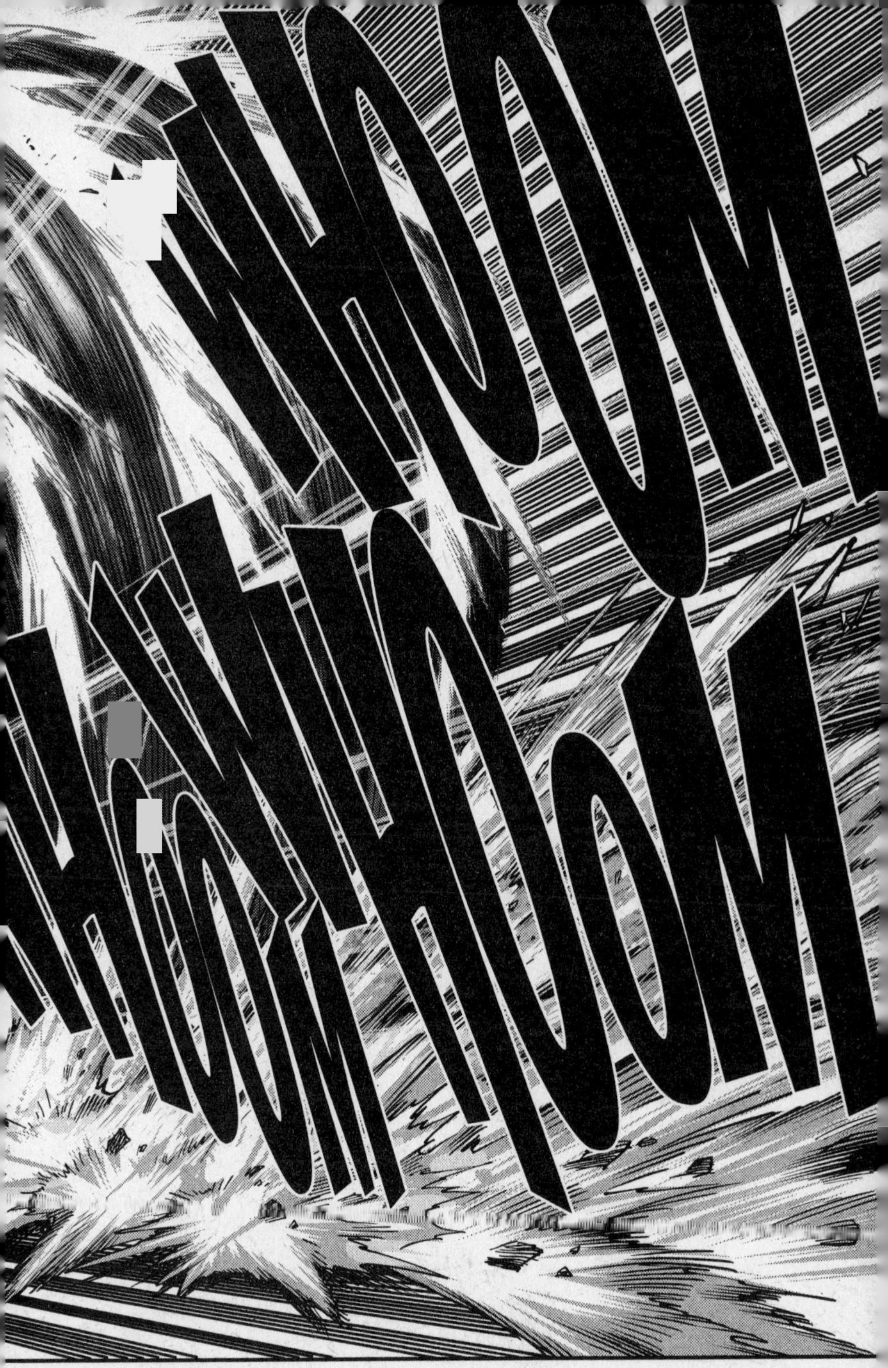

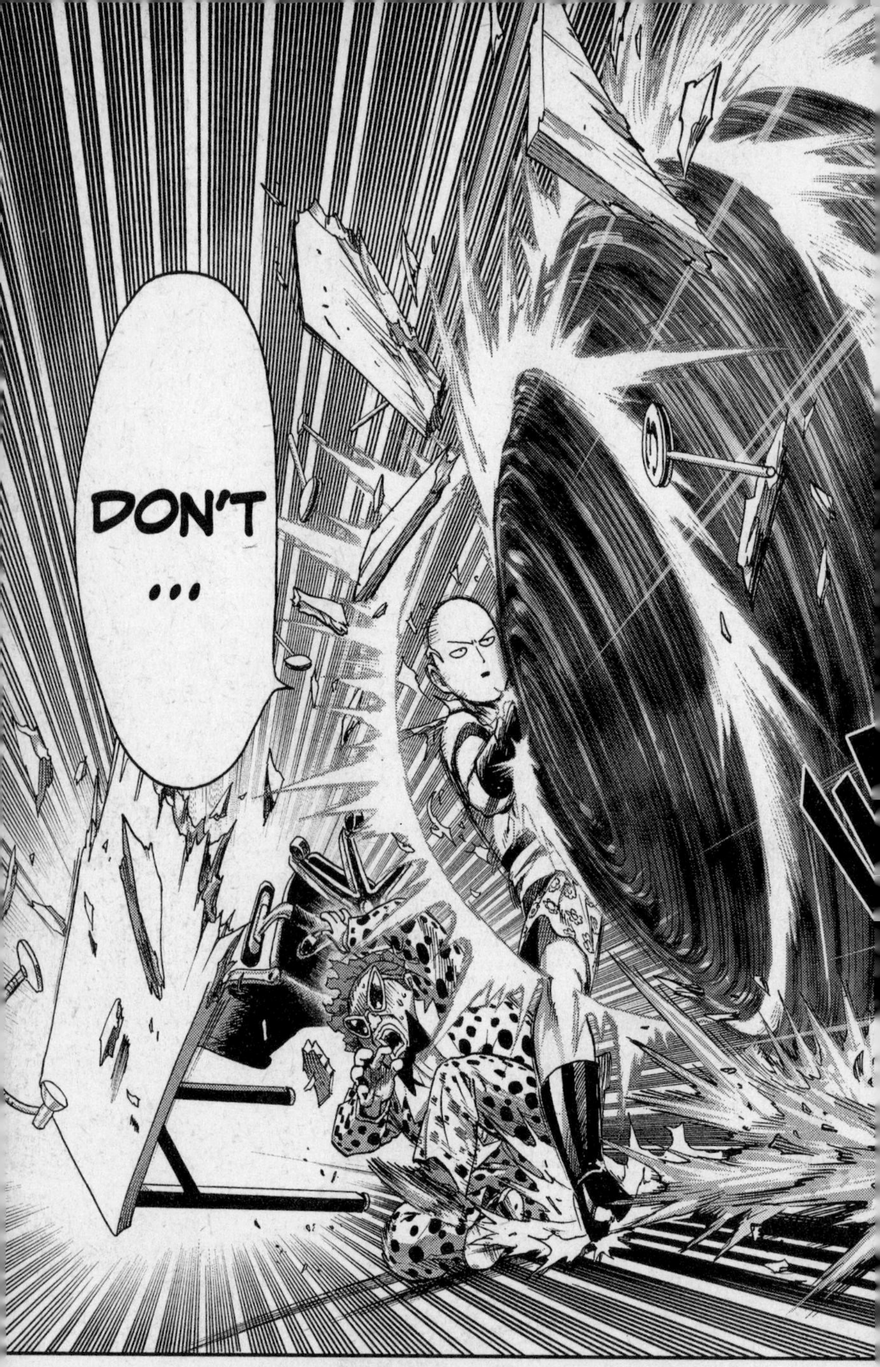
DON'T
...

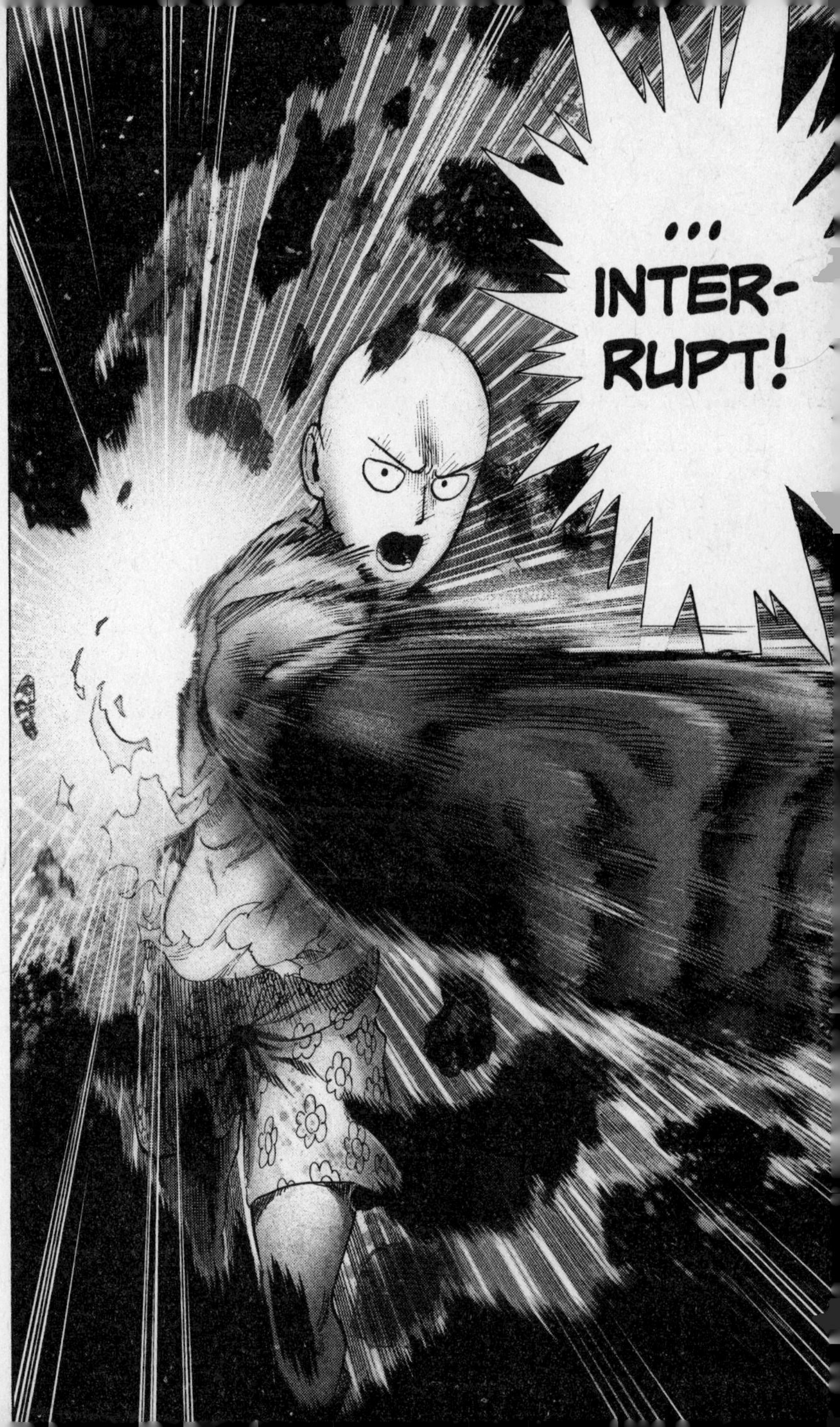
...INTER-RUPT!

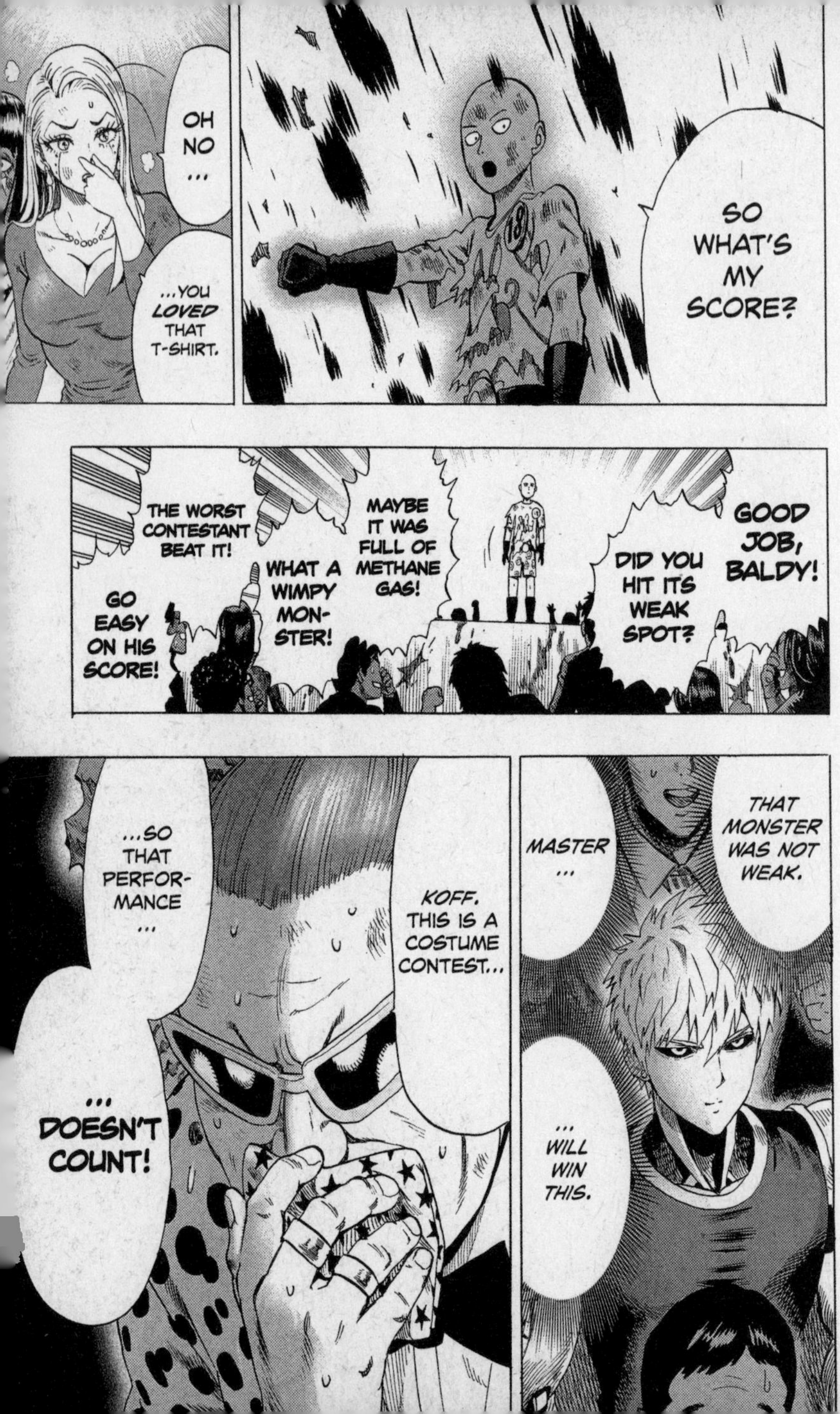
SO WHAT'S MY SCORE?
OH NO ...
...YOU *LOVED* THAT T-SHIRT.
GOOD JOB, BALDY!
DID YOU HIT ITS WEAK SPOT?
MAYBE IT WAS FULL OF METHANE GAS!
THE WORST CONTESTANT BEAT IT!
WHAT A WIMPY MONSTER!
GO EASY ON HIS SCORE!
THAT MONSTER WAS NOT WEAK.
MASTER ...
... WILL WIN THIS.
KOFF. THIS IS A COSTUME CONTEST...
...SO THAT PERFORMANCE ...
... DOESN'T COUNT!

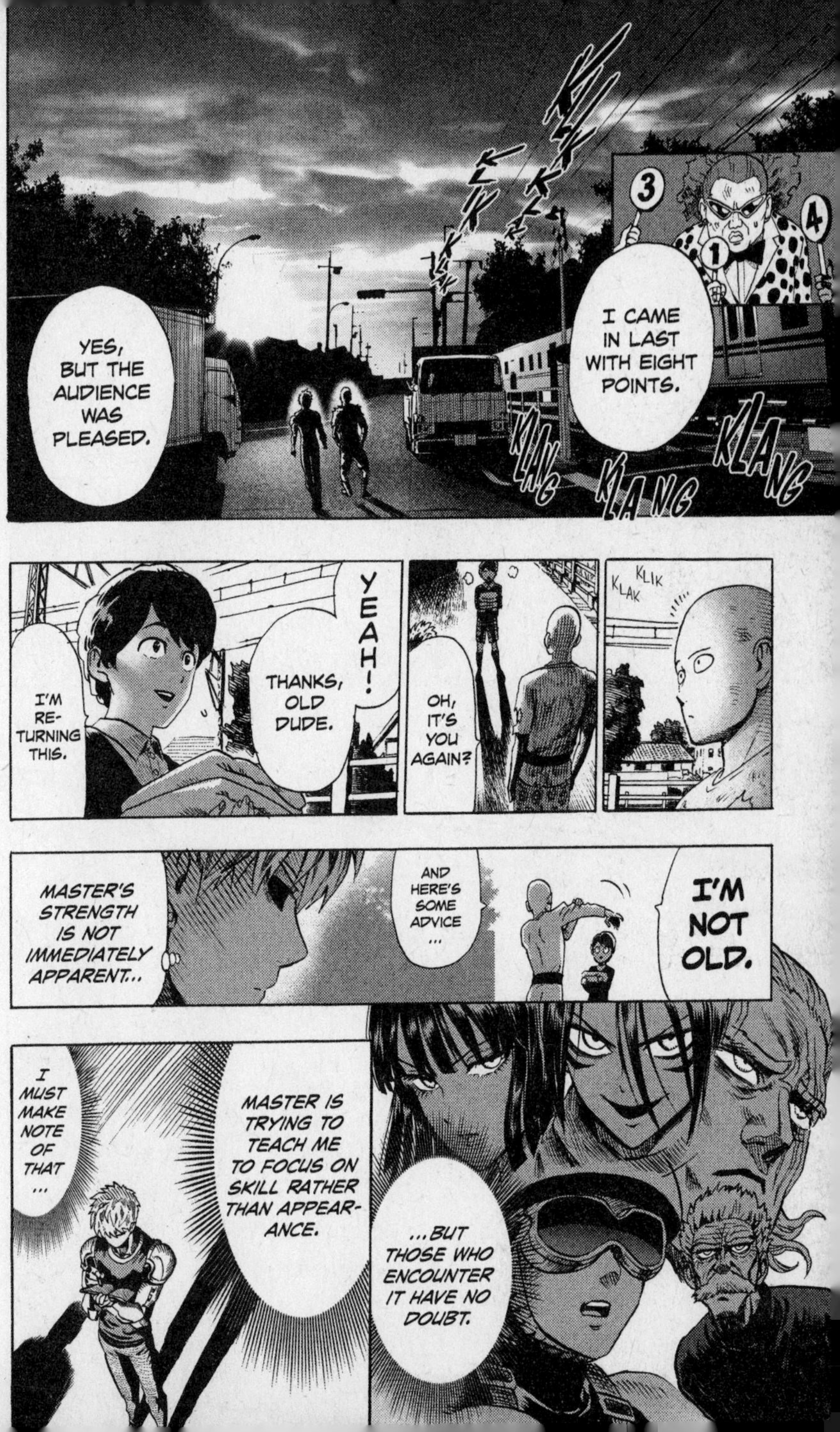
KLIK KLAK
3
1
4
I CAME IN LAST WITH EIGHT POINTS.
KLANG
KLANG
KLANG
YES, BUT THE AUDIENCE WAS PLEASED.
KLIK KLAK
OH, IT'S YOU AGAIN?
YEAH!
THANKS, OLD DUDE.
I'M RE-TURNING THIS.
I'M NOT OLD.
AND HERE'S SOME ADVICE...
MASTER'S STRENGTH IS NOT IMMEDIATELY APPARENT...
...BUT THOSE WHO ENCOUNTER IT HAVE NO DOUBT.
MASTER IS TRYING TO TEACH ME TO FOCUS ON SKILL RATHER THAN APPEAR-ANCE.
I MUST MAKE NOTE OF THAT...

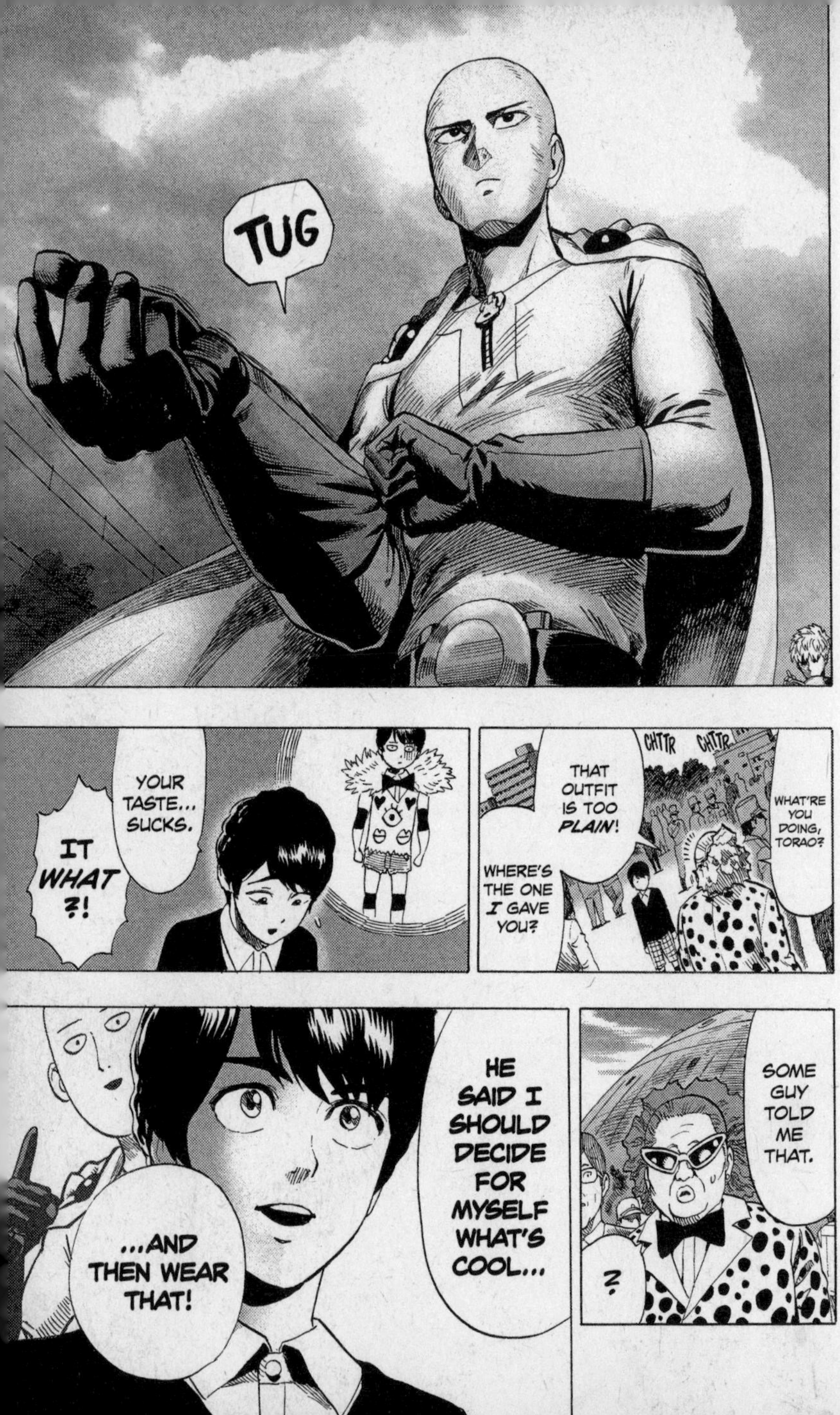
TUG
CHTTR
CHTTR
WHAT'RE YOU DOING, TORAO?
THAT OUTFIT IS TOO *PLAIN*!
WHERE'S THE ONE *I* GAVE YOU?
YOUR TASTE... SUCKS.
IT *WHAT*?!
SOME GUY TOLD ME THAT.
?
HE SAID I SHOULD DECIDE FOR MYSELF WHAT'S COOL...
...AND THEN WEAR THAT!

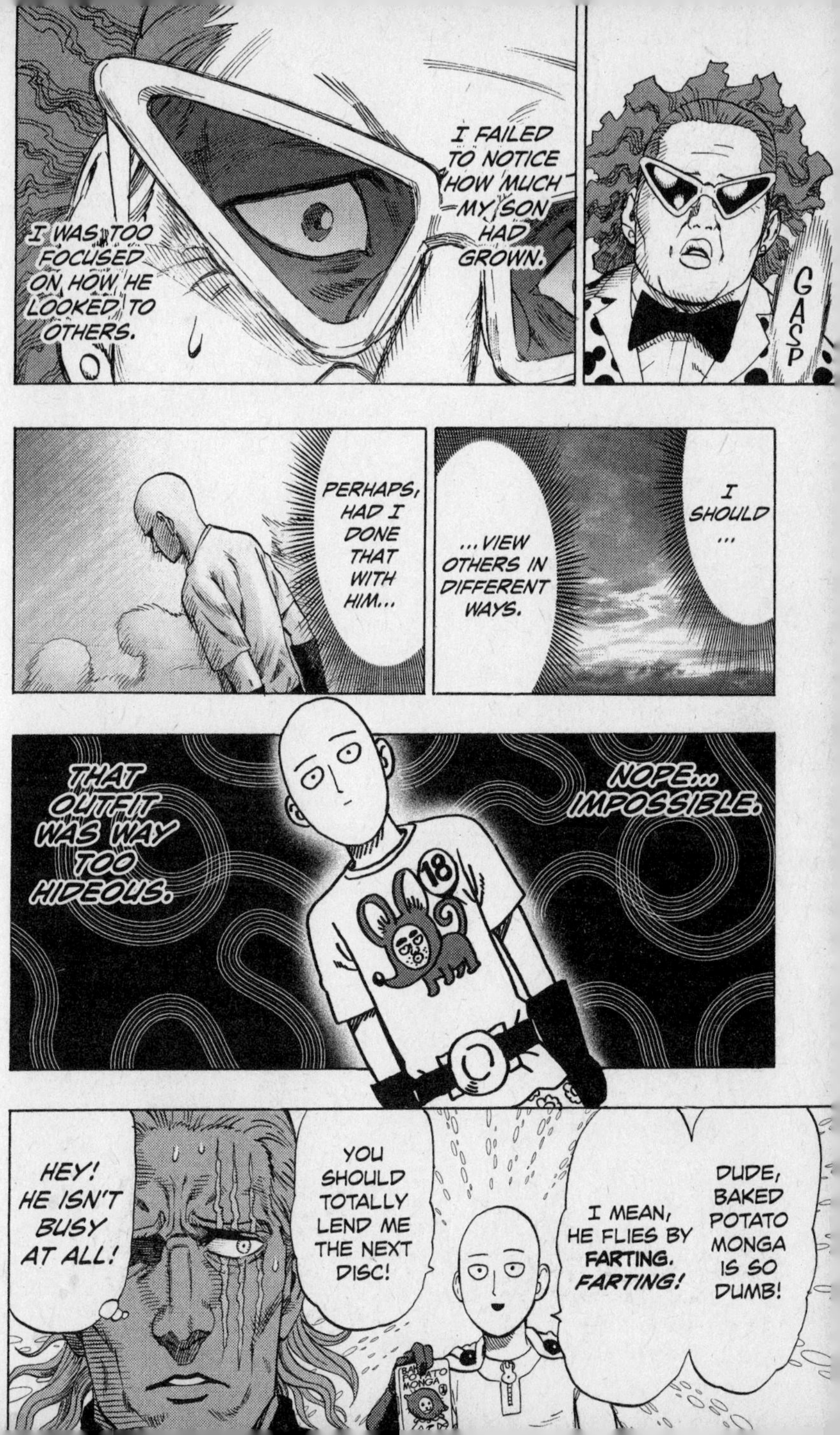
GASP
I FAILED TO NOTICE HOW MUCH MY SON HAD GROWN.
I WAS TOO FOCUSED ON HOW HE LOOKED TO OTHERS.
I SHOULD ...
...VIEW OTHERS IN DIFFERENT WAYS.
PERHAPS, HAD I DONE THAT WITH HIM...
NOPE... IMPOSSIBLE.
THAT OUTFIT WAS WAY TOO HIDEOUS.
DUDE, BAKED POTATO MONGA IS SO DUMB!
I MEAN, HE FLIES BY **FARTING**. *FARTING!*
YOU SHOULD TOTALLY LEND ME THE NEXT DISC!
HEY! HE ISN'T BUSY AT ALL!

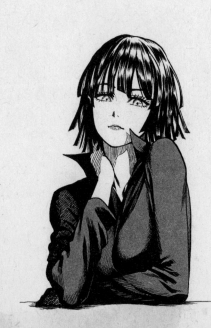

ONE-PUNCH MAN|10
ONE + YUSUKE MURATA

BONUS MANGA 3: NUMBERS

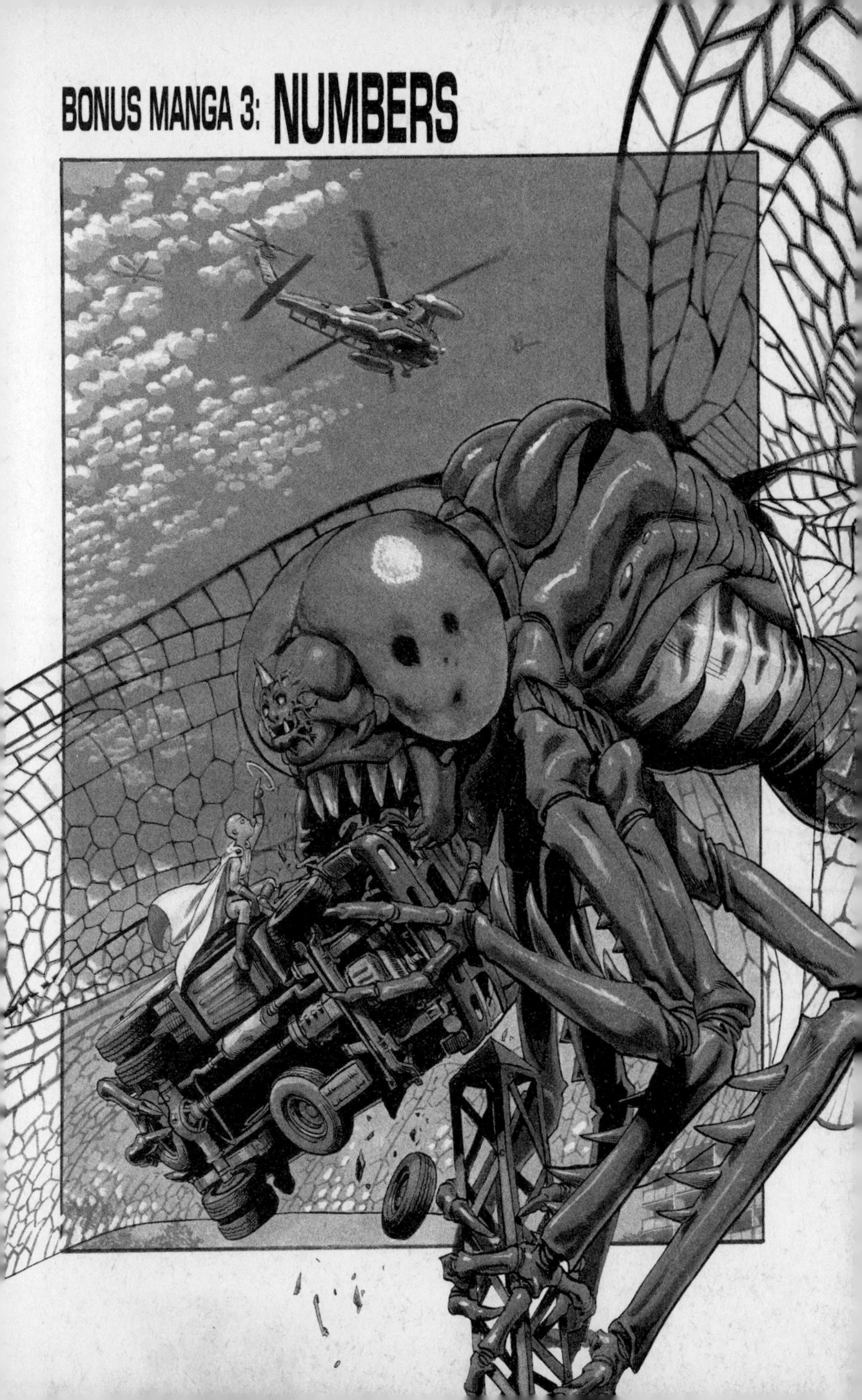

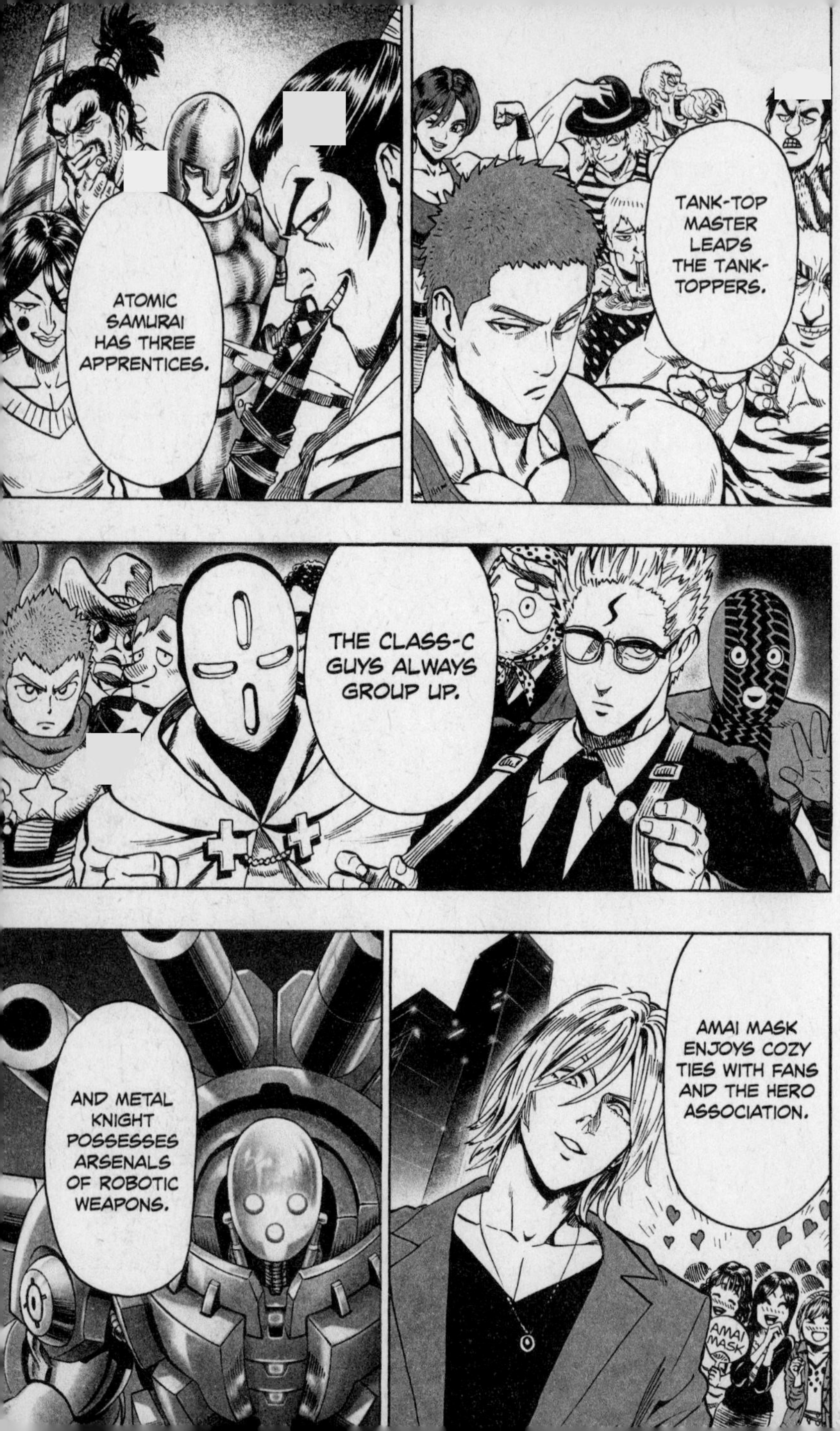
TANK-TOP MASTER LEADS THE TANK-TOPPERS.
ATOMIC SAMURAI HAS THREE APPRENTICES.
THE CLASS-C GUYS ALWAYS GROUP UP.
AMAI MASK ENJOYS COZY TIES WITH FANS AND THE HERO ASSOCIATION.
AMAI MASK
AND METAL KNIGHT POSSESSES ARSENALS OF ROBOTIC WEAPONS.

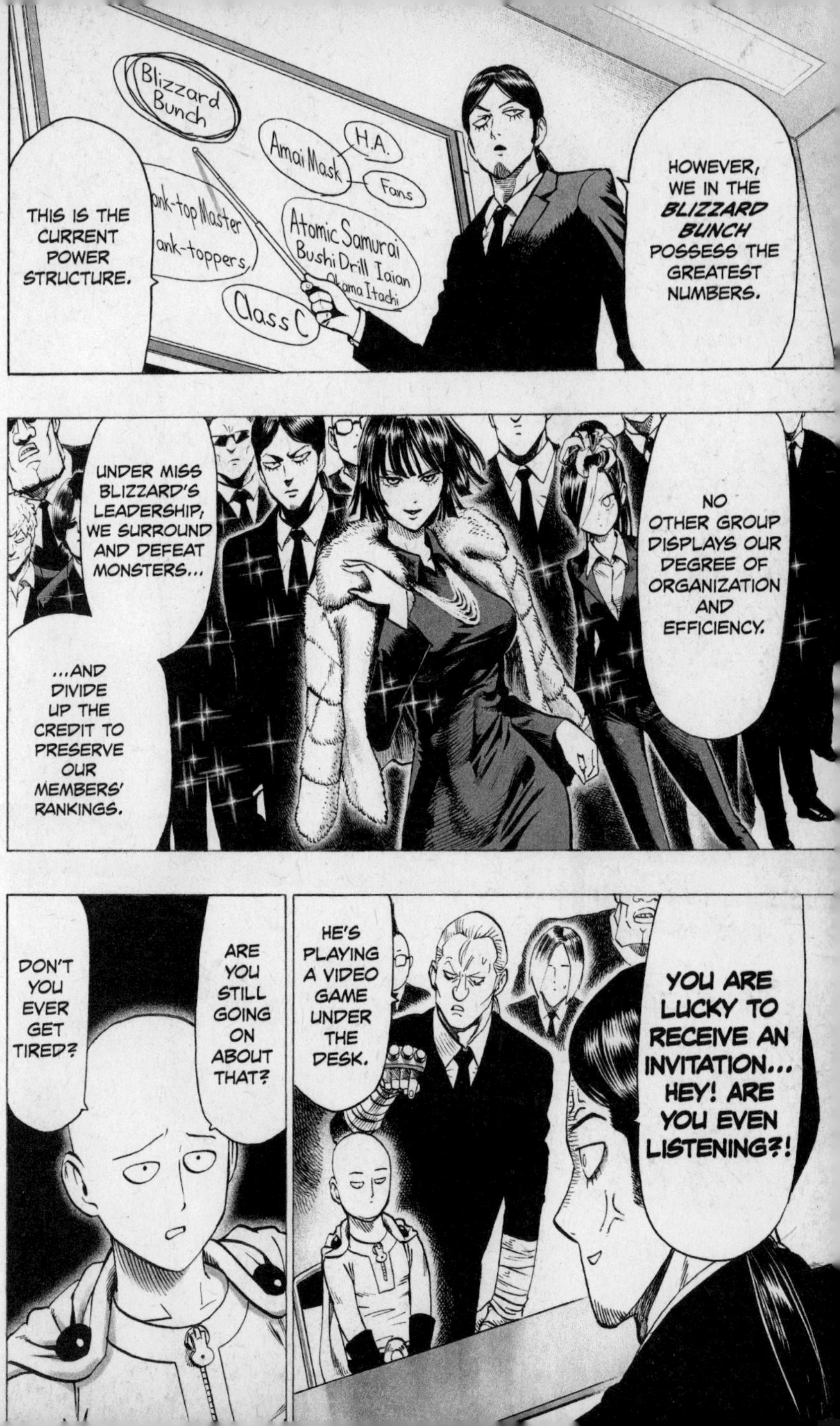
HOWEVER, WE IN THE *BLIZZARD BUNCH* POSSESS THE GREATEST NUMBERS.
Blizzard Bunch
H.A.
Amai Mask
Fans
ank-top Master
ank-toppers
Atomic Samurai
Bushi Drill Iaian
Okama Itachi
Class C
THIS IS THE CURRENT POWER STRUCTURE.
NO OTHER GROUP DISPLAYS OUR DEGREE OF ORGANIZATION AND EFFICIENCY.
UNDER MISS BLIZZARD'S LEADERSHIP, WE SURROUND AND DEFEAT MONSTERS...
...AND DIVIDE UP THE CREDIT TO PRESERVE OUR MEMBERS' RANKINGS.
YOU ARE LUCKY TO RECEIVE AN INVITATION... HEY! ARE YOU EVEN LISTENING?!
HE'S PLAYING A VIDEO GAME UNDER THE DESK.
ARE YOU STILL GOING ON ABOUT THAT?
DON'T YOU EVER GET TIRED?

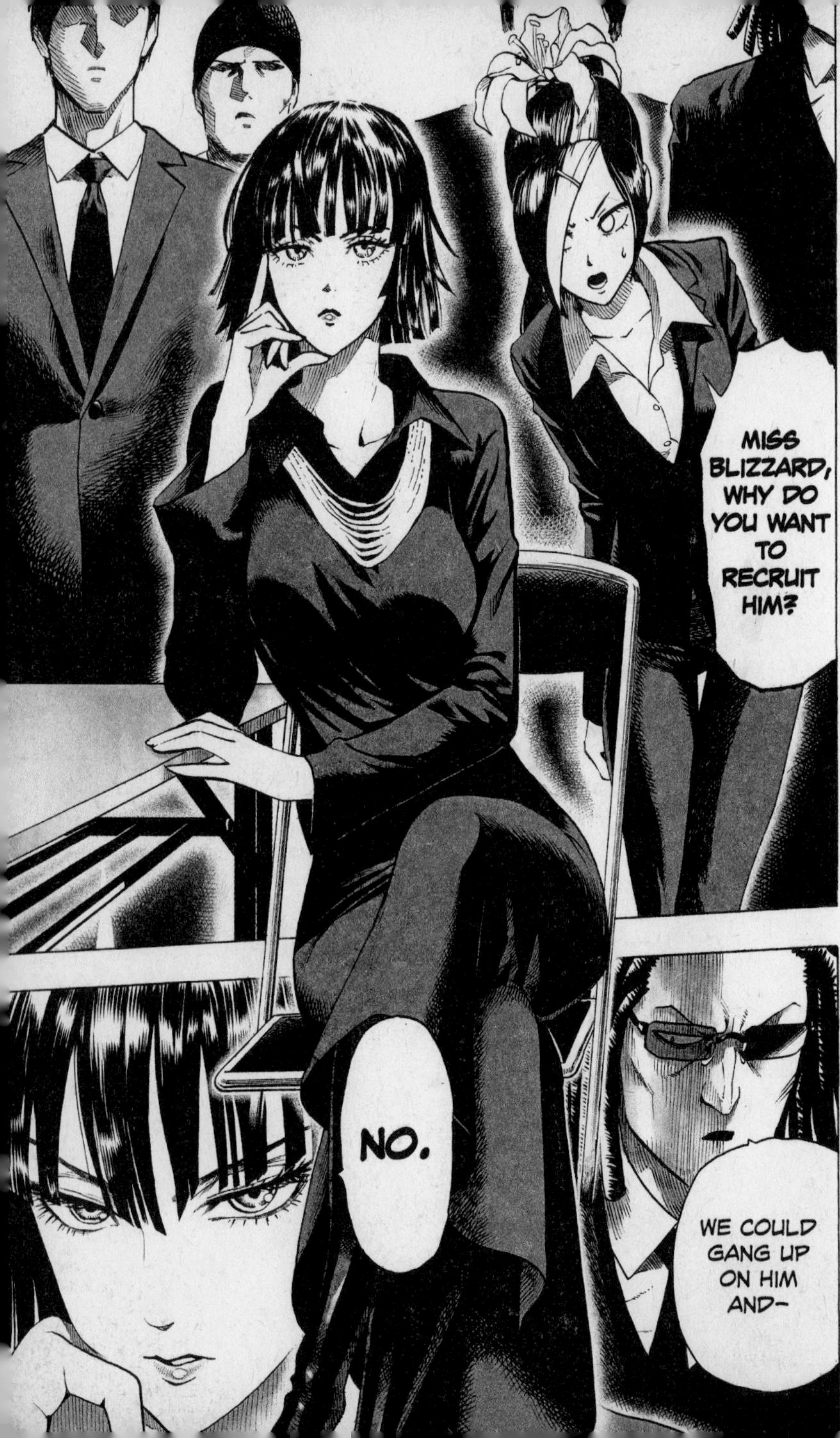
MISS BLIZZARD, WHY DO YOU WANT TO RECRUIT HIM?
WE COULD GANG UP ON HIM AND-
NO.

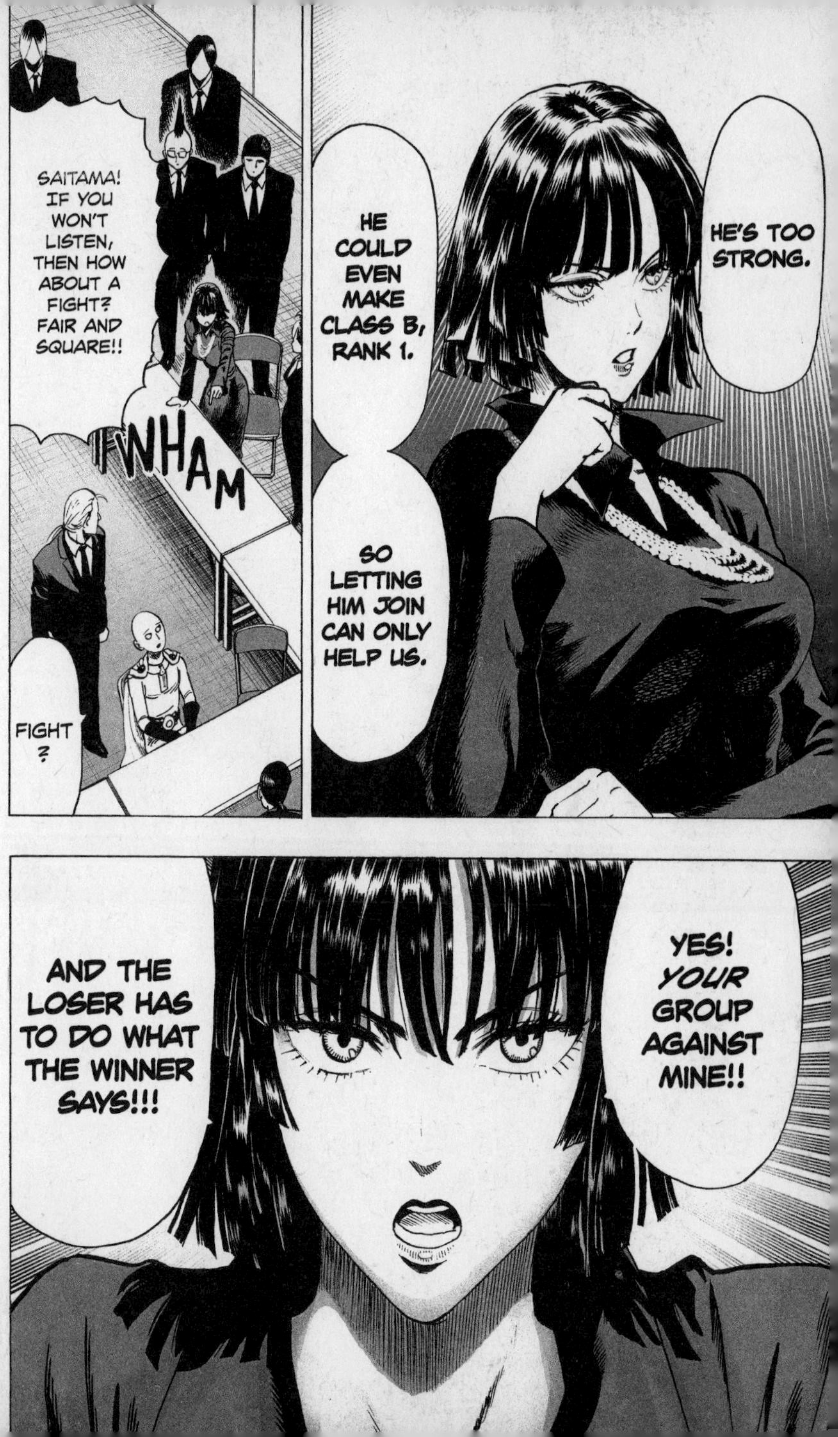
HE'S TOO STRONG.
HE COULD EVEN MAKE CLASS B, RANK 1.
SO LETTING HIM JOIN CAN ONLY HELP US.
SAITAMA! IF YOU WON'T LISTEN, THEN HOW ABOUT A FIGHT? FAIR AND SQUARE!!
WHAM
FIGHT?
YES! *YOUR* GROUP AGAINST MINE!!
AND THE LOSER HAS TO DO WHAT THE WINNER SAYS!!!

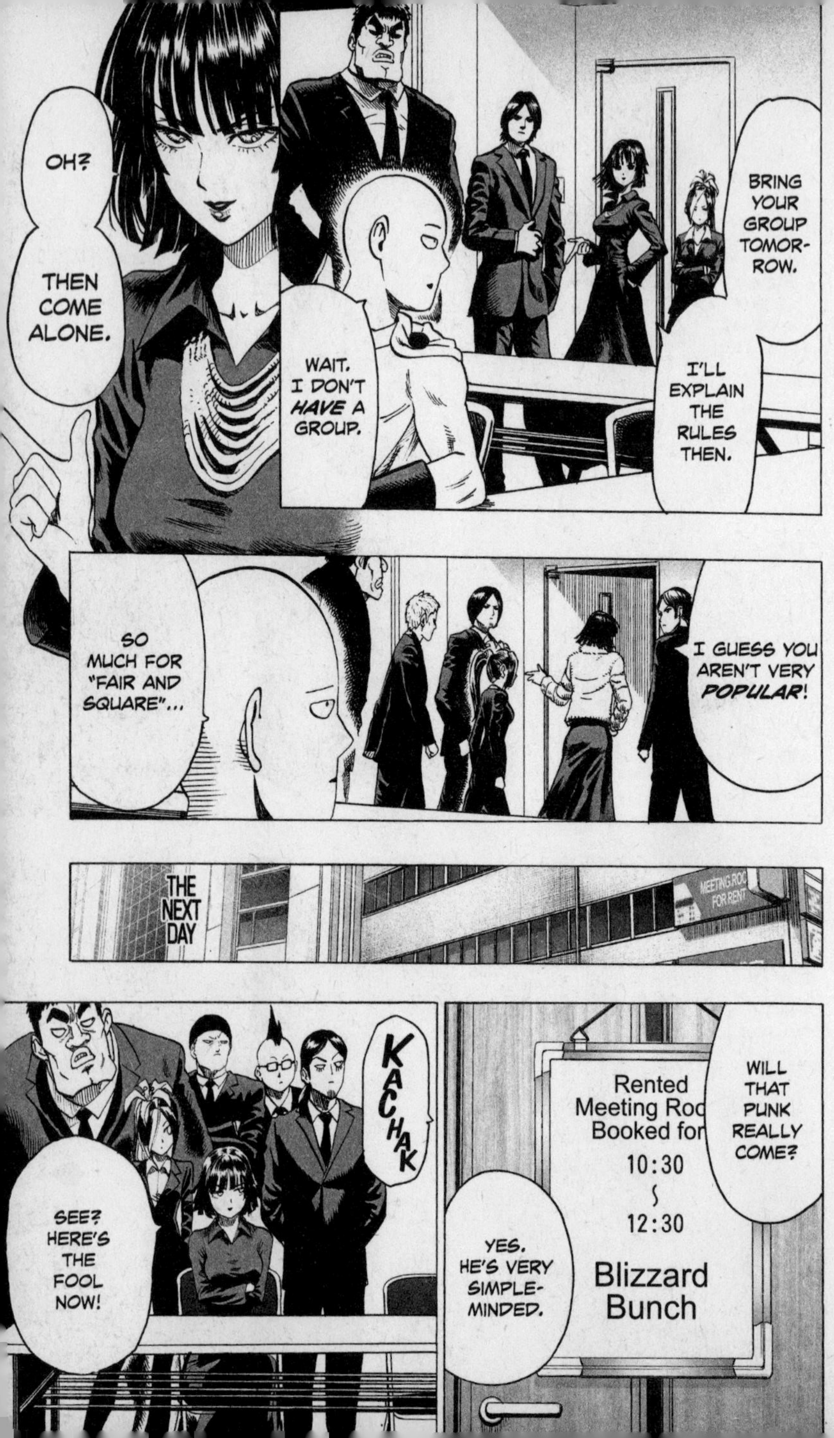
BRING YOUR GROUP TOMORROW.
I'LL EXPLAIN THE RULES THEN.
WAIT. I DON'T *HAVE* A GROUP.
OH?
THEN COME ALONE.
I GUESS YOU AREN'T VERY *POPULAR*!
SO MUCH FOR "FAIR AND SQUARE"...
MEETING ROC FOR RENT
THE NEXT DAY
WILL THAT PUNK REALLY COME?
Rented Meeting Roc Booked for 10:30 ~ 12:30 Blizzard Bunch
YES. HE'S VERY SIMPLE-MINDED.
KACHAK
SEE? HERE'S THE FOOL NOW!

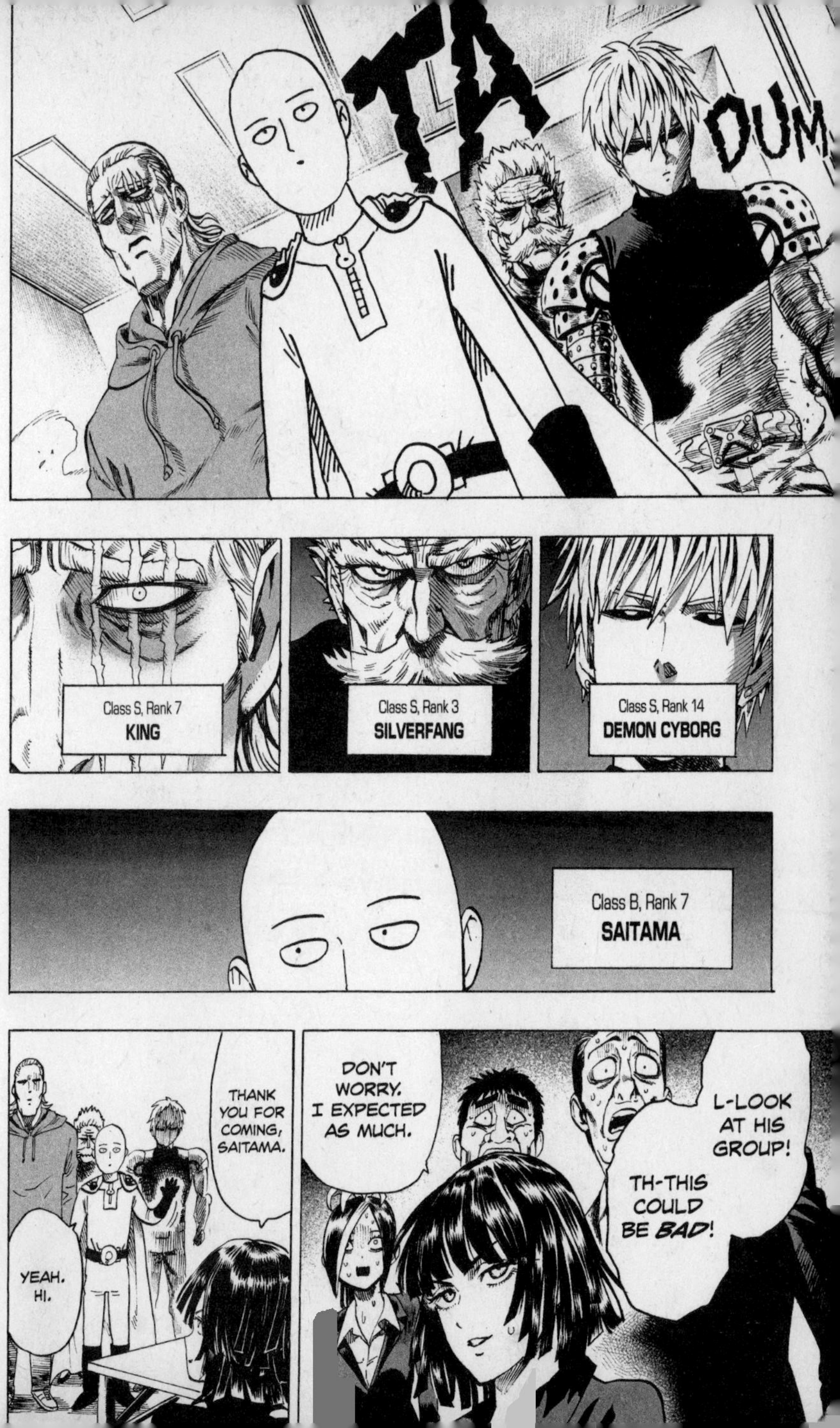
TA DUM
Class S, Rank 14
DEMON CYBORG
Class S, Rank 3
SILVERFANG
Class S, Rank 7
KING
Class B, Rank 7
SAITAMA
L-LOOK AT HIS GROUP!
TH-THIS COULD BE *BAD*!
DON'T WORRY. I EXPECTED AS MUCH.
THANK YOU FOR COMING, SAITAMA.
YEAH. HI.

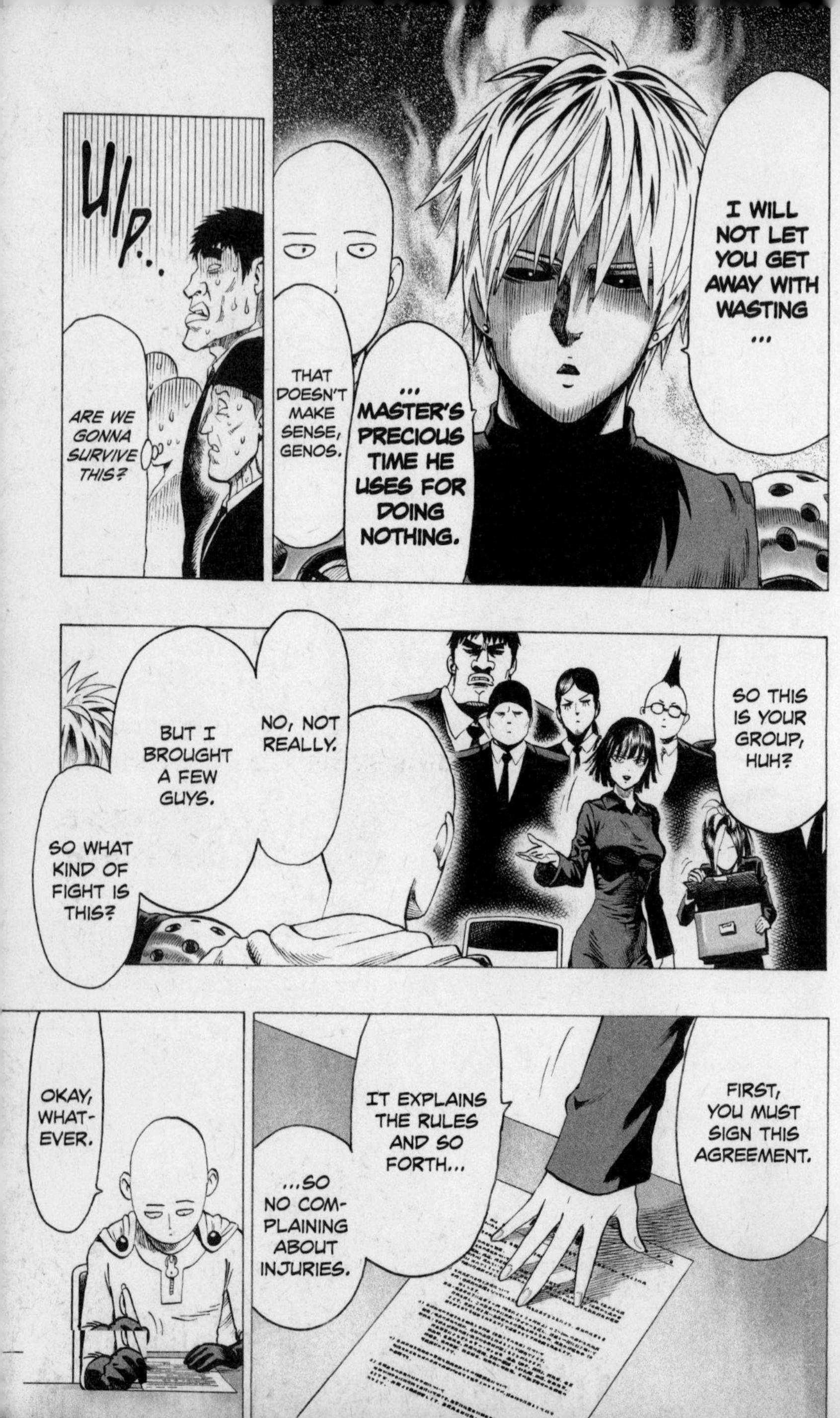
I WILL NOT LET YOU GET AWAY WITH WASTING ...
... MASTER'S PRECIOUS TIME HE USES FOR DOING NOTHING.
THAT DOESN'T MAKE SENSE, GENOS.
UIP...
ARE WE GONNA SURVIVE THIS?
SO THIS IS YOUR GROUP, HUH?
NO, NOT REALLY.
BUT I BROUGHT A FEW GUYS.
SO WHAT KIND OF FIGHT IS THIS?
FIRST, YOU MUST SIGN THIS AGREEMENT.
IT EXPLAINS THE RULES AND SO FORTH...
...SO NO COM-PLAINING ABOUT INJURIES.
OKAY, WHAT-EVER.

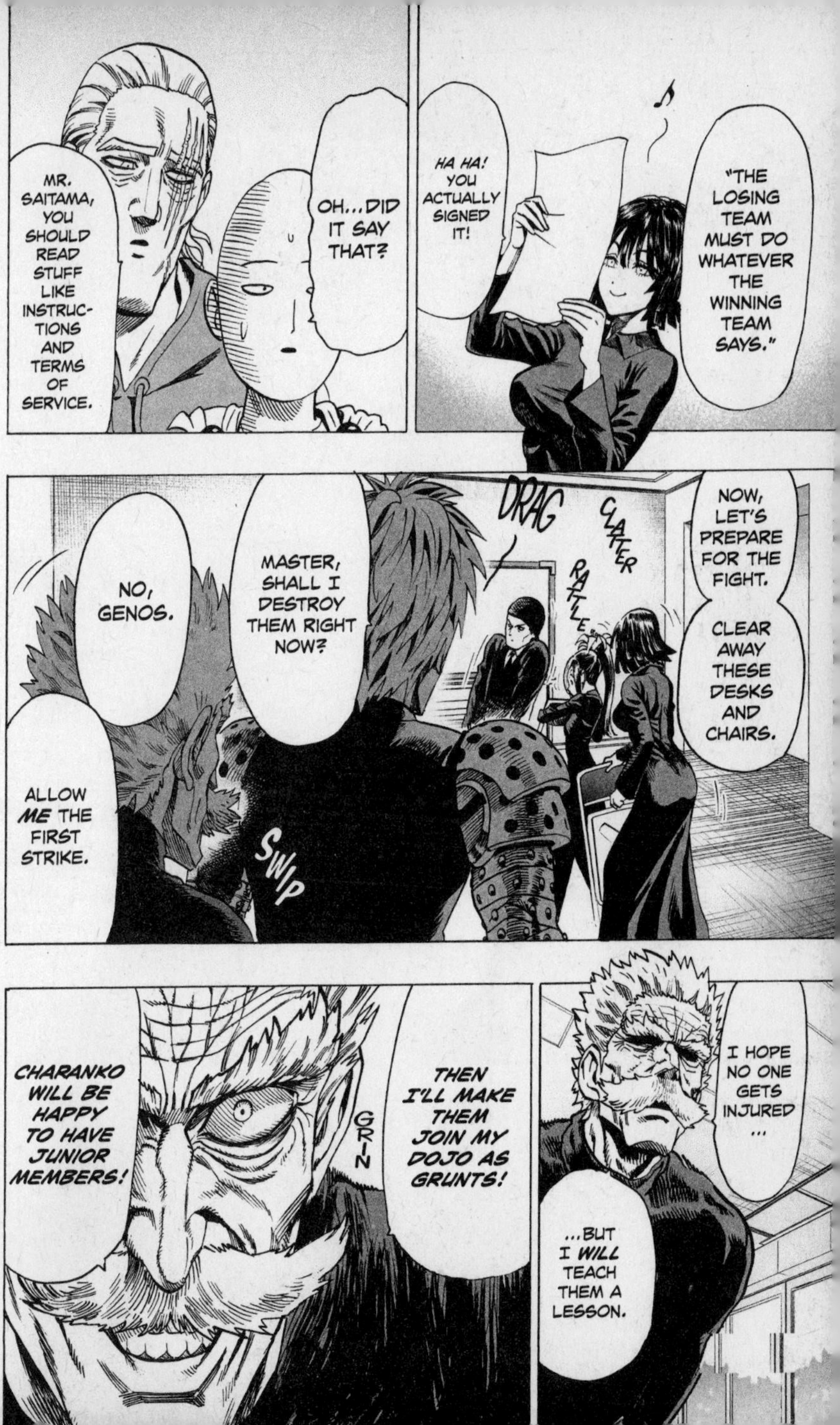
"THE LOSING TEAM MUST DO WHATEVER THE WINNING TEAM SAYS."
HA HA! YOU ACTUALLY SIGNED IT!
OH...DID IT SAY THAT?
MR. SAITAMA, YOU SHOULD READ STUFF LIKE INSTRUCTIONS AND TERMS OF SERVICE.
NOW, LET'S PREPARE FOR THE FIGHT.
CLEAR AWAY THESE DESKS AND CHAIRS.
DRAG
CLATTER
RATTLE
MASTER, SHALL I DESTROY THEM RIGHT NOW?
NO, GENOS.
ALLOW *ME* THE FIRST STRIKE.
SWIP
I HOPE NO ONE GETS INJURED...
...BUT I *WILL* TEACH THEM A LESSON.
THEN I'LL MAKE THEM JOIN MY DOJO AS GRUNTS!
GRIN
CHARANKO WILL BE HAPPY TO HAVE JUNIOR MEMBERS!

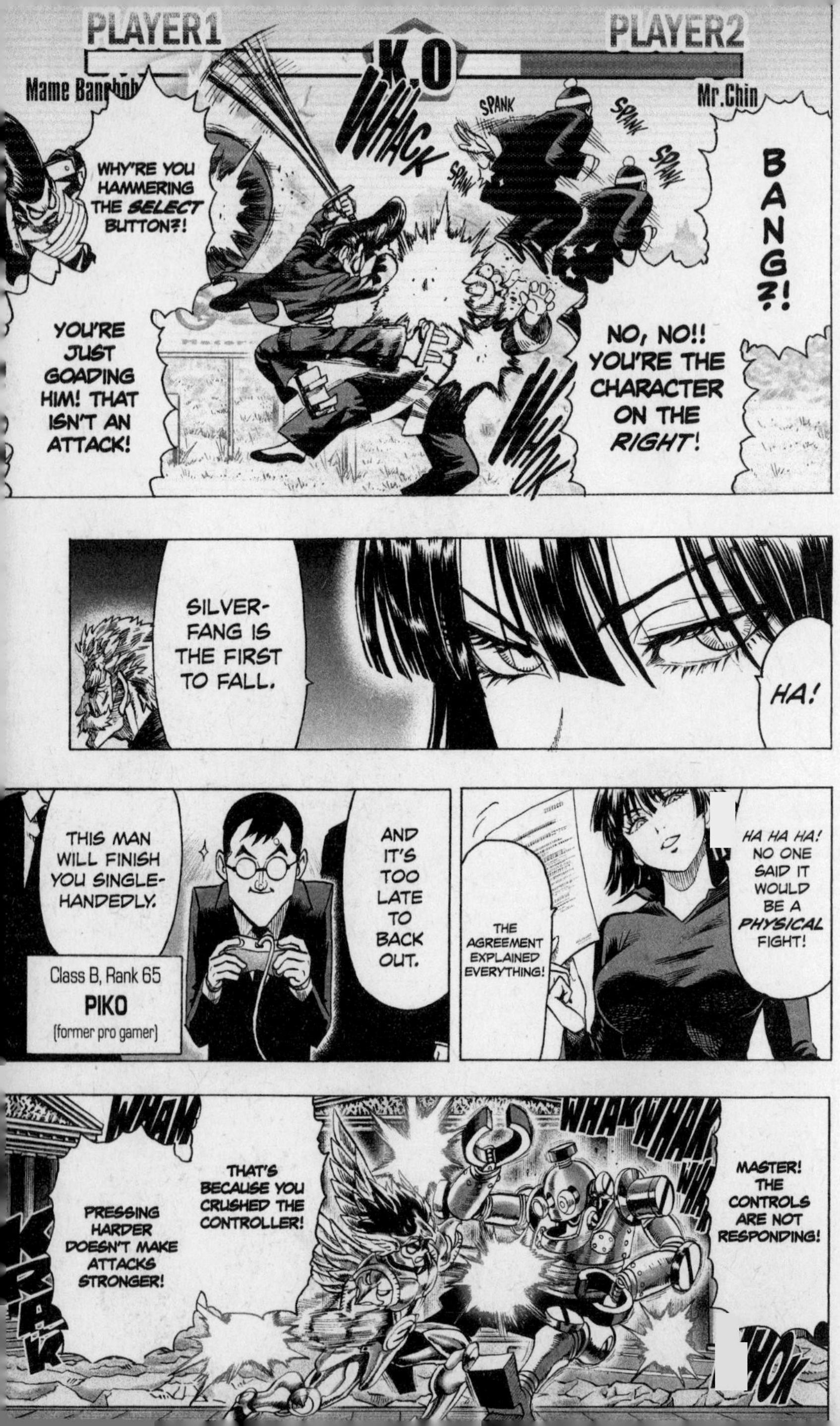
PLAYER2
Mr.Chin
BANG?!
NO, NO!! YOU'RE THE CHARACTER ON THE *RIGHT*!
SPANK
SPANK
SPANK
SPANK
K.O
PLAYER1
WHACK
WHY'RE YOU HAMMERING THE *SELECT* BUTTON?!
YOU'RE JUST GOADING HIM! THAT ISN'T AN ATTACK!
HA!
SILVER-FANG IS THE FIRST TO FALL.
HA HA HA! NO ONE SAID IT WOULD BE A *PHYSICAL* FIGHT!
THE AGREEMENT EXPLAINED EVERYTHING!
AND IT'S TOO LATE TO BACK OUT.
THIS MAN WILL FINISH YOU SINGLE-HANDEDLY.
Class B, Rank 65
PIKO
(former pro gamer)
MASTER! THE CONTROLS ARE NOT RESPONDING!
WHAK WHAK
THAT'S BECAUSE YOU CRUSHED THE CONTROLLER!
PRESSING HARDER DOESN'T MAKE ATTACKS STRONGER!
WHAM

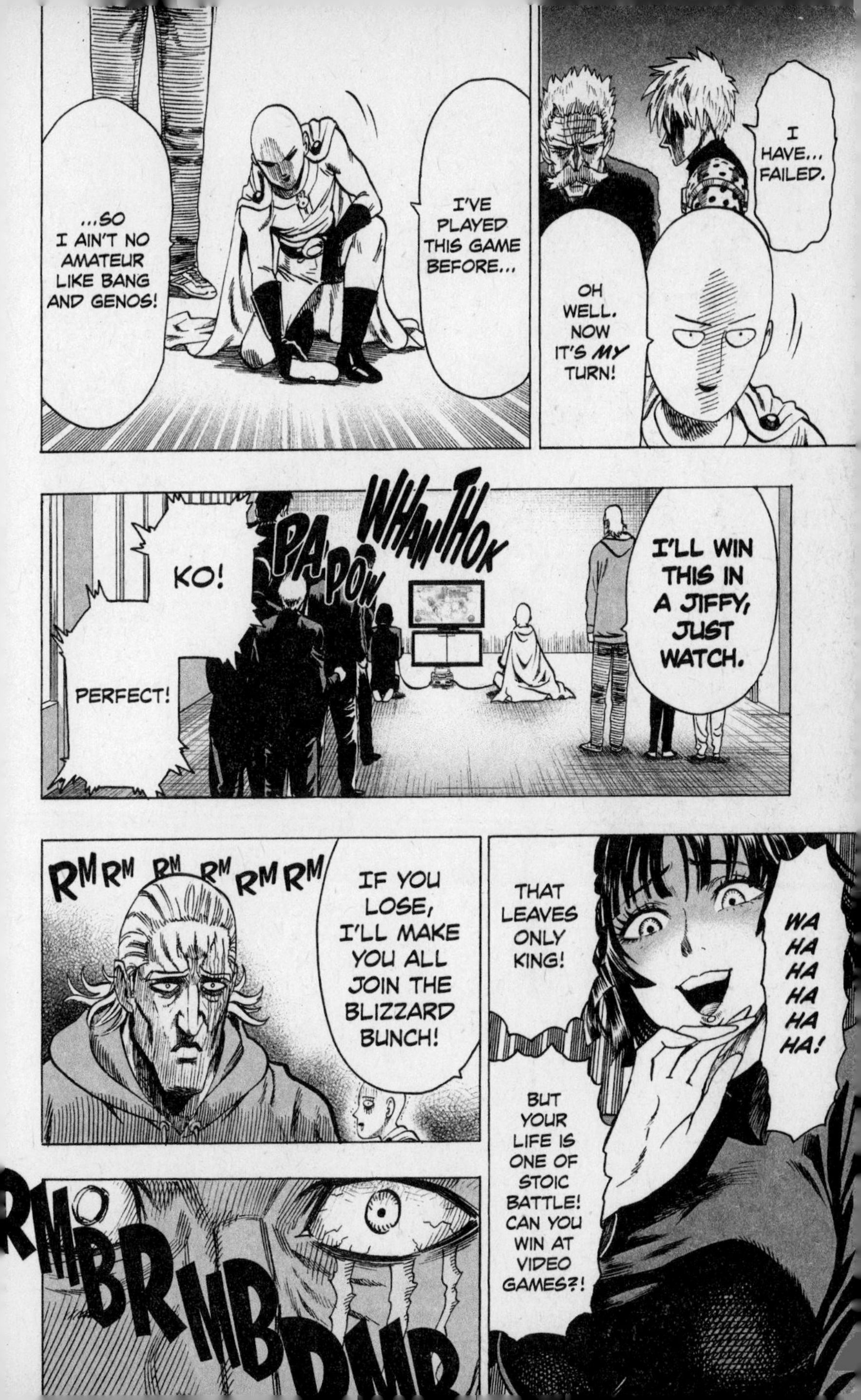
I HAVE... FAILED.
OH WELL. NOW IT'S *MY* TURN!
I'VE PLAYED THIS GAME BEFORE...
...SO I AIN'T NO AMATEUR LIKE BANG AND GENOS!
I'LL WIN THIS IN A JIFFY, JUST WATCH.
WHAM THOK
PA POW
KO!
PERFECT!
THAT LEAVES ONLY KING!
WA HA HA HA HA HA!
BUT YOUR LIFE IS ONE OF STOIC BATTLE! CAN YOU WIN AT VIDEO GAMES?!
RM RM RM RM RM RM
IF YOU LOSE, I'LL MAKE YOU ALL JOIN THE BLIZZARD BUNCH!
RMB BRMB DMB

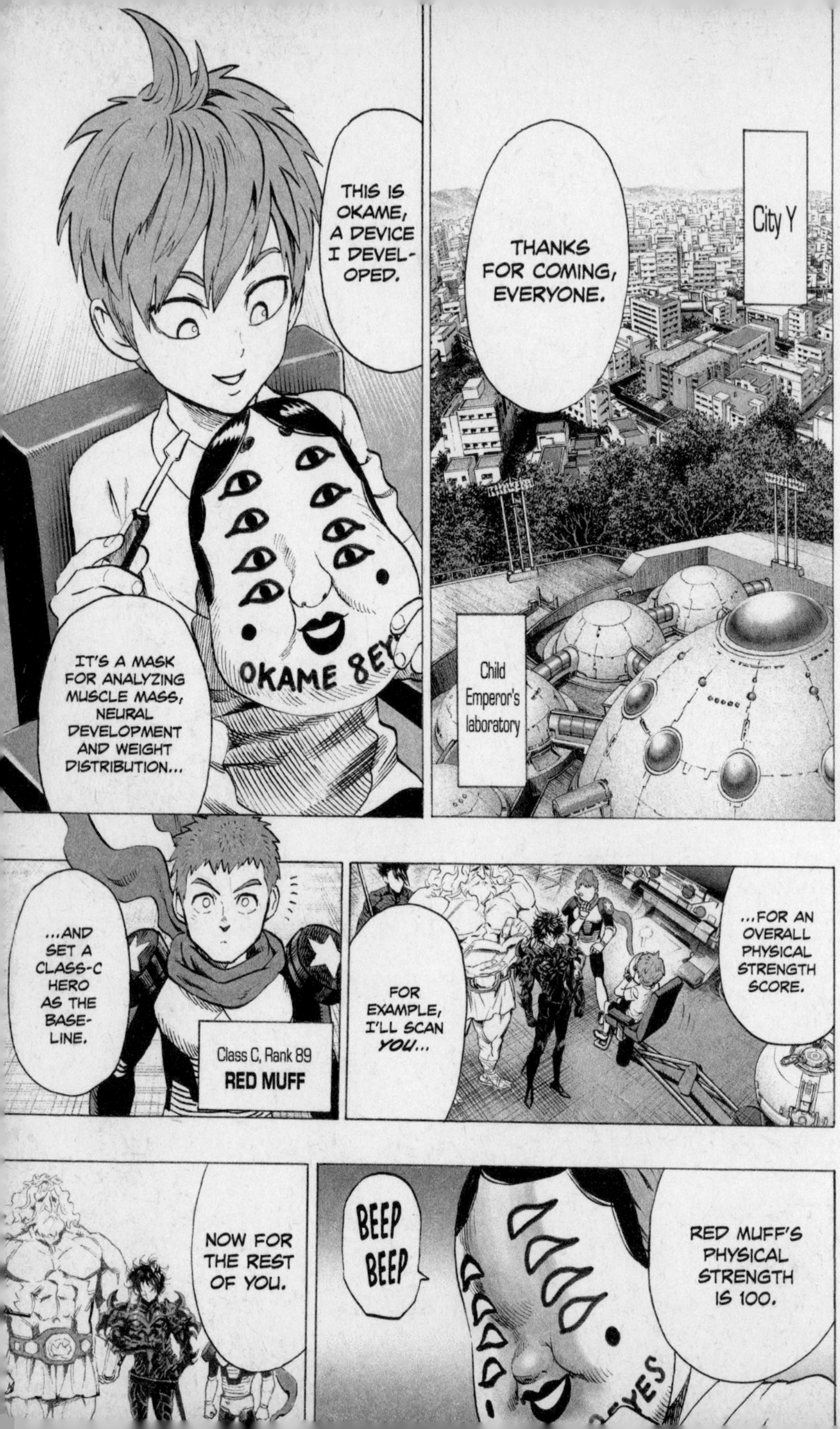
City Y
THANKS FOR COMING, EVERYONE.
Child Emperor's laboratory
THIS IS OKAME, A DEVICE I DEVEL-OPED.
OKAME 8EY
IT'S A MASK FOR ANALYZING MUSCLE MASS, NEURAL DEVELOPMENT AND WEIGHT DISTRIBUTION...
...FOR AN OVERALL PHYSICAL STRENGTH SCORE.
FOR EXAMPLE, I'LL SCAN *YOU*...
...AND SET A CLASS-C HERO AS THE BASE-LINE.
Class C, Rank 89
RED MUFF
BEEP BEEP
RED MUFF'S PHYSICAL STRENGTH IS 100.
NOW FOR THE REST OF YOU.

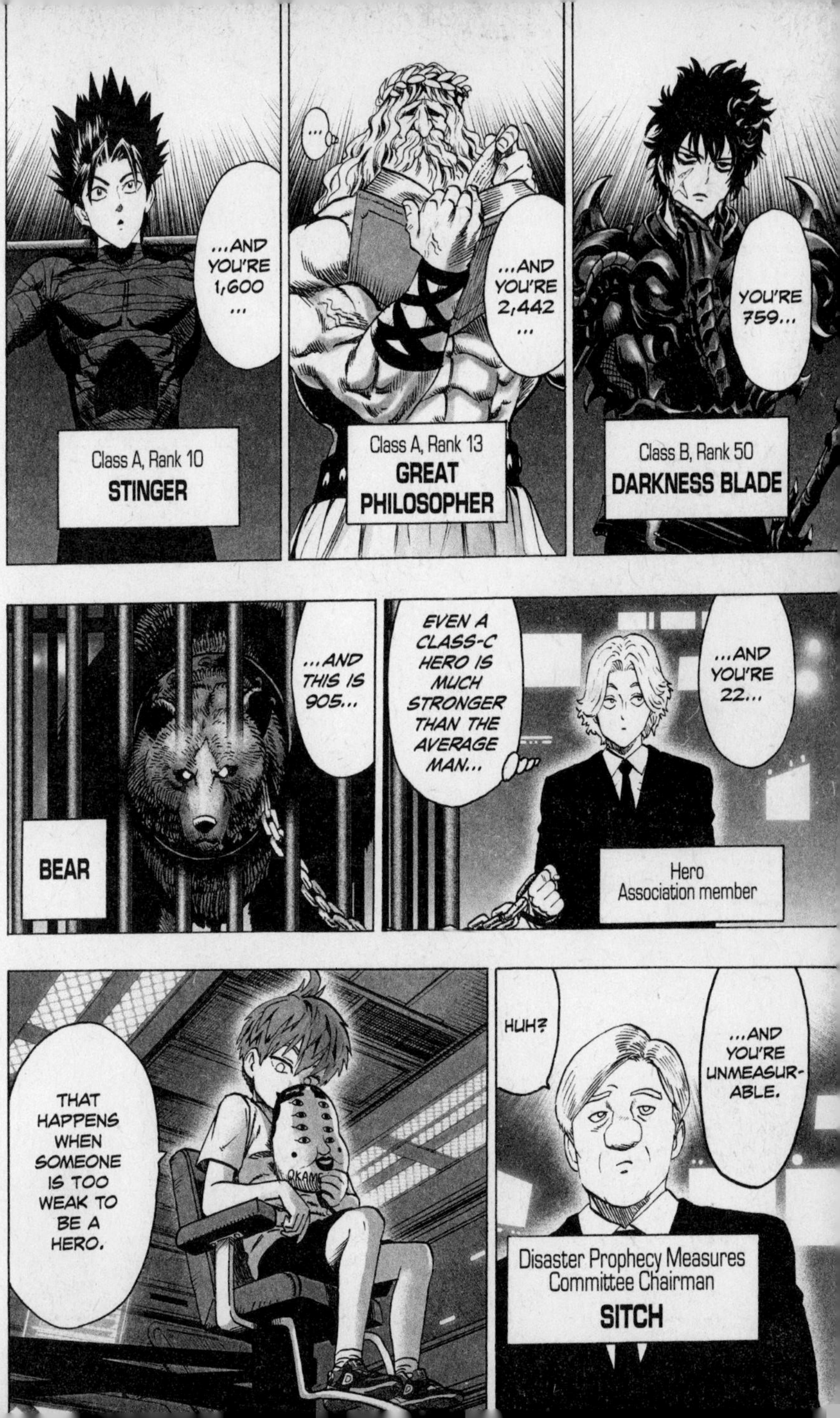
YOU'RE 759...
Class B, Rank 50
DARKNESS BLADE
...
...AND YOU'RE 2,442 ...
Class A, Rank 13
GREAT PHILOSOPHER
...AND YOU'RE 1,600 ...
Class A, Rank 10
STINGER
...AND YOU'RE 22...
EVEN A CLASS-C HERO IS MUCH STRONGER THAN THE AVERAGE MAN...
Hero Association member
...AND THIS IS 905...
BEAR
...AND YOU'RE UNMEASUR-ABLE.
HUH?
Disaster Prophecy Measures Committee Chairman
SITCH
OKAME
THAT HAPPENS WHEN SOMEONE IS TOO WEAK TO BE A HERO.

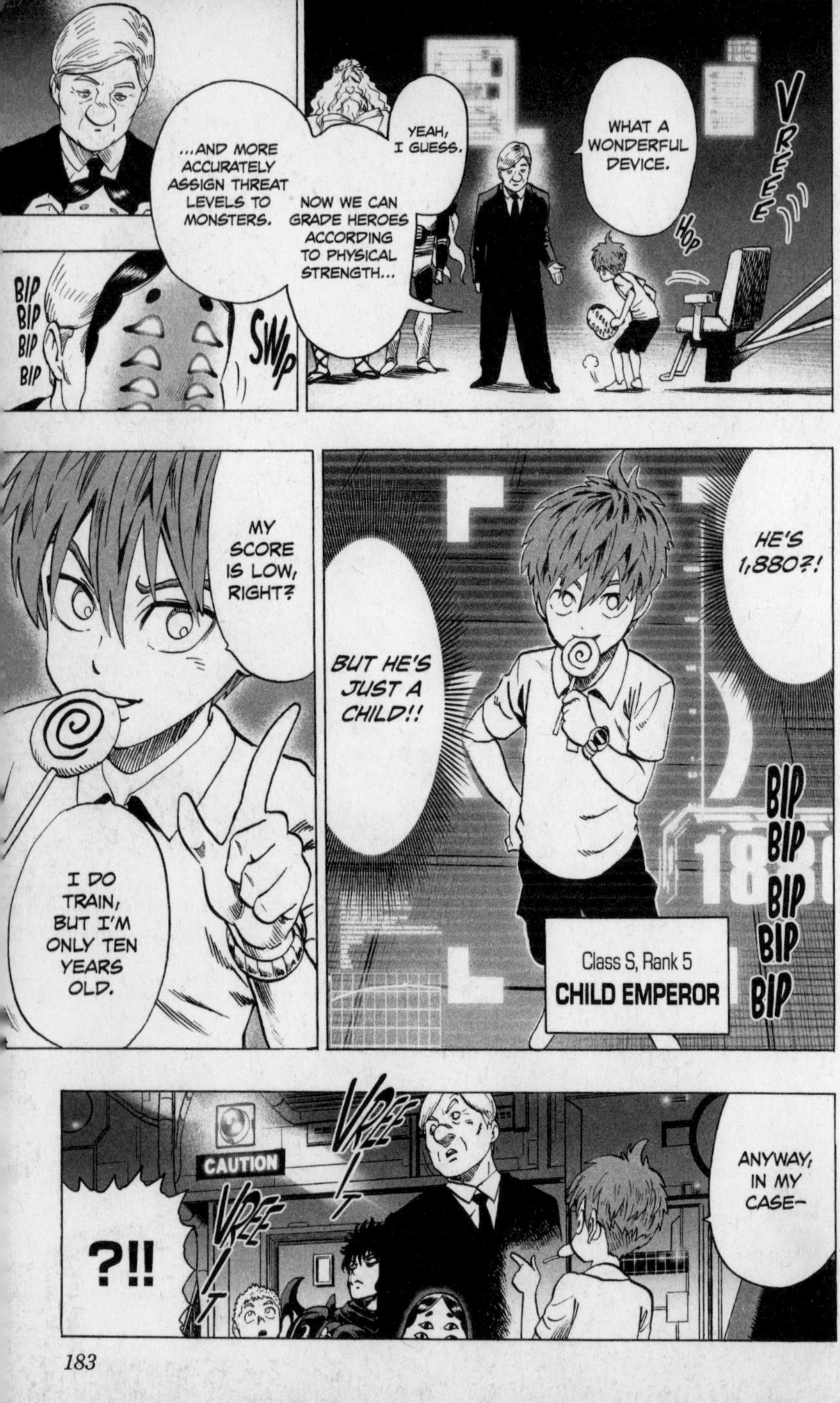
WHAT A WONDERFUL DEVICE.
VREEE
HOP
YEAH, I GUESS.
NOW WE CAN GRADE HEROES ACCORDING TO PHYSICAL STRENGTH...
...AND MORE ACCURATELY ASSIGN THREAT LEVELS TO MONSTERS.
SWIP
BIP BIP BIP BIP
HE'S 1,880?!
BUT HE'S JUST A CHILD!!
Class S, Rank 5
CHILD EMPEROR
1880
BIP BIP BIP BIP BIP
MY SCORE IS LOW, RIGHT?
I DO TRAIN, BUT I'M ONLY TEN YEARS OLD.
ANYWAY, IN MY CASE-
VREE-IT
VREE-IT
CAUTION
?!!

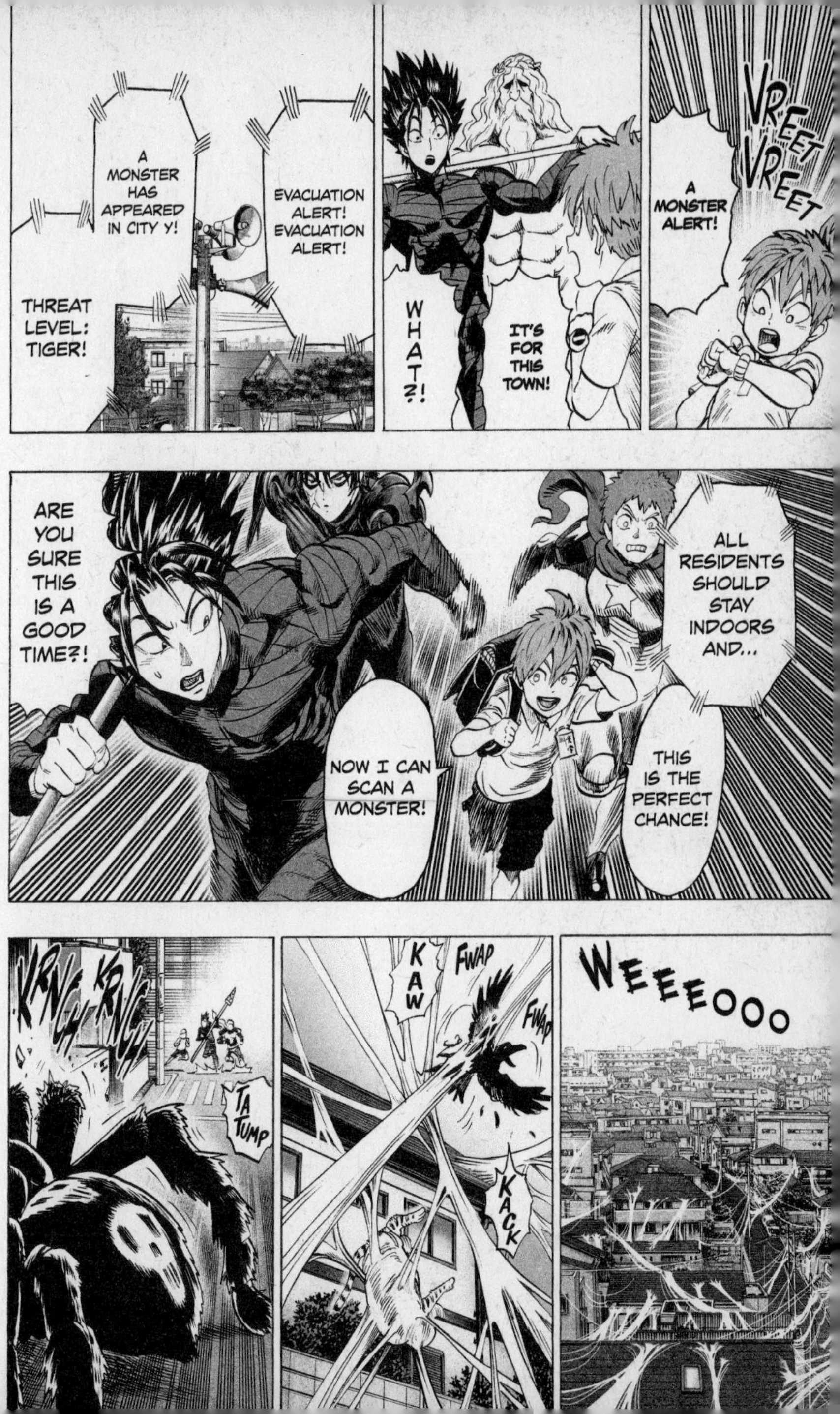
VREET VREET
A MONSTER ALERT!
IT'S FOR THIS TOWN!
WHAT?!
EVACUATION ALERT! EVACUATION ALERT!
A MONSTER HAS APPEARED IN CITY Y!
THREAT LEVEL: TIGER!
ALL RESIDENTS SHOULD STAY INDOORS AND...
THIS IS THE PERFECT CHANCE!
NOW I CAN SCAN A MONSTER!
ARE YOU SURE THIS IS A GOOD TIME?!
WEEEOOO
KAW
FWAP
FWAP
KACK
KRNCH KRNCH
TA TUMP

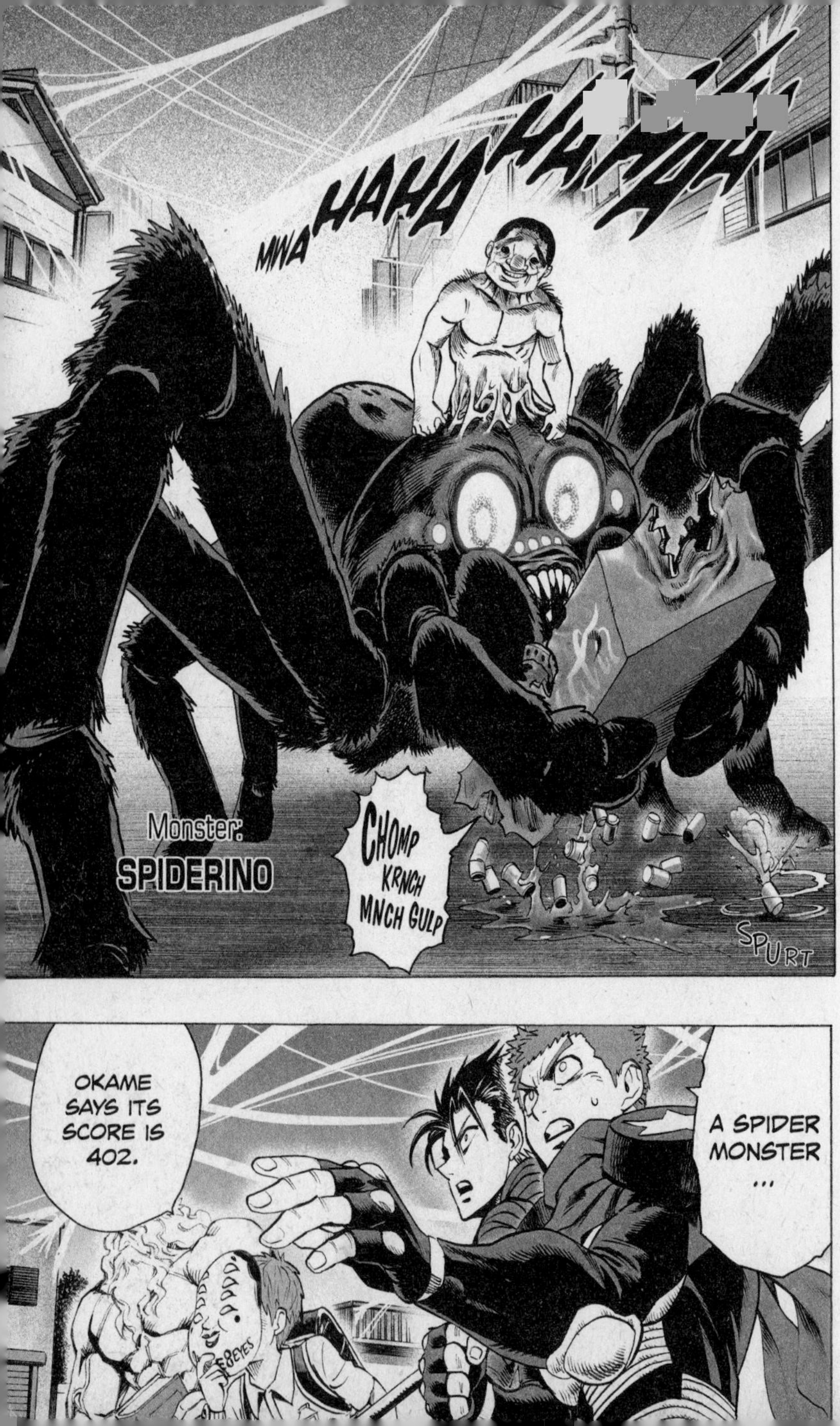
MWAHAHAHAHAH
Monster:
SPIDERINO
CHOMP KRNCH MNCH GULP
SPURT
A SPIDER MONSTER ...
OKAME SAYS ITS SCORE IS 402.

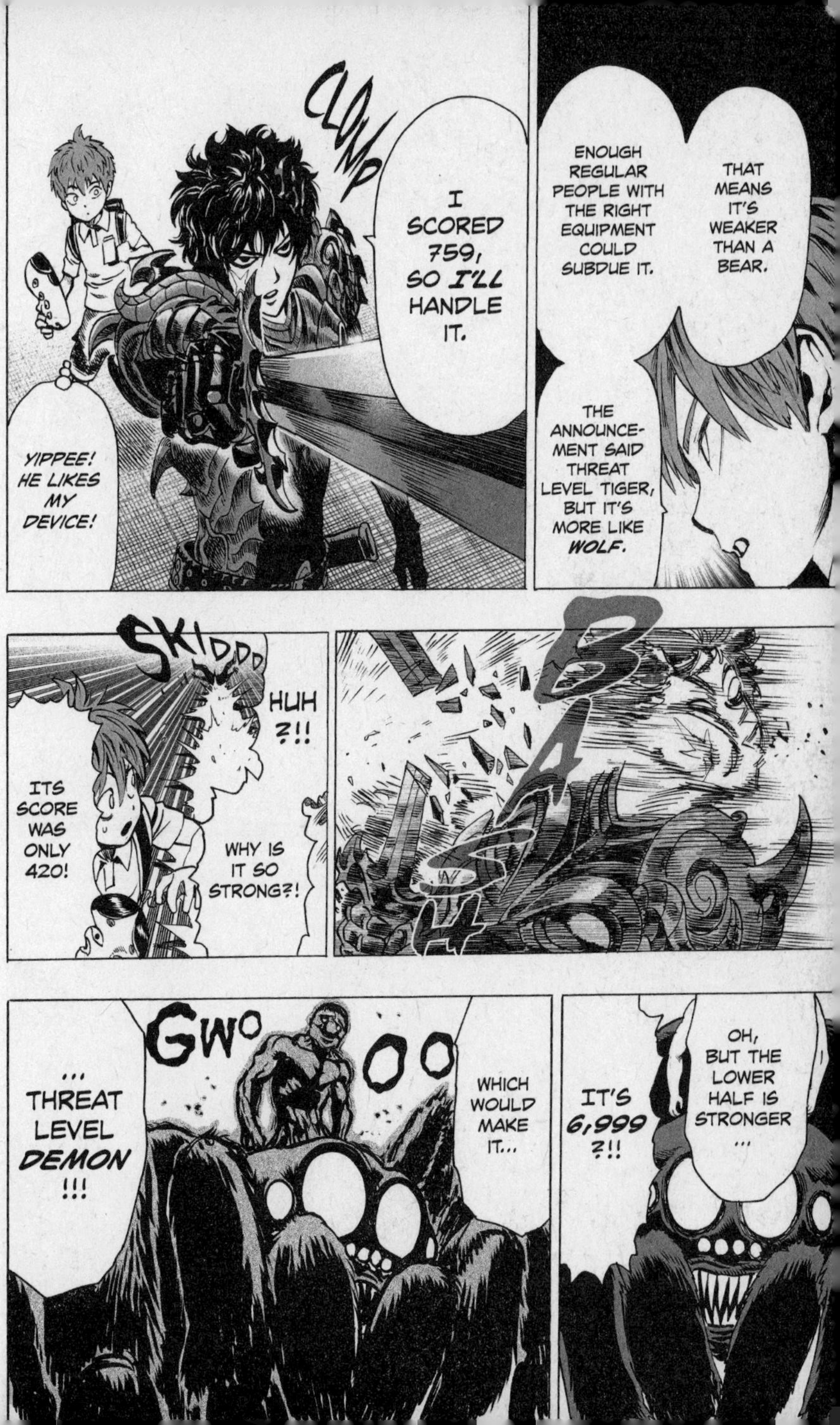
THAT MEANS IT'S WEAKER THAN A BEAR.
ENOUGH REGULAR PEOPLE WITH THE RIGHT EQUIPMENT COULD SUBDUE IT.
THE ANNOUNCE-MENT SAID THREAT LEVEL TIGER, BUT IT'S MORE LIKE *WOLF*.
CLOMP
I SCORED 759, SO *I'LL* HANDLE IT.
YIPPEE! HE LIKES MY DEVICE!
BASH
SKIDDD
HUH ?!!
WHY IS IT SO STRONG?!
ITS SCORE WAS ONLY 420!
OH, BUT THE LOWER HALF IS STRONGER...
IT'S *6,999* ?!!
WHICH WOULD MAKE IT...
GWOOO
...THREAT LEVEL *DEMON* !!!

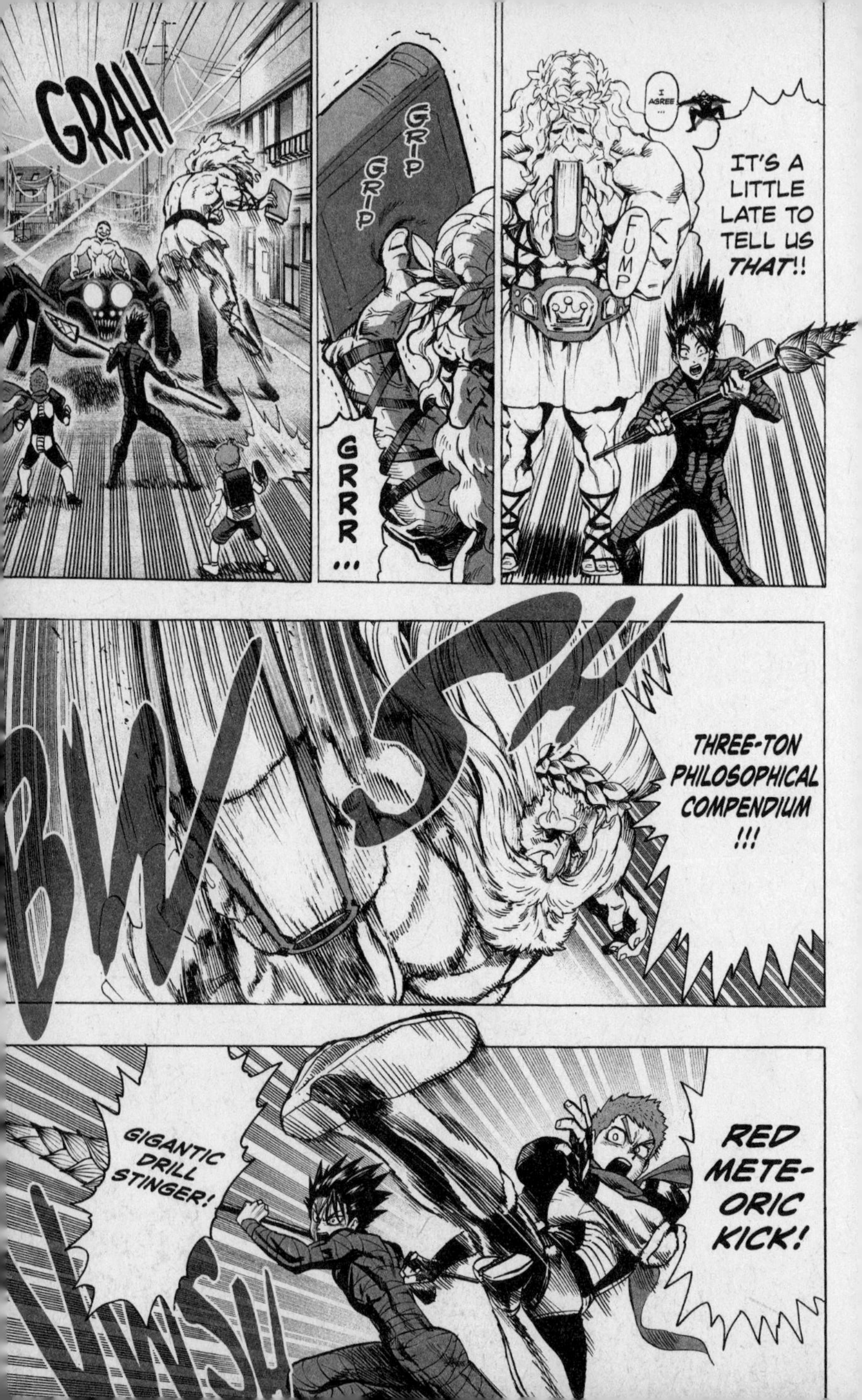
I AGREE ...
IT'S A LITTLE LATE TO TELL US *THAT*!!
FUMP
GRIP
GRIP
GRRR ...
GRAH
THREE-TON PHILOSOPHICAL COMPENDIUM !!!
RED METE-ORIC KICK!
GIGANTIC DRILL STINGER!

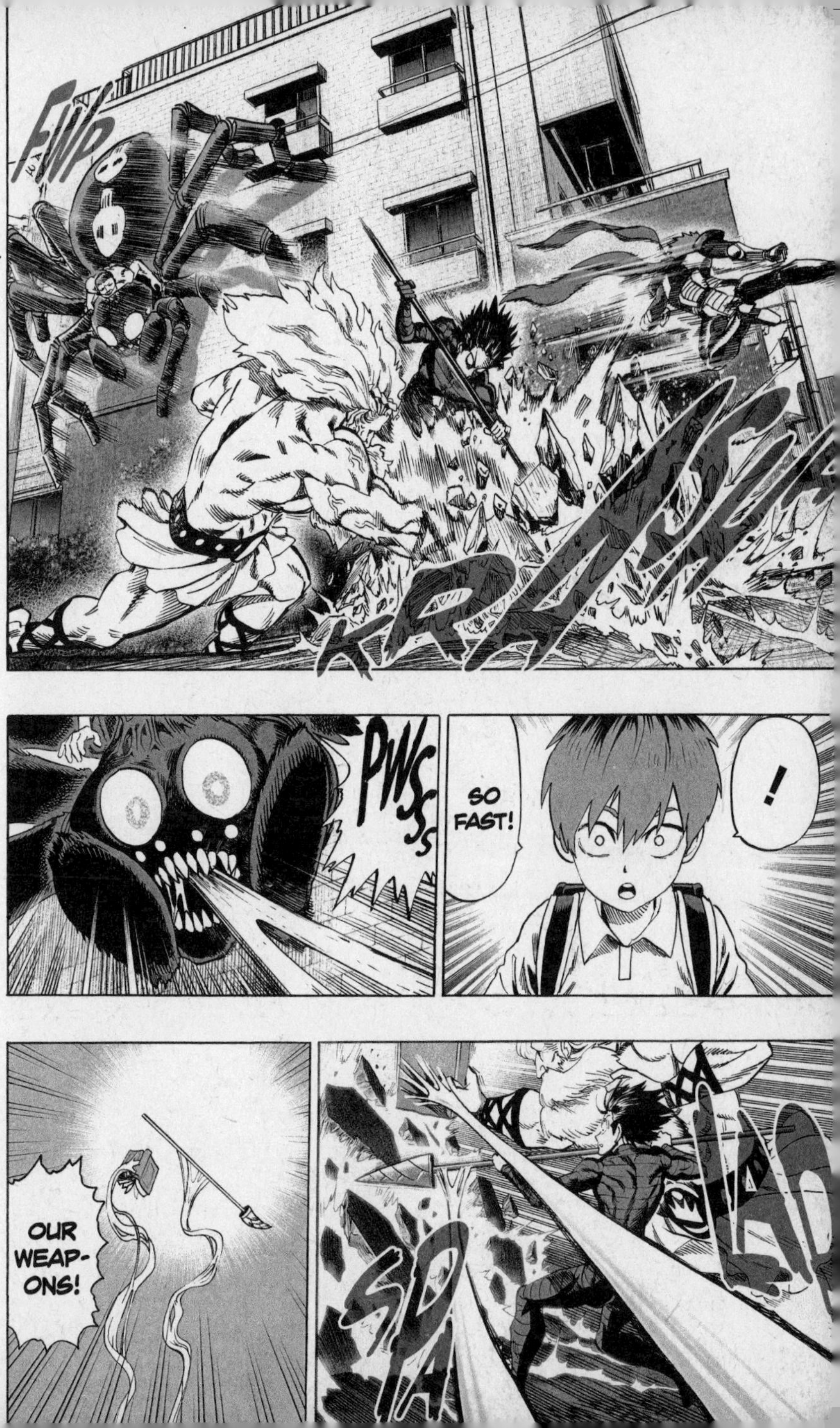
FWP
KRAM
!
SO FAST!
PWSSS
OUR WEAP-ONS!

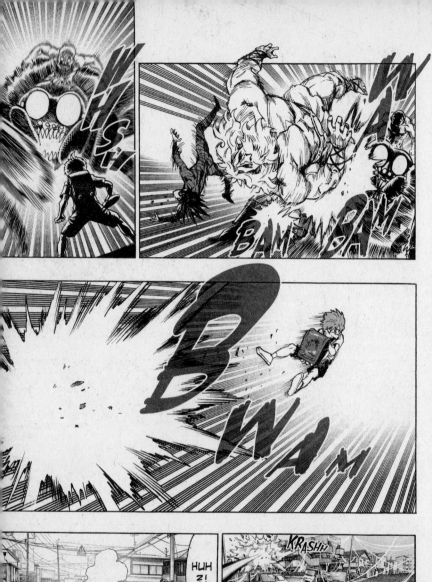

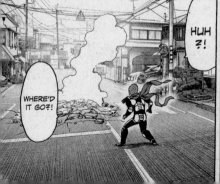

WHERE'D IT GO?!

HUH
?!

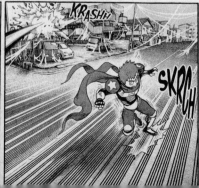

KRASHH

SKRCH

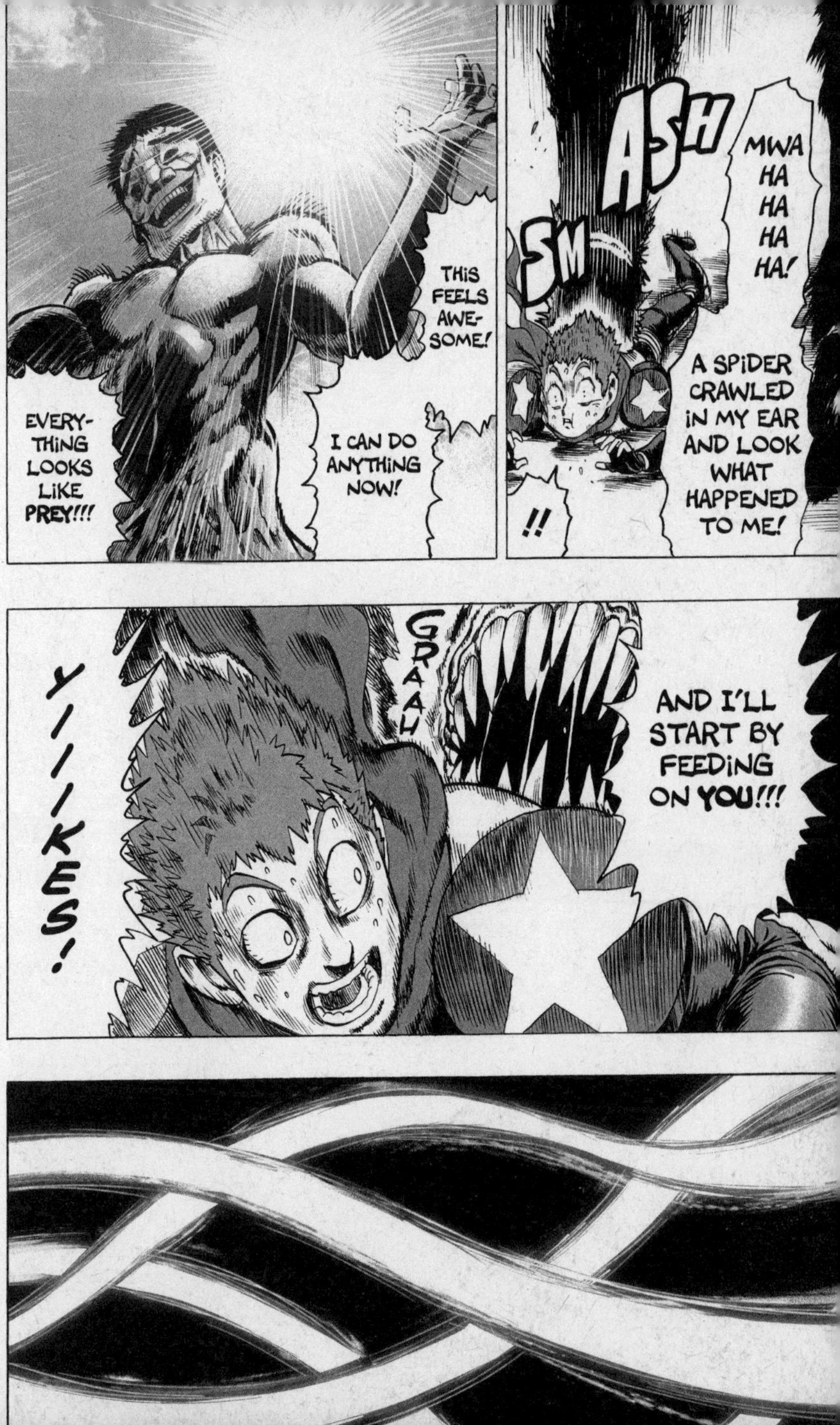
MWA HA HA HA HA!
SMASH
A SPIDER CRAWLED IN MY EAR AND LOOK WHAT HAPPENED TO ME!
!!
THIS FEELS AWE-SOME!
I CAN DO ANYTHING NOW!
EVERY-THING LOOKS LIKE **PREY**!!!
GRAAH
AND I'LL START BY FEEDING ON **YOU**!!!
YIIIIKES!

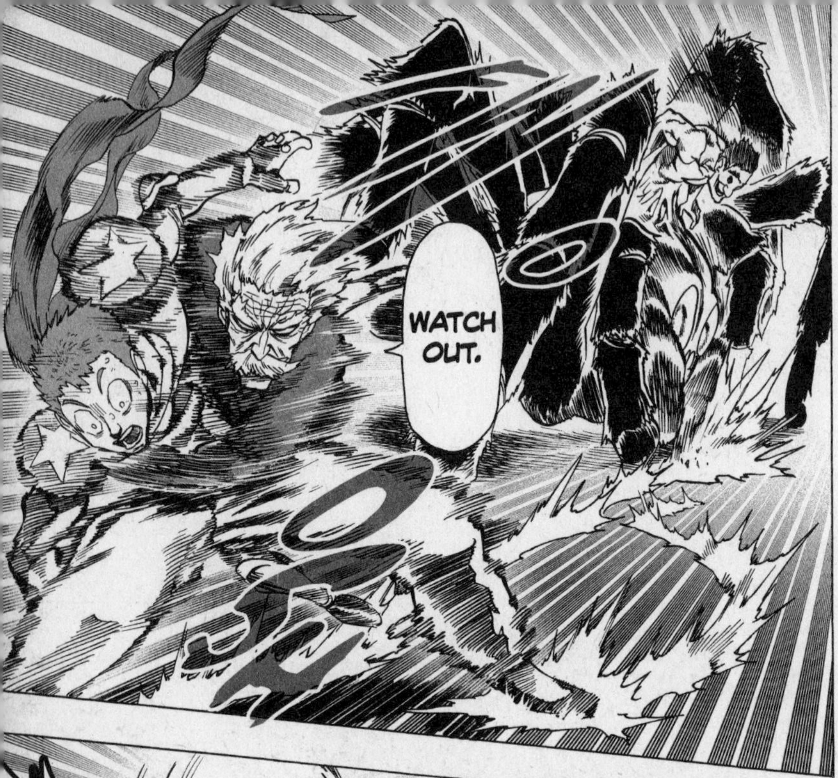
WATCH OUT.
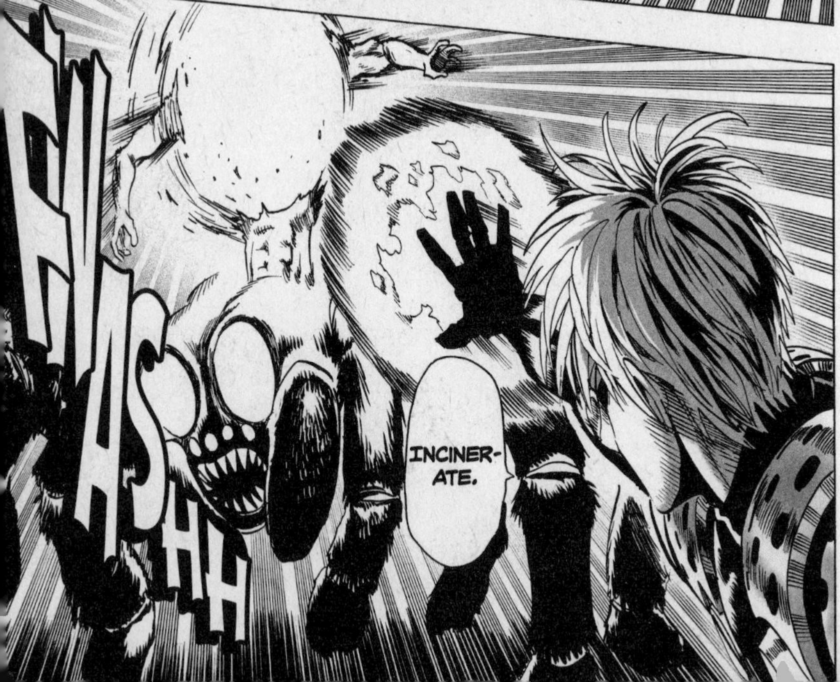
INCINER-ATE.

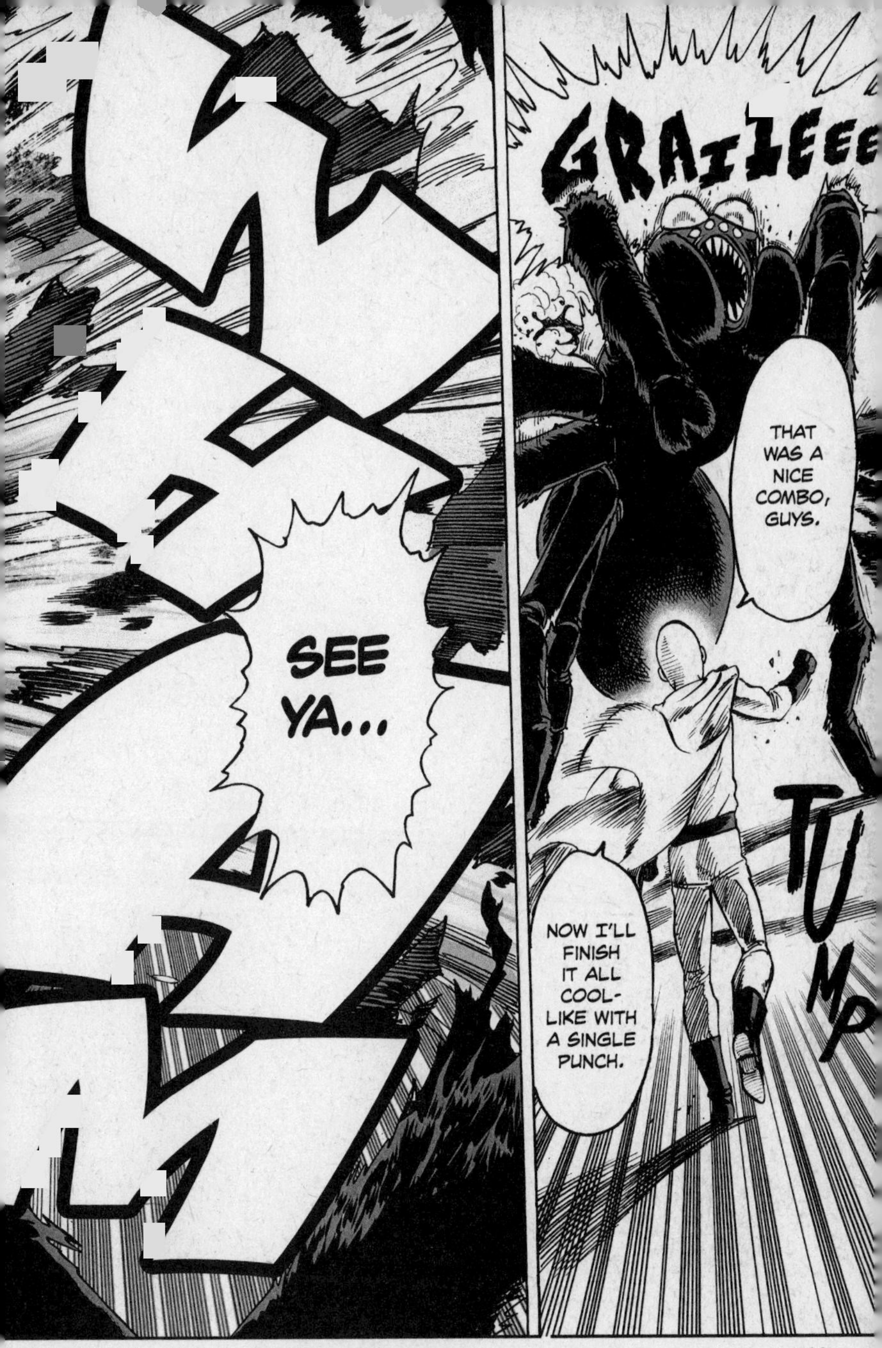
GRAIEEE
THAT WAS A NICE COMBO, GUYS.
NOW I'LL FINISH IT ALL COOL-LIKE WITH A SINGLE PUNCH.
TUMP
SEE YA...

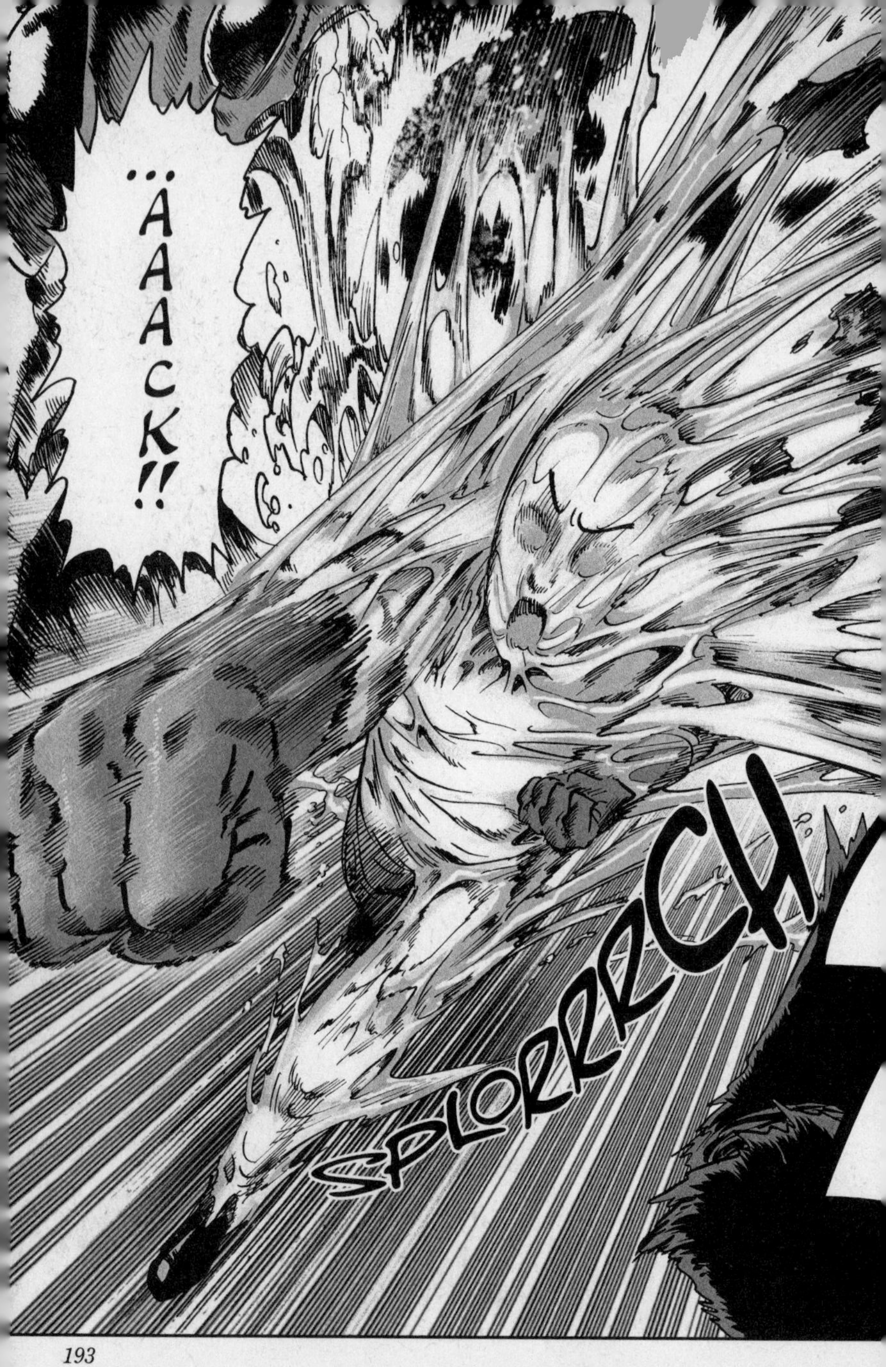
...ÄAAACK!!
SPLORRRCH

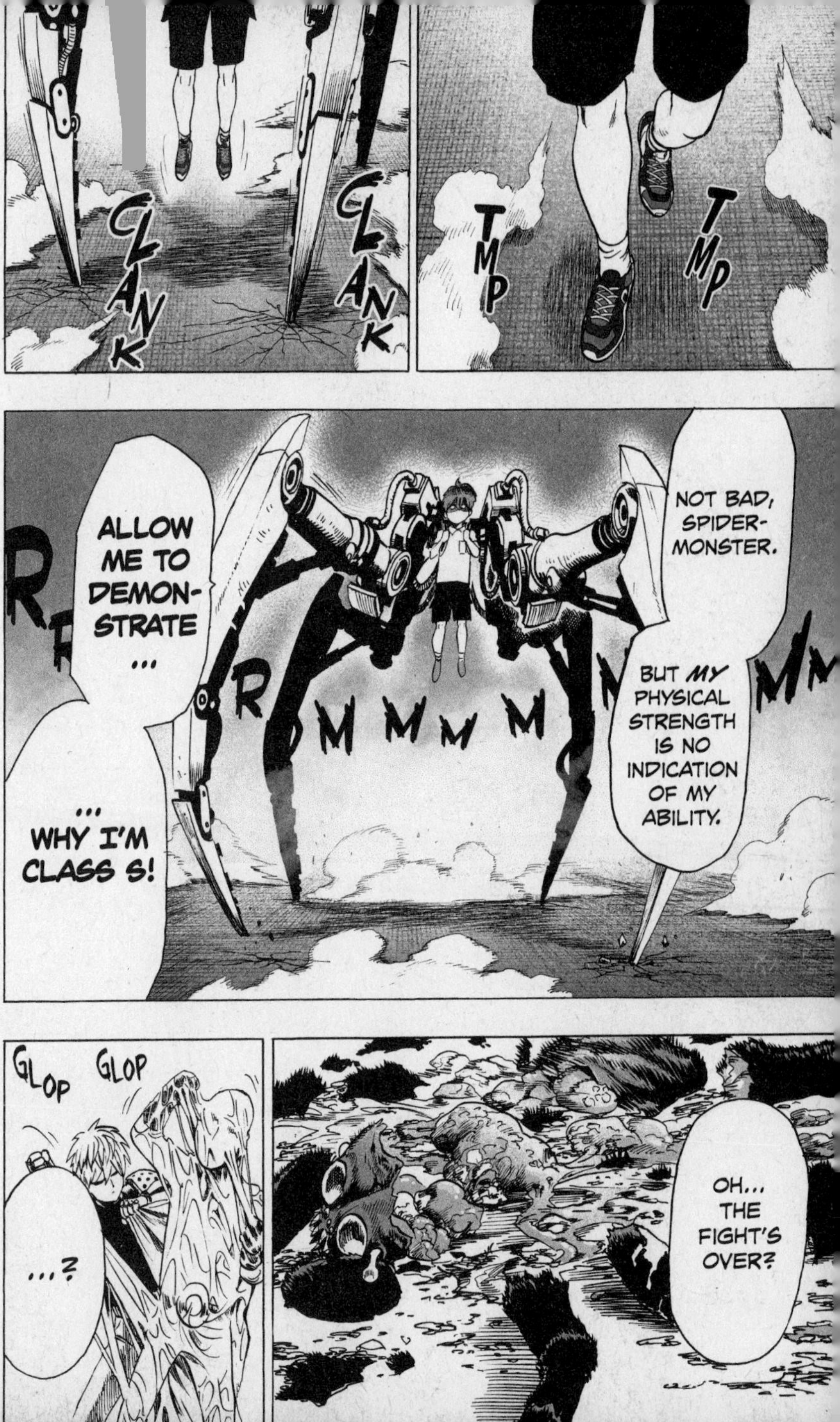
TMP
TMP
CLANK
CLANK
NOT BAD, SPIDER-MONSTER.
BUT MY PHYSICAL STRENGTH IS NO INDICATION OF MY ABILITY.
RRRRMMMMMMM
ALLOW ME TO DEMONSTRATE ...
... WHY I'M CLASS S!
OH... THE FIGHT'S OVER?
GLOP GLOP
...?

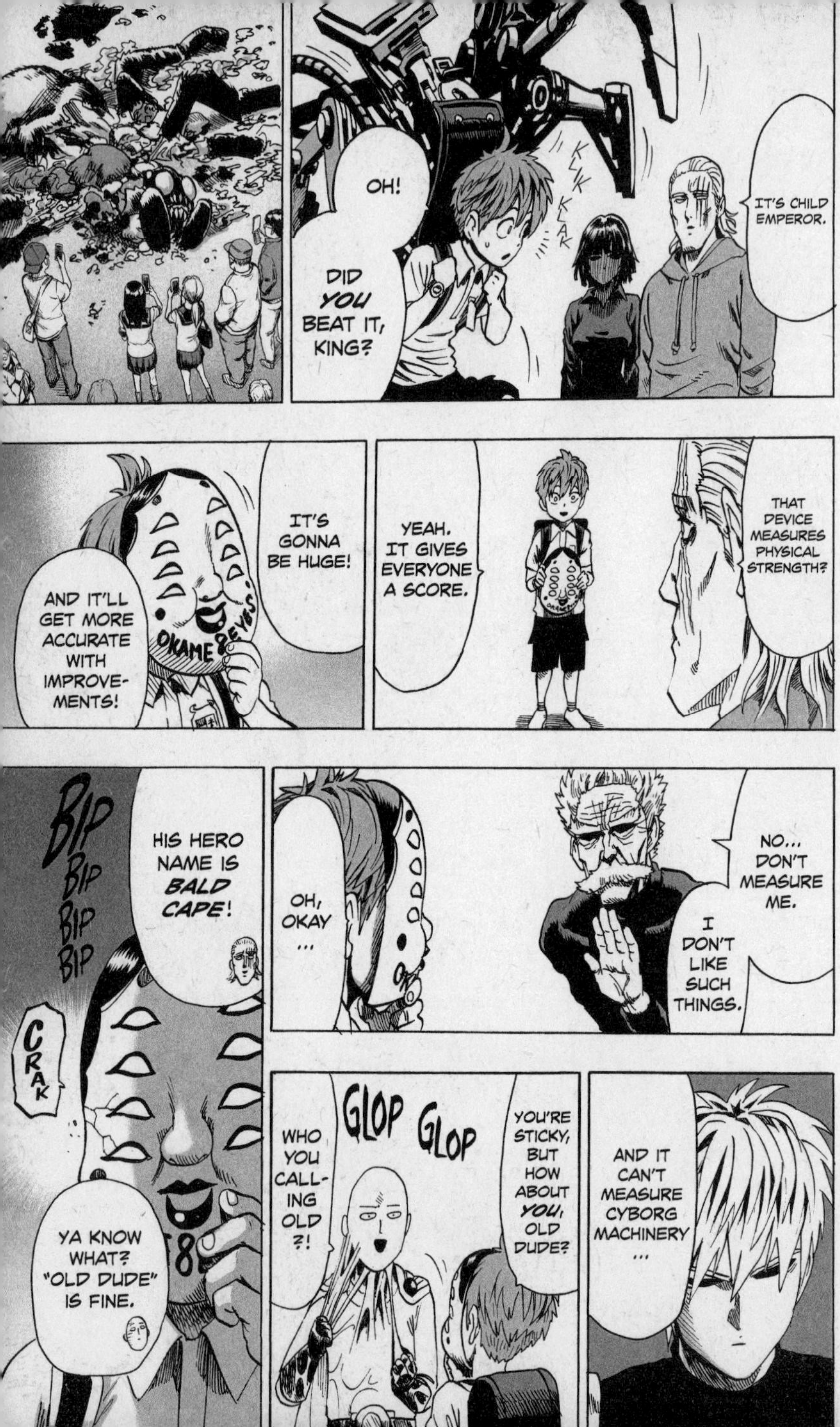
IT'S CHILD EMPEROR.
KLAK KLAK
OH!
DID *YOU* BEAT IT, KING?
THAT DEVICE MEASURES PHYSICAL STRENGTH?
YEAH. IT GIVES EVERYONE A SCORE.
IT'S GONNA BE HUGE!
AND IT'LL GET MORE ACCURATE WITH IMPROVE-MENTS!
OKAME 8EYES
NO... DON'T MEASURE ME.
I DON'T LIKE SUCH THINGS.
OH, OKAY ...
AND IT CAN'T MEASURE CYBORG MACHINERY ...
YOU'RE STICKY, BUT HOW ABOUT *YOU*, OLD DUDE?
GLOP GLOP
WHO YOU CALLING OLD?!
BIP BIP BIP BIP
HIS HERO NAME IS *BALD CAPE*!
CRAK
YA KNOW WHAT? "OLD DUDE" IS FINE.

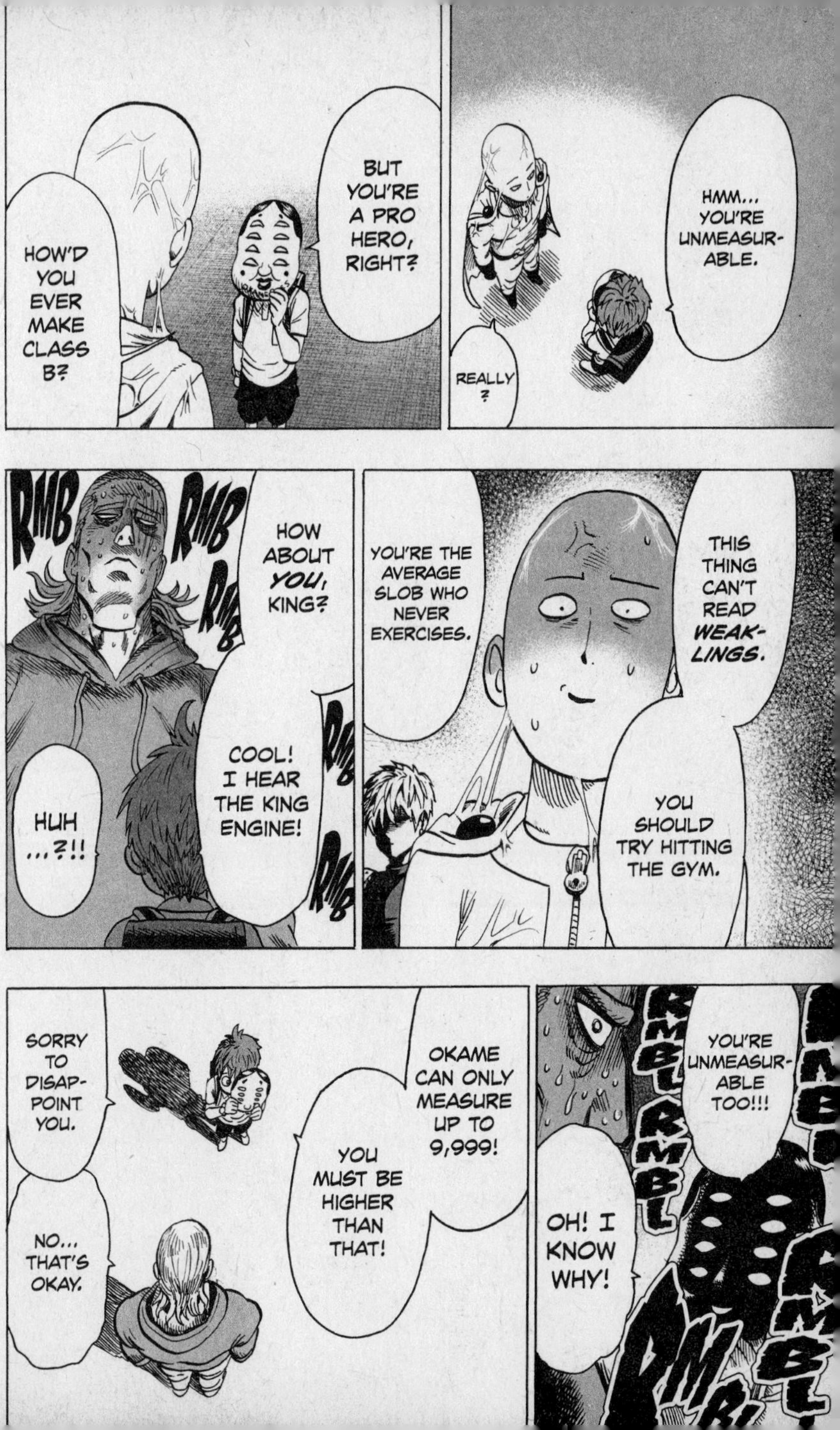
HMM... YOU'RE UNMEASUR-ABLE.
REALLY?
BUT YOU'RE A PRO HERO, RIGHT?
HOW'D YOU EVER MAKE CLASS B?
THIS THING CAN'T READ *WEAK-LINGS*.
YOU SHOULD TRY HITTING THE GYM.
YOU'RE THE AVERAGE SLOB WHO NEVER EXERCISES.
RMB
RMB
RMB
HOW ABOUT *YOU*, KING?
COOL! I HEAR THE KING ENGINE!
RMB
RMB
HUH ...?!!
YOU'RE UNMEASUR-ABLE TOO!!!
RMBL
RMBL
OH! I KNOW WHY!
OKAME CAN ONLY MEASURE UP TO 9,999!
YOU MUST BE HIGHER THAN THAT!
SORRY TO DISAP-POINT YOU.
NO... THAT'S OKAY.

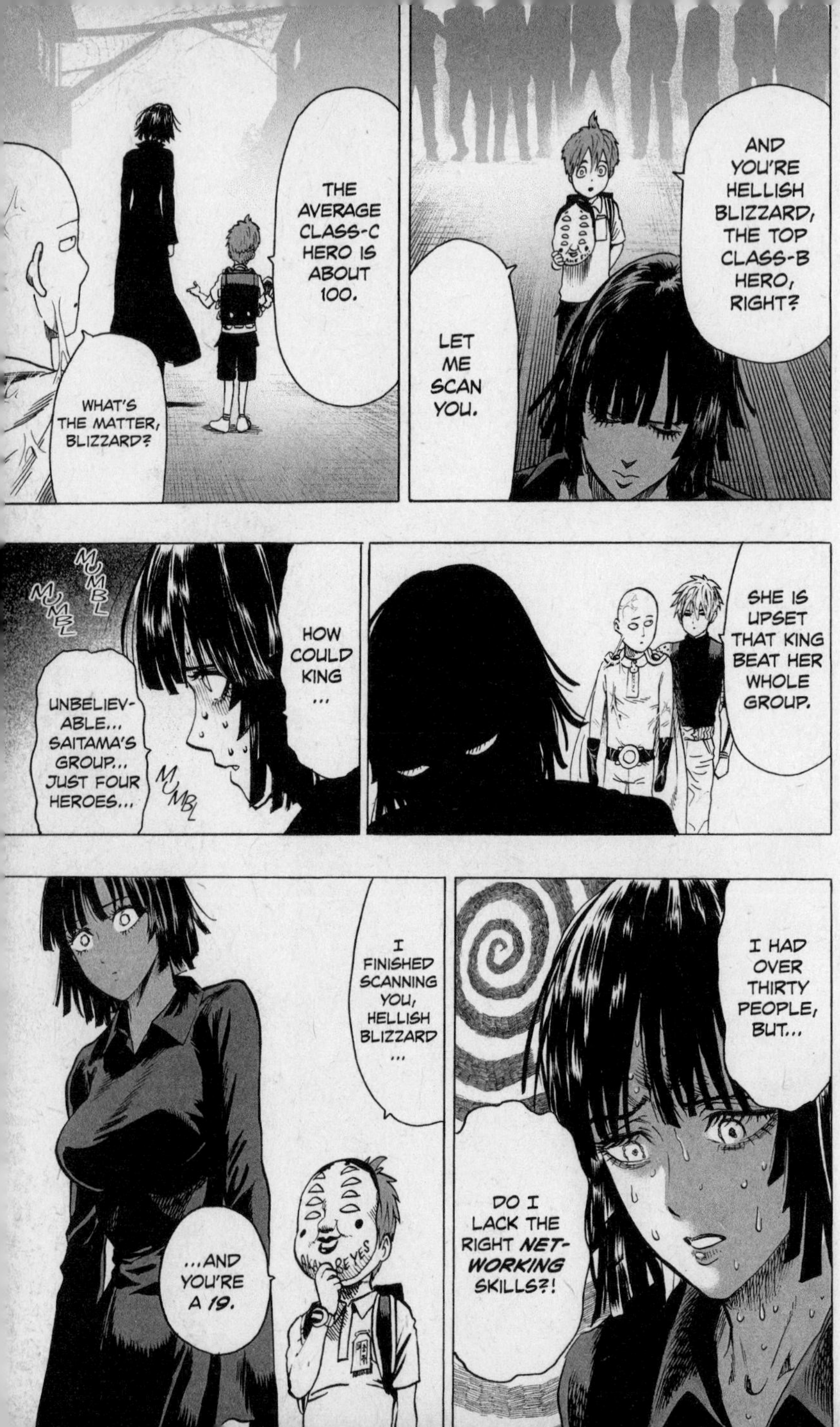
AND YOU'RE HELLISH BLIZZARD, THE TOP CLASS-B HERO, RIGHT?
LET ME SCAN YOU.
THE AVERAGE CLASS-C HERO IS ABOUT 100.
WHAT'S THE MATTER, BLIZZARD?
SHE IS UPSET THAT KING BEAT HER WHOLE GROUP.
HOW COULD KING ...
MUMBL
MUMBL
UNBELIEV-ABLE... SAITAMA'S GROUP... JUST FOUR HEROES...
MUMBL
I HAD OVER THIRTY PEOPLE, BUT...
DO I LACK THE RIGHT NET-WORKING SKILLS?!
I FINISHED SCANNING YOU, HELLISH BLIZZARD ...
...AND YOU'RE A 19.

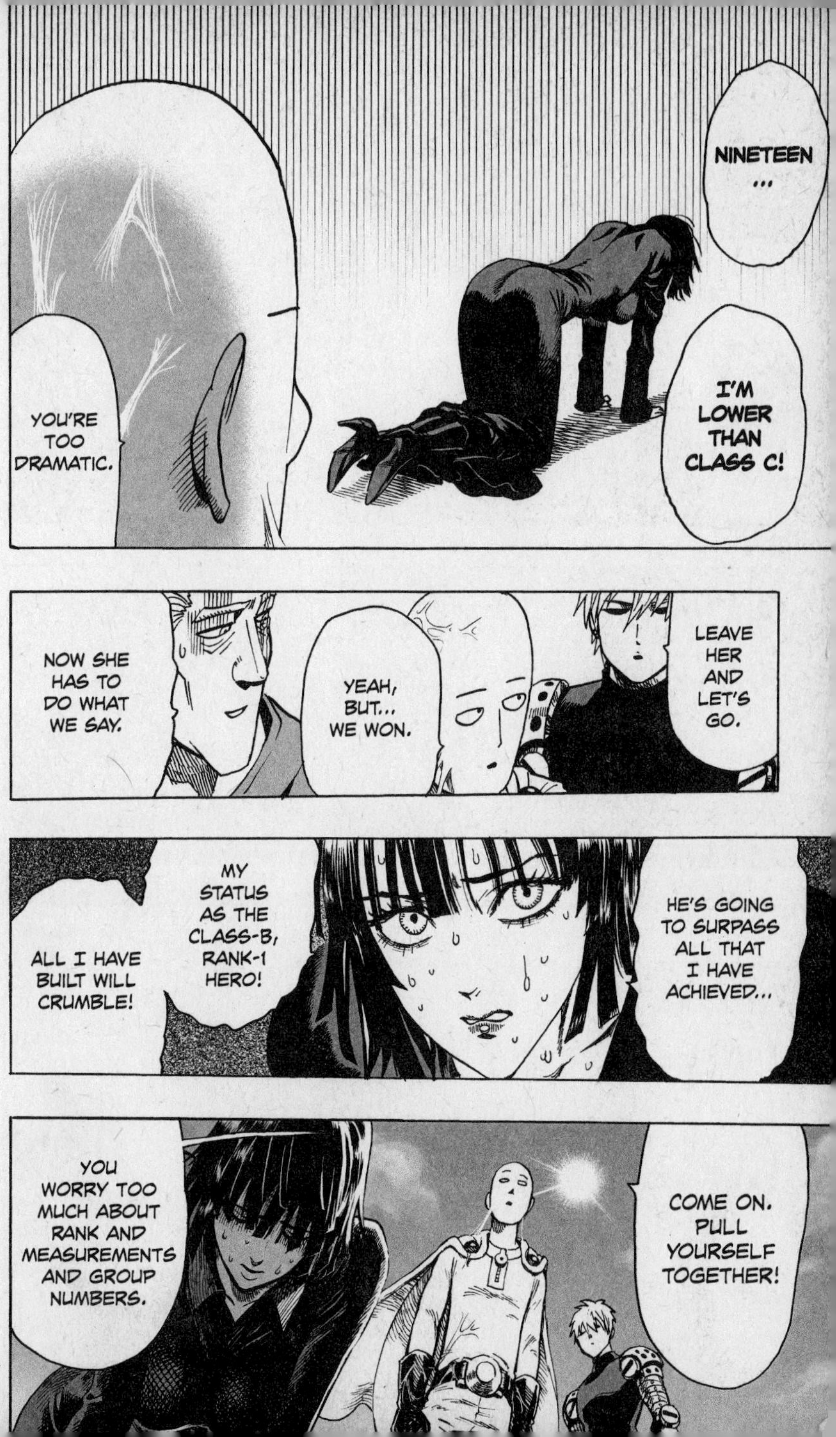
NINETEEN ...
I'M LOWER THAN CLASS C!
YOU'RE TOO DRAMATIC.
LEAVE HER AND LET'S GO.
YEAH, BUT... WE WON.
NOW SHE HAS TO DO WHAT WE SAY.
HE'S GOING TO SURPASS ALL THAT I HAVE ACHIEVED...
MY STATUS AS THE CLASS-B, RANK-1 HERO!
ALL I HAVE BUILT WILL CRUMBLE!
COME ON. PULL YOURSELF TOGETHER!
YOU WORRY TOO MUCH ABOUT RANK AND MEASUREMENTS AND GROUP NUMBERS.

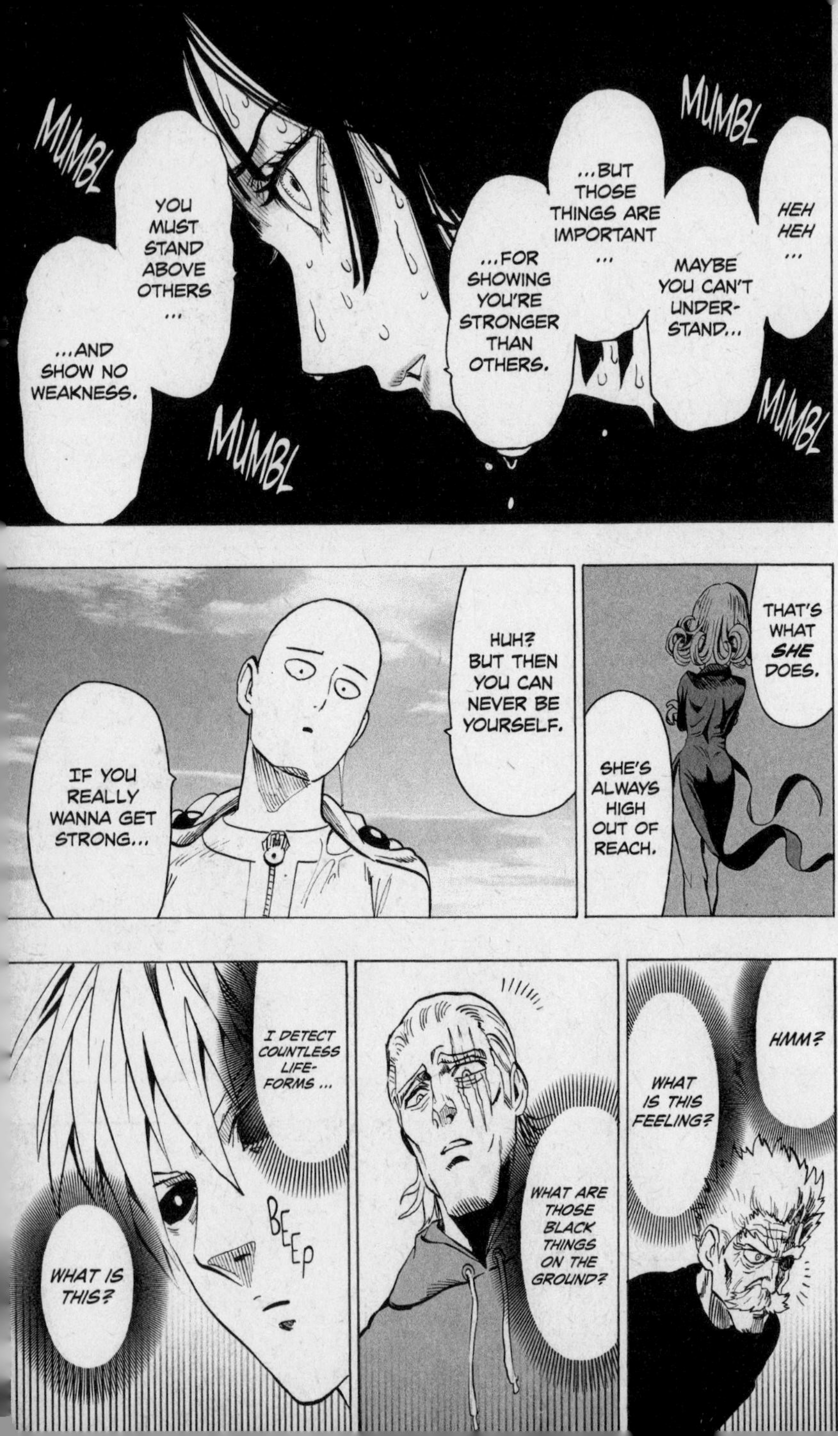
HEH HEH ...
MUMBL
MAYBE YOU CAN'T UNDER-STAND...
...BUT THOSE THINGS ARE IMPORTANT ...
...FOR SHOWING YOU'RE STRONGER THAN OTHERS.
MUMBL
YOU MUST STAND ABOVE OTHERS ...
...AND SHOW NO WEAKNESS.
MUMBL
MUMBL
THAT'S WHAT SHE DOES.
SHE'S ALWAYS HIGH OUT OF REACH.
HUH? BUT THEN YOU CAN NEVER BE YOURSELF.
IF YOU REALLY WANNA GET STRONG...
HMM?
WHAT IS THIS FEELING?
WHAT ARE THOSE BLACK THINGS ON THE GROUND?
I DETECT COUNTLESS LIFE-FORMS ...
BEEP
WHAT IS THIS?

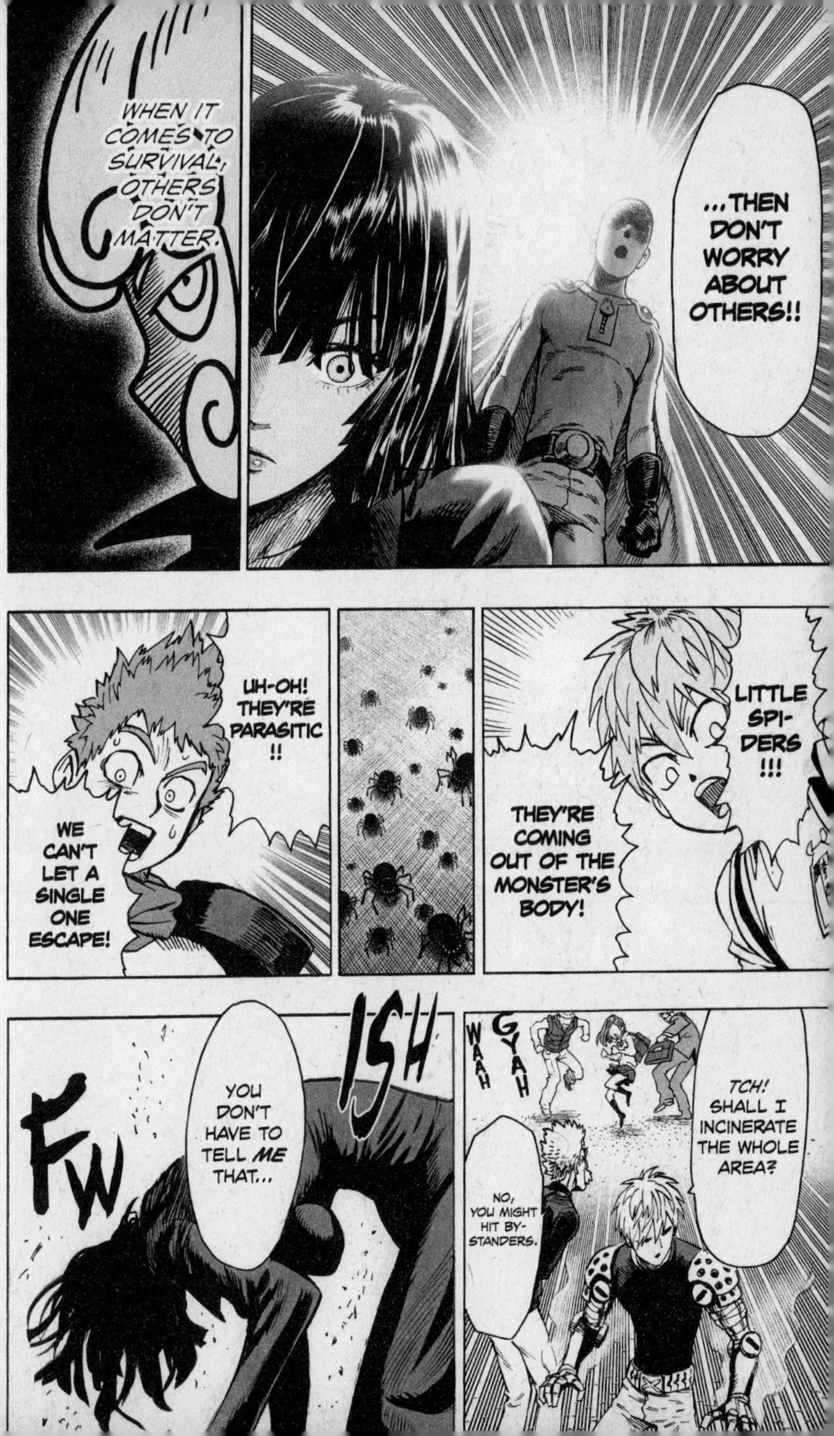
...THEN DON'T WORRY ABOUT OTHERS!!
WHEN IT COMES TO SURVIVAL, OTHERS DON'T MATTER.
LITTLE SPI-DERS!!!
THEY'RE COMING OUT OF THE MONSTER'S BODY!
UH-OH! THEY'RE PARASITIC!!
WE CAN'T LET A SINGLE ONE ESCAPE!
TCH! SHALL I INCINERATE THE WHOLE AREA?
GYAH
WAAH
NO, YOU MIGHT HIT BY-STANDERS.
ISH
YOU DON'T HAVE TO TELL *ME* THAT...
FW

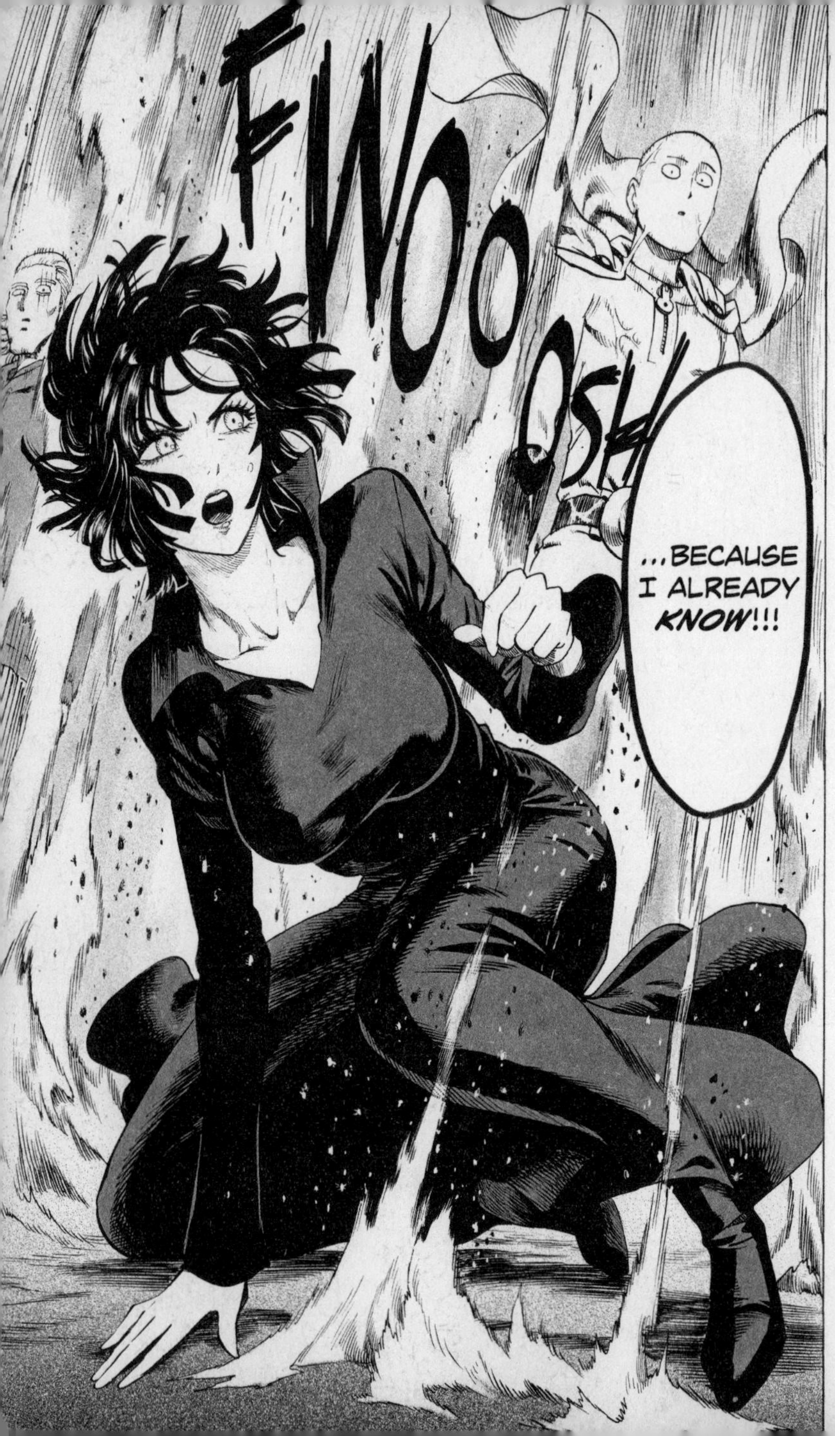
FWOOOSH
...BECAUSE I ALREADY KNOW!!!

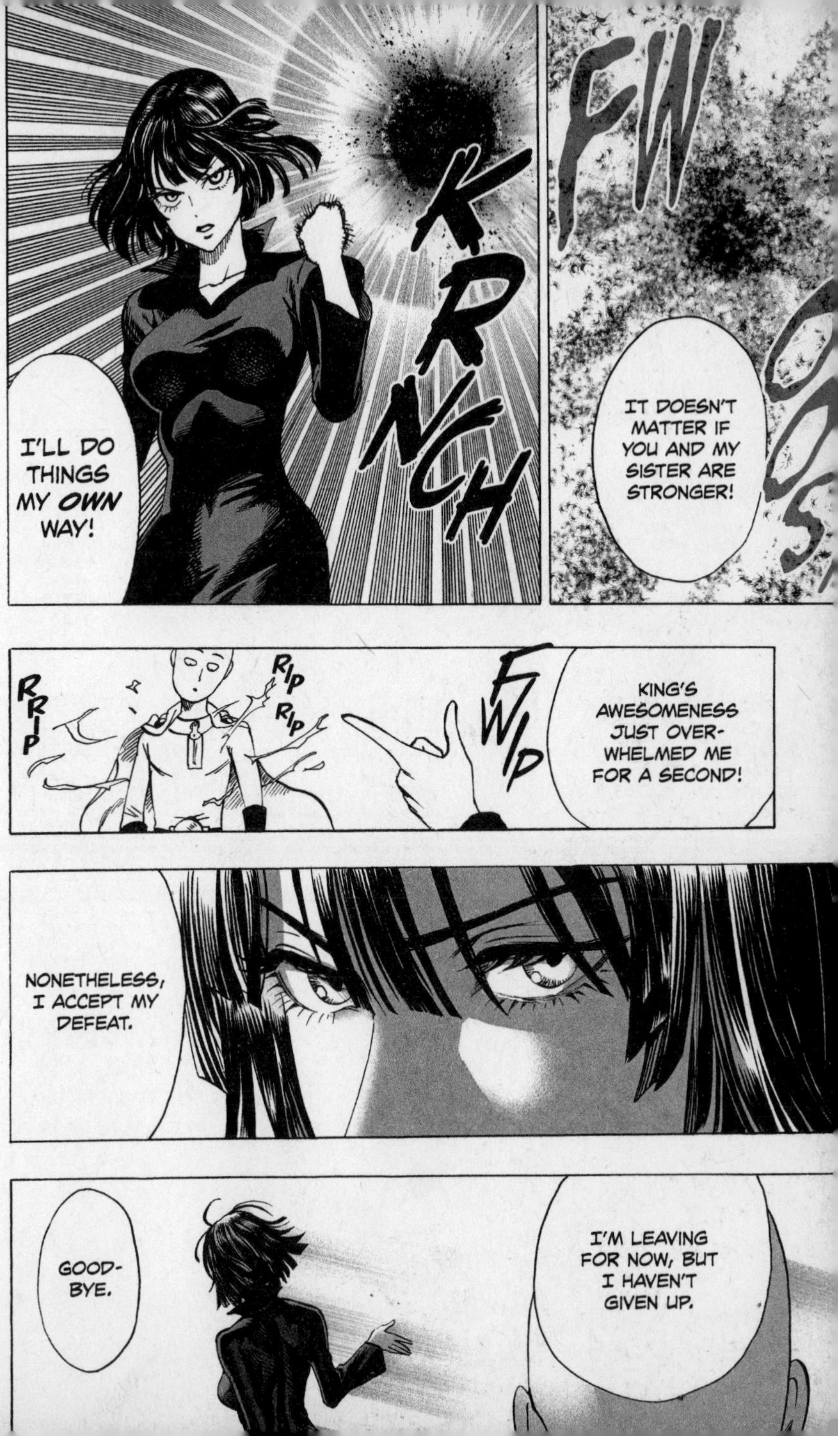
FW
IT DOESN'T MATTER IF YOU AND MY SISTER ARE STRONGER!
KRRNCH
I'LL DO THINGS MY *OWN* WAY!
KING'S AWESOMENESS JUST OVER-WHELMED ME FOR A SECOND!
FWIP
RIP RIP
RRIP
NONETHELESS, I ACCEPT MY DEFEAT.
I'M LEAVING FOR NOW, BUT I HAVEN'T GIVEN UP.
GOOD-BYE.

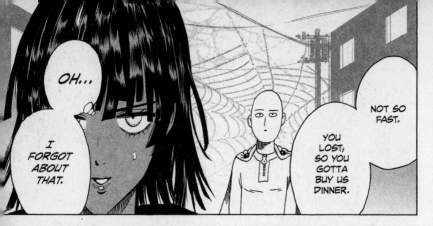

NOT SO FAST.
YOU LOST, SO YOU GOTTA BUY US DINNER.
OH...
I FORGOT ABOUT THAT.
HMM... TORNADO'S YOUR SISTER, HUH?
I GUESS THERE ARE ABILITIES THIS DEVICE CAN'T MEASURE.
THEN IT ISN'T ANY USE IN A REAL FIGHT.
OKAME 8 EYES
CURRENT TECH-NOLOGY CAN'T QUANTIFY STRENGTH.
IT LOOKS LIKE IT'S BROKEN ANYWAY.
I WONDER WHAT CAUSED THAT CRACK?
OKAME 8EYES

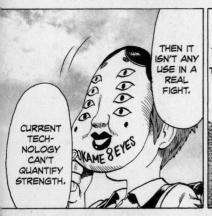

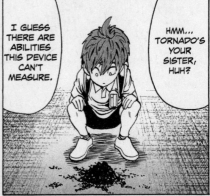

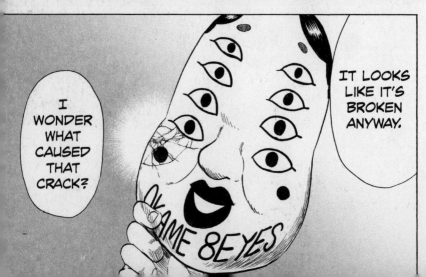

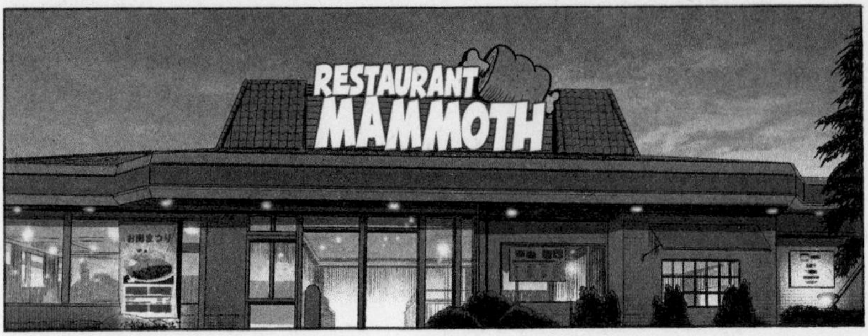
RESTAURANT MAMMOTH

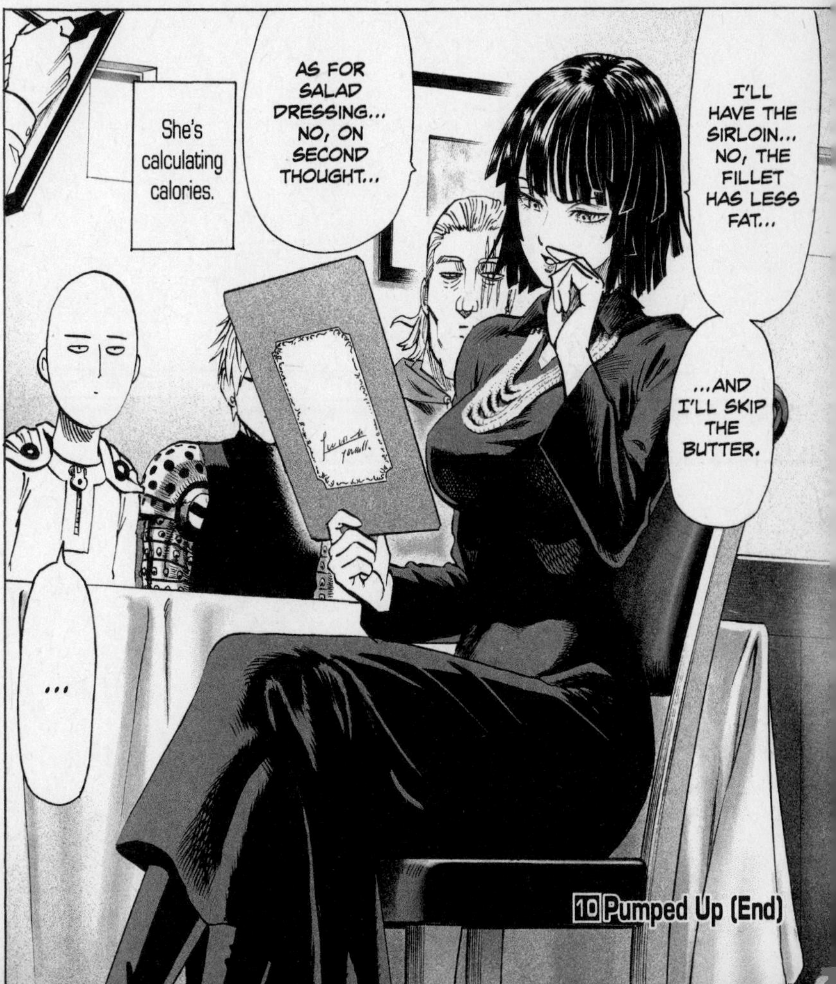
I'LL HAVE THE SIRLOIN... NO, THE FILLET HAS LESS FAT...
...AND I'LL SKIP THE BUTTER.
AS FOR SALAD DRESSING... NO, ON SECOND THOUGHT...
She's calculating calories.
...
10 Pumped Up (End)

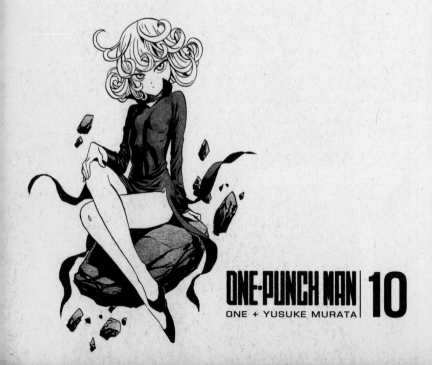

ONE-PUNCH MAN | 10

ONE + YUSUKE MURATA

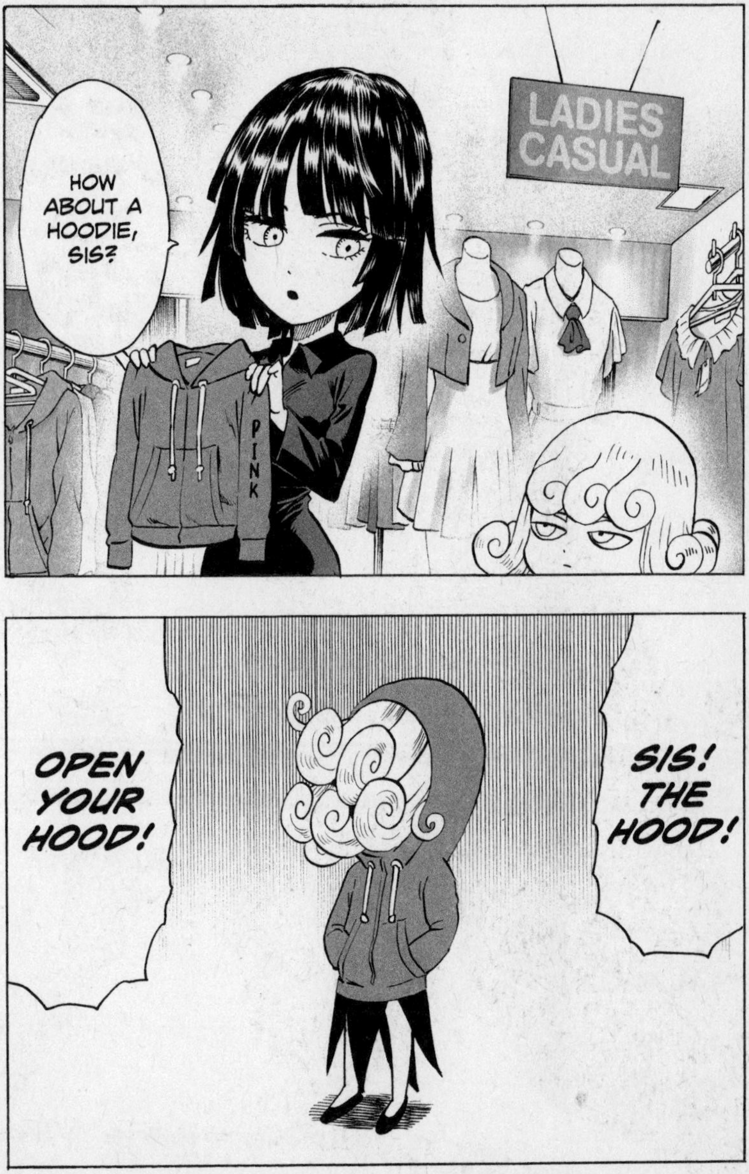
LADIES CASUAL
HOW ABOUT A HOODIE, SIS?
PINK
SIS! THE HOOD!
OPEN YOUR HOOD!

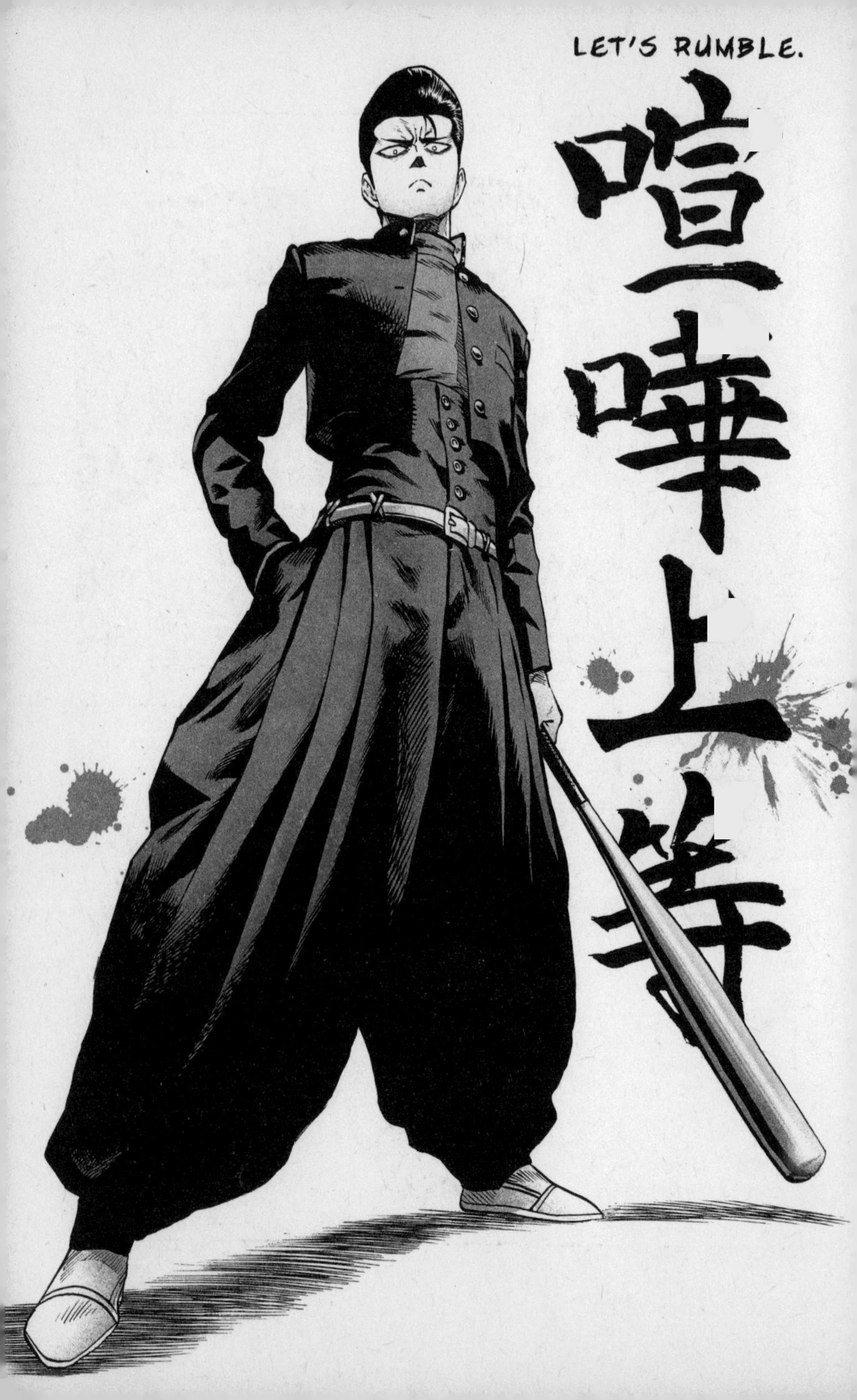
喧嘩上等
LET'S RUMBLE.

END NOTES

PAGE 73, PANEL 1:
The title of the book at the top is a reference to *Tonari no Young Jump*, the Japanese web magazine *One-Punch Man* is serialized in. The book below it is titled *Hamitsu*, which is a parody of the video game magazine *Famitsu*.

PAGE 78, PANEL 2:
King's shirt says "fish cake!"

PAGE 149, PANEL 2:
Saitama's shirt has the characters for "cliff" and "person" on it. This is possibly a reference to a shirt in Japan meant to imply one should "live life on the edge!"

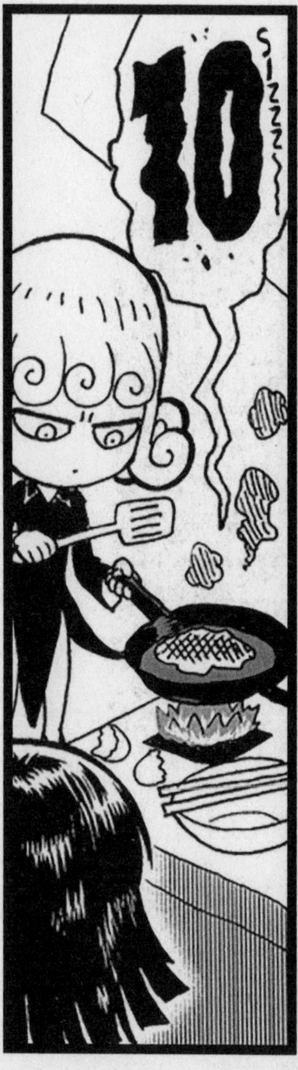
10
SIZZZ~~

ONE-PUNCH MAN

VOLUME 10

SHONEN JUMP MANGA EDITION

STORY BY | ONE
ART BY | YUSUKE MURATA

TRANSLATION | JOHN WERRY
TOUCH-UP ART AND LETTERING | JAMES GAUBATZ
DESIGN | FAWN LAU
SHONEN JUMP SERIES EDITOR | JOHN BAE
GRAPHIC NOVEL EDITOR | JENNIFER LEBLANC

First published in Japan in 2012 by SHUEISHA Inc., Tokyo.
English translation rights arranged by SHUEISHA Inc.

Printed in the U.S.A.

Published by VIZ Media, LLC
P.O. Box 77010
San Francisco, CA 94107

10 9 8 7 6 5 4 3 2 1
First printing, January 2017

www.viz.com

www.shonenjump.com

PARENTAL ADVISORY
ONE-PUNCH MAN is rated T for Teen and is recommended for ages 13 and up. This volume contains realistic and fantasy violence.

RATED T FOR TEEN

ratings.viz.com

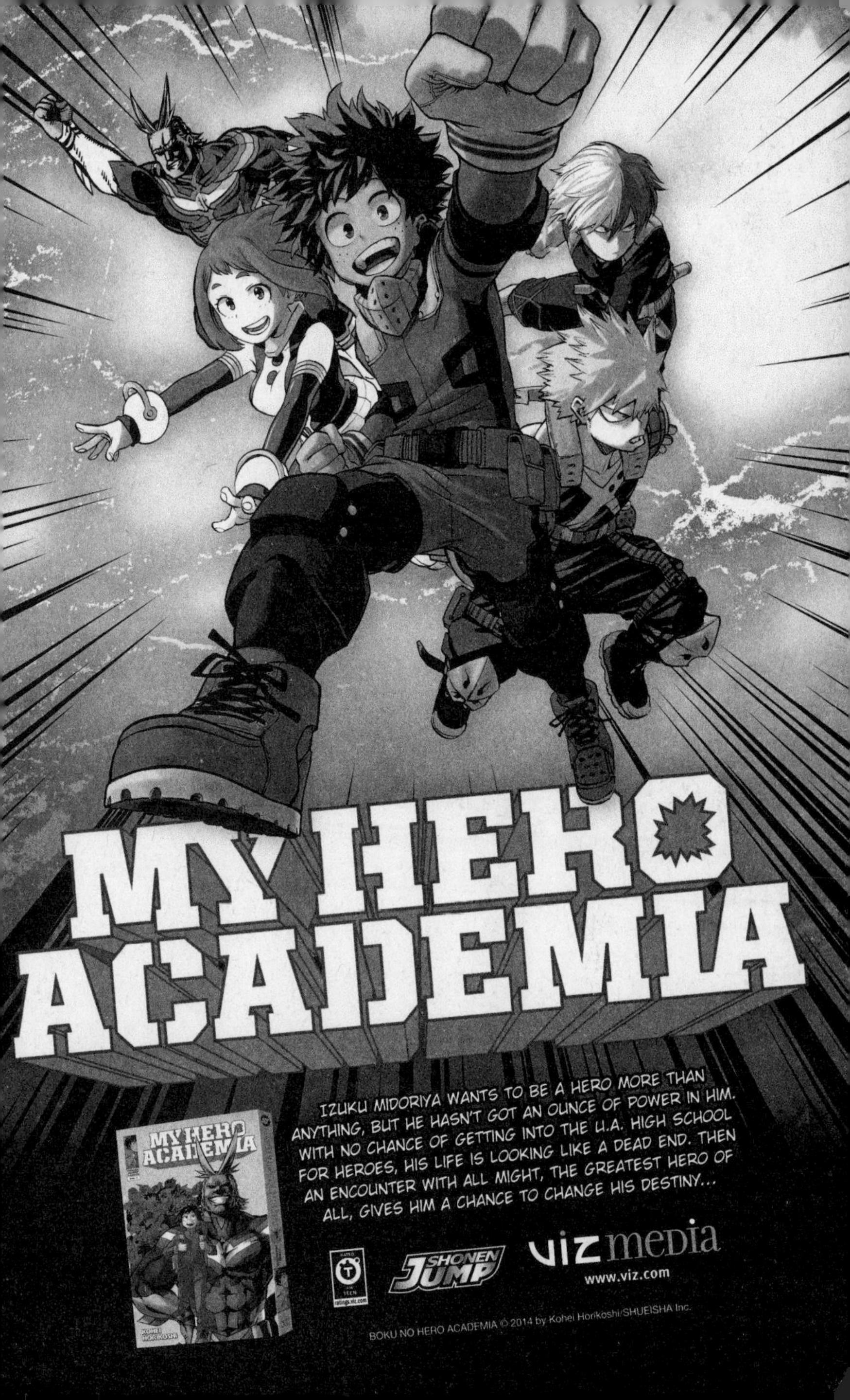
MY HERO ACADEMIA
IZUKU MIDORIYA WANTS TO BE A HERO MORE THAN ANYTHING, BUT HE HASN'T GOT AN OUNCE OF POWER IN HIM. WITH NO CHANCE OF GETTING INTO THE U.A. HIGH SCHOOL FOR HEROES, HIS LIFE IS LOOKING LIKE A DEAD END. THEN AN ENCOUNTER WITH ALL MIGHT, THE GREATEST HERO OF ALL, GIVES HIM A CHANCE TO CHANGE HIS DESTINY…
MY HERO ACADEMIA
KOHEI HORIKOSHI
RATED T TEEN
ratings.viz.com
SHONEN JUMP
viz media
www.viz.com
BOKU NO HERO ACADEMIA © 2014 by Kohei Horikoshi/SHUEISHA Inc.

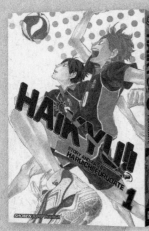
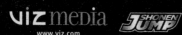

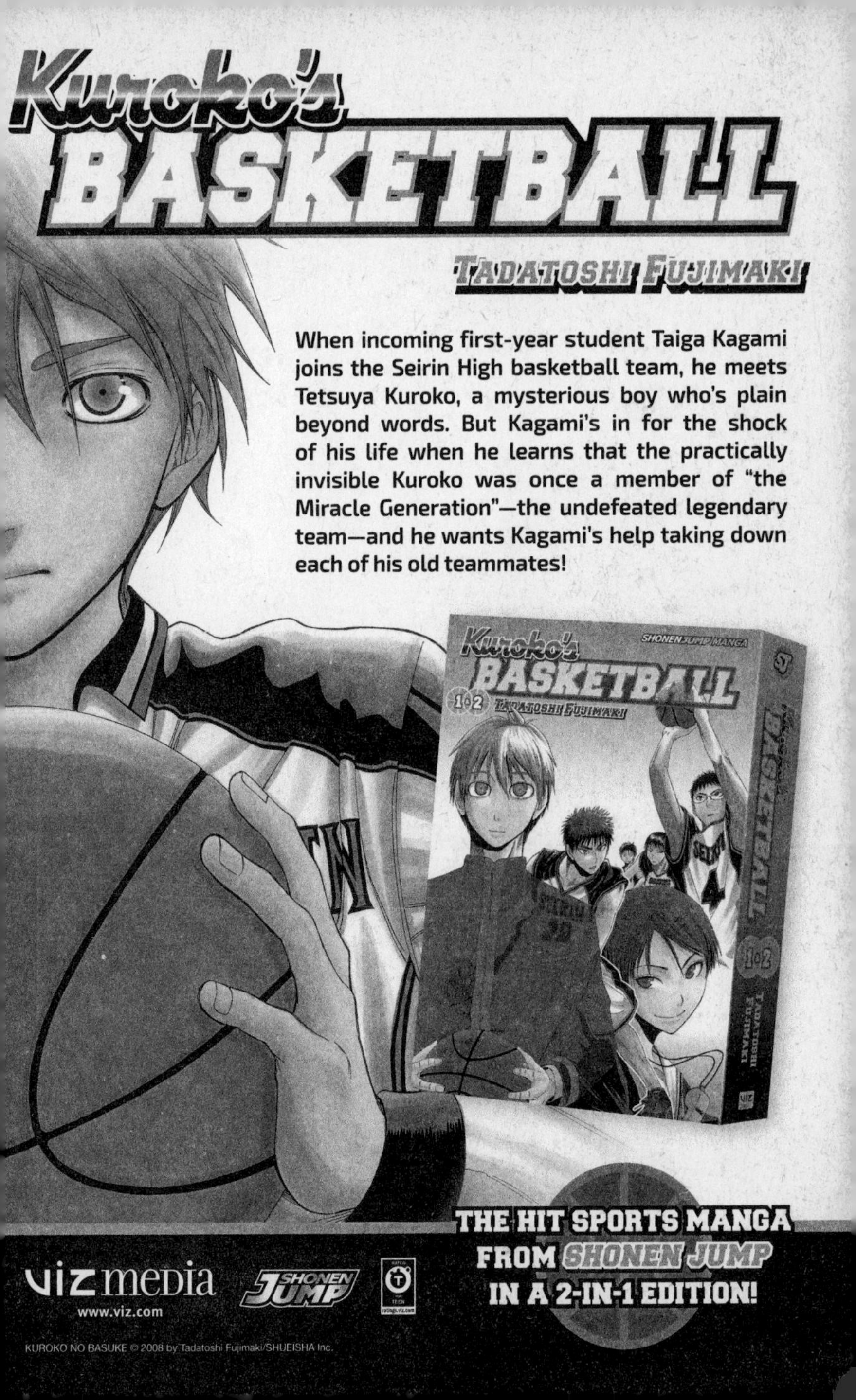
Kuroko's BASKETBALL
TADATOSHI FUJIMAKI
When incoming first-year student Taiga Kagami joins the Seirin High basketball team, he meets Tetsuya Kuroko, a mysterious boy who's plain beyond words. But Kagami's in for the shock of his life when he learns that the practically invisible Kuroko was once a member of "the Miracle Generation"—the undefeated legendary team—and he wants Kagami's help taking down each of his old teammates!
SHONEN JUMP MANGA
Kuroko's BASKETBALL
1•2
TADATOSHI FUJIMAKI
THE HIT SPORTS MANGA FROM SHONEN JUMP IN A 2-IN-1 EDITION!
viz media
www.viz.com
SHONEN JUMP
KUROKO NO BASUKE © 2008 by Tadatoshi Fujimaki/SHUEISHA Inc.

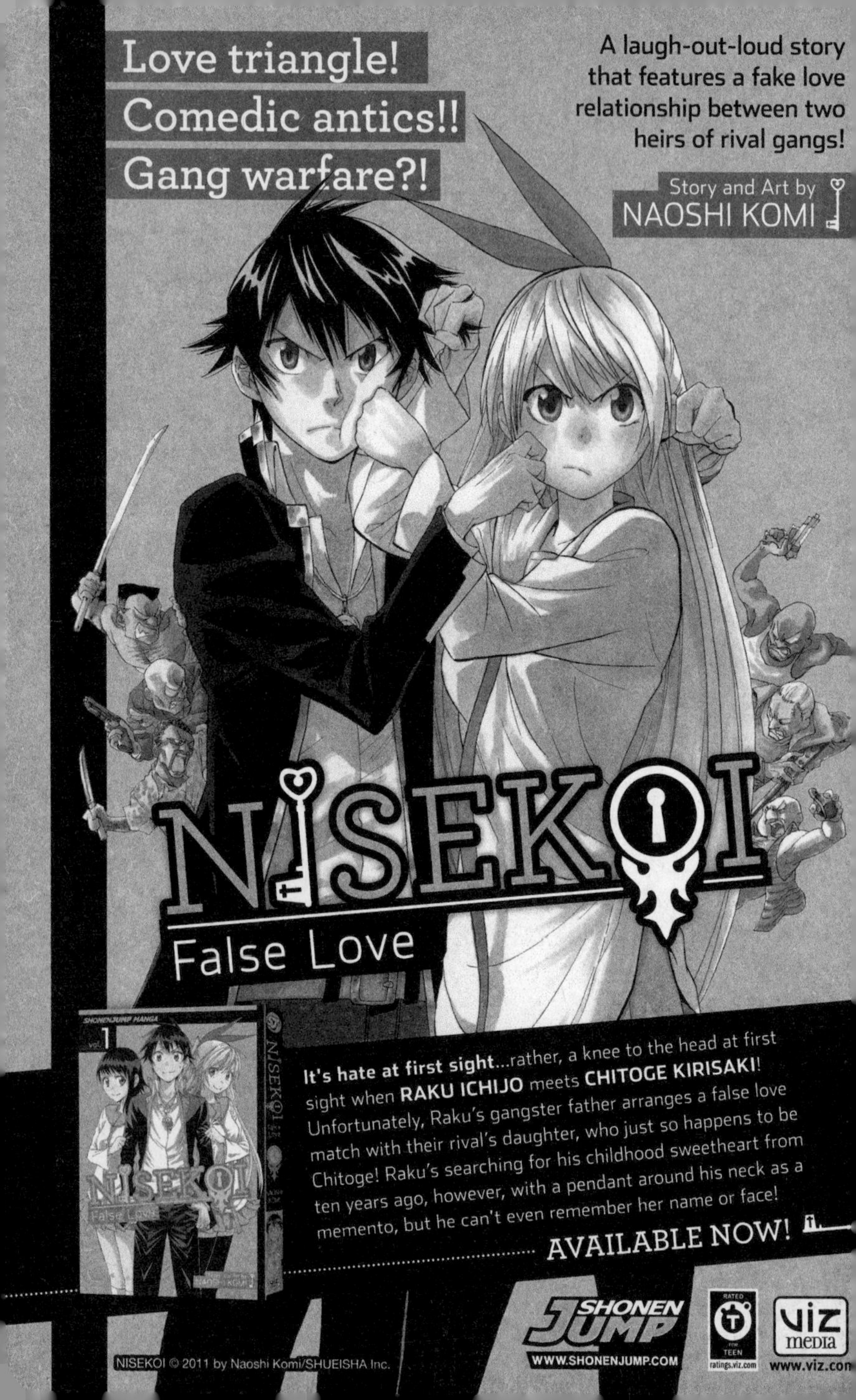

Love triangle!
Comedic antics!!
Gang warfare?!
A laugh-out-loud story that features a fake love relationship between two heirs of rival gangs!
Story and Art by
NAOSHI KOMI
NISEKOI
False Love
SHONENJUMP MANGA
vol. 1
NISEKOI
False Love
NAOSHI KOMI
It's hate at first sight...rather, a knee to the head at first sight when RAKU ICHIJO meets CHITOGE KIRISAKI! Unfortunately, Raku's gangster father arranges a false love match with their rival's daughter, who just so happens to be Chitoge! Raku's searching for his childhood sweetheart from ten years ago, however, with a pendant around his neck as a memento, but he can't even remember her name or face!
AVAILABLE NOW!
SHONEN JUMP
WWW.SHONENJUMP.COM
RATED T FOR TEEN
ratings.viz.com
viz media
www.viz.com
NISEKOI © 2011 by Naoshi Komi/SHUEISHA Inc.

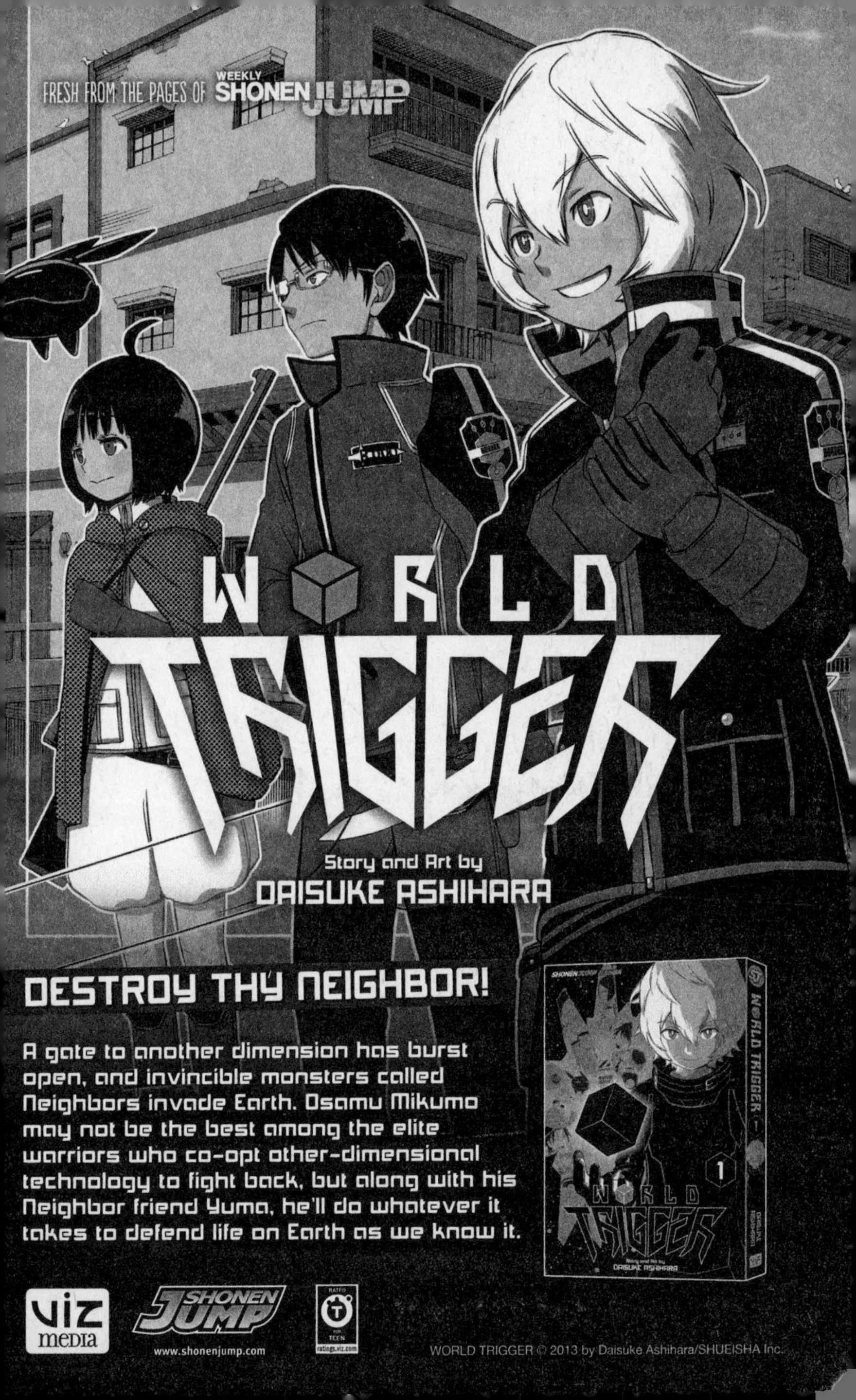
FRESH FROM THE PAGES OF WEEKLY SHONEN JUMP
WORLD TRIGGER
Story and Art by
DAISUKE ASHIHARA
DESTROY THY NEIGHBOR!
A gate to another dimension has burst open, and invincible monsters called Neighbors invade Earth. Osamu Mikumo may not be the best among the elite warriors who co-opt other-dimensional technology to fight back, but along with his Neighbor friend Yuma, he'll do whatever it takes to defend life on Earth as we know it.
WORLD TRIGGER
1
Story and Art by DAISUKE ASHIHARA
viz media
SHONEN JUMP
www.shonenjump.com
RATED T FOR TEEN
ratings.viz.com
WORLD TRIGGER © 2013 by Daisuke Ashihara/SHUEISHA Inc.

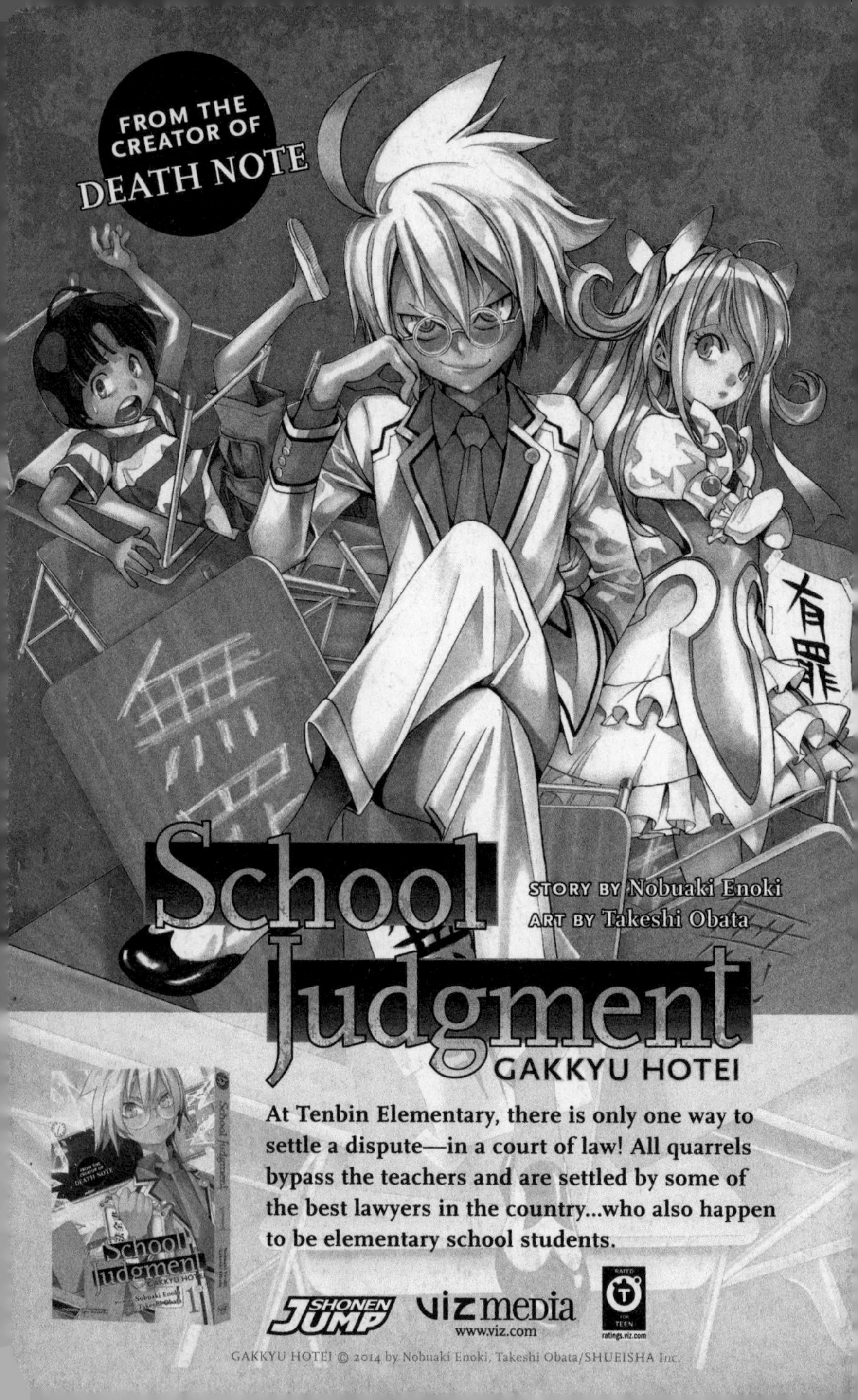
FROM THE CREATOR OF DEATH NOTE
School Judgment
STORY BY Nobuaki Enoki
ART BY Takeshi Obata
GAKKYU HOTEI
At Tenbin Elementary, there is only one way to settle a dispute—in a court of law! All quarrels bypass the teachers and are settled by some of the best lawyers in the country...who also happen to be elementary school students.
SHONEN JUMP
viz media
www.viz.com
RATED T FOR TEEN
ratings.viz.com
GAKKYU HOTEI © 2014 by Nobuaki Enoki, Takeshi Obata/SHUEISHA Inc.

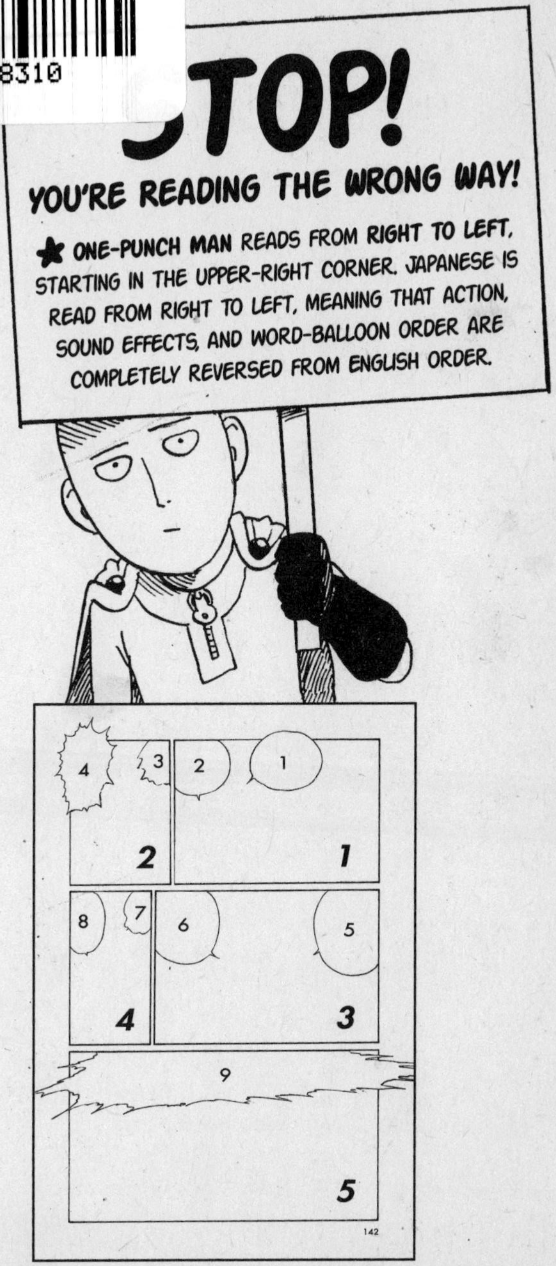
STOP!
YOU'RE READING THE WRONG WAY!
ONE-PUNCH MAN READS FROM RIGHT TO LEFT, STARTING IN THE UPPER-RIGHT CORNER. JAPANESE IS READ FROM RIGHT TO LEFT, MEANING THAT ACTION, SOUND EFFECTS, AND WORD-BALLOON ORDER ARE COMPLETELY REVERSED FROM ENGLISH ORDER.